Militant Democracy

This book aims to present a comprehensive theory of militant democracy and to answer questions such as: How can a democracy protect itself against its own downfall? And when is intervention against antidemocrats justified?

Against the backdrop of historical and current examples, this book examines a variety of theories from philosophers and legal scholars such as Karl Loewenstein, Karl Popper and Carl Schmitt as well as contemporary alternatives. It compares their interpretations of democracy and militant democracy, discusses how helpful these references are, and introduces two largely forgotten theorists to the militant democracy debate: George van den Bergh and Milan Markovitch. *Militant Democracy* then sets out to build a novel theory of democratic self-defence on the basis of democracy's capacity for self-correction. In doing so, it addresses the more classic and current criticisms of the concept, while paying specific attention to the position of the judge, the legal design and effectiveness of party bans, and the national and supranational procedural safeguards that can safeguard the careful application of militant democracy instruments.

Militant Democracy seamlessly combines political philosophy, political science and constitutional law to offer a new perspective on democratic self-defence. This book is essential reading for scholars and students of political theory, jurisprudence, democracy, extremism and the history of ideas.

Bastiaan Rijpkema is Assistant Professor of Jurisprudence at Leiden University, the Netherlands. He received his LLB in Law at Erasmus University Rotterdam (2010) and his LLM in Jurisprudence and Philosophy of Law (cum laude) from Leiden University (2011). In 2015 he obtained his PhD at Leiden University with a dissertation on militant democracy, which was published in Dutch as *Weerbare democratie: de grenzen van democratische tolerantie* (Nieuw Amsterdam, 2015). For *Weerbare democratie* he was awarded the prize for the best Dutch political book of the year in 2016, the *Prinsjesboekenprijs*. In 2017 he won the *New Scientist Wetenschapstalentprijs 2017* (New Scientist Science Talent Prize), the prize for the most talented young researcher of the Netherlands and Flanders (Dutch-speaking Belgium).

Routledge Studies in Extremism and Democracy
Series Editors: Roger Eatwell, *University of Bath,* and Matthew Goodwin, *University of Kent.*

Founding Series Editors: Roger Eatwell, *University of Bath* and Cas Mudde, *University of Antwerp-UFSIA.*

https://www.routledge.com/politics/series/ED

This new series encompasses academic studies within the broad fields of 'extremism' and 'democracy'. These topics have traditionally been considered largely in isolation by academics. A key focus of the series, therefore, is the (inter-)*relation* between extremism and democracy. Works will seek to answer questions such as to what extent 'extremist' groups pose a major threat to democratic parties, or how democracy can respond to extremism without undermining its own democratic credentials.

The books encompass two strands:

Routledge Studies in Extremism and Democracy includes books with an introductory and broad focus which are aimed at students and teachers. These books will be available in hardback and paperback. Titles include:

The Populist Radical Reader
A Reader
Edited by Cas Mudde

The Far Right in America
Cas Mudde

Routledge Research in Extremism and Democracy offers a forum for innovative new research intended for a more specialist readership. These books will be in hardback only. Titles include:

43. **Fascism, Populism and American Democracy**
Leonard Weinberg

44. **Militant Democracy**
The Limits of Democratic Tolerance
Bastiaan Rijpkema

Militant Democracy

The Limits of Democratic Tolerance

Bastiaan Rijpkema
translated by Anna Asbury

Routledge
Taylor & Francis Group
LONDON AND NEW YORK

First published 2018
by Routledge
2 Park Square, Milton Park, Abingdon, Oxon OX14 4RN

and by Routledge
711 Third Avenue, New York, NY 10017

Routledge is an imprint of the Taylor & Francis Group, an informa business

British Library Cataloguing in Publication Data
A catalogue record for this book is available from the British Library

Library of Congress Cataloging in Publication Data
A catalog record has been requested for this book

ISBN: 978-1-138-54296-9 (hbk)
ISBN: 978-0-429-42737-4 (ebk)

Typeset in Times NR MT Pro
by Cenveo® Publisher Services

MIX
Paper from responsible sources
FSC www.fsc.org FSC® C013056

Printed and bound in Great Britain by
TJ International Ltd, Padstow, Cornwall

Brief contents

Contents

Acknowledgements

This book is the English edition of my *Weerbare democratie: de grenzen van democratische tolerantie* (Nieuw Amsterdam, 2015). I want to thank Rebecca McPhee and Craig Fowlie, and the series editors Roger Eatwell and Matthew Goodwin, at Routledge for their excellent assistance in this project. I also want to thank Raisa Blommestijn, Niels Graaf, and the external reviewer solicited by the publisher, for their insightful comments and suggestions on the English manuscript. All errors naturally remain mine only. I am very grateful to the *Prinsjesboekenprijs* 2016 (for the best Dutch political book of the year), the *New Scientist Science Talent Prize* 2017, the Institute for the Interdisciplinary Study of the Law and the Profile Area Political Legitimacy (both at Leiden University), whose financial contributions made the English translation possible. Also, I want to thank Sarah de Lange for introducing me to the editors of the magnificent and very fitting *Democracy and Extremism* series at Routledge.

Anna Asbury translated the book from Dutch to English. All quotes from (original) Dutch, German and French sources have been translated to English for the purpose of this edition. I have updated the translated manuscript on certain points, mainly when there were developments that could not be ignored, such as the election of Donald Trump in 2016 and the German Federal Constitutional Court decision regarding the Nationaldemokratische Partei Deutschlands (NPD) in 2017, but also to clarify some issues that could be considered familiar to a Dutch audience, but not to international readers.

A previous version of chapter 1 has appeared in two parts as 'Democratie als doel: de weerbare democratie van George van den Bergh' ('Democracy as a goal: the militant democracy of George van den Bergh', introduction) and 'De juridische erfenis van *De democratische staat en de niet-democratische partijen*' ('The legal heritage of *The democratic state and the non-democratic parties*', appendix to the introduction), p. 21–119, in *Wat te doen met anti-democratische partijen? De oratie van George van den Bergh* (What to do with antidemocratic parties? The inaugural lecture of George van den Bergh),

Amsterdam: Elsevier Boeken 2014. An abridged and edited version of the first chapter of this English edition was published as 'Militant Democracy *beyond* Loewenstein: George van den Bergh's 1936 Inaugural Lecture', in Afshin Ellian and Bastiaan Rijpkema (eds.), *Militant Democracy: Political Science, Law and Philosophy*, *forthcoming* Springer 2018.

Introduction

So anspruchslos wird doch wohl niemand sein, daß er mit einem 'Was sonst?' eine geistige Grundlage oder eine moralische Wahrheit für erwiesen hielte.[1]

Carl Schmitt, *Die geistesgeschichtliche Lage des heutigen Parlamentarismus*, 1926

1. Weimar

The NSDAP's intended 'national revolution' ends in a debacle.[2] Instead of a 'march on Berlin', there is a confrontation with heavily armed police in Munich: fourteen Nazis are killed, Göring is wounded, Hitler dislocates his shoulder.[3] The unheroic flight of the 'revolution leader' while his men are still under fire completes the fiasco.[4] Hitler is locked up in Landsberg.[5] The failed Beer Hall Putsch in the autumn of 1923 would radically change the tactics of the NSDAP. At Landsberg Hitler comes to the conclusion that the modern state is too strong to attack head-on.[6] Power must be seized *from within*, so as to use the 'machinery of the state' in support of the National Socialist revolution.[7] They will have to play along with the 'game of democratic politics' in order to grasp power.[8] Central to this idea is the freedom of the press, along with freedom of association and expression, in order to build up a loyal mass following; elections ensure that these numbers can subsequently be converted into power.[9] The 'constitutional freedoms and democratic rights' of the Weimar Republic would make a *legal* revolution possible.[10]

Initially progress is slow. In 1924 the Nazis gain only 5 percent of the vote in parliamentary elections and not even 1 percent in the presidential elections a year later.[11] They are political outcasts.[12] With fourteen seats in parliament, they are nothing more than a splinter group 'on its way to political obscurity'.[13] But on 14 September 1930 everything changes: the NSDAP achieves 18 percent of the vote, making it the second parliamentary party.[14] The Reichstag, already somewhat ineffectual, is now decisively crippled.[15]

From 1932 on the NSDAP is Germany's largest party.[16] In the last more or less 'free' elections in March 1933 the party gains almost half of the vote.[17]

Parties hostile to the Weimar Republic (besides the NSDAP, these include the Communists) now have 65 percent of the seats in parliament.[18] On 23 March 1933 Hitler, who has been chancellor since January, addresses the Reichstag;[19] on the agenda is the *Ermächtigungsgesetz*, the Enabling Act that will make him a *de facto* dictator. The separation of powers is abolished: Hitler will be able to issue laws without parliamentary approval, laws that can also deviate from the constitution.[20] Since this means changing the constitution, he needs a two-thirds majority.[21] The Communist members of parliament are against this, but after the Reichstag fire they are arrested and unable to vote.[22] Even without the Communists, though, Hitler still needs the support of a party loyal to the Weimar Republic.[23] Despite enormous pressure, the Social Democrats continue to resist and vote against the change.[24] Hitler is eventually aided in attaining the required majority by the Catholic Centre Party,[25] with a number of smaller parties loyal to Weimar following their example. The Enabling Act is passed at eight o'clock in the evening.[26] In his diary that evening, Goebbels notes, 'Now we are lord and master.'[27] The Weimar democracy has come to an end.[28]

2. Beyond the *locus classicus*

The dismantling of the Weimar democracy is the prototypical 'legal revolution', the overthrow of democracy using democratic rights and freedoms,[29] devised after a failed violent revolution, meticulously executed, and completed ten years later, with the Enabling Act as the final stroke and 'legal burial of the Republic'.[30]

Weimar is therefore the *locus classicus* in militant democracy thought, the ultimate example of the way in which antidemocratic powers can abuse excessive democratic tolerance, and the scenario that militant democracy aims to prevent. But the story is not unique. Benito Mussolini, too, succeeded in coming to power 'legally' in Italy in the twenties,[31] and on 10 July 1940 the French parliament, having fled to Vichy, voted with an overwhelming majority for an unconditional transfer of power to Marshal Philippe Pétain and his programme of 'moral and intellectual restoration'.[32] Even the very cradle of democracy was familiar with the phenomenon of 'democratic suicide': in 411 BC the Athenians voted for the abolition of their democracy, in exchange for support from the Persian king and others in the war with Sparta.[33]

Then there is the stormy rise of the *Front Islamique du Salut* (FIS) in Algeria. On 26 December 1991 the FIS won 189 of 231 parliamentary seats in the first round of elections.[34] The party was thus effectively certain of a two-thirds majority in the second round, thereby opening the way to changing the Algerian constitution.[35] The FIS had announced that if it won it would turn Algeria into an Islamic state—proclamations such as 'It is in democracy that darkness lies,' and 'democracy is blasphemy' made it clear that there would be little room for democracy in this new state.[36]

Intervention came at the very last minute: the president stepped down and the army took over power; the second round of elections was cancelled.[37] The country sank into a civil war which would cost many lives.[38] Human rights minister Ali Haroun would later claim that he saw no other choice:

> As a minister of human rights, my question is: who is there to defend the notion of human rights? Am I going to allow a situation where, in a month or two, people will no longer have any rights? I cannot do that.[39]

As a former American ambassador once noted, the transfer from colonial government to a democracy often results in 'one man, one vote, one time'.[40]

Turkish democracy has also been seriously challenged by Islamist parties. In 1995 the Refah Party became the largest party in Turkey with an undemocratic programme of sharia law and parallel legal systems.[41] Refah founder and later prime minister Necmettin Erbakan had called on Turkish Muslims to vote for his party in order to establish 'supremacy of the Quran' through a holy war.[42] The party was banned in 1998 by Turkey's Constitutional Court, a judgement approved by the European Court of Human Rights.[43]

Another example is the very short-lived 'democratic moment' in the Middle East, which has come to be known as the 'Arab Spring'. After its election victory in Egypt in 2012, the Muslim Brotherhood gradually began to gather increasing power, a process that was reversed a year later when the army deposed President Mohamed Morsi.[44] In Europe there are concerns over EU member states Hungary and Poland. In Viktor Orbán's Hungary, among other things, the powers of the Constitutional Court were restricted, regular political issues were placed outside the realm of day-to-day politics in 'cardinal laws' (which can only be amended by a two-thirds majority) and media pluralism was strongly diminished.[45] Orbán also had redrawn the electoral districts, a form of gerrymandering on steroids, gaining him a *two-thirds majority* in parliament with less than half of the votes cast in 2014,[46] winning a two-thirds majority again in 2018.[47] Orbán's policies have repeatedly led to fierce criticism from the European Parliament, up to starting the 'Article 7'-sanction procedure against Hungary in September 2018.[48] When it comes to Poland, the European Commission already triggered the 'Article 7'-sanction procedure in December 2017, in response to the 'politicization' of the judiciary by the ruling Prawo i Sprawiedliwosc (PiS, the Law and Justice Party).[49]

3. The problem

The examples above, varied as they may be, plainly reveal an uncomfortable truth: democracy can do itself serious damage and can, in some cases, even usher in its own downfall.[50] It has a number of inherent weaknesses that, if effectively abused, can turn the system against itself. Democracy is characterized by compromise and consensus—easy targets in times of economic crisis. Democratic rights such as freedom of association and expression apply to everyone equally, including antidemocrats. Finally, after the elections democracy also allows its antidemocratic enemies into the heart of its system, namely, parliament. This was the analysis of German political scientist and lawyer Karl Loewenstein (1891-1973) in 1935.[51] Loewenstein reminded us that democratic government is the exception in history.[52] If this fragile form of government is to survive, its weak spots must be fortified. Two years later Loewenstein wrote that democracy 'has to become militant'; a democracy must actively defend itself against its enemies.[53] It must relinquish its neutrality; a democracy is not a 'suicide pact'. A democracy must be able to ban antidemocratic parties.

After World War II 'militant democracy' became an influential constitutional concept, embedded in many constitutions and treaties.[54] And, in fact, parties *are* banned, often with the approval of the European Court of Human Rights.[55]

An urgent problem remains, though. How can a democracy turn to such a fundamentally 'undemocratic' measure as banning a party? It seems difficult to reconcile with the essence of democracy, which starts out from the equal battle of ideas. Loewenstein addresses this topic too briefly: in times of emergency 'legality takes a vacation', he argues.[56] The question of justification thus remained largely unanswered, and the theory of militant democracy was born with a lacuna at its heart. Similarly, most literature arising in Loewenstein's wake passes over this question of justification, and not without consequences. The justification (*why* is it permissible for a democracy, in the name of democracy, to limit democracy?) should be the foundation of any militant democracy theory. After all, this is the cornerstone of the theory: on the basis of this justification one can determine which cases justify action and which cases do not, or, to put it another way, when a ban on a party is well founded and when it is nothing more than abuse of power against unwelcome ideas. The justification directly affects the grounds for banning a political party. For example, if we support a broad justification (such as protection of certain fundamental rights), this leads to a broad legal basis for banning parties, with all the associated disadvantages that entails, namely: problems with interpretation and a greater likelihood of abuse.[57] When formulating a theory of militant democracy, one also needs to consider these consequences; the literature in line with Loewenstein, however, largely does not.

Its absence is no new discovery: several authors have pointed out the troubling lack of a coherent, normative theory for a concept that has become so influential.[58] Jan-Werner Müller expresses it as follows:

> It might seem somewhat surprising, then, that there exists no general legal or, for that matter, proper normative theory of militant democracy—a theory, that is, which could solve, or even just address,

> what is often referred to as the 'democratic paradox' or the 'democratic dilemma', namely the possibility of a democracy destroying itself in the process of defending itself.[59]

This book starts out from the assumption that a coherent militant democracy theory depends on the question of justification. This is an attempt to develop such a coherent theory. Any comprehensive theory of militant democracy must at least pay attention to three questions. First, is it permissible for a democracy to ban antidemocratic parties, and, if so, in what cases (the question of justification)? Second, do party bans work? And third, how do we ensure that a judge can actually *work* with a party ban, or, in other words: how do we translate the justification into a legally workable banning provision? These questions show the multidisciplinary nature of militant democracy theory, positioned at the intersection of three closely related disciplines: political philosophy (is it permissible?), political science (does it work?) and law (how do you effectuate militant democracy in law?). Answering these questions should deliver a theory that contains four elements: a justification, clearly delineated grounds for banning parties, procedural safeguards and attention to the design of party bans.

4. Preliminary exploration

Of all possible measures, prohibiting a political party is probably the most difficult to justify in a democracy. It is the classic, million-dollar question of militant democracy: is it permissible for a democracy to ban antidemocratic parties? This book focuses primarily on this question. That does not mean that other measures are not relevant, but when it comes to the question of justification, I primarily refer to the justification for banning a political party. In this way I hope to avoid the confusion of concepts and vagueness from which theories of militant democracy tend to suffer. If the question of party bans *can* be answered satisfactorily, the justification can also in principle be used for other, less radical militant democracy measures, such as excluding antidemocrats from political office or outlawing political uniforms.

Moreover, the justification will start out from the assumption of *non-violent* antidemocratic parties. From the perspective of political philosophy this is the most interesting question, and it substantially raises the burden of proof: action against a party that has a gang of thugs, after all, is less controversial than action against a party without one.[60] However, *if* that burden of proof can be met, it provides a stronger justification. Acting against an antidemocratic party that commits or incites violent acts and confronting an antidemocratic party that keeps to the letter of the law can be based on the same foundation: their *antidemocratic* efforts. That might also offer advantages in terms of legal proof: violent activities are not always easy to link to the antidemocratic party itself or its members. This does not mean that violent parties will be omitted from consideration in the discussion to follow; far from it. It *does*, however, mean that when we discuss the justification for banning parties, in principle it should be assumed that it is a justification for action against both kinds of antidemocrats.

Consequently, militant democracy must also be viewed in a broader context of 'democracy-limiting' measures. Judicial review of legislation, eternity clauses and supranational oversight by the European Court for Human Rights (ECHR) and even the European Union (EU) all (in part) go back to the same fact: the post-war consensus that an unbridled 'Rousseauian' democracy would eventually turn into something very undemocratic; limits must therefore be set on democracy.[61] The lesson of Weimar was one of mistrust with respect to majorities. Democracy must allow itself to be curbed by the rule of law, among other things: 'democracy and constitutionalism are not available separately', as former Dutch minister of justice and professor of constitutional law Ernst Hirsch Ballin says.[62] We do not just live in a democracy, but in a democracy under the rule of law.[63] Here too the justification for banning parties can be employed more broadly, this time outside the traditional terrain of militant democracy theory, in other measures to curb democracy. That makes the justification relevant to a whole range of measures that limit democracy to a greater or lesser extent. The next question, of course, is which of the democracy-limiting measures is the most effective. One might, for instance, argue that judicial review of legislation could be useful in the fine-tuning of the rules of the democratic game (does flag burning fall under freedom of expression, for example?), but that it will not be particularly effective once antidemocratic powers have succeeded in organizing themselves.[64] If a Constitutional Court had declared Hitler's Enabling Act unconstitutional, would the NSDAP have accepted that decision?

But will it really come to that? Of course, one can make a completely different assessment when it comes to militant democracy. For example, Weimar was not a 'lesson', but rather a very specific, traumatic case; things will generally turn out fine when democracies are confronted by antidemocrats. There are various possible answers to such a view.

The first is pragmatic. Parties *are* banned, so the practice should be studied.[65] Germany is not the only state to ban parties: countries as diverse as Belgium, Spain and Turkey, for example, do so too. Furthermore, France, Greece, Hungary, Bulgaria, Russia, Italy and Portugal also have regulations making it possible to act against antidemocrats.[66] Party bans are not always reasonably applied either, as in Turkey, where by 2004 eighteen parties had already been banned because of their Kurdish perspectives, and the ECHR consistently rejected Turkish party bans (before the Refah case).[67] Furthermore, it is often hard to see the use of party bans in Africa as a defence of democracy.[68] This practice of banning political parties is in need of justification *and* a theory for judging the legitimacy of specific party bans: which ones are just, and which merely conceal abuse of power?

The idea that 'in most cases it will not come to that' may come from the belief that a militant democracy is constructed exclusively to deal with a scenario in which an antidemocratic party neatly complies with all procedures in abolishing democracy. That is a misunderstanding. The point is that, under the guise of legality, antidemocratic parties can undermine democracy until it is on the verge of collapse. Whether the final push comes from a *coup d'état* or a 'collective abdication' is of little importance.[69]

To put it differently, antidemocratic parties can also do great damage when holding (only) a substantial minority. The NSDAP, for example, created the problem for which it professed to be the solution (unrest and the threat of civil war) not only in the street, but also in parliament—by effectively paralysing its most important institution, democracy could be accused of indecision and brought further into discredit.[70] As the American political scientist Robert Dahl writes:

> Even a large minority of militant and violent antidemocrats would probably be sufficient to destroy a country's capacity for maintaining its democratic institutions.[71]

That can easily be forgotten. In 2009 a very thorough report was drawn up, *Democratische waarborgen* (Democratic safeguards), after a discussion on democratic self-defence in the Dutch House of Representatives.[72] The report is unique in its kind in the Netherlands, describing all hurdles that must be overcome before Dutch democracy can actually be abolished. However, from this overview one might draw the conclusion that, taken together, all these hurdles form such a substantial obstacle to antidemocratic parties that it will never come to that. That might be the case, but such a view misses the point that antidemocratic parties do not always need a majority, and that they do not always need to comply with all democratic procedures to severely damage democracy.[73]

Even then, assuming all that is true, surely we are still talking about a theory designed for a very specific situation, associated with a traumatized European continent? In other words: is militant democracy not a typically European, un-American, problem? This has been suggested in American literature on the subject.[74] The answer is yes, but *not* because the problem is alien to American democracy. American exceptionalism assumes that American democracy offers the most freedom to divergent ideas; see the *First Amendment*, a monument to this conviction.[75] Banning parties is completely out of the question. The United States, however, can only afford this 'freedom' by employing one of the most restrictive party systems.[76] To be sure, the United States gives extremism more freedom, but this is only possible because in practice extremists have no chance whatsoever of participating in elections. They are *de facto* excluded early on by the 'duopoly' of Democrats and Republicans. However, the 2016 election of political eccentric Donald Trump as president, with a track record of dubious remarks when it comes to liberal democracy,[77] does provide (at least) a nuance to this theory. One might even argue that a two-party system is—from a militant democracy perspective—actually quite vulnerable once one of the two parties is 'seized' by an antidemocratic candidate or faction.[78] The difference with militant democracies, in any case, is that the exclusion is not informal or implicit, but imposed in complete openness, by judges who have to explain why they are keeping antidemocrats out of the electoral arena.[79]

Interestingly enough, Dutch democracy quite fairly resembles the American system, at least in terms of its degree of militancy. The Netherlands is traditionally seen as a primarily *procedural* democracy: the majority decides, and there is no extensive substantive framework it has to adhere to, although changing the constitution does require two readings in both houses of parliament, with a two-thirds majority in the second reading.[80] As a result, the Netherlands plays an insignificant role in comparative studies of militant democracy.[81] In some sense that is unwarranted. The Dutch system includes the possibility of banning parties via Article 20, Book 2 of the Civil Code—a rather odd place for such a fundamental regulation, which makes it easy to overlook.[82] And parties have indeed been banned in the Netherlands, as in the case of the extreme right CP'86 party in 1998. Actually, between 1944 and the present the Netherlands even banned *more* parties than the prototypical militant democracy of Germany.[83] The Dutch system, despite being essentially a procedural democracy, contains a number of good, quite coincidental solutions for the legal design of militant democracy, that is, the way in which the procedures concerning a party ban are designed. The focus of this study will, of course, not be on the precise technical details of the Dutch system. Nevertheless, the Dutch militant democracy will figure more than once as an example, as its procedural design may be of interest to scholars of militant democracy.

A study of militant democracy touches on the *concepts* of democracy: what sort of democracy are we defending? Of course, democracy, at a minimum, means a system in which the people govern themselves. But the procedural and substantive notions of democracy shape the further discussion on its precise meaning.[84] A procedural democracy sees democracy exclusively as a decision-making procedure, a 'market of ideas', in which all ideas are equal.[85] A substantive democracy sees democracy as founded on a number of fundamental values and is therefore emphatically *not* neutral with respect to ideas.[86] I do not propose to make a choice in advance between these notions of democracy. This book is an attempt to offer a new insight into what characterizes democracy, in order to use it as a foundation for the self-defence of democracy. Subsequently I will consider how the idea of democracy developed here relates to the procedural and substantive approaches, and why it provides a better foundation for a theory of militant democracy. The procedural and substantive models of democracy serve as the two 'beacons' in the discussion, and I will situate my conception of militant democracy on a scale between them. To be sure, *purely* procedural and substantive democracies are ideal types, to be used in political-philosophical argument; in reality, democracies show all kinds of degrees of 'substantiveness' (which is the subject of scholars of comparative constitutional law).[87]

The scope of militant democracy is not limited to protecting democracies that are already stable. After World War II West Germany was in fact a country in transition from a destructive dictatorship to a democracy. It sought support in the concept of militant democracy, which soon, in the 1950s, resulted in banning the Socialist Reich Party (the NSDAP's informal successor) and the Communist Party of Germany.[88] From the beginning militant democracy was presumed to be of use in 'transitional democracies'. If we assume that the presence of a democratic tradition really is the best guarantee of the survival of a democracy (Loewenstein),[89] or even constitutes one of the three necessary conditions for the existence of a democracy (Dahl),[90] then it can indeed play a role in strengthening new democracies. A democracy appears to be particularly vulnerable in its early days; when the memory of the undemocratic regime is still alive, its supporters are still powerful or tribal scores remain to be settled.[91] Militant democracy theory can help steer a democracy through this uncertain early phase, giving a democratic tradition and culture time to mature.

The Israeli-American sociologist Amitai Etzioni (born 1929) argues for what could be called a form of militant democracy in the Middle East,[92] viewing it as a third way between pessimistic realism (the idea that democracy in the Middle East inevitably leads to oppressive Islamist regimes) and naive non-realism (accept Islamism as a 'childhood disease' on the way to developing a mature democracy). Instead new democracies must be established slowly. Antidemocrats should initially be excluded, in order to give the more liberal, democratic powers the opportunity to develop. This is all the more necessary given that Islamist factions have generally already organized themselves, as in the case of the Muslim Brotherhood in Egypt.

Militant democracy also has some common ground with counterterrorism. Some antidemocratic or extremist parties have a clandestine terrorist branch, or, vice versa, some terrorist groups gain political ambitions. In Spain Batasuna, the political branch of the terrorist separatist movement ETA, was banned in 2003.[93] Ireland has Sinn Fein, the political branch of the IRA.[94] A statement by Danny Morrison, one of Sinn Fein's leaders, makes it clear why militant democracy sometimes enters the territory of counterterrorism. In 1981 Morrison, continuously entangled in a shadow dance between legality and illegality, said of Sinn Fein's strategy:

> Who here really believes we can win the war through the ballot box? But will anyone object if, with a ballot paper in one hand and the Armalite in the other, we take power in Ireland?[95]

It would be wise, by way of preliminary demarcation, to indicate what forms of intervention cannot take place in a militant democracy *under any circumstances.*

Misunderstandings can easily occur here. The first is intervention by an army in a democracy. The role of the Turkish army as protector of democracy and secularism in Turkey cannot be deemed a legitimate application of militant democracy.[96] The same goes for intervention by the Algerian army in 1991.[97] Even in its most basic form, militant democracy relies on a *judge* to decide when to intervene, as a minimal procedural safeguard. Moreover, for a democracy to even function, it is probably necessary that the army submits to *elected* government officials.[98]

Second, let us turn to the Guantanamo Bay detention of terrorist suspects. An 'extrajudicial space' of this kind cannot be justified on the basis of militant democracy.[99] The assumption of militant democracy, after all, is that action against the enemies of democracy is taken *within* the boundaries of the 'normal' constitutional order.[100] An issue like Guantanamo Bay, by contrast, belongs to the theory of the state of exception, with its far-reaching and general suspension of civil rights.[101]

Finally, a few words on the different terms used in different languages for the concept. Militant democracy, as it is referred to in English, is a term with different connotations from the *Streitbare* (or *Wehrhafte*) *Demokratie* commonly used in Germany, which expresses more of a 'defensive', than a 'militant or aggressive', attitude.[102] The Dutch *weerbare* also indicates a more reserved attitude, rather than an active or combative one. Both the German and the Dutch terms fit better with what is meant by a *defensive* democracy, at least here: a democracy that defends itself against antidemocratic powers. With *militant democracy* that nuance, reflecting a more reactive than proactive stance, is lost. Seen in that light, it is unfortunate that Loewenstein launched the idea in the 1930s as *militant democracy* and the literature in English tends to follow him in this, although it does tell us something about Loewenstein's temperament, particularly his views on democracy, as will be made clear later on. Here I will submit to the custom in the English literature and use the term 'militant democracy'.

5. This book

If you were to ask a random passerby, 'Why exactly are you pro-democracy?' the answer might be, 'Well, we don't have anything better, do we?' or words to that effect. It is an often heard answer, which goes back to an endlessly repeated cliché spoken by Winston Churchill (1874-1965) in 1947, labelling democracy 'the worst form of Government except all those others that have been tried.'[103] Instead of representing profundity, this appears to be what philosopher Daniel Dennett (born 1942) calls a *deepity*: it appears profound, because of the apparent opposition, but some reflection will quickly reveal it to be a superficial statement.[104] More importantly, it is an indulgent defence that not only reinforces technocrats in their sometimes barely concealed disgust at democracy, but also more generally hampers the defence of democratic values. That is remarkable coming from a statesman who in other respects has been so significant for democracy. But if *that* is the intellectual defence, a democracy can never be truly resilient. More is needed: how can you really defend a democracy in word and deed if you believe you are merely supporting the least bad system out there?

In that case, we have more to learn from a strong enemy of (parliamentary) democracy, the German lawyer and political philosopher Carl Schmitt (1888-1985). In the 1920s he launched a vicious attack on parliamentary democracy. Schmitt challenges democrats to make explicit the intellectual foundations of their system and asks:

> Certainly no one would be so undemanding that he regarded an intellectual foundation or a moral truth as proven by the question, what else?[105]

Churchill's popular pearl of wisdom does precisely that: we are *for* democracy, but *only* because nothing else works. Schmitt is right, and that is why we must attempt to provide Schmitt with an answer. This book takes up the gauntlet and attempts to present a positive defence of democracy: what makes democracy unique? What is so special about democracy that we want to defend it? The answer cannot be that we don't have anything better. The quest for a justification for banning parties, and for militant democracy, is therefore also a quest for the essence of democracy.

That is precisely the way in which Amsterdam professor of constitutional law George van den Bergh (1890-1966) approached this question. In 1936 he was the first to formulate a political-philosophical answer to the question, is it permissible for a democracy to ban antidemocratic parties?[106] His answer was: yes, a democracy can ban parties. Van den Bergh's defence rests on a principle I would like to call 'democracy as self-correction',[107] an idea that we come across, before him, in part in the work of the French legal scholar Milan Markovitch, and after Van den Bergh only in a limited form in Karl Popper's work. In a democracy all decisions are *revocable*. The people govern themselves by means of continuous self-correction.[108] There is, however, one decision that evades that self-correction: the decision to abolish democracy. That decision overthrows the framework that enables self-correction in the first place; it is a decision that the people can never revoke in a peaceful, *democratic* manner. That is why democrats are permitted to resist that one decision. This principle forms the foundation of the theory of militant democracy in this book.

First we will examine in detail George van den Bergh's theory and the intellectual context in which he formulated it, the explicitly antidemocratic atmosphere of the 1930s. I also compare Van den Bergh's work with that of his contemporary Karl Loewenstein, the 'father' of militant democracy, the current interpretation of Loewenstein by ECHR judge and constitutional lawyer András Sajó and the criticism of Loewenstein's work by historian Udi Greenberg. I contrast Van den Bergh with his most important opponent, the Austrian philosopher of law Hans Kelsen, which will result in two possible interpretations of Van den Bergh's theory: 'principled democracy' and 'democracy as self-correction'. Under the latter interpretation I will also discuss Milan Markovitch's variant. Chapter 1 closes with a comparison between both interpretations of Van den Bergh and a preliminary formulation of democracy as self-correction as a theory of militant democracy.

Chapter 2 addresses alternatives and criticism. In the literature on militant democracy, in the absence of a general theory, authors tend to seek the support of various lawyers and political philosophers. Normally they pick Karl Popper, the philosopher of 'intolerance of the intolerant', while Carl Schmitt, John Stuart Mill and John Rawls are also regularly mentioned. Chapter 2 investigates whether these references are really helpful: can a militant democracy theory really be distilled from the theories of these thinkers? I then discuss two important contemporary attempts to come to a fully-fledged theory of militant democracy: Alexander Kirshner's political science study and Svetlana Tyulkina's comparative legal and theoretical study.

I proceed to address several critiques of militant democracy. They fall into two categories: pragmatic criticism ('it doesn't work') and principled criticism ('the concept of militant democracy is not sound'). Following British political scientist Tim Bale, the discussion of pragmatic criticism focuses on two questions. First, will banned parties not simply re-establish themselves? In other words, are party bans *ineffective*? Second, will antidemocrats not go underground, thereby leading to more violence? That is to say, are party bans *counterproductive*? The pragmatic criticism is answered in this chapter; the principled criticism is answered in chapter 3.

Chapter 3 elaborates on 'democracy as self-correction' to form a comprehensive theory of militant democracy, first by connecting Van den Bergh and Popper's ideas more explicitly, then by consulting other authors who support democracy as self-correction. These authors each map out a specific aspect of democracy as self-correction: the *learning* capacity of democracy, the *revocability* of decisions and the *temporary nature* of majorities.

We then put ourselves in the place of the judge who is called upon to ban a party. How do we ensure that a militant democracy is 'workable' from the perspective of a judge? First, that means that the justification for a party ban, and with it the *reason for the ban*, must be as concrete as possible. How can a judge assess whether a party is antidemocratic? In other words, when is self-correction so threatened that it may be said that the framework itself will sustain lasting damage? To answer this question, we take inspiration from two high-level European judicial institutions, beginning with the court that may well have the most clearly worked-out theory of militant democracy, namely, the highest court in Germany, the Federal Constitutional Court. This will be followed by the court with a European helicopter view, which reviews party bans from all over Europe, the European Court for Human Rights. How do they define such a fundamental concept as 'democracy', and how is it subsequently assessed? What elements do they distinguish within the concept of 'democracy'? And what elements are relevant to the capacity to self-correct, to the idea that the people govern themselves through self-correction?

I also look at procedural safeguards. It is regularly stated that judicial supervision is essential to a militant democracy; it is even what distinguishes it to an important extent from the state of exception, for example. But where should we look for those safeguards? They may be sought in the institution calling for a ban and an independent judge deciding on the requested ban. But it will become apparent that, in Europe, these safeguards can also increasingly be sought on a supranational level. The ECHR is a good example of such external supervision of democracy. In Europe it is not the judge embedded in the national democracy who has the final word on the legitimacy of party bans, but a more distant supranational court. Is that a desirable development? Furthermore, we will look at the remarkable situation with respect to militant democracy in the EU: on the one hand there is a development in the direction of more intensive EU control over national democracies, while on the other hand there is actual and potential resistance to the progression of European integration from national judges 'in the name' of militant democracy. Can a country that has cast its democracy in stone with an eternity clause, as Germany has done, really be absorbed into a federal European Union? The chapter concludes with a reply to the principled criticism left unanswered in chapter 2; with the theory of democracy as self-correction in hand, it must now be possible to answer this satisfactorily.

The conclusion summarizes the theory of democracy as self-correction on the basis of the previous chapters, while the epilogue looks ahead at a question that could not be addressed within the scope of this book: what does a militant democracy demand of democratic citizens and officials? In short, what do militant democracy and democracy as self-correction mean in a *political* and *cultural* sense; what should our democratic ethos be?

That is the path that lies before us. The ultimate goal is a coherent theory of militant democracy *and* a better answer to the fundamental question, why do we want democracy? We start in the 1930s, with one of the most distinguished intellectuals of the time, who remains a much-read socialist critic of society to this day—and his plan for an order of 'liberal fascists'.

Notes

1. Carl Schmitt, *Die geistesgeschichtliche Lage des heutigen Parlamentarismus*, München/Leipzig: Duncker and Humblot 1926, p. 7. The first edition of this work appeared in 1923; the quotation comes from the new *Vorbemerkung* in the 1926 edition. The English translation reads as follows: 'Certainly no one would be so undemanding that he regarded an intellectual foundation or a moral truth as proven by the question, What else?' See Carl Schmitt, *The Crisis of Parliamentary Democracy* (*Die geistesgeschichtliche Lage des heutigen Parlamentarismus*), Cambridge (M.A.): MIT Press 1988, p. 3.

2. Joseph W. Bendersky, *A Concise History of Nazi Germany*, Lanham: Rowman and Littlefield 2014, p. 44.
3. Bendersky 2014, p. 44; Frank McDonough, *Hitler and the Rise of the Nazi Party*, Abingdon/New York: Routledge 2014, p. 48.
4. McDonough 2014, p. 48.
5. McDonough 2014, p. 48.
6. Bendersky 2014, p. 45–46.
7. Bendersky 2014, p. 46.
8. Bendersky 2014, p. 46.
9. Eric D. Weitz, *Weimar Germany: Promise and Tragedy*, Princeton: Princeton University Press 2013, p. 342–343.
10. Bendersky 2014, p. 46; see also p. 84: in the end, the 'Nazi revolution' was completed 'through a series of legal, pseudolegal, and clearly illegal maneuvers' (see also p. 85).
11. Bendersky 2014, p. 47.
12. Ivan Ermakoff, *Ruling Oneself Out: A Theory of Collective Abdications*, Durham and London: Duke University Press 2008, p. 6; Weitz 2013, p. 351.
13. Bendersky 2014, p. 54.
14. Ermakoff 2008, p. 6.
15. Weitz 2013, p. 351.
16. From 1932 the elections follow in quick succession: on 31 July 1932 the NSDAP wins 37.4 percent of the vote, on 6 November 1932, 33.1 percent and on 5 March 1933, 45 percent. See Ermakoff 2008, p. 15–17, and Bendersky 2014, p. 75–80 and 86–87 (Bendersky makes the figure at the last elections 43.9 percent).
17. These elections take place on 5 March 1933; the NSDAP receives 45 percent of the vote. See Ermakoff 2008, p. 17; Willem Melching and Marcel Stuivenga, 'Revolutie en consolidatie 1933-1934' ('Revolution and consolidation 1933-1934'), p. 34–38 (36), in Willem Melching and Marcel Stuivenga (eds.), *Joseph Goebbels: Hitlers spindoctor, een selectie uit de dagboeken 1933-1945* (Joseph Goebbels: Hitler's spin doctor, a selection from the diaries 1933-1945), Amsterdam: Bert Bakker 2011. On the restrictions, intimidation and atmosphere of fear under which these elections took place, see Ermakoff 2008, p. 16–17, and for an extensive discussion: Bendersky 2014, p. 85–86. The best result that the NSDAP achieved in *free* elections is therefore the 37.4 percent on 31 July 1932 (Bendersky 2014, p. 75). See also Afshin Ellian, 'Op de grens van vrijheid: ketterij in de vrije samenleving' ('On the boundary of freedom: heresy in free society'), p. 89–115 (106–107), in Afshin Ellian, Gelijn Molier and Tom Zwart (eds.), *Mag ik dit zeggen? Beschouwingen over de vrijheid van meningsuiting* (May I say this? Views on freedom of expression), The Hague: Boom Juridische Uitgevers 2011.
18. In 1930 the share of seats occupied by parties hostile to Weimar was still 39 percent; after the elections of 31 July 1932 it was 59 percent. See Ermakoff 2008, p. 11 and 15; for 1933 see p. 18.
19. Ermakoff 2008, p. 20.
20. Bendersky 2014, p. 88. Moreover, such emergency legislation could also no longer be revoked by the Reichstag, whereas on the basis of Article 48 of the Weimar constitution this was still possible. Formally the president could still function as a check: he maintained the option of dismissing the chancellor, but the elderly Paul von Hindenburg (deteriorating physically and psychologically) never made use of this option. When Hindenburg died on 2 August 1934, Hitler immediately announced the merging of the offices of president and chancellor (Bendersky 2014, p. 96).
21. Ermakoff 2008, p. 18.
22. Bendersky 2014, p. 87.

23. Bendersky 2014, p. 87.
24. Bendersky 2014, p. 88.
25. Ermakoff 2008, p. 20; on this decision by the Centre Party, see in more detail: Ivan Ermakoff, 'Frail Democracy', in Afshin Ellian and Bastiaan Rijpkema (eds.), *Militant Democracy: Political Science, Law and Philosophy, forthcoming* Springer 2018.
26. Ermakoff 2008, p. 20.
27. Diary of Joseph Goebbels, 25-3-1933, p. 44, in Melching and Stuivenga 2011.
28. Bendersky 2014, p. 87: 'Its passage [that of the Enabling Act, BR] was nothing less than a political revolution that finally ended the Weimar Republic.' Of course there are nuances to the Weimar story; or rather, the story could be told in many different ways. Had Weimar's fate not already been sealed, for instance, with the choice of Hitler as chancellor in January 1933 (Marc de Wilde, *Verwantschap in Extremen: Politieke Theologie bij Walter Benjamin en Carl Schmitt* [Affinity in Extremes: Political theology of Walter Benjamin and Carl Schmitt, diss. Amsterdam UvA], Amsterdam: Vossiuspers/Amsterdam University Press 2008, p. 93), or the issuing of very restrictive emergency decrees on 28 February 1933, after the Reichstag fire (Ermakoff 2008, p. 21), or earlier, when the last normally functioning majority government failed on 27 March 1930 (De Wilde 2008, p. 94)? Did Weimar not really come to an end because of abuse of Article 48, which, although it was meant to protect the constitution, was in fact used to invoke a sort of unconstitutional presidential system, paving the way for Hitler (De Wilde 2008, p. 93)? It might be pointed out that Hindenburg did not need Article 48 to help Hitler to power, although, on the other hand, parliament was largely sidelined due to governing on the basis of this article (De Wilde 2008, p. 93–94). This, in combination with the machinations of Franz von Papen to achieve 'containment', enabled Hitler to do something that he had not yet achieved through elections and revolution: to seize power, at a moment when a majority (55 percent) of the German people were still against the NSDAP and Hitler (or at least not *for* them) (Bendersky 2014, p. 82–83). It should, however, be observed as a side note that at the start of 1933 Hindenburg felt *compelled* to appoint Hitler as chancellor, because, even without a majority, the NSDAP had recently become the largest party for the second time in succession (De Wilde 2008, p. 93 and note 4). It should also be remembered that in July 1932 the *antidemocratic* (anti-Weimar) part of the Reichstag (consisting of the Communist Party [KPD], the German National People's Party [DNVP] and the NSDAP) already held 59 percent of the seats and that this share would eventually grow to 65 percent in March 1933 (Ermakoff 2008, p. 15 and 18). Perhaps then there was never a full majority for the NSDAP; a large proportion of the German population were behind an undemocratic alternative to Weimar (see also Mark Chou, *Theorising Democide: Why and How Democracies Fail*, Basingstoke: Palgrave Macmillan 2013, p. 67). Finally, one might wonder to what extent the Enabling Act was a 'blank cheque' involving complete transfer of power to Hitler. For a discussion of this issue, see Ermakoff 2008, p. 37–42, who answers in the affirmative: the Enabling Act was indeed a blank cheque; see p. 37 and 41.
29. Ermakoff 2008, p. 21–23.
30. As the *Frankfurter Zeitung* aptly put it at the time; see Ermakoff 2008, p. 42.
31. See Ermakoff 2008, p. xxi and 23–34. In 1923 the Acerbo Law was adopted, stating that the largest party (or candidate list) would automatically receive two thirds of seats in parliament, as long as it gained at least a quarter of all votes. According to Ermakoff, this cleared the way to legal assumption of power by the fascists (p. xxi). The Acerbo Law received broad support; only the Catholics resisted. In the elections of April 1924 the government list

(including right-wing liberals alongside Mussolini's fascists) received 66 percent of the vote (and thus did not require the Acerbo Law in the end); more than half of the new members of parliament were fascists. For all of this, see Christopher Duggan, *A Concise History of Italy*, Cambridge: Cambridge University Press 2014, p. 210–211.

32. See Ermakoff 2008, p. 23–34. See also Jan-Werner Müller, 'Defending Democracy within the EU', *Journal of Democracy* 2013, vol. 24 no. 2, p. 138–149 (143) (henceforth Müller 2013a).
33. John Keane, *The Life and Death of Democracy*, London: Pocket Books 2010, p. 96, and extensive treatment in Robert J. Buck, *Thrasybulus and the Athenian Democracy*, Stuttgart: Franz Steiner Verlag 1998, p. 24, and Martha Taylor, 'Implicating the Demos: A Reading of Thucydides on the Rise of the Four Hundred', *Journal of Hellenic Studies* 2002, vol. 122, p. 91–108.
34. Gregory H. Fox and Georg Nolte, 'Intolerant Democracies', *Harvard International Law Journal* 1995, vol. 36 no. 1, p. 1–70 (6).
35. Fox and Nolte 1995, p. 6.
36. Fox and Nolte 1995, p. 6, note 19.
37. Fox and Nolte 1995, p. 7.
38. Samuel Issacharoff, 'Fragile Democracies', *Harvard Law Review* 2007, vol. 120, p. 1405–1467 (1450–1451, note 197). With respect to the intervention, Issacharoff also states, 'Even the most extreme cases, such as the Algerian military intervention to prevent a parliament from forming around a platform of eliminating democracy, are not so readily dismissed as simply counterproductive exercises, despite the resulting military confrontation.'
39. Quoted in Fox and Nolte 1995, p. 7.
40. Issacharoff 2007, p. 1465 and note 251.
41. Gregory Tardi, 'Political Parties' Right to Engage in Politics', p. 81–111 (103), in András Sajó (ed.), *Militant Democracy,* Utrecht: Eleven Publishing 2004; for the party programme, see ECHR 13 February 2003, 41340/98, 41342/98 and 41344/98, *NJ* 2005, 73, incl. note E.A. Alkema (Refah Partisi/Turkey), §116-127, in particular §123.
42. He did so in a speech as early as January 1991; see Banu Eligür, *The Mobilization of Political Islam in Turkey*, Cambridge: Cambridge University Press 2010, p. 217 (for other statements by several party members and their context, see p. 218–219).
43. See EHRM Refah Partisi.
44. See 'Egypt's Tragedy: Islam, Democracy and Soldiers', *The Economist*, 6 July 2013, and Daniel Steinvorth and Volkhard Windfuhr, 'Morsi's Grab for Power: Egyptian Revolutionaries Take on Radical Islam', *Der Spiegel* (online), 26 November 2012.
45. See *De wil van het volk? Erosie van de democratische rechtsstaat in Europa* (The will of the people? Erosion of democracy under the rule of law in Europe) (no. 104), Advisory Council on International Affairs (AIV), June 2017, The Hague, p. 43–44, 47–48; an English translation of the report is available at https://aiv-advice.nl/download/efa5b666-1301-45ef-8702-360939cb4b6a.pdf; 'Opinion on the new constitution of Hungary', *Commission for Democracy through Law* (Venice Commission), adopted in the 87e plenary session, 17-18 June 2011, p. 6–7; see also Susanna Mancini, 'The Tempting of Europe, the Political Seduction of the Cross: A Schmittian Reading of Christianity and Islam in European Constitutionalism', p. 111–135 (132), in Susanna Mancini and Michel Rosenfeld (eds.), *Constitutional Secularism in an Age of Religious Revival,* Oxford: Oxford University Press 2014, and James Kirchick, 'Wrong Way Down the Danube: How Hungary's Democratic Backsliding Threatens Europe', *Foreign Affairs* (online), 10 July 2012. A growing literature

documents the deteriorations of the rule of law and democracy under Fidesz in Hungary; for an overview, see Bastiaan Rijpkema, 'Democratie als zelfcorrectie *revisited*: nadere aantekeningen bij de weerbare democratie' (Democracy as self-correction revisited: further remarks on militant democracy), p. 31–59, in Afshin Ellian, Gelijn Molier and Bastiaan Rijpkema (eds.), *De strijd om de democratie: essays over democratische zelfverdediging* (The battle for democracy: essays on democratic self-defence), Amsterdam: Boom 2018.

46. Mitchell A. Orenstein, Péter Krekó, and Attila Juhász, 'The Hungarian Putin?', *Foreign Affairs* (online), 8 February 2015; János Kornai, 'Hungary's U-turn: Retreating from Democracy', *Journal of Democracy* 2015, vol. 26 no. 3, p. 34–48 (41–42).
47. James McAuley, 'Hungary Votes to Keep Prime Minister and Right Wing in Power', *The Washington Post* (online), 8 April 2018; 'Anti-migrant PM Claims Election Win, Vows to "Defend Hungary"', *CBC.ca/The Associated Press*, 8 April 2018.
48. 'Hungary in the Crossfire: Orbán Lashes Out at Critics in European Parliament', *Der Spiegel* (online), 19 January 2012; Lily Bayer and Maïa de la Baume, 'European Parliament Report Calls for Sanctions Procedure against Hungary', *Politico.com*, 12 April 2018; 'EU Parliament votes to punish Hungary over "breaches" of core values', *BBC.com*, 12 September 2018.
49. 'Rule of Law: European Commission Acts to Defend Judicial Independence in Poland', *European Commission Press Release*, 20 December 2017, http://europa.eu/rapid/press-release_IP-17-5367_en.htm; Maïa de la Baume, 'European Commission "Very Close" to Triggering Article 7 on Poland', *Politico.com*, 19 July 2017.
50. See also Chou 2013, in particular p. 12, 44, 64–65, 75 and 78, who speaks in this context, following John Keane, of 'democide': a democracy can commit suicide because of *too much* democracy (no restriction whatsoever on 'ideas and perspectives') and *too little* democracy (very extensive restrictions); this 'tragedy' is part and parcel of democracy. Chou builds on political science research that suggests that in 40 percent of the cases in which a democracy comes to an end it is due to 'endogenous' factors; that is, the cause of the downfall lies in the government and administration (and thus in the democratic system itself); see Ko Meada, 'Two Modes of Democratic Breakdown: A Competing Risks Analysis of Democratic Durability', *Journal of Politics* 2010, vol. 72 no. 4, p. 1129–1143 (1130), in Chou 2013; see p. 10–11.
51. Karl Loewenstein, 'Autocracy versus Democracy in Contemporary Europe, I', *American Political Science Review* 1935, vol. 29 no. 4, p. 571–593 (577–588) (henceforth Loewenstein 1935a). For the summary of three weaknesses given here, see Paul Cliteur and Bastiaan Rijpkema, 'The Foundations of Militant Democracy', p. 227–272 (235–236), in Afshin Ellian and Gelijn Molier, *The State of Exception and Militant Democracy in a Time of Terror*, Dordrecht: Republic of Letters Publishing 2012.
52. Loewenstein 1935a, p. 571.
53. Karl Loewenstein, 'Militant Democracy and Fundamental Rights, I', *American Political Science Review* 1937, vol. 31 no. 3, p. 417–432 (423) (henceforth Loewenstein 1937a).
54. See, for example, Markus Thiel (ed.), *The 'Militant Democracy' Principle in Modern Democracies*, Farnham: Ashgate 2009.
55. For an overview, see Angela Bourne, 'Militant Democracy and the Banning of Political Parties in Democratic States: Why Some Do and Why Some Don't', in Ellian and Rijpkema *forthcoming* 2018.
56. Loewenstein 1937a, p. 432.

57. Chou 2013, p. 68, also points more generally to this risk of Loewenstein's ideas.
58. See Jan-Werner Müller, 'A "Practical Dilemma Which Philosophy Alone Cannot Resolve?" Rethinking Militant Democracy: An Introduction', *Constellations* 2012, vol. 19 no. 4, p. 536–539 (536–537); Gur Bligh, 'Defending Democracy: A New Understanding of the Party-Banning Phenomenon', *Vanderbilt Journal of Transnational Law* 2013, vol. 46 no. 5, p. 1321–1379 (1326–1327); Nancy Rosenblum, 'Banning Parties: Religious and Ethnic Partisanship in Multicultural Democracies', *Law and Ethics of Human Rights* 2007, vol. 1 no. 1, p. 17–57 (18), note 2; see also recently: Carlo Invernizzi Accetti and Ian Zuckerman, 'What's Wrong with Militant Democracy?', *Political Studies* 2017, vol. 65, p. 182–199 (183).
59. Müller 2012, p. 536–537. Recently normative dimensions of the militant democracy discussion have attracted increasing attention; see Jan-Werner Müller, 'Protecting Popular Self-Government from the People? New Normative Perspectives on Militant Democracy', *Annual Review of Political Science* 2016, vol. 19, p. 249–265. Two important monographs attempt to fill the void and attempt to offer *mutatis mutandis* a theory of militant democracy; they are discussed at length below (see chapter 2): Alexander Kirshner's *A Theory of Militant Democracy: The Ethics of Combatting Political Extremism,* New Haven and London: Yale University Press 2014, and Svetlana Tyulkina's *Militant Democracy: Undemocratic Political Parties and Beyond*, London/New York: Routledge 2015.
60. This distinction was first clearly put into words by George van den Bergh in 1936; see chapter 1 for a detailed discussion.
61. See Jan-Werner Müller, 'Who Is the European Prince? A More or Less Machiavellian Meditation on the European Union', *Social Research: An International Quarterly* 2014, vol. 81 no. 1, p. 243–267 (251–252), and Müller 2013a, p. 142–143.
62. Ernst Hirsch Ballin, *De Grondwet in politiek en samenleving. Rechtsstaatlezing 2013* (The Constitution in politics and society. Rule of law lecture 2013), The Hague: Boom Lemma Uitgevers 2013, p. 36.
63. 'Democracy under the rule of law' is taken here to be equivalent to the Dutch concept of 'democratische rechtsstaat'. See on these notions, more specifically the 'rule of law': Erik Jurgens, 'Het verschil tussen *rechtsstaat* en *rule of law*: inzichtelijk rapport van de Venice Commission van de Raad van Europa' (The difference between *rechtsstaat* and the *rule of law*: insightful report by the Venice Commission of the Council of Europe), *NTM/NJCM-bulletin* 2011, p. 867–872; *Report on the Rule of Law*, European Commission for Democracy Through Law (Venice Commission), 10-11 March 2011 (86th Plenary Session), p. 4; Paul Cliteur and Afshin Ellian, *Legaliteit en legitimiteit: de grondslagen van het recht* (Legality and legitimacy: the foundations of law), Leiden: Leiden University Press 2016, p. 53–54.
64. See Kirshner 2014, p. 14.
65. See also Tyulkina 2015, p. 21.
66. See Pieter Vanden Heede, 'Het Europees Hof voor de Rechten van de Mens en het Partijverbod: dansen op een slap koord' ('The European Court of Human Rights and the Party Ban: dancing on a slack rope'), p. 193–232 (193 and note 2), in Maurice Adams and Patricia Popelier (eds.), *Recht en democratie: de democratische verbeelding in het recht* (Law and democracy: the democratic illusion of law), Antwerp: Intersentia 2004; see also Issacharoff 2007, p. 1409–1410, and for a detailed discussion Martin Klamt, 'Militant Democracy and the Democratic Dilemma: Different Ways of Protecting Democratic Constitutions',

p. 133–158 (133–134), in Fred Bruinsma and David Nelken (eds.), *Explorations in Legal Cultures,* Reed Business NV 2007.

67. See Tyulkina 2015, p. 171 and 180.
68. Matthijs Bogaards, Matthias Basedau and Christof Hartmann, 'Ethnic Party Bans in Africa: An Introduction', *Democratization* 2010, vol. 17 no. 4, p. 599–617 (611–612), and Matthias Basedau and Anika Moroff, 'Parties in Chains: Do Ethnic Party Bans in Africa Promote Peace?', *Party Politics* 2011, vol. 17 no. 2, p. 205–222 (217).
69. This is also Loewenstein's view. See Loewenstein 1935a, p. 579–580; see also Bendersky 2014, p. 46. 'Collective abdication' is a term coined by Ivan Ermakoff; see Ermakoff 2008.
70. See also Issacharoff 2007, 1410.
71. Robert A. Dahl, *On Democracy*, Yale: Yale University Press 2000, p. 158; see also Issacharoff 2007, p. 1410.
72. W. van der Woude, *Democratische waarborgen* (Democratic safeguards), Deventer: Kluwer 2009. The report was drawn up after a debate about statements by Minister of Justice Donner; see p. 9. Donner had claimed that if a two-thirds majority wanted to introduce sharia law in the Netherlands, this should be possible. See Max van Weezel and Margalith Kleijwegt, 'Piet Hein Donner: "De meerderheid telt!"' ('Piet Hein Donner: "The Majority Counts!"'), *Vrij Nederland*, 16 September 2006: 'It must be possible for Muslim groups to come to power by democratic means. Every citizen can make a case for changing the law as long as he complies with the law in the meantime. To me it is clear: if two thirds of all Dutch citizens wanted to introduce Sharia law tomorrow, then surely that possibility must exist? You cannot legally prevent such a thing. It would be scandalous to say, "That is not allowed!" The majority counts. That is the very essence of democracy.'
73. See extensively: Kirshner 2014, p. 12–14, as discussed below in chapter 2; Loewenstein 1935a, p. 579–580; and Van der Woude 2009, in the report itself, making a disclaimer at p. 64–65.
74. See Stephen Holmes, 'Andras Sajó (ed.), Militant Democracy' (review), *International Journal of Constitutional Law* 2006, vol. 4 no. 3, p. 586–591 (589).
75. Gur Bligh, 'Extremism in the Electoral Arena: Challenging the Myth of American Exceptionalism', *Brigham Young University Law Review* 2008, p. 1367–1440. In full the *First Amendment* states, 'Congress shall make no law respecting an establishment of religion, or prohibiting the free exercise thereof; or abridging the freedom of speech, or of the press; or the right of the people peaceably to assemble, and to petition the government for a redress of grievances.'
76. See Bligh 2008, p. 1390, 1396 and 1413, Issacharoff 2007, p. 1420–1421, and Suzie Navot, 'Fighting Terrorism in the Political Arena: the Banning of Political Parties', *Party Politics* 2008, vol. 14 no. 6, p. 745–762 (747).
77. For an overview, see Adam Liptak, 'Trump vs. the Constitution', *The New York Times* (online), 29 November 2016.
78. The political eccentric Trump could not win outside the two-party system; but the Republican Party, after a certain point, did not dare to let him run as an independent candidate and risk losing the 2016 elections, or even the elections thereafter if an independent candidate Trump would cause a rupture in the Republican Party (which is fatal in a two-party system); see Jan-Werner Müller in the preface to the Dutch edition of *What Is Populism?*, Jan-Werner Müller, *Wat is populisme?*, Amsterdam: Nieuw Amsterdam 2017, p. 12–13.
79. See also Bligh 2008, p. 1440: 'Only when we are truly aware of the nature of these limitations can we avoid their misuse and over-reaching and ensure that we are drawing the restrictive line in the proper place.'

80. Van der Woude 2009, p. 76.
81. See, for example, Tyulkina 2015; Martin Klamt, *Die Europäische Union als Streitbare Demokratie: Rechtsvergleichende und europarechtliche Dimensionen einer Idee*, München: Herbert Utz Verlag 2012; and Thiel 2009.
82. See in detail: Gelijn Molier and Bastiaan Rijpkema, 'Naar een afzonderlijke bepaling inzake het partijverbod' (Towards an independent legal provision regarding party bans), *Nederlands Juristenblad* 2017, vol. 92 no. 10, p. 662–664.
83. Depending on the definitions used, of course; see the overview of banned parties in Europe in Bourne *forthcoming* 2018.
84. See Th. L. Bellekom, 'Partijverboden' ('Party Bans'), p. 113–146 (114–119), in A.W. Heringa, R.E. de Winter and W.J. Witteveen, *Staatkundig Jaarboek 1982-1983* (Political almanac 1982-1983), Leiden 1982.
85. See Bellekom 1982, p. 118.
86. See Bellekom 1982, p. 117.
87. R. de Lange, N. Efthymiou and F. van Tienen, *Risico's voor de democratie: een juridische verkenning van het gevaar-criterium in het democratisch verdedigingsrepertoire in vijf landen: Duitsland, Frankrijk, Spanje, het Verenigd Koninkrijk en de Verenigde Staten* (Risks for democracy: a legal exploration of the 'threat'-criterion in the democratic defense repertoire of five countries: Germany, France, Spain, the United Kingdom, and the United States), Rotterdam: Erasmus Universiteit Rotterdam 2016, p. 13 and note 25.
88. See A.J. Nieuwenhuis, 'Partijverbod en supraconstitutionalisme in rechtsvergelijkend perspectief' ('Party bans and supraconstitutionalism from a comparative legal perspective'), p. 199–213 (201–202), in J.L. de Reede and J.H. Reestman (eds.), *Op het snijvlak van recht en politiek: Opstellen aangeboden aan prof. mr. L. Prakke* (On the cutting edge of law and politics: Papers presented to Professor L. Prakke), Deventer: Kluwer 2003.
89. Loewenstein 1935a, p. 588.
90. Dahl 2000, p. 147. The other essential factors are 'control military and police by elected officials' and 'no strong foreign control hostile to democracy'.
91. See Issacharoff 2007, p. 1465 and note 251.
92. Amitai Etzioni, 'Democracy Is Not a Suicide Pact', *The National Interest* (online), 7 January 2007, the introduction to which appeared in *The National Interest* 2007, no. 90, p. 13.
93. See Thomas Ayres, 'Batasuna Banned: The Dissolution of Political Parties under the European Convention of Human Rights', *Boston College International and Comparative Law Review* 2004, vol. 27, p. 99–113. For a timeline, see 'Batasuna Banned Permanently', BBC (online), 17 March 2003.
94. Rosenblum 2007, p. 45.
95. Clive Walker, 'Militant Speech about Terrorism in a Smart Militant Democracy', *Mississippi Law Journal* 2011, vol. 80 no. 4, p. 1395–1453 (1404–1405); on his description of 'walking on eggshells' between legality and illegality, see p. 1405.
96. Klamt 2007, p. 153.
97. See Issacharoff 2007, p. 1450–1451.
98. Dahl 2000, p. 148–149.
99. See Klamt 2007, p. 153.
100. See also Tyulkina 2015, p. 157 and 217–218.
101. That is not to say that Guantanamo Bay can be justified within the theory of the state of exception (in fact, it probably cannot); see, for example, Marc de Wilde, 'Safeguarding the Constitution with and against Carl Schmitt' (discussion of Ellen Kennedy, *Constitutional Failure: Carl Schmitt in Weimar*, Durham: Duke University Press 2004, and Giorgio Agamben, *State of Exception*,

Chicago: University of Chicago Press 2005), *Political Theory* 2006, vol. 34 no. 4, p. 510–515 (514).

102. Klamt 2007, p. 133, and note 2.
103. Roland Quinault, 'Winston Churchill and Democracy', p. 27–46 (44), in David Cannadine and Roland Quinault (eds.), *Winston Churchill in the Twenty First Century*, Cambridge: Cambridge University Press 2004.
104. See Daniel Dennett, *Intuition Pumps and Other Tools for Thinking*, New York: W.W. Norton 2014, p. 56–57.
105. Schmitt 1988, p. 3; see also p. 76.
106. He did so in George van den Bergh, *De democratische Staat en de niet-democratische partijen* (The democratic state and the nondemocratic parties), Amsterdam: De Arbeiderspers 1936 (henceforth Van den Bergh 1936a), later republished as *Wat te doen met antidemocratische partijen? De oratie van George van den Bergh uit 1936* (What to do with antidemocratic parties? The inaugural lecture of George van den Bergh, 1936), Amsterdam: Elsevier Boeken 2014. Here I refer to the 1936 edition.
107. The term 'democracy as self-correction' was introduced in Cliteur and Rijpkema 2012 to describe Van den Bergh's notion of militant democracy. The term is also used by Ivan Krastev in a paper for the Transatlantic Academy on the decline of trust in democratic institutions and the effect on the self-corrective potential of democracies, see Ivan Krastev, 'Democracy as Self-Correction', *Transatlantic Academy Paper Series 2012-2013*, 10 December 2012.
108. See Van den Bergh 1936a, p. 9–10.

1 Origins and development

1. The antidemocratic interbellum

In the summer of 1932 H.G. Wells (1866-1946), a prominent British writer and intellectual, gave a lecture in Oxford. The occasion was a summer school for liberal youths. Wells was there by his own account to aid 'a kind of "Phoenix Rebirth" of Liberalism',[1] a statement that turned out to be no exaggeration. The liberal youths had to leave behind the 'sentimental casualness' of nineteenth-century liberalism. The new ideal was that of the 'Liberal *Fascisti*'.[2] Like Mussolini's Italian *Fascisti* the new liberal vanguard had to ensure that state and party became one. Liberalism would thus completely replace the slow, indecisive parliamentary democracy.

These might seem surprising ideas for a progressive socialist critic such as Wells. Nevertheless, he meant every word. Wells saw fascism as a necessary instrument for creating a 'liberal' utopia, a world state without the evil influences of private property and individualism.[3] Essential to this vision was the quest for a so-called 'competent receiver', an alliance consisting of only exceptional people, capable of leading human society.[4] Mussolini's *Fascisti* were a concrete example of this receiver.[5]

Wells emphasized that these ideas were directly opposed to the principles of parliamentary democracy.[6] Ultimately to Wells the idea of 'democracy' was a hopelessly anachronistic relic;[7] a powerful organization such as the liberal *Fascisti* would have to take its place.

Wells was not alone in his aversion to democracy. A large number of British intellectuals, including Sydney Webb (1859-1947), economist and cofounder of the London School of Economics and Political Science, and Nobel Prize winner George Bernard Shaw (1856-1950), also turned against parliamentary democracy.[8] The same antidemocratic mood also had continental Europe firmly in its grip. In 1933 in *The Shape of Things to Come*, Wells states that the idea that 'parliamentary democracy had come to an end' appeared to have spread everywhere.[9]

There was a good deal of truth in that claim.[10] In Austria Robert Musil (1880-1942), author of *Der Mann ohne Eigenschaften*, made it clear that he would not resist fascism; parliamentary democracy no longer had any future.[11]

The Romanian intellectual Emil Cioran (1911-1995) praised the 'totalitarian attack on "democratic rationalism"'.[12] In the Netherlands Catholics devised drastic alternatives to parliamentary democracy.[13] Edmund Burke's criticism echoed on the continent: a 'pure democracy' would lead to the exercise of the 'most cruel oppressions upon the minority'.[14] A subtle attack came from the German sociologist Max Weber (1864-1920): in Europe a 'universal trend towards bureaucracy' had arisen.[15] That trend could not be stopped; a complex society requires government by large organizations of technically able experts.[16] In such a future there is certainly decreasing space for parliamentary democracy, with its inefficiency, irrationality and unskilled leaders. Weber, however, appears not to have come to that conclusion himself and remained a moderate supporter of parliamentary democracy.[17]

His compatriot and critic, the influential lawyer and political philosopher Carl Schmitt (1888-1985), launched a less subtle attack on parliamentary democracy.[18] In Schmitt's view, the idea that naked power and violence could be conquered by discussion and openness was outdated, as the Weimar experience had shown, and with it parliament as an institution.[19] Democracy was also possible without 'parliamentarianism', or even made possible by its absence. 'The secret ballot and parliamentary decision making procedures' could be replaced by the '"original democratic phenomenon" of acclamation': the shouts of a crowd.[20] In the second imprint of his *Die geistesgeschichtliche Lage des heutigen Parlamentarismus*, he writes:

> Bolshevism and Fascism by contrast are, like all dictatorships, certainly antiliberal but not necessarily antidemocratic.... Compared to a democracy that is direct ... parliament appears an artificial machinery, produced by liberal reasoning, while dictatorial and Caesaristic methods not only can produce the acclamation of the people but can also be a direct expression of democratic substance and power.[21]

In 1933 Schmitt became a member of the NSDAP. It was the beginning of a meteoric rise within the new regime. His success was short-lived, as he became entangled in the internal power politics of the Third Reich; the SS put an end to Schmitt's career in 1936.[22] After the war ended, following stays in various internment camps, he was freed in 1947 and, so the story goes, declared to his Russian interrogators, 'I drank of the Nazi bacillus, but I was not infected.'[23]

Antidemocratic thinking under Weimar did not remain limited to those who, like Schmitt, at some point felt attracted to the NSDAP. Even more than other countries on the continent, the paralysed Weimar Republic (1918-1933), permanently in crisis, appeared to be particularly fertile ground for ideas hostile to democracy.[24] Historian Friedrich Meinecke (1862-1954) saw a 'Vertrauensdiktatur', a 'dictatorship of trust', as the only solution.[25] War hero and writer Ernst Jünger (1895-1998), and with him a large proportion of Germany's youth, on whom he had a significant influence at the time, rejected democracy outright.[26] And as early as 1918, when it became clear that the new Germany would become a parliamentary democracy, Thomas Mann (1875-1955), later winner of the Nobel Prize, wrote:

> I want the monarchy, I want a passionately independent government, because only it offers protection for freedom in the intellectual as well as the economic sphere.... I don't want this parliament and party business that will sour the whole life of the nation with its politics.... I don't want politics. I want competence, order and decency.[27]

Weimar and the Europe of the 1930s had lost their confidence in parliamentary democracy on a large scale. One budding democracy after another collapsed: Albania (1923), Yugoslavia (1929), Portugal (1925), Poland (1926 to 1935) and Romania (1938) became dictatorships.[28] In 1936, the year of Van den Bergh's inaugural lecture, the British newspaper *The Times* concluded, 'it may be that the system of parliamentary Government which suits Great Britain suits few other countries besides.'[29] Democratic pessimism lay like an oppressive blanket over large swathes of the continent.[30]

2. George van den Bergh's inaugural lecture

At this undemocratic point in time, beset by pessimism, on 28 September 1936 the young Amsterdam law professor George van den Bergh (1890-1966) gave his inaugural lecture. He refused to conform to the intellectual trend in Europe, united in fatalism and dislike of democracy. It was no lament or utopian alternative to democracy that he presented. The title read, *De democratische staat en de niet-democratische partijen* (The democratic state and the non-democratic parties).[31]

There was overwhelming interest. All seats were taken in the auditorium of the University of Amsterdam. Former minister of justice Donner, Leiden professor of law Kranenburg, the mayor of Amsterdam, aldermen, members of the House of Representatives, judges and lawyers had all come to hear what this new professor had to say on such a sensitive topic.

Putting his arguments calmly, Van den Bergh led those present along to his conclusion: the prohibition of antidemocratic parties can be justified both from the perspective of political philosophy and that of the law. It was effectively a preliminary formulation of the idea of militant democracy. The audience listened attentively. The words with which Van den Bergh addressed the students present made a big impression:

> We live in a terrible time. Even more than in the Great War, which you are privileged not to have lived through, or in any case not to have been aware of, *everything* of value appears to be teetering on the brink. In a number of great states in our part of the world justice has lost its validity, and power, violence and capriciousness prevail. In the Great War

> our country was one of the few places on earth where peace, humanity and rationality found refuge. Now that is the case once again, but the danger now is greater than it was then. The majority of our people oppose the delusions of the day, and Justice still prevails here, as does a Constitution which according to the time-honoured principle attempts to grant every man his own. We want to keep Holland! Ladies and Gentlemen Students, I see it as my mission to instil in you respect and love for our democratic government institutions.[32]

The words give an impression of the urgency. After all, it was 1936. The previous year Nazi Germany had shown its true face with the Nuremberg Race Laws.

After the ceremony there was quite a storm. The speech was to keep many newspaper editorial offices and commentators busy for weeks, even months. 'An interesting presentation of the question', 'sharp' and 'impressive' was the verdict, but also, 'dangerous' and 'political'.[33]

Then things went quiet. Van den Bergh did not publish any more on the subject himself, and after the war the lecture that had caused such a stir at the time was rarely mentioned.[34] Outside the Netherlands, in the meantime, in the wake of the emigrated German lawyer Karl Loewenstein a new, influential tradition of democracy known as militant democracy developed. Although Van den Bergh formulated his idea of a militant democracy around the same time as Loewenstein,[35] his inaugural lecture, presumably because of the language barrier, never made its way into the international academic debate on militant democracy,[36] and it was largely forgotten in the Netherlands.[37] This is unfortunate. Van den Bergh's inaugural lecture has some important insights to offer on militant democracy. Most importantly, it presents an original and cogent political-philosophical justification for militant democracy, which is absent from Loewenstein's work and much of the literature that follows.[38]

3. Karl Loewenstein: father of militant democracy

The weak spots of democracy

Karl Loewenstein (1891-1973) was a political scientist and legal scholar at the University of Munich. After Hitler assumed power he was initially permitted to stay on and his students (with one exception) remained loyal, but in October 1933 he received a letter from the state of Bavaria informing him that he was to be made redundant: 'constitutional theory and law cannot be taught by a Non-Aryan in the National Socialist State'.[39] Two months later Loewenstein and his wife left for the United States.[40] The American legal historian Rande Kostal sums up Loewenstein's precarious position in Germany:

> When the Nazis came to power in 1933, Loewenstein's Jewish ancestry, liberal cast of mind, and fine English were three compelling reasons to leave Munich for a lectureship at Yale University.[41]

In the Germany of the interbellum 'liberalism' was primarily another word for endless discussion in the impotent parliament, 'government by discussion'.[42] Loewenstein's liberalism, however, was of a different sort, at least when it came to his views on democracy. Loewenstein's most important claim to fame comes precisely from the fact that he wanted to arm democracy against its enemies. He saw that democracy was losing ground to authoritarian regimes. Democracy could no longer be pacifist; it needed to become militant.[43]

Loewenstein came to his theory in two stages. First of all, in 1935 he published a pair of articles in the prominent *American Political Science Review* in which he outlined the threat to democracy in Europe.[44] Democracy on the old continent was entangled in an existential battle with the competing, historically dominant, autocratic concept of government,[45] which lacked separation of powers or mutual checks; power was concentrated in the hands of one or more individuals.[46] Autocratic regimes can be fascist, but they might also be communist, for example. In Europe the autocratic threat revealed itself primarily in the form of fascism,[47] and it is this fascism that Loewenstein wanted to understand in order to gain a grip on the worrying situation in Europe.

In Loewenstein's view fascism is not a political ideology with any *content*; it is simply a means to an end, a technique.[48] It has come into being in reaction to, and in interaction with, democracy. It is parasitic, in the sense that it can only exist by the grace of the democratic system. If one follows Loewenstein, one might thus argue that fascism could *only* come about because of the rise of democracy. It is a systemic negative effect of democracy, and in particular mass democracy, stimulated by the advent of mass media and the unprecedented expansion of voting rights. It is a new phenomenon, which also spurred on contemporaries such as Michael Oakeshott (1901-1990) and José Ortega y Gasset (1883-1955) to sharp analyses of their time.[49]

This is different from stating that fascism stems from the 'failure' of democracy, from a 'political' or 'economic crisis' that forms a 'breeding ground' for fascism, as the French intellectual Thierry Maulnier argued.[50] Loewenstein would say that these circumstances can *hasten* the establishment of an autocratic regime, but that it is the inherent weaknesses of a democracy that eventually make it vulnerable to fascism. Those are systemic effects, independent of the performance of the democracy in a material sense. Loewenstein's early analysis of fascism would later stand up rather well, at least on the points of 'fighting democracy by democratic methods', fascism's relatively contentless character and the use of modern forms of mass organization. Nevertheless, later on somewhat more content was attributed to fascism; at the very least it involved 'a particular emotional and intellectual approach', revolving around issues such as the leadership principle, the notion of the elite and nationalism.[51]

Fascism is thus tailored to the inherent weaknesses of the democratic system and capable of exploiting them to the maximum. Loewenstein himself does not put it so explicitly, but from his analysis it follows that democracy is vulnerable in three different ways.[52] First, it is vulnerable in its traits of compromise and consensus.[53] Normally we consider this to be a praiseworthy aspect of a democracy, but in times of crisis its consultation-oriented character is less attractive; democracy then becomes what Schmitt called the 'endless conversation', an outpouring of 'politische Romantik'.[54] Second, constitutional freedoms offer elements hostile to democracy every opportunity to organize and spread their hostile propaganda.[55] Third, after elections the parliament and other democratic organs open their doors to those who previously preached the downfall of the democratic system.[56]

Whenever fascist parties are permitted to exploit these weaknesses, Loewenstein believes, the establishment of an autocratic regime will follow. Loewenstein sees this as a fundamental defect of the system; particular circumstances, such as economic crises, are secondary; they can only accelerate or delay the process.[57] These weak spots must be fortified if democracy is to arm itself sustainably against fascism.

Sajó's interpretation: a theory of emotionalism

We find an interesting perspective on this analysis in the work of the Hungarian lawyer and European Court of Human Rights (ECHR) judge András Sajó (born 1949). Sajó is currently the most important 'interpreter of Loewenstein' and defends militant democracy along the lines set out by Loewenstein.[58] In Sajó's view Loewenstein's analysis of fascism is correct, but we can distil a more general principle from it: 'emotionalism'. Fascism is merely the 'ultimate form' of this principle.[59] Emotionalism is characterized as the 'politics of emotional manipulation', as opposed to the 'more or less rational' approach to problems in 'constitutional institutions'.[60] Sajó uses that distinction as an argument, for example, to refuse referenda, as 'reputable democracies' do in his view.[61] Sajó describes emotionalism as a 'fundamental contradiction' within democracy:

> Loewenstein's concerns about emotionalism pertain to a fundamental contradiction of democracy, a problem that has prominent practical importance in the contemporary world: emotionalism is inherent in democracy, but democracy, especially in the form of representative government, was designed as a characteristically non-emotional institution.[62]

The 'manipulation of the masses' is about creating and calling on public emotions that are not expressed in the system of rational 'democratic decision making'.[63] According to Sajó this coincides with what we now call 'identity politics', making fascism, with its leader cult, a clear example of the phenomenon.[64] Also today we also encounter emotionalism, Sajó argues, albeit in two new guises: a religious extremist variant and an ethnic, nationalist variant.[65]

The mechanism of emotionalism goes against Weber's view of democracy, against the 'legal-rational *Herrschaft*', and against the 'rule of law'.[66] Under emotionalism, all of this, particularly rational decision making, is replaced by capricious expressions of an assumed 'will of the people' that is no longer shaped by formal procedures and representation, but by listening to the direct 'verdict of the people',[67] something that someone like Schmitt would in fact appreciate.

Sajó does contend that Loewenstein's theory ultimately is elitist, in the sense that little can be expected from the people, the 'masses', when it comes to rational decision making; Loewenstein writes that he fears that 'political aristocrats' will lose ground everywhere to the 'awakened masses'. And although Sajó agrees with sociologists, who tear to shreds this fear of the 'masses', he nevertheless argues for a 'militant anti-majoritarianism', involving measures to prevent the current will of the people from being heard *too* clearly, or, to put it more sympathetically, to prevent decision making from becoming mired in emotionalism.[68] The problem with democracy is that it contains certain inherent characteristics, the weaknesses that Loewenstein identified, that encourage emotionalism.[69] Democracy must therefore find a solution to the emotionalism it produces. That is the 'fundamental contradiction' to which Sajó refers.[70]

'Democracy must become militant'

With the weaknesses of democracy in mind, two years later Loewenstein took the next step. In 1937 he published his famous call to action for European democracies, again in the *American Political Science Review*,[71] recommending that they adopt legislation that would fortify democracy's weak spots: 'democracy must become militant'.[72] Loewenstein gives an extensive overview of the measures that different European countries have already taken.[73] These are a range of different legislative restrictions on fundamental freedoms such as that of the press, individual expression and association,[74] as well as legislation against glorification of political criminals.[75] If these measures are taken, they render fascism powerless.[76] This might seem satisfying from an empirical, comparative and even legal perspective, but something does not sit right. Is it not remarkable that a democracy, the system of the level playing field and equality of beliefs, should suddenly deprive a particular group of its citizens of their liberties? That requires a theoretical justification. How is the restriction of 'democratic rights' reconcilable with the essence of democracy?

Loewenstein is aware of this tension,[77] and even ventures a solution, but he does not entirely succeed.[78] In his view, the restriction of freedoms in a democracy would be justified by analogy with emergency measures against an external enemy in a war: in emergency situations 'legality takes a vacation'.[79] His comparison with an 'external war', however, appears to be on the wrong track for two reasons.

First, in a war of that kind there is an external enemy. In that situation the democracy in question defends itself, as a whole, against an external entity as a whole. In the case of powers that threaten democracy *from within*, the democracy fights an internal battle. The enemy is an intrinsic part of the democracy, of its own state. Can a democracy, in such a battle against an 'internal enemy', deprive a *specific* group of citizens of their fundamental rights? It seems that we need a better justification.

There is another important difference between a war and an internal antidemocratic threat. In a war the survival of the state, its sovereignty, is threatened, generally by violence, for an identifiable period, from the declaration of war until peace, ceasefire or surrender. In the case of an antidemocratic threat it is not so much sovereignty that is threatened, but the *form* of government, democracy, by citizens hostile to democracy, not necessarily using violence, and for a period that is not clearly limited. When does the threat begin and when does it end? Surely there will *always* be groups or individuals who hold antidemocratic ideas. When is the expression of those sympathies sufficient to form a threat? Under Loewenstein's justification, one could, in principle, always continue to fight internal antidemocratic forces; no population is 100 percent pro-democracy. The answer is therefore elastic and vague, which is never a good thing when it comes to intervention. As a result, citizens hostile to democracy are threatened with the loss of their fundamental rights in the long term, if not permanently.

Greenberg's criticism

It is also possible to criticize Loewenstein's work on other grounds. In *The Weimar Century* historian Udi Greenberg discusses the influence of the refugee German intellectuals, the academic *émigrés*, on (American) thinking during World War II and the Cold War.[80] Besides Karl Loewenstein, this group includes Carl Friedrich and Hans Morgenthau, among others. The ideas of these *émigrés*, Greenberg acknowledges, played an important role in reconstructing Germany as a stable democracy and in part determined its new, cooperative and modest international profile.[81] The same goes for Loewenstein's ideas, but Greenberg also shows how his idea of militant democracy can be derailed. During World War II Loewenstein's ideas formed the basis for a harsh internment campaign against suspected sympathizers of the Axis powers in Latin America.[82] The Emergency Advisory Committee for Political Defense, a union of all twenty-one American states, coordinated these activities, and Loewenstein held an important advisory role on the committee.[83] In the end it led to the internment of thousands of German, Japanese and Italian citizens from Latin America.[84] For this reason Greenberg criticizes Loewenstein particularly fiercely.[85]

This criticism is in part fair, but Greenberg pays little attention to the actual threat from the Axis powers at that point, which was during the war. Greenberg is also rather disparaging about the period *after* the war, when he continues to write unreservedly about 'paranoid' and 'virulent' anti-communism.[86] As historian Michael Kimmage remarks, this does little justice to the (geo)political reality of the day; in Greenberg's work, Joseph Stalin's 'tyrannical, murderous and expansionary' Soviet Union is remarkably distant.[87] In fact, Stalin is only mentioned twice,[88] but more important than that is the question, can the overreaction in Latin America really be traced so *directly* back to Loewenstein's ideas? Is that reaction not in part explained by the usual 'wartime paranoia', a factor that Greenberg also mentions?[89] And is it fair to judge the concept of militant democracy based on an application in a global war by a power that looks around nervously and at times feels it needs to intervene?

Nevertheless, Greenberg has raised an important point. Loewenstein's militant democracy *is* vulnerable to abuse. Its application in Latin America, in an interpretation provided in part by Loewenstein *himself*, demonstrates that all too clearly. This vulnerability to abuse is caused by two fundamental weaknesses in Loewenstein's theory.

The first is his unconditional faith in political elites, something that Greenberg also observes. Shocked as Loewenstein is by the implications of the 'radical' Rousseauian democracy and the awakened 'masses', he himself in turn assigns exorbitant power to the 'responsible elites' who are to rule the people.[90] These elites are tasked with protecting individual freedoms and at the same time 'taming the masses'.[91] The assumption is that elites do not abuse power, but in fact increase the 'stability and health of democracy'.[92] That is a naive assumption, which also leads Loewenstein to neglect the justification for interventions in a militant democracy, the reason for 'responsible elites' taking action. This brief justification, as we have seen, does not stand up. Nowhere does he identify the problem in all this.[93] Loewenstein thus unintentionally gives almost unlimited power to those with their fingers on the buttons of democratic self-defence, an invitation to abuse.

The second weak point is the poor definition of the concept of militant democracy (a point not elucidated by Greenberg). In his articles Loewenstein describes a large number of measures that can be seen as militant. Without sharp criteria, more or less all militant measures, from banning films to preventive detention and party bans, can be included under the concept of militant democracy. Thus governments can employ far-reaching measures violating civil rights under the guise of making the democracy militant, when such measures are really only applicable in exceptional circumstances. That, too, increases the risk of abuse. Not only do governors enjoy almost unrestricted application of measures from the arsenal of militant democracy (after all, we have to *trust* them), but they can also expand this arsenal unchecked, according to their own insight, with new militant democratic measures.

Father of militant democracy

Despite these shortcomings, Loewenstein has internationally come to be seen as the father of the concept of militant democracy.[94] Much work on the subject points to him as the person who introduced the concept, or at least the one who coined the term.[95] In a 2004 collection of essays on the subject by András Sajó, Loewenstein's article is even included as an appendix.[96] There are various possible explanations for Loewenstein's predominance. The fact that Loewenstein wrote in English, and in a leading, easily accessible American journal, undoubtedly plays a role. His articles from the 1930s were also impressive in their analyses and predictive power. No doubt a further contributing factor was the international reputation he enjoyed because of his work as a constitutional lawyer. In fact, some even see him as 'one of the most important thinkers on the rule of law in the twentieth century'.[97] As a member of the American occupying force, he also had a leading role in the judicial reconstruction and the denazification of post-war Germany.[98]

In Loewenstein, however, militant democracy has had a somewhat unfortunate father.[99] That is particularly palpable in the literature on the subject. Many writers follow in Loewenstein's wake, with ideas on positive law, and provide interesting contributions,[100] but the theoretical side of the problem tends to be short-changed. This makes it all the more interesting that in 1936 Van den Bergh's *De democratische Staat en de niet-democratische partijen* (The democratic state and the non-democratic parties) was published, which does address the problem from the angle of political philosophy.

Loewenstein himself seems unaware of this. In an article published in 1938 he actually mentions Van den Bergh's speech in a footnote in discussing legal measures against extremism in the Netherlands.[101] Loewenstein praises Van den Bergh: 'The legal aspect of excluding anti-democratic parties inimical to the existing constitutional order of the state from participation in public life in the Netherlands is competently discussed.'[102] What is more interesting is that Loewenstein also remarks that, to his knowledge, Van den Bergh's lecture is the only European contribution on militant democracy that comes to conclusions comparable to his own articles. That is a remarkable statement, for Van den Bergh's lecture differs significantly from Loewenstein's article. Substantial attention is focused on the very points that were absent from Loewenstein's work: the political-philosophical justification for militant democracy.

4. George van den Bergh's concept of militant democracy

In the opening paragraphs of his inaugural lecture, Van den Bergh first outlines what is at stake in the defence of democracy by referring to a definition given by professor of criminology and sociology Willem Bonger, in his influential work *Problemen der demokratie* (Problems of democracy) (1934):

> Democracy is a form of government involving collectivity and self-government, in which a large proportion of its members participate either directly or indirectly, freedom of conscience and equality before the law are safeguarded, and the members are convinced of this idea.[103]

Van den Bergh's lecture can be seen as an extension of Bonger's *Problemen der demokratie*, as Van den Bergh starts out from a question that Bonger touched upon but left open in his book: what do we need to do, concretely, with antidemocratic forces?[104] What measures can be taken? And how can they be justified?

Violent and non-violent parties

What the measures should be is clear to Van den Bergh: the prohibition of antidemocratic political associations. But what makes a political party antidemocratic? It is propagation of 'the idea of dictatorship'; dictatorship to Van den Bergh is as autocracy was to Loewenstein. Concretely that means wanting to change the democratic system into a *non*-democratic variant, be it the German, Italian or Russian style. This definition of dictatorship, however, is not entirely pure, as Van den Bergh observes. After all, a dictatorship, in an academic, legal sense, means the *temporary* transfer of the 'fullness of power' by a community to one individual.[105] It is what Carl Schmitt calls a 'commissarial dictatorship', a constitutional form known since the Romans, which had as its aim the safeguarding of the constitution by temporarily suspending that same constitution.[106] In order to avoid confusion, Van den Bergh nevertheless opts to use the popular terminology, thus making dictatorship synonymous with autocracy, and the polar opposite of democracy.

Confusion also lies in wait elsewhere. Two issues must be stated clearly. First, those who do not openly preach dictatorship but who try to sell it under the guise of 'true democracy' should be reprimanded: it should not make any difference to us whether they attack democracy openly or secretly.[107] To put it another way, we must not allow ourselves to be misled into Giovanni Gentile's idea that the fascist state is the 'democratic State *par excellence*'.[108]

The second clarification is the most important and can be contrasted with Loewenstein's work. There is a great deal of literature on which measures a democracy can take against *violent* antidemocratic parties. The answer to that question is simple: that's what we have criminal law for.[109] One might debate the best methods of combat, Van den Bergh suggests, but it is not a matter of principle.[110] The really interesting question pertains to antidemocratic parties that are in principle *non-violent*, parties that claim to be willing to play the democratic game.

How does one respond to such parties? According to Van den Bergh, it is these parties who form the 'great, fundamental problem', not the violent parties. This sets the discussion on the right track. The importance of this distinction can hardly be overestimated; until this moment the easiest question (that of the violent antidemocratic party) and the most difficult (that of the non-violent) were muddled. An answer to the easier question was seen as valid for both, as 'antidemocratic' seemed to coincide with 'violent', at least in Loewenstein's work,[111] but this would render one powerless against a party that professed to be non-violent, or would impose exhausting burdens of proof.

Hans Kelsen: relativist democracy

Despite the paradoxical nature of non-violent antidemocratic parties (they demand all the rights of democracy that they wish to deny to their opponents), democrats still tend to believe that they must be respected. They must be recognized alongside other parties as 'holding equal rights'.[112] In the view of some democrats this is in fact an indisputable truth, 'an axiom'.[113]

Van den Bergh acknowledges that he himself had 'until recently been tempted' by these ideas.[114] At a conference of the Social Democratic Workers' Party (SDAP), of which he was a prominent member, in spring 1936 he even plainly stated that democracy can only be defended by democratic means.[115]

This dominant view was represented by the Austrian legal philosopher Hans Kelsen (1881-1973), one of the key figures in the democracy debate in the Weimar Republic of the 1930s[116]—and also the main target of Loewenstein's Weimar polemics.[117] In a key passage from *Vom Wesen und Wert der Demokratie* (2nd edition, 1929), Kelsen deals with the theoretical basis for the democratic idea:

> For that is the great question: *whether* there is cognition of absolute truth, insight into absolute values. That is the basic conflict between *Weltanschauungs* and views of life under which the conflict between autocracy and democracy can be subsumed.... Those who hold absolute truth and absolute values to be inaccessible to human cognition must consider not only their own, but also foreign, opposing opinions to be at least possible. Thus *relativism* is the *Weltanschauung* that the *democratic idea* presumes. Democracy values each person's political will *equally*, just as it respects equally any political belief, any political opinion, which is after all expressed by the political will. It therefore gives every political conviction the same chance to be articulated and to *compete* freely for people's minds and hearts.[118]

When Van den Bergh discusses the *communis opinio* among democrats, it is *these* thoughts that he means, represented here in their most authoritative formulation, by an ideologically related thinker.[119] Without attaching the same relativism to this as Kelsen and without explicitly mentioning him, Van den Bergh states that for many democrats 'the pride and glory of democracy' appear to be that 'all honest beliefs are equal', or 'all principles are of equal value'. It is the 'peaceful battle of intellects' that must decide between them.[120]

From this hard logic it follows that even non-violent antidemocratic parties must be admitted to the 'peaceful battle of minds'.[121] For Kelsen this seems to be the (somewhat ironic) strength of a 'pure' conception of democracy, just as is his 'pure theory of law', a conception without *any* substantive values.[122] Antidemocrats argued that a democracy must be overthrown in order to realize their antidemocratic goals; a pure democracy proves them wrong. Democracy's value-neutrality allows antidemocrats to realize their aims *within* the constitutional order. In his 'Foundations of Democracy' (1955) Kelsen further elaborates on this (ultimate) consequence of a value-neutral democracy:

> Democracy seems to have less power of resistance than autocracy, which without any consideration destroys every opponent, whereas democracy, with its principle of legality, freedom of opinion, protection of minorities, tolerance, directly favors its enemy. It is a paradoxical privilege of this form of government, a doubtful advantage which it has over autocracy that it may, by its own specific methods of forming the will of the state, abolish itself.[123]

In an essay entitled *Verteidigung der Demokratie* (1932), Kelsen is even more explicit on the issue of democratic self-abolition:

> But with this situation in mind the question also arises of whether one should restrict oneself to defending democracy theoretically. Whether democracy should not defend itself, even against the people who no longer want it, even against a majority which is united in nothing other than its will to destroy democracy. To ask the question is to answer it in the negative. A democracy that seeks to act against the will of the majority, *that has even tried to act by force, has ceased to be a democracy*.[124]

So, in Kelsen's view, a democracy cannot act against the will of the majority, even when the majority wants to abolish democracy altogether. A democracy that tries to resist such a decision ceases to be a democracy.[125]

In the pre-war European debate on democracy we then find three rough categories. There are outspoken, sometimes plainly hostile critics, who believe that (parliamentary) democracy itself is the problem. A second category consists of supporters, *democrats*, who combine fundamentalist characteristics with passivity—fundamentalist in the sense that they maintain an uncompromising focus on one single element of the democratic idea, its tolerance, to the end, even when the survival of democracy is at stake. They are passive in the sense that they view and accept the destruction of democracy with stoical resignation. Kelsen belongs to this category. He closes *Verteidigung der Demokratie* with the following words:

> One must remain faithful to one's flag, even when the ship is sinking; when entering the abyss one can only take the hope that the ideal of freedom is indestructible and that the deeper it sinks the more passionately it will be revived.[126]

If democracy comes to an end, then so be it; all that remains to us is hope. Van den Bergh, too, admits that he was 'tempted' by these ideas, but after 'much contemplation and long hesitation' he came to the conclusion that this position is untenable.[127] Van den Bergh and Loewenstein represent a third category of democrats who do not accept this supposed logic. Tolerance is good, but a democracy is not a 'suicide pact'.

A first answer to relativist democracy: principled democracy

What, then, has Van den Bergh to offer in response to the relativist or procedural conception of democracy? In his inaugural lecture Van den Bergh pays substantial attention to the question of whether it is possible to ban *non-violent* antidemocratic parties under the Dutch law of the time. Although Van den Bergh is very critical of the banning provision, which he deems too vague, and thereby inadequate for such a far-reaching measure as the banning of a political party, he concludes that a ban is indeed possible.[128] But Van den Bergh is not satisfied with this legal answer alone. A theoretical justification of militant democracy is needed. This requires a different type of argumentation and, moreover, a theory of what democracy is. In short, we need to answer Hans Kelsen.

First, the aim of antidemocratic parties is built on contradictions. Van den Bergh brings this paradoxical character to the reader's attention several times.[129] The antidemocrats demand respect from democracy for their conviction while denying that same respect to others.

This attitude gives rise to contradictory statements, such as 'In a democracy everyone is equal before the law, including those who want to abolish this equality',[130] and 'Democracy is tolerant towards everyone, including the intolerant',[131] a forerunner of Karl Popper's renowned 'paradox of tolerance' in *The Open Society and Its Enemies.*[132] It might be seen as an early version of Popper's 'paradox of democracy'. As Van den Bergh puts it, 'In a democracy the people make the final decision on government policy. The people can thus also decide that they will no longer decide on government policy.'[133]

The paradoxical nature is clear, or at least feels that way, but what precisely is paradoxical about it? On closer inspection, it is possible to distinguish a formal and a substantive level. On the formal level beliefs are equal in their capacity as 'belief', for the simple reason that they are beliefs. On a substantive level those beliefs differ in *content*: from 'adjusting the retirement age' to 'abolishing democracy'. A democracy, defined as 'majority decision' or 'majority rule', only pays attention to the formal aspect: all beliefs are equal in its eyes (Kelsen's 'value relativism').

On a formal level, there is thus no obvious paradox; at most, one could say, the ambition to democracy itself is unsettling. From an analytical perspective, it is only a paradox if the definition of democracy *merges* the formal and substantive levels, that is, by not only looking at the formal status of beliefs as 'beliefs', but also assessing their content: the substantive level. For that, one would indeed need to interpret democracy differently. As 'majority rule' it *cannot* 'inspect' the content of decisions; it remains at the formal level.

Van den Bergh makes a first attempt at this by citing a French saying: 'Pour discuter il faut être d'accord.'[134] For an exchange of views it is necessary that: 1) there is agreement on *wanting* an exchange of views, and 2) there is consensus on at least one fundamental principle.[135] More or less the same applies to democracy. If we assume that a democracy is intended to result in 'peaceful coexistence in society and state', we see that the same principles apply there: 1) one must first *want* that peaceful coexistence, and 2) there must be a fundamental principle against which ideals can be tested.[136]

For a democracy, according to Van den Bergh, that fundamental principle is formed by a pair of 'inviolable principles': freedom of conscience (comprising freedom of religion and freedom of belief) and equality before the law. Van den Bergh sums it up as follows:

> With these principles as *touchstone* and *foundation* the peaceful battle of minds is decided. Acceptance of this touchstone and foundation is a condition of admittance to the peaceful battle. Parties which attack these pillars of our state are its enemies. The state must do everything in its power to oppose them.[137]

Under this definition a democracy is no longer characterized by 'majority rule'; instead its essence lies in the fundamental principles of freedom of conscience and equality before the law. These two principles form the gateway to the democratic arena. Parties that fail to recognize these principles are denied entry. This is now possible: democracy has been given substantive content and is thus equipped with a substantive criterion. This interpretation fits with Van den Bergh's remarks elsewhere in his inaugural lecture: 'In my view the deepest essence of democracy can be found in its tolerance, in its respect for the individuality of every human being, rather than in the majority principle.'[138]

The answer to Kelsen here is that he has not properly understood the essence of democracy. If we assume that democracy is purely 'majority rule', that leads to the misplaced supposition that 'anything goes'.[139] If we understand democracy instead as being characterized by the principles of freedom of conscience and equality before the law, it naturally follows that the boundaries of the democratic arena are also defined, so it is *not* simply a case of 'anything goes'. This notion of democracy exhibits characteristics of natural law: democracy is founded on a number of absolute principles with 'the presumption of permanence'.[140] We might call it 'principled democracy'.

However, we can also imagine Kelsen's criticism of this reply. Does this not stretch the principle of democracy much too far? Is it not an overspecification, risking the open, non-absolute quality of democracy? Is it not based on a confusion of the concepts of democracy and rule of law, the latter being the proper place where fundamental rights are to be located? In fact, does this not, as it were, smuggle moral judgements into law via the back door, by elevating them to legally inviolable principles?

Without fully embracing this criticism, one may argue that this solution 'substantializes' the concept of democracy too much. If we assume that a democracy in any case should allow *as much freedom as possible* to different beliefs, we might wonder, is it really necessary to go so far to defend a democracy as to formulate such a broad touchstone, as this interpretation of Van den Bergh does?

A second answer to relativist democracy: democracy as self-correction

There is an alternative interpretation of Van den Bergh's notion of democracy. Elsewhere in his lecture he creates an original and more fruitful conception of militant democracy. His other observations are valuable, but this may be his most important innovation in the defence of democracy against antidemocrats.

British philosopher James Mill centred his powerful and influential argument for representative democracy, the 'grand discovery of modern times', around the concept of an 'identity of interests' between governors and those governed.[141] Only if this identity of interests is in place can the government serve the greatest happiness for the greatest possible number of people.[142] Regular elections ensure that those interests do not diverge.[143] This idea of an 'identity of interests' can also be found in Van den Bergh's work:

> In democracy the circles of the stakeholders and those who make the decisions coincide in the final instance. The people make the decisions and feel the consequences directly.[144]

However, Van den Bergh does not stop at the 'identity of interests'. Governors and those governed having the same interests means something else too: the people make their *own* decisions, albeit through their representatives. In a democracy citizens are thus also responsible for the consequences of their decisions, a serious task, but one with great advantages: because they make their own decisions, the people can also revoke them *themselves*.[145]

'More than any other system', Van den Bergh contends, democracy offers the safeguards that ensure that incorrect decisions can actually be revised—claiming that 'one of the most powerful characteristics of democracy is its "self-correction"'.[146] Van den Bergh puts the core of the matter as follows:

> [The people] know their responsibility, they correct their own mistakes. In principle every democratic decision is revocable, although it is not always possible to undo all the consequences.[147]

The essence of democracy in this interpretation no longer lies in the majority principle (Kelsen), or the protection of inviolable fundamental principles (the first interpretation), but in the *capacity for self-correction*, in government by means of self-correction by the people.

This has consequences for the problem of antidemocratic parties. Is there perhaps, in the light of democracy's capacity for self-correction, something exceptional about the aspirations of antidemocratic parties? Van den Bergh thinks so, and we can see that if we imagine the spectrum of possible decisions in a democracy. It then becomes clear that one decision differs radically from all other possible decisions, namely, the decision to abolish democracy. It is the only decision that is not open to democratic self-correction,[148] and it is precisely what the antidemocratic parties aspire to. Their ambitions thus go directly against the essence of democracy, and *that* is also the reason to deny them entry to the democratic arena.[149]

Now one might wonder whether this is really the only irrevocable decision in a democracy. A comparison might clarify this question. Take, for example, the democratic decision to demolish a monument.[150] That seems a fairly definitive decision. Even if we were to decide on reconstruction, the predicate 'monument' would no longer naturally apply—the original stones and such are gone.[151] Nevertheless, there is a subtle difference between the two decisions. Of course, the actual consequences of a democratic decision cannot be completely restored. The monument has been demolished, but that does not make the decision itself irrevocable. Within the framework of democracy we can revoke the decision and attempt to alleviate the consequences as far as possible. The decision to abolish democracy, by contrast, leads to the loss of the entire framework, making the decision not only irreparable, but also *irrevocable*. It is permissible for a democracy to oppose that decision. We might call this second interpretation of Van den Bergh 'democracy as self-correction'.

Markovitch and the law of reaction

Van den Bergh ingeniously deployed the self-correction principle he developed to defend democracy. He was also the first to make it part of a more comprehensive *theory* of militant democracy, which, for instance, also pays attention to procedural safeguards—which I will discuss in more detail below. Van den Bergh thus gave a political-philosophical, but concrete, answer to a current problem. In formulating the self-correction mechanism, however, he turned out not to be alone. On 6 October 1936, a week and a half after the inaugural lecture, his fellow SDAP party member and lawyer Marinus van der Goes van Naters (1900-2005) sent Van den Bergh a letter.[152] He regretted that he had been unable to attend the ceremony, but he had nevertheless read the lecture 'with great interest'. As evidence of his interest, Van der Goes van Naters referred to *La doctrine sociale de Duguit* by Milan Markovitch, a Sorbonne doctoral dissertation written in 1933 that he had before him at that moment, probably while he worked on his *Socialistische Staatsvernieuwing* (Socialist state revival), which was to appear a year later, in which Duguit is briefly discussed.[153] Why does he make this suggestion? According to Van der Goes van Naters, Markovitch has an idea similar to Van den Bergh's.

La doctrine sociale de Duguit: ses idées sur le syndicalisme et la représentation professionnelle, as the full title reads, is first and foremost an exposition of the ideas of the French jurist Léon Duguit (1859-1928).[154] Duguit's thinking does not square well with democracy,[155] and it is precisely that aspect that is sharply criticized by Markovitch in a remarkable concluding chapter.[156]

Duguit fails to understand the value of democracy, and Markovitch seeks to counter his arguments by demonstrating that value. He therefore goes in search of what makes democracy unique, finding that special quality in the 'law of reaction'. New political systems are always a 'reaction' to existing forms of government: they are an adaptation or even rejection of those systems.[157] Such a reaction can only take place in two ways: with or without bloodshed.[158] The latter option is always preferable; in the former case society is, after all, thrown into chaos and tyranny, leaving no essential difference between humans and animals.[159] It is unworthy of man, the only self-aware and thinking being.[160] The possibility of accepting, approving and rejecting a political system must therefore be guaranteed 'whatever the price'.[161] That is what Markovitch calls the 'law of reaction'. 'The ability to change systems of political organization' is a 'fundamental law for all societies', founded in *humanity*.[162] Democracy is the only system that does not deny this law of reaction, nor opposes it.[163] In fact it actively applies the law of reaction, via periodical elections.[164] Measured against the yardstick of the law of reaction, democracy is 'superior to all other forms of political organization'.[165] It is 'inviolable'.[166]

But Markovitch does not stop here, and that is where Van den Bergh comes into the picture. Markovitch anticipates critics who, in defence of Duguit, seek to relativize the inviolability of democracy. What happens if the reaction is that we want to replace democracy? On the basis of the law of reaction a democracy must surely allow that?[167] This would leave the way open to less democratic alternatives, such as that of Duguit. Markovitch's reply is, 'superficially yes, but in reality no'.[168] A democracy is not obliged to allow *all* reactions: the reaction that excludes a new reaction, whether intentionally or unintentionally, thus 'ignoring and practically destroying' the reaction, is one that a democracy need not tolerate.[169] Such a reaction against democracy 'justifies and codifies the revolution, the fire and the blood', precisely that which does not befit the ambitions of man to be *more* than a 'common animal, without mind or consciousness', in other words: his humanity.[170]

The common ground is unmistakable. Markovitch too feels that democracy could oppose the one decision that makes all other decisions impossible, namely, the decision to abolish democracy.[171] What should be done with parties seeking to bring down democracy by legal means? By his own admission, after 'diligent searching in Dutch and foreign literature', Van den Bergh had failed to find anything significant on the subject.[172] Even in a personal account of the writing of the inaugural lecture we find nothing on specific sources of inspiration,[173] to his own disappointment, in fact: 'I am aware of how dangerous it is not to be able to connect one's own ideas with those of others.'[174] Van den Bergh missed this book, which is not surprising. A book about Duguit, after all, is not the first source one would consult when it comes to the defence of democracy, or democracy in general. Van den Bergh and Markovitch, as Van der Goes van Naters writes to Van den Bergh, probably stumbled across the same fundamental democratic mechanism of self-correction completely independently of one another.

That is a shame. It would have been interesting to know what Van den Bergh thought of Markovitch's theory, because besides common ground there are also differences. First, there are conceptual differences: where Markovitch speaks more generally of the 'law of reaction' and 'reactions' to political systems, Van den Bergh thinks much more *within* democracy; he talks about the 'self-correction of democracy' and 'decisions'. These conceptual differences, however, point to a subtle, but more fundamental, contrast. Markovitch develops an *external* criterion, the law of reaction, that all political systems must fulfil. Democracy scores the highest on that criterion, giving it an inviolable status. But it remains an *external* criterion, and Markovitch must then acknowledge elsewhere that a democracy has to allow itself to be replaced under certain circumstances, namely, if the full law of reaction is ensured in the *new* political system.[175] He in fact directly admits that it is difficult to think of another such system and that a system that respects the law of reaction is democratic *in essence*.[176] An external criterion, or external justification, has a clear advantage. In addition to acting against antidemocrats within a democracy, it also justifies opposition to an undemocratic system outside a democracy. To put it a different way, it legitimizes revolution in order to establish a democracy. This advantage, however, comes at a price: we must find support for this external criterion. Markovitch appears to seek such a basis for his law of reaction in what makes us human, our 'humanity', our capacity to distinguish ourselves from animals, without mind or consciousness. That gives such a justification the characteristics of natural law, raising the burden of proof; after all, someone might conceivably argue that no binding laws can be derived from our humanity, let alone one as concrete as the law of reaction. It is the least convincing part of Markovitch's argument. We only read about the compelling force of 'humanity', and *thus* the compelling force of the law of reaction: the political system is there for man, and not the other way around; 'man, that is life'. Every political system must take into account that aspect of life, because 'man is everything and everywhere'.[177]

To Van den Bergh the point of departure is democracy as an *established* system. Is it inconsistent of a democracy, that is, does it betray its own principles, if it bans a party? Van den Bergh's answer is no: a democracy does not have to take an antidemocratic threat lying down. That is a smaller claim. It is only stated that there is nothing inherently illogical about a democracy that opposes its own abolition. When Van den Bergh writes that all decisions except one are acceptable in a democracy, he engages in a polemic against a *procedural* notion of democracy in the work of Kelsen and others;

when Markovitch makes the same claim, he opposes a supposed consequence of his law of reaction in a democracy. Van den Bergh thus offers no justification for revolution in the name of democracy, but neither does he incorporate natural law into his argumentation. Of course, that is *one* interpretation—to be more precise, the second interpretation outlined previously: democracy as self-correction. In the first interpretation, the principled democracy, on the other hand, there are starting points for a defence of democracy charged with more value and thus also more in line with natural law. Van den Bergh, after all, *also* speaks of the 'individuality of every human being'. In order to clarify this very point, it would be interesting to know what he thought of Markovitch's theory.

There are other differences too. Van den Bergh emphasizes the revocability of decisions and with it the unique opportunity a democracy offers to *learn* from mistakes;[178] Markovitch thinks instead of preventing bloodshed, which is only guaranteed in a democracy in which a *legal* 'reaction' to a political system is possible. Nonetheless, the core of the self-corrective mechanism (all decisions are permitted except one) is brought into sharp focus by both Markovitch and Van den Bergh.[179]

The interpretations compared

The second interpretation, democracy as self-correction, differs from the first on a number of points. Where the first interpretation might obscure the concept of democracy, by incorporating a large array of fundamental principles into its definition, the second interpretation is further removed from the concept of the rule of law, leaves the 'all-but-one-decision' open, and is thus, in a strict sense, the 'more democratic' democracy. One may also consider it in this order: 'majority rule' offers (and is) a decision mechanism, democracy as self-correction offers 'majority rule' plus a mechanism for facilitating *and* protecting 'self-correction', while principled democracy offers 'majority rule' plus a number of inviolable, fundamental rights. Democracy as self-correction thus leaves more freedom for public, democratic debate; principled democracy has less faith in debate and excludes a specific 'core' of principles from it.

The basis for party bans under democracy as self-correction is considerably smaller than in principled democracy. The reason for prohibition is thus more restricted, with the important advantage that undesirable repression is less likely.[180] The only test is: does the targeted party aim to overturn the democratic model of decision making, the framework? Or, in other words: does it want to make democratic self-correction impossible? That leaves little room for interpretation. Under 'principled democracy' that is different: does this party aspire to erode freedom of conscience or equality before the law? It is a broader foundation with greater interpretative freedom.

In the first interpretation of Van den Bergh we find one of the first theoretical formulations of a militant democracy concept. It is a notion of militant democracy that fits seamlessly with what is now constitutionally established in Germany.[181] There the inviolable core of principles appears in the form of an 'eternity clause' (Art. 79 para. 3 of the German Constitution): certain democratic principles *plus* the principle of 'human dignity' lie outside the legislator's reach, regardless of any majority.[182] The democratic route is thus shut off; a revolution is the only option, and for that there is criminal law.[183] We find variations on this theme in countries such as Israel, Spain and Italy.[184]

In the second interpretation of the inaugural lecture we find an original idea of what democracy is, a notion of democracy, furthermore, that is equipped for the battle with antidemocratic parties, but without leaving democracy too little space to function in the process.

Procedural safeguards

In his speech Van den Bergh also covers the concrete execution and application of his ideas. First of all, 'One should be careful of allowing too much latitude in the interpretation of, in the above mentioned sense, inviolable principles!'[185] For this problem democracy as self-correction, given its formulation, appears to offer the most guarantees: the grounds for prohibition are narrower. Secondly, one should trust, as far as possible, in 'the moral conscience of the vast majority of our people'.[186] In other words, he proposes an 'opportunity principle'. An antidemocratic party need not always be directly banned. It is not a mechanical construct, a guillotine set to fall at the first antidemocratic expression. The democratic state itself can thus choose the appropriate moment to apply its most powerful means of defence.

In order to ensure careful application, Van den Bergh also argues that decisions on party bans should be made exclusively by a Supreme Court, in a unanimous verdict, on the basis of an independent 'Political Parties Act' that contains carefully formulated grounds for prohibition.[187] In fact, according to Van den Bergh, such a law should also oblige parties to practise complete openness with respect to their finances; recently this last proposal was taken up in the Netherlands in the form of the 2013 Political Parties Funding Act.[188]

The reception of Van den Bergh's inaugural lecture

The reception of Van den Bergh's inaugural lecture was overwhelming. 'Much talked about' would be an understatement. A day after the ceremony, more or less all the newspapers and journals of any note published summaries, from *De Tijd, Het Vaderland*, *De Telegraaf* and the *Algemeen Handelsblad* to *De Rotterdammer* and the *Provinciale Drentsche en Asser Courant*. There followed a deluge of comments and reviews in local papers, as well as in all the big publications, often in several articles.

The liberal *Nieuwe Rotterdamsche Courant* was outspokenly critical. Under the title 'Political science' Van den Bergh was accused of having given a political, and hence unscientific, speech.[189] For convenience' sake it was assumed that Van den Bergh's lecture was targeted exclusively at a specific party, the Nationaal-Socialistiche Beweging (National Socialist Movement, NSB), a suspect action for an SDAP member. What, then, are we supposed to make of the SDAP itself, with its doctrine of class war, its antimonarchical stance and its undermining of authority in the army? Moreover, according to some, socialism even demands a transitional dictatorship on the way to the ideal socialist state.

The similarly liberal *De Avondpost* felt able to agree with Van den Bergh's notion of militant democracy, but exhibited dissatisfaction over his legal argumentation, accusing him of pinning a ban 'on a contrived interpretation of an existing article which was not written for a case such as this'. It would be better to produce legislation specifically for the purpose.[190] The newspaper also expressed the expectation that the new professor would be roundly criticized by his colleagues in law. Neither could his opportunity principle count on support; the newspaper declared it 'weak'.

The frontal assault from the socialist newspaper *Het Volk* was more painful still, expressing concern as to what Van den Bergh's theory would mean for the position of the social democrats themselves:

> We consider this a highly dubious stance [banning antidemocratic parties on the basis of 'public morality' (goede zeden), BR]. In essence it is the foundation of any strict conservatism. With this proposition in hand a judge might for example succeed in banning the Neo-Malthusian League or the association of free thinkers 'De Dageraad'. It would only be a small stretch to ban the S.D.A.P., if a judge were permitted to assume that the right to private property belonged to the 'fundamental moral principles' of our people, an idea for which he could find support in decades of election results.[191]

Many commentaries also simply put forward the prevailing relativist notion of democracy. The *Algemeen Handelsblad* wrote that a state that protects freedom of conscience should never adopt authoritarian methods, not even in its own self-defence: 'The democratic state would destroy itself by this method.'[192]

The *Haagsche Post,* which was not unsympathetic to the inaugural lecture,[193] concluded in an overview article, 'Now that a few weeks have passed, we must observe that the idea has not been received with approval.'[194] The *Dagblad van Noord-Brabant* wrote, 'Much has now been written on these propositions by Professor Van den Bergh, in the mainstream literature as well as the anti-revolutionary papers, but neither side declares warm approval.'[195] That is unmistakably true. But other voices also made themselves heard, some of them positive.

In *De Groene Amsterdammer* the speech was favourably discussed by the chief editor, Delft professor of constitutional law C.A. Josephus Jitta.[196]

He first addressed those who believed the topic of the speech showed that it was a political treatise: anyone who really familiarized themselves with the speech would be fully reassured to find that it exhibits a 'purely scholarly character'. It is not the subject that is decisive, but rather the methodology that is used. Josephus Jitta did, however, wonder how the judge's power to ban a party could be delimited. One must be willing to grant the judge almost unlimited power, or else provide a sharper formulation for the grounds for prohibition, which is the very point that seems impossible to provide. He considered Van den Bergh's most important innovation to be the distinction between non-violent and violent parties, which sharpens the formulation of the problem compared with previous treatment. Josephus Jitta concluded:

> The speaker has exhibited the unusual merit, in a short timeframe, of shedding new and surprising light on a problem which has repeatedly been debated. What more could one ask of an inaugural lecture?[197]

A few days earlier, as main speaker at a free-thinking democratic conference, Josephus Jitta had recommended to his audience that they study Van den Bergh's lecture. The socialist *Het Volk* made much of this with the headline:

> Professor Josephus Jitta on democracy. Approval of the inaugural lecture of Professor van den Bergh.[198]

On the opening of the Liberal State Party's election campaign, another colleague, professor of constitutional law, C.W. de Vries, looked in detail at Van den Bergh's speech.[199] He endorsed the condemnation of national socialism and communism as conflicting with 'the morals of our people', but he felt unable to agree with what followed: 'We want to overrule political wrong with what is right and not by force and prohibition.' Nonetheless, De Vries was sufficiently satisfied with the lecture to order 225 copies for his Rotterdam students.[200]

There was also commentary in the communist and national socialist press. In two articles seething with vile antisemitism, the national socialist mouthpiece *Volk en Vaderland* dismissed the inaugural lecture as a 'propaganda speech'.[201] A while later Henri Polak, a prominent Jewish SDAP member and union leader, was sent a dozen copies of the national socialist newspaper uninvited, something that often happened, but in this case each copy had the article about the lecture marked out.[202] In the article it was suggested that Van den Bergh, who was Jewish, owed his appointment to a 'Jewish clique'. Some time later Polak settled the score with this antisemitism brilliantly in a column for the newspaper *Het Volk*:

> This clearly shows how great the power of this Jewish clique is. In the entire Faculty of Law there is only one Jewish professor to be found.

> Of the five members of the University Board of Governors not one is Jewish. In spite of all that the Polaks and co succeeded in imposing their will on both boards.[203]

The communist press was more argumentative. In *De Tribune*, Van den Bergh was accused of lumping fascists together with communists, in true 'SDAP tradition'.[204] The picture he had painted of dictatorship lacked nuance, for it lacked any consideration of its nature or aim: which form would it take, or which classes would support it?[205] In this, *De Tribune* contended, the fascist and communist dictatorships, besides their names, have nothing in common. Van den Bergh's conclusion, however, could be endorsed, at least as far as it applied to fascists. *De Tribune* thought the precise legal argumentation for these measures could be thrown overboard; it would only be of interest to jurists and their formal concepts.[206]

Let me add a few observations. The daily newspapers were manifestly critical or negative. Ideological colour certainly played no small role in their assessment.[207] Van den Bergh had taken a scholarly view on political subject matter. It turned out to be a hornets' nest. Much of the press hurried to interpret the speech in exclusively political terms, leading to predictable criticism, with that of *Het Volk* standing out most of all. Some newspapers betrayed their political interpretation by explaining Van den Bergh's proposal without reservation as a plea for the prohibition of the National Socialist Movement and communist parties, when nowhere in Van den Bergh's speech does he mention concrete parties.[208] It was perhaps naive to think that in such politicized times such political interpretations would not be forthcoming, but it could also be explained as a sign of Van den Bergh's courage to discuss such a topical and controversial subject from a scholarly perspective at such a moment.

Moreover, good answers were conceivable for the more serious points of criticism. Take, for example, the variants of 'What should be done with party or association X?' It would have been sufficient for Van den Bergh to reply that if its *aim* was in conflict with the essence of democracy (in the first or second interpretation), then party X could indeed be banned; that simply follows from the concept of militant democracy he was outlining. The fact that this would mean banning the NSB in no way reduces the consistency of that argument. It is then up to the critics to show why an outcome such as the prohibition of the NSB would be undesirable. A simple reference to the concept of relativist democracy is not sufficient here, as that is the notion that Van den Bergh argues against. It would thus be necessary to come up with arguments to defend one's own concept of relativist democracy against Van den Bergh's militant democracy.

The condemnation of the legal argument as a 'contrived interpretation' is also dubious. From a technical legal perspective, Van den Bergh had indisputably set his sights on the right law: according to Dutch law the political party was (and still is) nothing other than an ordinary association. The fact that Van den Bergh then has to go to some lengths to properly delimit the concept of 'public morality' [goede zeden] is true, but one can hardly blame him for that, as legal history offered almost no points of departure. The proposition that Van den Bergh would have been better off seeking salvation in new legislation is similarly easy to refute: in his speech Van den Bergh explicitly argues that new legislation of this kind would be highly desirable. And so it goes, with the odd exception, for many of the objections.

It is a shame that Van den Bergh neglected to discuss and counter these points of criticism explicitly.[209] Deep into the defence, in a personal account in *Het Vaderland*, he expressed his profound indignation regarding the treatment he received:

> I find it undeniably distasteful to have to write it now. Once again, all this really is of no concern to anyone, but I will not allow my scholarly reputation to be insulted without defending it.[210]

The scholarly reception was more positive.[211] The speech was discussed in the leading legal journal *Nederlands Juristenblad* by H.L.M. Kramer, who supported Van den Bergh's idea and 'warmly' recommended studying it; he had only a few 'modest objections on some subordinate points'.[212] The eminent jurist and later Leiden professor Gerard Langemeijer also enters the debate at this point. His criticism: Van den Bergh's idea leads to the possible will of a future majority prevailing over 'the established will of the majority of today'.[213] Kramer writes a firm response: Langemeijer misunderstands the 'essential characteristic' of democracy. He mistakes the majority principle, merely a necessary method of decision making, for the key principle on which democracy rests—'an overly simplistic proposal', according to Kramer.[214] At the end of 1936 the discussion among legal scholars even ended up in the daily press via a piece submitted to *De Tijd*: under the title 'legal polemic', 'Van den Bergh's bulldog' debated on, this time with jurist C.Ch.A. van Haren.[215] This was a modest restitution for Van den Bergh, just before the storm surrounding his inaugural lecture died down.

Democracy as an end, not as a means

In the 1930s three books on democracy appeared within a short period of time. All three were written at the University of Amsterdam; the authors were all SDAP members. In 1933 Bastiaan van den Tempel was granted his PhD on *Democratische vrijheid en socialistisch recht* (Democratic freedom and socialist justice). A year later the previously mentioned *Problemen der demokratie* (Problems of democracy) by Professor Willem Bonger was published. The trio of books was completed the following year by Van den Bergh's *De democratische Staat en de niet-democratische partijen* (The democratic state and the non-democratic parties). The three books illustrate the divisions within the SDAP on a prominent question: what is the relationship between democracy and socialism? Which is the end and which the means?

Van den Tempel is explicitly named in Van den Bergh's inaugural lecture. The mention is anything but approving:

> I have forcefully contested Mr Van den Tempel's proposal: I reject it completely.[216]

This sharply rejected proposal was that under certain circumstances a dictatorship can be justified in order to realize socialism.[217] In Van den Tempel's view the order was clear: socialism is an end because it is *objectively* right; democracy was an interchangeable means.[218] That is not to say that they were equal, but if democracy did not lead to socialism, a transitional dictatorship was an acceptable alternative.[219]

Bonger was of a very different opinion. In opposition to the trend of youthful revolutionary zeal, he clung to the social democratic tradition, which in his view had always defended the attainments of democracy.[220] In Bonger's work democracy held a special position. With reference to associations and 'natural peoples', *Problemen der demokratie* described democracy as the 'natural' form of government for humans.[221] To Bonger democracy might still be a means, but it is the *only* means; there are no alternatives.[222]

Van den Bergh takes the opposite view to Van den Tempel. For him democracy is always an end, socialism the means.[223] At the SDAP Easter conference in 1936 he had already explained this position, and in his inaugural lecture he repeated it.[224] Van den Bergh resists the temptation to which so many other world-improving intellectuals of the time fell prey: enforcement of a utopian ideal by an elite who sidestep the indecisive democracy, working without the people but 'for the people', on the way to the 'true democracy' or another ideal. In his view socialism is the means to fully realize the democratic promise of respect for the individuality of every human being. Freedom of belief and religion, and equality before the law, can only reach maturity through socialism, but that society will be *democratic* above all. Van den Bergh words this relationship as follows:

> He who does not accept socialism is free in his belief; but he who rejects freedom of belief will be the victim of his own doctrine![225]

This characterizes the place of socialism within the boundaries of a militant democracy: socialism is merely one of the options, and has Van den Bergh's strong preference, but it can never replace democracy.

These were remarks of no small significance. In *Vijandige Broeders?* (Enemy brothers?) Dutch historian Rob Hartmans shows that Van den Bergh and Bonger firmly set the SDAP on the tracks to democracy by dispensing with the antidemocratic Marxist direction.[226] The SDAP was ultimately a party that often struggled with a militant, revolutionary left wing.[227] This was particularly disadvantageous for a party that still needed to work on its democratic credibility after its former leader Pieter Jelles Troelstra's failed attempt at revolution in 1918.[228] Within the SDAP's long-standing 'dual character', revolutionary in origin and reform oriented in practice, the parliamentary democratic direction now definitively had the upper hand.[229]

At the same time, of the Bonger-Van den Bergh duo, it was Van den Bergh who formulated the idea of democracy as an end *in itself*. Ultimately in his view we wanted to live a democratic life above all. Freedom of conscience was central. Socialism could subsequently make a democracy flourish. This unique and heartfelt commitment to democracy probably explains why it became George van den Bergh who would lay the foundation for the idea of militant democracy in the Netherlands.

Freedom of conscience also played an important role in the speech with which Van den Bergh bade farewell to the University of Amsterdam in 1960. The central idea of that speech is concentrated in the figure of a French army rabbi; on the battlefield he held up a crucifix for a dying Catholic soldier.[230] It was symbolic for Van den Bergh's interpretation of freedom of conscience and his respect for the individuality of every person.[231] The title of his farewell lecture is *De demokratische staat en de demokratische partijen* (The democratic state and the democratic parties). His collected work begins with his inaugural lecture and ends with this farewell lecture, both on the defence of democracy. In the intervening period (1936-1960) Van den Bergh, who during the war had been incarcerated in Buchenwald, published nothing on the subject.[232] In his farewell lecture Van den Bergh explicitly reflects on the initial reception, as well as the later vindication, of his ideas. We end this contribution with Van den Bergh looking back on his inaugural lecture:

> The reception of my lecture by the press was generally anything but friendly.... Even circles of otherwise kindred spirits were far from enthusiastic. There the accusation was frequently, 'Undemocratic!' But everything turned out all right in the end. Eyes have been opened by the worst possible misery. In the spring of 1941 I gave a lecture with the same content to the law faculty of Buchenwald, a faculty with more public law professors than any Dutch university. There, where a large number of the victims of the antidemocratic Nazi practices were present, my thoughts were welcomed with willingness and enthusiasm. There they were pleased to hear their daily reflections on practice supported by a lucid theory.
>
> And now! I merely have to read you the closing article of the renowned Universal Declaration of Human Rights, unanimously accepted in 1948 by the General Assembly of the UN: (Art. 30) 'Nothing in this Declaration may be interpreted as implying for any state, group or person any right to engage in any activity or to perform any act aimed at the destruction of any of the rights and the freedoms set forth herein.'
>
> And also from the European Convention on Human Rights (Rome 1950), which directly binds the undersigned, including our country. Article 17 states in almost the same words: 'Nothing in this convention

may be interpreted as implying for any state, group or person any right to engage in any activity or perform any act aimed at the destruction of the rights and freedoms set forth herein or at their limitation to a greater extent than is provided for in the convention.' That, in a nutshell, is what I meant to say in my inaugural lecture, so I am not dissatisfied.[233]

Notes

1. Philip Coupland, 'H.G. Wells's "Liberal Fascism"', *Journal of Contemporary History* 2000, vol. 35 no. 4, p. 541–558 (542–543), which is about H.G. Wells, 'Liberalism and the Revolutionary Spirit', p. 1–28 (with the phoenix metaphor on p. 2–3), in H.G. Wells, *After Democracy: Addresses and Papers on the Present World Situation*, London: Watts and Co 1932.
2. Or, in another designation, 'enlightened Nazis'; see Wells 1932, p. 24. See Coupland 2000, p. 543; see also Keane 2010, p. 570.
3. See Coupland 2000, p. 543; Edward Mead Earle, 'H. G. Wells, British Patriot in Search of a World State', *World Politics* 1950, vol. 2 no. 2, p. 181–208 (183, 201–202), and John S. Parrington, 'H.G. Wells and the World State: A Liberal Cosmopolitan in a Totalitarian Age', *International Relations* 2003, vol. 17 no. 2, p. 233–246 (242–243). This was a constant in his thinking. In *Anticipations* (1901, new edition 1914) he writes, 'And so it is I infer that, whether violently as a revolution or quietly and slowly, this grey confusion that is democracy must pass away inevitably by its own inherent conditions, as the twilight passes, as the embryonic of the cocoon creature passes, into the higher stage, into the higher organism, the world-state of the coming years', and, 'I know of no case for the elective Democratic government of modern States that cannot be knocked to pieces in five minutes' (see H.G. Wells, *Anticipations,* London: Chapman and Hall 1914, p. 175 and 147, respectively). It must be acknowledged, as Michael Sherborne argues, that Wells was not primarily interested in the ideology of the fascists—after all, he remained a (somewhat unusual) 'liberal'—but to write that he meant this merely metaphorically, to suggest that liberals must organize themselves better (as Sherborne has written), glosses over and oversimplifies matters (see Michael Sherborne, *H.G. Wells: Another Kind of Life*, London/Chester Springs: Peter Owen 2010, p. 289–290). His manifest, oft-repeated aversion to democracy is too clearly present. On this subject Earle says, 'Wells's contempt for democracy—perhaps contempt is too strong a word—is disturbing but cannot be overlooked. It recurs often in his writings but can be summarized in the sentence, "Muddle isn't ended by transferring power from the muddle-headed few to the muddle-headed many"'; see Earle 1950, p. 202 (note 64). On his 'liberal *Fascisti'* Wells himself writes (in supplementary materials for the summer school lecture), 'It acknowledges no more than a conditional loyalty to any established government or authority. It repudiates the belief that majority decisions, whether embodied in parliamentary or suchlike institutions or expressed by mass or mob action, are necessarily right, or necessarily to be respected. It seeks its ends irrespective of the numbers of its supporters.' See H.G. Wells, 'A Liberal World Organization', p. 29–39 (37), in Wells 1932.
4. See Earle 1950, p. 207: 'He [Wells, BR] was under the illusion that an elite of scientists, intellectuals, and others could build a world independent of politics, in which the national state and other political forms would be immaterial and irrelevant. If democracy stood in the way, democracy, too, must be

circumvented and perhaps discarded.' Beatrice Webb wrote in her diary about a lunch with Wells: 'He was obsessed with his own vague vision of a world order, with his search for a "competent receiver" of the power to organize mankind. The mass electorate and its representatives were totally unfit for the job. But he utterly failed to make me understand what kind of social institution he had in mind'; see W. Boyd Rayward, 'H.G. Wells's World Brain: a Critical Re-Assessment', *Journal of the American Society for Information Science* 1999, vol. 50 no. 7, p. 557–573 (568); on Wells' notion of democracy, see also p. 569. Wells had in any case previously made it clear who would not belong to this new world state: 'And for the rest, those swarms of black and brown, and dirty-white, and yellow people, who do not come into the new needs of efficiency? Well, the world is a world, not a charitable institution, and I take it they will have to go. The whole tenor and meaning of the world, as I see it, is that they have to go.' See Wells 1914, p. 317. Sherborne argues that *Anticipations* was both the starting point (his breakthrough as a social critic) and the nadir of Wells' career: afterwards he developed in a radically different direction, arguing against racism, although he never explicitly (publically) distanced himself from these passages (see Sherborne 2010, p. 152).

5. See Coupland 2000, p. 543.
6. See Coupland 2000, p. 543. See also Tom Gibbons, 'Modernism and Reactionary Politics', *Journal of Modern Literature* 1974, vol. 3 no. 5, p. 1140–1157 (1149–1150).
7. In *Anticipations* Wells also speaks of democracy as a 'grey confusion' that will inevitably need to step aside (as a result of its 'own inherent contradictions'); see Wells 1914, p. 175.
8. Coupland 2000, p. 542. For George Bernard Shaw, see Piers J. Hale, 'Of Mice and Men: Evolution and the Socialist Utopia: William Morris, H.G. Wells, and George Bernard Shaw', *Journal of the History of Biology* 2010, vol. 43 no.1, p. 17–66 (58–60).
9. Coupland 2000, p. 548.
10. See also Coupland 2000, p. 548.
11. Keane 2010, p. 570.
12. Keane 2010, p. 570.
13. Henk te Velde, *Van regentenmentaliteit tot populisme: politieke tradities in Nederland* (From 'governor's mentality' to populism: political traditions in the Netherlands), Amsterdam: Bert Bakker 2010, p. 66. For a detailed discussion of one such proposal, see A.A. de Jonge, *Crisis en critiek der democratie, anti-democratische stromingen en de daarin levende denkbeelden over de staat in Nederland tussen de wereldoorlogen* (Crisis and criticism of democracy, antidemocratic trends and their inherent concepts of the state in the Netherlands in the interbellum), Assen: Van Gorcum 1968 (diss. UvA), p. 295–299.
14. Keane 2010, p. 570–571; for a detailed discussion see Edmund Burke, *Reflections on the Revolution in France*, New Haven/London: Yale University Press 2003, p. 105–106.
15. Keane 2010, p. 571.
16. See Keane 2010, p. 571–572. This technocratic turn had already been predicted by Auguste Comte and Saint-Simon; see Isaiah Berlin, 'The Bent Twig: A Note on Nationalism', *Foreign Affairs* 1972, vol. 51 no. 1, p. 11–30 (12). See also Harvey Mansfield, *A Student's Guide to Political Philosophy*, Wilmington: ISI Books 2001, p. 5–6, on the difference between political philosophy and political science, essentially an echo of Leo Strauss' criticism of positivism, on which see David Janssens, 'Leo Strauss: filosofie, protectie, tirannie en de vraag naar

het kwaad' ('Leo Strauss: philosophy, protection, tyranny and the demand for evil'), p. 93–107 (94–98), in G.J. Buijs and H.E.S. Woldring, *Grote politieke denkers. Hun strijd tussen goed en kwaad: een rondblik* (Great political thinkers. Their battle between good and evil: an exploration), Zoetermeer: Uitgeverij Meinema 2001.

17. See Anthony McElligott, *Rethinking the Weimar Republic: Authority and Authoritarianism 1916-1936*, London: Bloomsbury 2014, p. 182, and Ellen Kennedy, 'Introduction: Carl Schmitt's Parlementarismus in Its Historical Context', p. xiii-l (xxii-xxiii, xxiv and xxvi), in Schmitt 1988.
18. Schmitt fiercely criticized Weber for his technical, bureaucratic subjection of law to 'science'. Schmitt wanted to rescue law as an independent discipline from Weber's instrumental 'scientific approach'. See Catherine Colliot-Thélène, 'Carl Schmitt versus Max Weber: Juridical Rationality and Economic Rationality', p. 138–154, in Chantal Mouffe (ed.), *The Challenge of Carl Schmitt*, London/New York: Verso 1999. For a discussion of the political influence of (part of) Schmitt's work, see McElligott 2014, p. 191–192.
19. See Kennedy 1988, p. xviii, and McElligott 2014, p. 183. For Schmitt the criticism of parliament as an institution went hand in hand with his criticism of nineteenth-century liberalism. See also Volker Neumann, 'Carl Schmitt', p. 280–289 (285), in Arthur J. Jacobsen and Bernhard Schlink (eds.), *Weimar: A Jurisprudence of Crisis*, Berkeley: University of California Press 2002, and Chantal Mouffe, 'Carl Schmitt and the Paradox of Liberal Democracy', *Canadian Journal of Law and Jurisprudence* 1997, vol. 10 no. 1, p. 21–33.
20. Neumann 2002, p. 285. See also Ulrich K. Preuss, 'Political Order and Democracy: Carl Schmitt and His Influence', p. 155–179 (163), in Mouffe 1999.
21. Schmitt 1988, p. 16–17. Later in his *Verfassungslehre* he would repeat, 'The natural form of the direct expression of the people's will is the assembled multitude's declaration of their consent or their disapproval, the *acclamation*'; see Carl Schmitt, *Constitutional Theory* (*Verfassungslehre*), Durham: Duke University Press 2008, p. 131; it should then be seen in connection with the distinction that Schmitt makes between the *pouvoir constituant* and the *pouvoir constitué*; see William E. Scheuerman, *Carl Schmitt: The End of Law*, Oxford: Rowman and Littlefield 1999, p. 69–72. On this pair of concepts see also chapter 2 below, under 'Carl Schmitt'.
22. Neumann 2002, p. 281. There is a great deal of discussion as to the reasons for the conversion of the Catholic, conservative Schmitt to Nazism, for which see Neumann 2002, p. 281–282, and Afshin Ellian, 'De staat van uitzondering' ('The state of exception'), p. 177–213 (203–204), in Gelijn Molier and Timo Slootweg (eds.), *Soevereiniteit en recht: Rechtsfilosofische beschouwingen* (Sovereignty and justice: Legal philosophical views), The Hague: Boom Juridische Uitgevers 2009. On the post-war reception of Schmitt, see Neumann 2002, p. 286–289. On his period with the NSDAP, see also Tracy B. Strong, 'Foreword: The Sovereign and the Exception: Carl Schmitt, Politics, Theology, and Leadership', p. vii–xxxiii (vii–xi and xxxiii), in Carl Schmitt, *Political Theology: Four Chapters on the Concept of Sovereignty* (*Politische Theologie*), Chicago/London: Chicago University Press 2005; Guy Oakes, 'Translator's Introduction', p. ix–xxxv (x–xii), in Carl Schmitt, *Political Romanticism* (*Politische Romantik*), Massachusetts/London: MIT Press 1986; and Rob Hartmans, *Vaarwel dan! Essays over intellectuelen en hun illusies* (Farewell then! Essays on intellectuals and their illusions), Soesterberg: Aspekt 2000, p. 123–126.
23. Th. W.A. de Wit, 'Carl Schmitt: het risico van het politieke kwaad' ('Carl Schmitt: the risk of political evil'), p. 59–76 (60), in Buijs and Woldring 2001.

24. This crisis affected more or less the entire Weimar era, from 1919 to 1933; see Arthur J. Jacobsen and Bernhard Schlink, 'Constitutional Crisis: The German and the American Experience', p. 1–39 (1), in Jacobsen and Schlink 2002.
25. See McElligott 2014, p. 190.
26. See McElligott 2014, p. 203. See also Hartmans 2000, p. 153–163 (in particular p. 155 and 160).
27. Thomas Mann, *Betrachtungen eines Unpolitischen* (1914/1919), cited in Kennedy 1988, p. xxiv.
28. See Keane 2010, p. 570–575; Loewenstein 1935a, p. 574; and Liesbeth van der Grift, *Voorwaarts en vergeten. De overgang van fascisme naar communisme in Oost-Europa, 1944-1948* (Onwards and forgotten. The transition from fascism to communism in Eastern Europe, 1944-1948), Amsterdam: Ambo 2010, p. 21–28.
29. Cited in Keane 2010, p. 570.
30. British political theorist John Keane calls the antidemocratic intellectuals of the 1930s the 'gravediggers' of democracy; see Keane 2010, p. 570. A.A. de Jonge comes to a similar conclusion. He writes of a 'minor crisis' (in the functioning of government institutions) and a 'major crisis' that really 'damaged the idealistic foundations of democracy': 'firstly only among a few thinkers, but soon in broad swathes of society: instead of democratic thinking, the opinion gains ground that the average man on the street is *not* rational and thus not capable of political judgement, that the great mass is eternally immature and merely in need of hard guidance by the small host of the more highly talented, that political freedom is thus also harmful and that people are not equal but in fact *unequal* by nature.' See De Jonge 1968, p. 9–10.
31. Van den Bergh 1936a.
32. The description of the ceremony given here is based on a report in the newspaper *Het Volk*: 'Grote belangstelling voor prof. v.d. Bergh's rede' ('Great interest in Professor Van den Bergh's speech'), *Het Volk*, 29 September 1936, and 'Democratie en Dictatuur' ('Democracy and Dictatorship'), *Het Christelijk Historisch Weekblad*, 17 October 1936. The quote is the spoken version, taken from the report in *Het Volk*, which differs in a few points from the published version of the lecture. All newspaper and magazine articles relating to Van den Bergh can be found in the International Institute of Social History: G. van den Bergh, *Archief George van den Bergh* (Archive of George van den Bergh): ARCH00037, box 3, and/or digitally via the Delpher database: www.delpher.nl (up to 1995), and/or via LexisNexis Academic NL (covers 1990 to present).
33. 'An extremely interesting question', the newspaper the *Haagsche Post* thought, in 'Hoe kan ik u weer kwijt?' ('How can I get rid of you again?'), 3 October 1936; *Vrijheid, Arbeid, Brood* called it 'sharp' and 'impressive' in 'Een dictator aanstellen is gemakkelijk genoeg' ('Appointing a dictator is easy enough'), 1936 (exact date unknown, appears in G. van den Bergh, *Archief George van den Bergh* [Archive of George van den Bergh], International Institute of Social History: ARCH00037, box 3); 'Dangerous proposition' was the headline in *De Amsterdammer: Christelijk Volksdagblad* on 7 October 1936; 'Political science' was the title of a critical piece in the *Nieuw Rotterdamsche Courant* on 14 October 1936.
34. In 1956, for instance, Van den Bergh was mentioned in a Dutch news report on the banning of the Communist Party in West Germany referred to Van den Bergh's lecture; see 'Verboden partij' ('Banned party'), *Het Vrije Volk*, 6 October 1956. Van den Bergh has also been mentioned in a Dutch discussion of party bans; see, for instance: D.J. Elzinga, *De Politieke Partij en het*

Constitutionele Recht (The political party and constitutional law), Nijmegen: Ars Aequi Libri 1982; Bellekom 1982, p. 113–146; Nieuwenhuis 2003.

35. Greenberg shows that, even before his famous two-part article on militant democracy (published in 1937, as discussed below), Loewenstein already pleaded to ban antidemocratic parties in a conference of German constitutional scholars (with Jellinek, Kelsen and Radbruch present, among others); see Udi Greenberg, *The Weimar Century: German Émigrés and the Intellectual Foundations of the Cold War*, Princeton: Princeton University Press 2014, p. 180.
36. Van den Bergh's ideas on militant democracy are discussed in Bastiaan Rijpkema, 'Popper's Paradox of Democracy', *Think* 2012, vol. 11, p. 93–96; and Paul Cliteur and Bastiaan Rijpkema, 'The Foundations of Militant Democracy', p. 227–272 (240–244), in Ellian and Molier 2012.
37. Van den Bergh's inaugural lecture was re-issued (in Dutch) in Van den Bergh 2014.
38. However, as mentioned above, there is an increasing interest in the normative dimensions of militant democracy; see Müller 2016. Tyulkina 2015 and Kirshner 2014 offer theories of militant democracy, and both are discussed at length below.
39. Thilo Rensmann, 'Munich Alumni and the Evolution of International Human Rights Law', *European Journal of International Law* 2011, vol. 22 no. 4, p. 973–991 (980).
40. Rensmann 2011, p. 980.
41. R.W. Kostal, 'The Alchemy of Occupation: Karl Loewenstein and the Legal Reconstruction of Nazi Germany, 1945-1946', *Law and History Review* 2011, vol. 29 no. 1, p. 1–52 (3).
42. See Carl Schmitt, who sees 'parliamentarianism' as something liberal and not as something democratic: Schmitt 1988, p. 8. On the alleged inefficiency of the parliament under Weimar, see among others McElligott 2014, p. 199.
43. Loewenstein 1935a, p. 580 and 593.
44. Loewenstein 1935a and Karl Loewenstein, 'Autocracy versus Democracy in Contemporary Europe, II', *American Political Science Review* 1935, vol. 29 no. 5, p. 755–784 (henceforth Loewenstein 1935b).
45. See Cliteur and Rijpkema 2012, p. 230.
46. See Loewenstein 1935a, p. 571–572, and Cliteur and Rijpkema 2012, p. 230–231.
47. Cliteur and Rijpkema 2012, p. 231.
48. For a detailed discussion see Cliteur and Rijpkema 2012, p. 232–233 and 235. See also Peter Niesen, 'Anti-Extremism, Negative Republicanism, Civic Society: Three Paradigms for Banning Political Parties—Part I', *German Law Journal* 2002, vol. 3, §23; Tyulkina 2015, p. 13, 28 and 207; and recently: Anthoula Malkopoulou and Ludvig Norman, 'Three Models of Democratic Self-Defence: Militant Democracy and Its Alternatives', *Political Studies* 2017, vol. 66 no. 2, p. 442–458 (444).
49. For a summary of Michael Oakeshott's thoughts on 'mass democracy', see Perry Anderson, *Spectrum: From Right to Left in the World of Ideas*, London/New York: Verso 2005, p. 9–11; for Ortega y Gasset, see José Ortega y Gasset, *The Revolt of the Masses* (*La rebelión de las masas*), New York/London: W.W. Norton 1993; and on the same subject see Manuel Maldonado-Denis, 'Ortega y Gasset and the Theory of the Masses', *Western Political Quarterly* 1961, vol. 14 no. 3, p. 676–690, and Diederik Boomsma, 'Ortega's filosofie van de "vitale rede"' ('Ortega's philosophy of the "vital reason"'), p. 7–22, in the new Dutch translation of José Ortega y Gasset, *De opstand van de massamens* (The revolt of the masses), introduced, translated and annotated by Diederik Boomsma, with an afterword by Mario Vargas Llosa, Rotterdam: Lemniscaat 2015.

50. Van der Grift 2010, p. 28.
51. On this see De Jonge 1968, p. 14–15. In a later article Loewenstein indicates that he does see *Nazism* as a substantive political philosophy; see Karl Loewenstein, 'Legislation for the Defense of the State in Chile', *Columbia Law Review* 1944, vol. 44 no. 3, p. 366–407 (407).
52. For this interpretation of Loewenstein, see Cliteur and Rijpkema 2012, p. 230–236.
53. Cliteur and Rijpkema 2012, p. 235.
54. Schmitt 1986, p. 20, 139 (and the translator's introduction: xiii and xxvii). See also Anderson 2005, p. 21. It is this 'endless conversation' that becomes institutionalized by the 'parliament', the institution that Schmitt criticises so fiercely in *The Crisis of Parliamentary Democracy*, mentioned above (Schmitt 1988); see Michael Hoelzl and Graham Ward, 'Introduction', p. x–xxviii (xv), in Carl Schmitt, *Dictatorship* (*Die Diktatur. Von den Anfängen des modernen Souveränitätsgedankens bis zum proletarischen Klassenkampf*), Cambridge: Polity Press 2014.
55. Cliteur and Rijpkema 2012, p. 235.
56. Cliteur and Rijpkema 2012, p. 235.
57. See Cliteur and Rijpkema 2012, p. 235 and 236–237. On the national circumstances in the Netherlands, Loewenstein, for instance, writes, 'The uniform-wearing habit in Holland seems even more ridiculous than in the Scandinavian countries; for goose-stepping before a so-called leader is not in the least within the inclination of the slow, freedom-loving, anti-militaristic, and individualistic mentality of the Dutchman.' See Loewenstein 1935b, p. 764. See also Karl Loewenstein, 'It Is Later Than You Think; The Need for a Militant Democracy by Max Lerner' (discussion), *American Political Science Review* 1939, vol. 33 no. 3, p. 519–521 (521).
58. See, for example, András Sajó, 'Militant Democracy and the Transition towards Democracy', in Sajó 2004, and in particular Andras Sajó, 'Militant Democracy and Emotional Politics', *Constellations* 2012, vol. 19 no. 4, p. 562–574.
59. Sajó 2012, p. 562.
60. Sajó 2004, p. 211.
61. Sajó 2004, p. 211.
62. Sajó 2012, p. 563.
63. Sajó 2012, p. 563. This agrees quite closely with the way the Nazis themselves saw their propaganda. On this, see Bendersky 2014, p. 49: 'Hitler considered the correct use of propaganda an art.... The essence of the Nazi theory of propaganda was explained in *Mein Kampf*. Its first principle was that propaganda must always be addressed to the masses; its second precept was that effective propaganda must be aimed at the emotions and not the intellect. The underlying assumptions were that the masses had limited intelligence and that their behavior was determined more by feeling than rational thought.'
64. Sajó 2012, p. 563.
65. Sajó 2012, p. 564 and 571.
66. Sajó 2012, p. 563 and 569.
67. Sajó 2012, p. 563. This is where militant democracy comes into view: measures from the repertoire of militant democracy can shape that 'militant anti-majoritarianism'.
68. For all this, see Sajó 2012, p. 570–571. In his idea of the 'masses' Loewenstein was in fact not unique among liberal German lawyers; see Greenberg 2014, p. 175. For a recent critique of Loewenstein's *and* Sajó's militant democracy theories as elitist, see Malkopoulou and Norman 2017, p. 444–446, 455.

69. Sajó 2012, p. 563–564 and 572.
70. Sajó 2012, p. 563.
71. Loewenstein 1937a, and Karl Loewenstein, 'Militant Democracy and Fundamental Rights, II', *American Political Science Review* 1937, vol. 31 no. 4, p. 638–658 (henceforth Loewenstein 1937b).
72. Loewenstein 1937a, p. 423.
73. Loewenstein 1937b, with an overview of the different countries on p. 638–644 and a thematic discussion from p. 644.
74. See, for example, Loewenstein 1937b, p. 652–654. These measures are not unproblematic: due to vague concepts and narrow dividing lines between legal and illegal use of political rights, judges can be forced to pass judgement on what essentially are political problems (p. 654).
75. Loewenstein 1937b, p. 654. As an example of such glorification Loewenstein mentions Hitler's expression of support for a political murderer who had been condemned to death in 1933.
76. Cliteur and Rijpkema 2012, p. 238.
77. See Loewenstein 1937a, p. 431.
78. See also the criticism in Invernizzi Accetti and Zuckerman 2017, p. 185.
79. Loewenstein 1937a, p. 431–432; for part of the following discussion see Cliteur and Rijpkema 2012, p. 238–240.
80. Greenberg 2014.
81. Greenberg 2014, p. 9–10.
82. Greenberg 2014, p. 187–198.
83. Greenberg 2014, p. 189.
84. Greenberg 2014, p. 194.
85. Greenberg 2014, p. 207–209; a comparable criticism, albeit worked out in less detail, can be found in Chou 2013, p. 68 and 72.
86. See, for example, Greenberg 2014, p. 15, 23, 167 and 258.
87. Michael Kimmage, 'Do the Roots of the Cold War Alliance Lie in Weimar Germany?' (discussion of Greenberg 2014), *The New Republic* (online), 8 December 2014.
88. Kimmage 2014.
89. Greenberg 2014, p. 198.
90. Greenberg 2014, p. 176; see also p. 177 and 179.
91. Greenberg 2014, p. 179.
92. Greenberg 2014, p. 209.
93. Greenberg 2014, p. 198.
94. The Hungarian sociologist Karl Mannheim (1893-1947) is sometimes mentioned alongside him. In 1943 he argued for a 'militant democracy' in his *Diagnosis of Our Time: Wartime Essays of a Sociologist*; see Markus Thiel, 'Militant Democracy and State of Emergency in Germany', p. 273–327 (275), in Ellian and Molier 2012; and Klamt 2012, p. 31; Klamt sees Mannheim more as a descriptive sociologist who offers no clear solutions.
95. This involves more or less *all* literature on law and politics; to gain an impression, see among others Tyulkina 2015, p. 13; Kirshner 2014, p. 2; Giovanni Capoccia, 'Militant Democracy: The Institutional Bases of Democratic Self-Preservation', *Annual Review of Law and Social Science* 2013, vol. 9, p. 207–226 (208); Angela K. Bourne, 'Democratization and the Illegalization of Political Parties in Europe', *Democratization* 2012, vol. 19 no. 6, p. 1065–1085 (1080) (henceforth Bourne 2012a); Klamt 2012, p. 2; Markus Thiel, 'Introduction', p. 1–14 (4), in Thiel 2009 (henceforth Thiel 2009a); Issacharoff 2007, p. 1409; Sajó 2012, p. 562; Klamt 2007, p. 133–134; Sajó 2004, p. 210; Otto Pfersmann, 'Shaping Militant Democracy', p. 47–68 (48), in Sajó 2004.

96. Sajó 2004.
97. Hans-Jürgen Papier and Wolfgang Durner, 'Streitbare Demokratie', *Archiv des öffentlichen Rechts* 2003, vol. 128, p. 340–371 (345). See also Gerhard Loewenberg, 'The Influence of European Émigré Scholars on Comparative Politics, 1925-1965', *American Political Science Review*, vol. 100 no. 4, p. 597–604 (599–601).
98. Greenberg 2014, p. 198–200. Kostal 2011, p. 46–51, is more cautious, with more attention for Loewenstein's frustrations over American policy in occupied Germany.
99. See Cliteur and Rijpkema 2012, p. 240, see also Jan Eskes, 'Verbied partij voordat die de democratie ontwricht' ('Ban party before it disrupts democracy'), *Trouw*, 11 August 2011.
100. See, for instance, Thiel 2009 and Tyulkina 2015.
101. Karl Loewenstein, 'Legislative Control of Political Extremism in European Democracies I', *Columbia Law Review* 1938, vol. 38 no. 4, p. 591–622 (617, note 90); see Cliteur and Rijpkema 2012, p. 240–241.
102. Loewenstein 1938, p. 617, note 90.
103. Van den Bergh 1936a, p. 3–4; W.A. Bonger, *Problemen der demokratie: een sociologische en psychologische studie* (Problems of democracy: a sociological and psychological study), Groningen/Batavia: P. Noordhoff N.V. 1934, p. 17; for a discussion of the definition, see p. 10–17. Within the Social Democratic Workers' Party, Bonger's book became the most important work on democracy and was used as material on courses for party officials; see Rob Hartmans, *Vijandige broeders? De Nederlandse sociaal-democratie en het nationaal-socialisme, 1922-1940* (Enemy brothers? Dutch social democracy and National Socialism, 1922-1940), Amsterdam: Ambo 2012, p. 205. See also Bart van Heerikhuizen, *W.A. Bonger*, p. 114–146 (131), in Jan Bank, Paul Talma, Martin Ros and Bart Tromp (eds.), *Het vierde jaarboek voor het democratisch-socialisme* (The fourth yearbook for democratic socialism), Amsterdam: De Arbeiderspers/Wiardi Beckmann Stichting 1983.
104. Bonger 1934, p. 129.
105. Van den Bergh 1936a, p. 4.
106. See Schmitt 2014, p. 1–2 and 86–87; for the concept of 'commissarial dictatorship', as opposed to *sovereign* dictatorship, in Schmitt, see Marc de Wilde, *Verwantschap in Extremen: Politieke Theologie bij Walter Benjamin en Carl Schmitt* (Affinity in Extremes: Political Theology of Walter Benjamin and Carl Schmitt), Amsterdam: Vossiuspers/Amsterdam University Press 2008, p. 96; see also Schmitt's reading of Article 48 of the Weimar constitution in these terms: Carl Schmitt, 'The Dictatorship of the Reich President According to Art 48 of the Reich Constitution' (translated by Ellen Kennedy), *Constellations* 2011, vol. 18 no. 3, p. 299–323 (in particular p. 310–312), also published as an appendix in Schmitt 2014, and on this subject see Marc de Wilde, 'The State of Emergency in the Weimar Republic. Legal Disputes over Article 48 of the Weimar Constitution', *Legal History Review* 2010, vol. 78, p. 135–158 (144–145). See also Schreuerman 1999, p. 31–32.
107. Van den Bergh 1936a, p. 4–5. On the definition of 'antidemocratic parties' see also Bart Tromp, 'Anti-democratische stromingen' ('Antidemocratic movements'), p. 84–104 (85–87), in J.J.A Thomassen (ed.), *Hedendaagse democratie* (Contemporary democracy), Alphen aan den Rijn: Samsom/H.D. Tjeenk Willink 1991. Tromp also makes a distinction between groups that reject democracy outright on the one hand and those that support a *different* idea of democracy (the 'true democracy'). The former are groups that seek to go 'back in time', thus defending the *ancien regime*, while the latter are antidemocrats that want to move 'forward', towards a new 'democratic order', consisting of

a left-wing variant (anarchism and particular forms of socialism) and a right-wing variant (fascism and national socialism).

108. Giovanni Gentile, 'The Philosophic Basis of Fascism', *Foreign Affairs* 1928, vol. 6 no. 2, p. 290–304 (302). See also Müller 2012, p. 537.
109. And at the time criminal law was equipped for the task in more or less all European countries; see Loewenstein 1937b, p. 645.
110. Van den Bergh 1936a, p. 5–6. See also J.A.O. Eskes, Repressie van Politieke Bewegingen in Nederland: een juridisch-historische studie over het Nederlandse publiekrechtelijke verenigingsrecht gedurende het tijdvak 1798-1988 (Repression of Political Movements in the Netherlands: a legal historical study of the Dutch right of association in public law during the period 1798-1988, diss. Utrecht), Zwolle: W.E.J. Tjeenk Willink/NISER 1988, p. 248–249.
111. See, for example, Loewenstein 1937a, p. 424–425; see also Cliteur and Rijpkema 2012, p. 241–242.
112. See Van den Bergh 1936a, p. 7.
113. See Van den Bergh 1936a, p. 7. With respect to Germany, see also Greenberg 2014, p. 174: 'In the eyes of Germany's leading liberal scholars and politicians, democracy was founded on political relativism, the conviction that in a secular world no political ideology was superior to any other.'
114. See Van den Bergh 1936a, p. 8.
115. See 'Democratie. Ook jegens niet-democraten' ('Democracy. Towards non-democrats too'), *Vooruit*, 6 October 1936.
116. In 1940 Kelsen, like Loewenstein, left Europe, and after a stay at Harvard, became a professor at the University of California, Berkeley; see Clemens Jabloner, 'Hans Kelsen', p. 67–76 (68), in Jacobsen and Schlink 2002. As a representative of the idea of relativist democracy, Eskes primarily mentions Gustav Radbruch; see Eskes 1988, p. 249, note 616. On Loewenstein and Kelsen, see Greenberg 2014, p. 174–175.
117. Greenberg 2014, p. 174–175; see also Malkopoulou and Norman 2017, p. 448.
118. Hans Kelsen, 'On the Essence and Value of Democracy (*Vom Wesen und Wert der Demokratie*, 2nd edition, 1929)', p. 84–109 (107–108), in Jacobsen and Schlink 2002. The same line of reasoning can be found in the first edition of 1920: Hans Kelsen, *Vom Wesen und Wert der Demokratie*, Tübingen: Mohr 1920, p. 36–38. Kelsen connects democracy not only with relativism, but also with positivism and scientific thinking; see the observations in Schmitt 2005, p. 49. More problematic, for Schmitt, was the confusion of democracy (*not* equality of individuals) with liberalism (which *is* equality of individuals as individuals; an individualist-humanist ethics and worldview) in Kelsen's ideas; see Schmitt 1988, p. 13.
119. Kelsen never joined a political party, but he entertained a certain sympathy for the Austrian social democrats (see Jabloner 2002, p. 71–72).
120. Van den Bergh 1936a, p. 8.
121. See Van den Bergh 1936a, p. 8–9.
122. Nadia Urbinati and Carlo Invernizzi Accetti, 'Editor's Introduction', p. 6–40 (7), in Hans Kelsen, *Essence and Value of Democracy* (translated by Brian Graf), Lanham: Rowman & Littlefield 2013.
123. Hans Kelsen, 'Foundations of Democracy', *Ethics* 1955, vol. 66 no. 1, p. 1–101 (31).
124. Hans Kelsen, 'Verteidigung der Demokratie', p. 229–237 (237), in *Verteidigung der Demokratie: Abhandlungen zur Demokratietheorie*, Tübingen: Mohr Siebeck 2006 (1932).
125. Jabloner 2002, p. 74; Greenberg 2014, p. 174; see also the discussion in Malkopoulou and Norman 2017, p. 448. Jabloner stresses that Kelsen's attitude of 'non-opposition' to a democracy abolishing itself does not *necessarily*

follow from legal positivism, since, as for instance H.L.A. Hart argues in his well-known article 'Positivism and the Separation of Law and Morals', the legal status of a law is a different, and separate, question, next to the duty to obey that same law; this also holds for a law that would abolish a democracy (see Jabloner 2002, note 7 to p. 74).

126. Kelsen 2006, p. 237. A similar sentiment can be found in the work of American political philosopher Lawrence Hatab; see Chou 2013, p. 54.
127. Van den Bergh 1936a, p. 9.
128. Van den Bergh 1936a, p. 19–20, 22.
129. Van den Bergh 1936a, first on p. 6–7, and later in detail on p. 23–24.
130. Van den Bergh 1936a, p. 23–24.
131. Van den Bergh 1936a, p. 23.
132. Karl Popper, *The Open Society and Its Enemies*, Princeton/New York: Princeton University Press 2013, p. 581–582 (note 4 in chapter 7 of part 1).
133. Van den Bergh 1936a, p. 24; for Popper's variant, see Popper 2013, p. 581–582 (note 4 in chapter 7 of part 1). Popper's solution, however, is dissatisfying; see Rijpkema 2012, p. 93–96. See also Eric Weber's response, in which he suggests that John Dewey approached the problem in a manner comparable to Van den Bergh; see Eric Thomas Weber, *Democracy and Leadership: On Pragmatism and Virtue*, Plymouth: Lexington Books 2013, p. 177.
134. Van den Bergh 1936a, p. 24.
135. Van den Bergh 1936a, p. 24.
136. Van den Bergh 1936a, p. 25.
137. Van den Bergh 1936a, p. 25.
138. Van den Bergh 1936a, p. 8. In his interpretation of Van den Bergh, Gelijn Molier emphasizes this very aspect of the inaugural lecture, in particular Van den Bergh's insight that respect for the individuality of every human being can only exist by the grace of reciprocity. See Gelijn Molier, 'Syrië-gangers wacht "strijdbare democratie"' ('"Militant democracy" awaits Syria-goers'), *Civis Mundi* 2014, no. 22 (see under 4).
139. To Chou an 'anything-goes' mentality is an example of 'too much democracy', which can subsequently lead to democratic suicide; see Chou 2013, p. 69.
140. See Bellekom 1982, p. 117.
141. James Mill, 'Government', p. 857–889 (871–873), in Edwin A. Burtt, *The English Philosophers from Bacon to Mill*, New York: The Modern Library 1939; Leslie Stephen, *The English Utilitarians* (in three volumes; volume II: *James Mill*), London/New York: Continuum 2006 (reprint of the original from 1900), p. 79; Terence Ball, 'James Mill', under §4, in Edward N. Zalta (ed.), *The Stanford Encyclopedia of Philosophy*, edition: summer 2014, http://plato.stanford.edu/archives/sum2014/entries/james-mill/.
142. See Mill 1939, p. 857–859 and 885; Stephen 2006, p. 75.
143. Mill 1939, p. 873: 'This is an old and approved method of identifying as nearly as possible the interests of those who rule with the interest of those who are ruled' (p. 873). See also Stephen 2006, p. 79–80.
144. Van den Bergh 1936a, p. 9.
145. This is what I argue in Rijpkema 2012. See also Cliteur and Rijpkema 2012, p. 243–244.
146. Van den Bergh 1936a, p. 9
147. Van den Bergh 1936a, p. 9.
148. Van den Bergh 1936a, p. 9–10. Van Poelje and Hartmans also emphasize this aspect of the inaugural lecture; see G.A. van Poelje, 'Bewogen Staatsrecht' ('Turbulent Constitutional Law'), in G.A. van Poelje, *Opstellen aangeboden aan Prof. Mr. Van den Bergh ter gelegenheid van zijn aftreden als hoogleraar in*

het Nederlandse Staatsrecht aan de Universiteit van Amsterdam (Essays presented to Professor Van den Bergh on the occasion of his retirement from the position of professor of Dutch constitutional law at the University of Amsterdam), Alphen aan den Rijn: N. Samson 1960, p. 3, and Hartmans 2012, p. 185; see also Eskes 1988, p. 251, who sees this as a 'first justification'. Van den Bergh's idea was also noted in the first legal discussions; on the positive side, see H.L.M. Kramer, 'De democratische staat en de niet-democratische partijen' ('The democratic state and the non-democratic parties'), *Nederlands Juristenblad* 1936, p. 820–824 (821–822) (henceforth Kramer 1936a), and on the critical side, see G.E. Langemeijer, 'De democratische staat en de niet-democratische partijen', *Nederlands Juristenblad* 1936, p. 881–886 (883–884) (henceforth Langemeijer 1936a). In work relating to Van den Bergh's, the 'possibility of self-correction' is also mentioned in an interesting master's thesis by H.C. Wichers Hoeth; see H.C. Wichers Hoeth, *De democratie en niet-democratische partijen* (Democracy and non-democratic parties, master's thesis), 1980, p. 8–9 and 26.

149. Van den Bergh 1936a, p. 8–9.
150. I also use this example in Rijpkema 2012.
151. To illustrate this point: the Dutch minister of education, culture and science Jet Bussemaker initially refused to place a burned down but restored windmill dating back to 1787 back on the list of monuments, arguing that it was a 'replica'. Bussemaker: 'The essence of a monument is its authenticity, and this is not authentic. What would we do if *The Night Watch* were burned? Surely we would not suddenly pronounce a replica to be the true *Night Watch*?' Eventually, after protest from the House of Representatives, the minister revised her decision on the basis that it was a 'unique case'. See 'Molen Burum geen rijksmonument' ('Burum Windmill not a national monument'), *NOS* (online), 8 September 2014, and 'Molen Burum toch Rijksmonument' ('Burum Windmill a national monument after all'), *NOS* (online), 6 October 2014.
152. Marinus Van der Goes van Naters, letter to George van den Bergh, with attachment, 6 October 1936, in the personal archive of George van den Bergh, owned by Van den Bergh's heirs.
153. See Marinus van der Goes van Naters, *Socialistische Staatsvernieuwing* (Socialist state revival), Arnhem: Van Loghun Slaterus Uitgevers-maatschappij N.V. 1937, p. 118.
154. Milan P. Markovitch, La doctrine sociale de Duguit: ses idées sur le syndicalisme et représentation professionnelle, Paris: Éditions Pierre Bossuet 1933.
155. For an overview of Duguit's ideas, see Cécile Laborde, 'Pluralism, Syndicalism and Corporatism: Leon Duguit and the Crisis of the State (1900-25)', *History of European Ideas* 1996, vol. 22 no. 3, p. 227–244 (in particular p. 235–236 and 239–240); Duguit placed the 'functional representation' of economic and social groups in opposition to the 'individualistic basis' of the representative democracy. It would offer the French republic a more 'solid structure' than the 'democratic, individualistic and parliamentary framework'. Although Duguit saw himself as a democrat, and although part of the parliament would be elected by the regular democratic route, in his thinking citizens unmistakably fulfil a more passive role as 'those governed' without direct participation. Duguit's ideas also have technocratic characteristics, according to Laborde.
156. For a summary of that criticism, see Markovitch 1933, p. 275–277, including 'La représentation professionnelle est aux antipodes du parlementarisme rationalise qui est le couronnement logique et nécessaire de toute démocratie individualiste et de la souveraineté populaire. Ainsi, uniquement le système démocratique d'organisation politique conditionné par la

vie et adéquat à elle, ... Essayer de la remplacer par l'organisation de la représentation professionnelle est après cela, vraiment impossible. Introduire le mauvais, étant donné tous les défauts, vices et inconvénients de la représentation professionnelle, pour remplacer le bon est contraire à toute logique. Et la représentation professionnelle réalisée au Parlement le serait certainement. D'où et pour cette raison, la proposition de Duguit de donner aux professions organisées dans tous les syndicats les rênes pouvoirs est sans aucun doute impossible et inacceptable'; see also p. 255–256.

157. Markovitch 1933, p. 256–257.
158. Markovitch 1933, p. 257.
159. Markovitch 1933, p. 257.
160. Markovitch 1933, p. 257.
161. Markovitch 1933, p. 256, and also p. 258, with the elections as the instrument.
162. Markovitch 1933, p. 257–258: 'loi de réaction, c'est-à-dire la possibilité de changements de systèmes d'organisation politiques', p. 255: 'de la loi vitale de toute société qu'est la loi de reaction', and p. 256: 'Il est juste aussi bien logique que celui qui subit le poids d'un système soit l'arbitre souverain de sa valeur. Sans cela, l'homme sera enchaîné, opprimé, terrorisé, ce qui est tout à faire contraire a sa quaité [sic] d'homme, à son rôle social primordial, donc à toute la vie sociale.' On man, or humanity, as a point of departure, see also p. 256: 'L'homme, c'est la vie. Chaque système, s'il veut être tel, est nécessairement oblige de correspondre a cette vie, parce que l'homme est tout et partout,' and p. 251: 'L'individu est tout et partout. S'il n'est pas seul en dernier ressort, c'est toujours lui, l'individu. Donc, il est partout.'
163. Markovitch, 1933, p. 258: 'Seule, la démocratie, système d'organisation politique où le peuple est l'unique souverain, ne nie et ne s'oppose à la loi de réaction.'
164. Markovitch, 1933, p. 258.
165. Markovitch 1933, p. 255: 'La démocratie présente, en tant que système d'organisation politique, une valeur incontestablement supérieure à tous les autres modes d'organisation de la puissance politique. Ses qualités propres sont innombrables. Elle seul assure nettement la pleine expression de la loi vitale de toute société qu'est la loi de reaction.' See also p. 271.
166. Markovitch 1933, p. 276: 'Le principe de la démocratie est inattaquable' ; see also p. 255 and 258.
167. Markovitch 1933, p. 258.
168. Markovitch 1933, p. 258: 'Apparemment oui, mais au fond, non.'
169. Markovitch 1933, p. 258.
170. Markovitch 1933, p. 258–259: 'Toute réaction légale est possible, sauf une seule: la réaction qui veut consciemment ou non, peu importe, supprimer la possibilité d'une nouvelle réaction donc ignorer et pratiquement détruire la loi vitale de la société qu'est la loi de réaction, en justifiant et en codifiant ainsi la révolution, le feu et le sang, ce qui évidemment, ne doit nullement cadrer avec l'homme et son ambition d'être autre chose qu'un animal ordinaire, sans esprit et conscience.'
171. 'Here too the emphasis is on the legal reaction of those intending oppression, and here too every legal reaction is tolerated, except that which seeks to interrupt the possibility of a new reaction!' according to Van der Goes van Naters in his letter to Van den Bergh; see Van der Goes van Naters 1936.
172. Van den Bergh 1936a, p. 6.
173. 'De democratische Staat. Tegenover niet-democratische partijen' ('The democratic State. Against non-democratic parties'), *De Residentiebode*, 23 December 1936.
174. Van den Bergh 1936a, p. 6.

175. Markovitch 1933, p. 259.
176. Which taken *literally* is a circular argument: democracy is the best system because it fulfils the law of reaction, which in turn means it is a democracy; see Markovitch 1933, p. 259 and note 1. See also p. 258: 'La démocratie se présente comme le seul système politique compatible avec la vie, qu'elle doit rester dan tous les temps et chez tous les hommes.'
177. Markovitch 1933, p. 256: 'L'homme, c'est la vie. Chaque système, s'il veut être tel, est nécessairement oblige de correspondre a cette vie, parce que l'homme est tout et partout'; for comparable formulations see p. 251–252 and 273.
178. Van den Bergh 1936a, p. 9: 'One of the strongest elements of democracy can be attributed to its "self-correction". Every democrat admits that democracy often leads to erroneous decisions. However, it offers more safeguards than any other system to ensure that these decisions, as soon as it becomes apparent that they are incorrect, are revised. In democracy the circles of the stakeholders and those who make the decisions in the final instance overlap. The people make the decisions and feel the consequences directly. They know their responsibility, they correct their own mistakes.' Markovitch comes closest to this when he writes, 'L'homme, créateur du système et objet de son application, va être le seul juge de son opportunité et de son utilité. Il est juste aussi bien que logique que celui qui subit le poids d'un système soit l'arbitre souverain de sa valeur. Sans cela, l'homme sera enchaîné, opprimé, terrorisé, ce qui est tout à faire contraire a sa quaité [sic] d'homme, à son rôle social primordial, donc à toute la vie sociale' (Markovitch 1933, p. 256).
179. The Austrian judge and lawyer Rudolf Thienel also draws a distinction between possible changes in the law that fits closely with Van den Bergh's idea: 'There is an obvious difference between—for instance—a tax law, which is backed by the majority and can be changed by a future majority, and a constitutional change abolishing the democratic participation itself—without the possibility of returning to democratic rule if a future majority so wishes. The consequence is quite clear: In order to secure democratic participation for future generations, it is justified and necessary to deny radical political movements the possibility of destroying the democratic system—even if they try to achieve their goal not by violence, but by means of a "march through the institutions".' See Rudolf Thienel, 'Militant Democracy—Can Democracy Defend Itself?', p. 63–69 (64–65), in Harald Eberhard, Konrad Lachmayer, Gerald Ribarov and Gerhard Thallinger (eds.), *Perspectives and Limits of Democracy: Proceedings of the 3rd Vienna Workshop on International Constitutional Law*, Nomos/facultas.vuw 2008. Other 'approximations' of Van den Bergh's 'democracy as self-correction' are discussed at length in chapter 3. Interestingly enough, it could also be argued that the idea of 'self-correction' is approximated by Hans Kelsen (who was discussed as Van den Bergh's main 'antagonist' above); see Hong's interpretation of Kelsen called 'democracy as self-restraint', in Quoc Loc Hong, 'Democracy, Freedom of Speech and the Twin Challenges of the Exception', p. 329–366, in Ellian and Molier 2012, and the comparison in Gelijn Molier, 'Drie typen van weerbare democratie' (Three types of militant democracy), in Afshin Ellian, Gelijn Molier and Bastiaan Rijpkema (eds.), *De strijd om de democratie: essays over democratische zelfverdediging*, Amsterdam: Boom 2018.
180. Experiences in post-war Germany might serve as an illustration of these possibilities; see Jan-Werner Müller, 'Militant Democracy', p. 1253–1269 (1258–1260), in Michel Rosenfeld and Andras Sajó, *The Oxford Handbook of Comparative Constitutional Law*, Oxford: Oxford University Press 2013 (henceforth Müller 2013b).

181. See Müller 2013b, p. 1258, who speaks of the influence of Loewenstein's ideas on the German Constitution. H.C. Wichers Hoeth also links Van den Bergh expressly with the German 'streitbare Demokratie'; to my knowledge, this is the first interpretation of Van den Bergh in these post-war terms; see Wichers Hoeth 1980, p. 25). In 1995 Van den Bergh surfaces, along with the term 'weerbare democratie' (militant or defensive democracy), in an article for the newspaper *Trouw* on the AIVD, the General Intelligence and Security Service of the Netherlands (then the BVD): Louis Cornelisse, 'Met wc-rol was politieke baas BVD allang tevreden' ('Political boss of the BVD had long been satisfied with toilet roll'), *Trouw*, 6 September 1995. In response to the judgement of the ECHR on the Refah case, Eskes mentions Van den Bergh's inaugural lecture in *Trouw* and draws a direct line to the German 'streitbare Demokratie'; see Eskes 2011. In his comments on the same Refah case, in the context of militant democracy, Alkema too mentions Van den Bergh; see ECHR 13 February 2003, 41340/98, 41342/98 and 41344/98, *NJ* 2005, 73, incl. note E.A. Alkema (Refah Partisi/Turkey).
182. See Thiel 2012, p. 292.
183. See Thiel 2012, p. 293, and Klamt 2007, p. 137. The question, of course, is whether this means that the constitution can *never* be overturned. The answer is probably no, in the light of GG Article 146: if the people set up a new constitution and it comes into effect, the old one is deactivated. See P.P.T. Bovend'Eert and M.C. Burkens, 'De Bondsrepubliek Duitsland' ('The Federal Republic of Germany'), p. 69, in L.F.M. Besselink, P.P.T Bovend'Eert, J.L.W. Broeksteeg and R. de Lange, *Staatsrecht van landen van de Europese Unie* (Constitutional law of the countries of the European Union), Deventer: Kluwer 2012, and Ulrich Preuss, 'The Implications of "Eternity Clauses": The German Experience', *Israel Law Review* 2011, vol. 44, p. 429–448 (443). It can be argued, on the other hand, that, given the structure of the constitution, GG Article 146 anticipates the establishment and adoption of a constitution after a civil war (or at least, after a lengthy disturbance to public order), rather than the hypothetical situation in which a new constitution is written and adopted in parallel with the current constitution. At the same time the wording of the article does not rule this out. It creates the remarkable situation in which revision of certain *parts* of the Grundgesetz is impossible, but complete replacement might be formally permitted. This explanation appears also to be held by the Federal Constitutional Court: the eternity clause can only be overruled by the 'directly expressed will' of the German people (see Preuss 2011, p. 443).
184. See Müller 2013b, p. 1262–1266, and Klamt 2007, p. 150–152.
185. Van den Bergh 1936a, p. 26.
186. Van den Bergh 1936a, p. 31.
187. Van den Bergh 1936a, p. 28–29. For criticism of Van den Bergh's proposal only to allow the Supreme Court to ban a party on a unanimous vote, see Kramer 1936a, p. 824, who fears that this exacting requirement might 'endanger the intended protection of our democratic state institutions'; 'does this not put too much power in the hands of one single councillor?' That fear is not unfounded, as becomes apparent from experiences with the requirement for a *two-thirds majority* in Germany; see Thilo Rensmann, 'Procedural Fairness in a Militant Democracy: The "Uprising of the Decent" Fails before the Federal Constitutional Court', *German Law Journal* 2003, vol. 4 no. 11, p. 1117–1136 (1134): 'The real victim of the decision [in the case of the extreme right NPD, BR], however, is the normative authority of Article 21 para. 2 of the Basic Law. At least as long as the minority judges remain in office and wield their veto power, the possibility of a successful application to ban a political party in Germany is for all intents

and purposes excluded, save in exceptional cases of clear and present danger to the "free democratic basic order". Normativity is largely reduced to virtuality and symbolism. According to the minority a single informer in the party leadership is sufficient to thwart any attempt to dissolve a political party. On the other hand the minority opinion imposes a considerable burden on the applicants to substantiate the claim of unconstitutionality with sufficient evidence. Such evidence cannot, however, be obtained without the help of informers.'

188. Donations of 4500 euros and more have to be made public; see Article 25 of the 2013 Political Parties Funding Act (Wet financiering politieke partijen). Donations were first made public by the minister of the interior Ronald Plasterk on 1 October 2014; see 'Giften politieke partijen openbaar' ('Donations to political parties made public'), NOS (online), 1 October 2014.
189. 'Politieke wetenschap' ('Political science'), *Nieuwe Rotterdamsche Courant*, 14 October 1936. A day later this suggestion was repeated in a second piece on the lecture: 'Wet op de staatkundige partijen?' ('Political parties act?'), *Nieuwe Rotterdamsche Courant*, 15 October 1936.
190. 'Een lastig probleem' ('A difficult problem'), *De Avondpost*, 6 October 1936.
191. As cited in 'Gevaarlijke stelling' ('Dangerous proposition'), *De Amsterdammer: Christelijk Volksdagblad*, 7 October 1936. The example of *De Dageraad* (an organization now known as *De Vrije Gedachte*) turned out to be attractive. Had Thorbecke not named faith and religious piety 'the nation's most noble characteristic'? Would it not be possible, then, to ban the atheist *De Dageraad* by Van den Bergh's reasoning, *De Avondpost* asked a few weeks later? 'We are not arguing for that,' but 'not obstructing is not the same as encouraging'; see 'Twee gevaren' ('Two dangers'), *De Avondpost*, 20 October 1936. *De Vrijzinnig-democraat* came to the same conclusion as *Het Volk*; see 'Democratische Staatsbeleid: de houding tegenover dicatuur-stromingen' ('Democratic State Policy: the position on dictatorship trends'), *De Vrijzinnig-democraat*, 17 October 1936. In response to the review, the *Dagblad van Noord-Brabant* concluded, 'It is understandable that the social democrats prefer not to use this double-edged sword in defence of their democracy'. See 'Verbod van ondemocratische partijen?' ('Ban on undemocratic parties?'), *Dagblad van Noord-Brabant*, 16 October 1936.
192. See 'De zelfverdediging der democratie. Revolutionaire kiezers en revolutionaire Ambtsdragers' ('The self-defence of democracy. Revolutionary voters and revolutionary Officials'), *Algemeen Handelsblad*, 28 October 1936. To the same effect, see 'Niet aldus' ('Therefore no'), *De Standaard*, 8 October 1936; 'Democratie: ook jegens niet-democraten' ('Democracy: towards non-democrats too'), *Vooruit*, 6 October 1936; and 'Democratie en Dictatuur' ('Democracy and Dictatorship'), *Het Christelijk Historisch Weeklbad*, 17 October 1936.
193. 'We do not deceive ourselves that the execution of these propositions will provide wonderful possibilities; yet the writer's reasoning is fully deserving of attention.' See 'Hoe kan ik u weer kwijt?' ('How can I get rid of you again?'), *Haagsche Post*, 3 October 1936.
194. 'Het Probleem van deze Dagen' ('The Problem these Days'), *Haagsche Post*, 31 October 1936.
195. 'Verbod van ondemocratische partijen?' ('Ban on undemocratic parties?'), *Dagblad van Noord-Brabant*, 16 October 1936.
196. A.C. Josephus Jitta, 'Zelfverdediging der democratie' ('Self-defence of democracy'), *De Groene Amsterdammer*, 10 October 1936.
197. Josephus Jitta 1936. Previously Josephus Jitta expressed himself in similar words in a personal letter to Van den Bergh: 'I received your speech half an

hour ago and read it through in one breath. Yesterday evening I was somewhat shocked by the title. I thought, good heavens, has he indeed lost sight of the vague boundaries between politics and science. But that fear has been swept away.... An hour ago I still took the view that a democracy cannot [view] a dictatorial party as a prohibited association, although I felt dissatisfied with that. Now I am completely converted. Your speech, which is also in all respects praiseworthy, has thrown an entirely new light on a problem which we thought had been inspected from all sides. Is any greater praise imaginable for an inaugural lecture?' (A.C. Josephus Jitta, letter to George van den Bergh, 29 September 1936, in the personal archive of George van den Bergh, owned by Van den Bergh's heirs).

198. 'Prof Josephus Jitta over democratie. Instemming met de inaugurale rede van mr. dr. v.d. Bergh' ('Professor Josephus Jitta on democracy. Approval of the inaugural lecture of Professor van den Bergh'), *Het Volk*, 6 October 1936. See also 'Conferentie Vrijzinnig-Democr. Jongeren Organisatie' ('Conference of the Free-Thinking Democratic Youth Organization'), *Het Vaderland*, 6 October 1936.
199. A summary appeared as 'Liberale Staatspartij de Vrijheidsbond: Opening van de verkiezingscampagne te Amsterdam' ('Liberal State Party: Opening of the election campaign in Amsterdam'), *Nieuwe Rotterdamsche Courant*, 13 October 1936.
200. 'De democratische Staat. Tegenover niet-democratische partijen' ('The democratic State. Against non-democratic parties'), *Residentiebode*, 23 December 1936. In this connection the conditional approval of Willem Drees is also interesting; in a letter to Van den Bergh he writes, 'The argument which formed the main content of your speech stirs one to reflection. I am not yet at the point of complete endorsement, although I acknowledge the moral right of the democracy to oppose its enemies[,] even by methods different from those which have so far been considered normal' (Willem Drees, letter to George van den Bergh, 2 October 1936, in the personal archive of George van den Bergh, owned by Van den Bergh's heirs).
201. See 'Duys over de S.D.A.P. Vernietigend bewijsmateriaal' ('Duys on the S.D.A.P. Damning evidence'), *Volk en Vaderland*, 4 December 1936. The same goes for the earlier article, 'Een dankbare professor: de "objectieve wetenschap gediend"' ('A grateful professor: "serving objective science"'), *Volk en Vaderland*, 2 October 1936. The article by Duys (former SDAP member, and later NSB member), on which the former article was based, in fact gathered an unpleasant following when it was published as a separate booklet, *Democraten op Fascistenjacht* (Democrats on the hunt for fascists), from which his views on the (lack of) scientific content in Van den Bergh's inaugural lecture were sometimes adopted in other journals. It must have been a particularly traumatic experience, and Van den Bergh personally urged a number of editors to rectify the situation; he felt it was nothing less than slander (see 'Eer is teer' ['Honour is fragile'], *Deli Courant*, 12 March 1937). The editors generally reluctantly complied, the *Residentiebode* writing, 'Rereading the details, we must confess to having been swept along by Mr Duys' boisterous writing. It turns out that Professor van den Bergh's scientific character is in good working order, and we would therefore now like to withdraw the conclusions previously reached from Duys' book' (*Residentiebode*, 23 December 1936). Similarly, *De Tijd*: 'Professor van den Bergh is indignant at this term ['a stillborn child from a scientific perspective', BR] and on closer consideration we admit that these words would have been better omitted.' See 'Een verdediging. Prof. G. van den Bergh over zijn inaugurale rede' ('A defence. Professor G. Van den Bergh on his inaugural

lecture'), *De Tijd*, 22 December 1936. *Het Vaderland* refused to commit itself; see 'De inaugureele rede van prof. v.d. Bergh' ('The inaugural lecture of Professor van den Bergh'), *Het Vaderland*, 29 December 1936.

202. See Henri Polak, 'Kroniek' ('Chronicle'), *Het Volk*, 10 October 1936.
203. See Polak 1936.
204. 'Kroniek van de week' ('Chronicle of the week'), *De Tribune*, 10 October 1936.
205. 'Over democratie en dictatuur' ('On democracy and dictatorship'), *De Tribune*, 8 October 1936.
206. 'Over democratie en dictatuur' ('On democracy and dictatorship'), *De Tribune*, 8 October 1936.
207. Wichers Hoeth attributes the criticism of the daily newspapers entirely to party ideologies (Wichers Hoeth 1980, p. 22), which appears to me to be too strong a statement. We should not underestimate how widespread the relativist notion of democracy was at the time. The newspapers, as a rule, also go to great lengths to support their position with arguments.
208. In my view Hartmans also sees the speech too emphatically as being at the heart of the battle against the NSB when he writes in *Vijandige Broeders?* (Enemy brothers?), 'For what was now a very legalistic party like the SDAP it was therefore a natural step to see whether there were a legal means of calling a halt on the national socialists. That was why the most important constitutional lawyer of the SDAP, George van den Bergh, in September 1936 devoted his inaugural speech for acceptance of his professorship at the University of Amsterdam to the question of whether it was possible to ban the NSB.' See Hartmans 2012, p. 185. It seems justified to think that Van den Bergh would have firmly denied that. Besides the fact that the NSB is not mentioned at all in the speech, this coincides with what he himself stated in a piece submitted to *Het Vaderland*, included in 'De democratische Staat. Tegenover niet-democratische partijen' ('The democratic State. Against non-democratic parties'), *De Residentiebode*, 23 December 1936.
209. *De Tijd* came to the same conclusion: 'What good is it to the critics to be informed that Prof. C.W. de Vries has ordered 225 copies for his students?'; see 'Een verdediging. Prof. G. van den Bergh over zijn inaugurale rede' ('A defence. Prof. G. van den Bergh on his inaugural lecture'), *De Tijd*, 22 December 1936.
210. Included in 'De democratische Staat. Tegenover niet-democratische partijen' ('The democratic State. Against non-democratic parties'), *De Residentiebode*, 23 December 1936.
211. Eskes 1988, p. 254.
212. Kramer 1936a, p. 824; see Eskes 1988, p. 252–253. Kramer's main objection is directed at Van den Bergh's choice to base the legal part of his argument on the second part of Article 3 of the 1855 Wet vereniging en vergadering (Association and assembly act). Kramer sees the third part (which Van den Bergh ignores) as more appropriate; see p. 822–823. He later hones this argument in H.L.M. Kramer, 'Democratie en meerderheidsbeslissing' ('Democracy and majority decision'), *Nederlands Juristenblad* 1936, p. 991–995 (994) (henceforth Kramer 1936b).
213. Langemeijer 1936a, p. 884; see Eskes 1988, p. 254.
214. Kramer 1936b, p. 991; in a postscript Langemeijer denies that he sees the majority principle as the essential characteristic of democracy. See G.E. Langemeijer, 'Naschrift' ('Postscript'), *Nederlands Juristenblad* 1936, p. 995 (henceforth Langemeijer 1936b); for details on the debate between Kramer and Langemeijer, see Eskes 1988, p. 253–254.
215. 'Het begrip: "goede zeden". Een juridische polemiek' ('The concept of "public morality" [goede zeden]. A legal polemic'), *De Tijd*, 8 December 1936.

Thomas Henry Huxley (1825–1895), grandfather of author Aldous Huxley, called himself 'Darwin's Bulldog' and faithfully defended Darwin's ideas against 'the many attacks from ecclesiastical and other sides'; see Paul Cliteur, *Darwin, dier en recht* (Darwin, animal and justice), Amsterdam: Boom 2001, p. 11–12.

216. Van den Bergh 1936a, p. 27. Van den Bergh had reviewed Van den Tempel's PhD dissertation in *De Socialistische Gids*; see Hartmans 2012, p. 206.
217. Van den Bergh 1936a, p. 27.
218. See Bastiaan van den Tempel, *Democratische vrijheid en socialistisch recht* (Democratic freedom and socialist justice), Haarlem: Tjeenk Willink 1933, p. 54. For the objective principles, see p. 55–58. They are: 1) every human being must fight for the development of the entirety of humanity, and 2) the opportunity for sharing in this development must be shared as equally as possible among the individuals (the equality requirement). For a detailed discussion of Van den Tempel's dissertation, see Hartmans 2012, p. 203–207 (in particular 203).
219. See Van den Tempel 1933, p. 168 (transitional dictatorship) and 219–220 (dictatorship as last resort, if democracy is not sufficient). See also p. 93: 'Freedom [here assumed to be *democratic* freedom, BR] can only be a means for the socialist movement.'
220. See Ismee Tames, *'Oorlog voor onze gedachten': oorlog, neutraliteit en identiteit in het Nederlandse publieke debat, 1914-1918* ('War for our ideas': war, neutrality and identity in the Dutch public debate, 1914-1918), Hilversum: Uitgeverij Verloren 2006 (diss. UvA), p. 249, and Van Heerikhuizen 1983, p. 118.
221. See Bonger 1934, p. 80; Van Heerikhuizen 1983, p. 129–130. Bonger also defends democracy on technical grounds: only democracy is capable of enabling peaceful transfer of power; see Bonger 1934, p. 108.
222. The question is whether this puts democracy on an equal footing with socialism, or even places it higher. Van Heerikhuizen appears to suggest an equal footing (see Van Heerikhuizen 1983, p. 125–126); Tames seems to give it higher priority (see Tames 2006, p. 250). In my view there is more truth in Hartman's proposal that to Bonger, just as for Van den Tempel, democracy really was a means to an end, but that in Bonger's view, in contrast with Van den Tempel, any other means would be *inconceivable*; see Hartmans 2012, p. 205. What Bonger writes in his *Evolutie en Revolutie* (Evolution and revolution, 1919) fits in with this idea: 'The only means of achieving this great revolution which will be recognized in human history, is the gradual, peaceful way of democracy, springing from deep-rooted conviction. All other attempts, coups, dictatorships etc., since they are irreconcilable with the proper functioning of the economy, will necessarily fail, ending only in chaos and no higher order. May democracy thus conquer and be made complete and defended against attacks and never harmed', cited in Van Heerikhuizen 1983, p. 128.
223. See Ralph Pans, 'George van den Bergh, 1890-1966', p. 174–202, in Jan Bank, Paul Kalma, Martin Ros and Bart Tromp, *Het zesde jaarboek van het democratisch-socialisme* (The sixth yearbook of democratic socialism), Amsterdam: De Arbeiderspers/Wiardi Beckmanstichting 1985, p. 174.
224. In the speech at the Easter conference Van den Bergh puts it as follows: 'If I had to see democracy and socialism in a means-end relationship, then in my personal view socialism would have to be seen as the means and democracy as the end', and, 'We social democrats reject all tyranny, every dictatorship, even in order to achieve socialism'; see George van den Bergh, *Democratie: beginsel en doel, rede uitgesproken op het congres 1936 van de SDAP* (Democracy: principle and goal,

speech given at the 1936 SDAP conference), Amsterdam: De Arbeiderspers 1936 (henceforth Van den Bergh 1936b), p. 4 and 7 respectively. Van den Bergh also speaks about a certain 'young fellow party member' with different views on these issues (Van den Bergh 1936b, p. 6). On the Easter conference, see also Pans 1985, p. 191–192. For the relevant section in the inaugural lecture, see Van den Bergh 1936a, p. 20–21 and 26–28. An interesting parallel here is the recent theory of 'social democratic self-defence' as formulated by Malkopoulou and Norman on the basis of, among others, Van den Bergh's German contemporary (and fellow social democrat) Herman Heller, in which the inversion of the 'democracy-socialism'-relationship (still rather underdeveloped in Van den Bergh) leads to a theory of democratic self-defence that relies on citizens and puts the emphasis on the social conditions for defending democracy: '...the approach does not assume that democracy is instrumental for satisfying the objective needs of citizens, but rather the opposite that securing social non-domination is a precondition for citizens to be able to exercise their liberties. In other words, social justice is not an end in itself, but rather a precondition for political participation and for stabilising democracy' (Malkopoulou and Norman 2017, p. 454).

225. Van den Bergh 1936a, p. 28.
226. Hartmans 2012, p. 206–207. Other developments undoubtedly contributed (see Hartmans 2012, p. 207–211). For instance, there was a fourth influential book, the report *Het staatkundig stelsel der sociaal-democratie* (The political system of democracy, 1935), co-authored by Van den Bergh, which firmly rejects 'any form of dictatorship' in favour of a 'plea for parliamentary democracy with strong state authority'; see Peter-Jan Knegtmans, 'De jaren 1919-1946' ('The years 1919-1946'), p. 63–117, in Maarten Brinkman, Madelon de Keizer and Maarten van Rossem (eds.), *Honderd jaar sociaal-democratie in Nederland 1894-1994* (One hundred years of social democracy in the Netherlands 1894-1994), Amsterdam: Bert Bakker 1994, p. 100. On the basis of this report a resolution (adopted during the SDAP conference, April 1936) expressly states that the party honours democracy, 'not only as a method in the battle for socialism, but also as a principle and as a goal'; the resolution is included in Van den Bergh 1936b; see p. 15. To Josephus Jitta the report and the following SDAP conference were reasons to conclude in *De Groene Amsterdammer* that the SDAP had once again taken a step in the direction of becoming a true democratic party (see Hartmans 2012, p. 211). He was confronted with prickly commentary on this by SDAP leader J.W. Alberda in *Het Volk*: in what sense was it a step in the direction of a democratic party? Alberda attempts to demonstrate in detail that the SDAP has always been loyal to democracy, referring to a number of resolutions and reports. He also distances himself expressly from a few party members' 'personal views', including those of Bastiaan van den Tempel. See J.W. Alberda, 'Democratie: beginsel, middel en doel. Geen gelegenheidspolitiek' ('Democracy: principle, means and end. No opportunity politics'), *Het Volk*, 21 April 1936. The argument is not very convincing; one only need look to Alberda's predecessor Troelstra to see that the claim that they were '*always* purely democratic' requires some further qualification (on Troelstra in this connection, see Tames 2006, p. 249).
227. See Knegtmans 1994, p. 63–117, especially p. 82–117.
228. This famous 'mistake by Troelstra' was plainly perceived as an attack on democracy; see Tames 2006, p. 249.
229. On this 'dual character', see Jos Perry, 'De jaren 1849-1919' ('The years 1849-1919'), p. 10–61 (61), in Brinkman, De Keizer and Van Rossem 1994.

230. George van den Bergh, 'De demokratische staat en de demokratische partijen (afscheidsrede uitgesproken op 2 juli 1960)' ('The democratic state and the democratic parties [valedictory lecture of 2 July 1960]'), p. 82–90 (86), in George van den Bergh, *Verzamelde staatsrechtelijke opstellen (supplement bij de derde bundel)* (Collected constitutional law papers [supplement to the third collection]), Alphen aan den Rijn: Samsom N.V. 1961. The valedictory lecture is briefly mentioned in G.A.I. Schuijt, 'Ten geleide' ('Editorial'), p. 7–10 (7–8), in G.A.I. Schuijt and D. Voorhoof (eds.), *Vrijheid van meningsuiting, racisme en revisionisme* (Freedom of expression, racism and revisionism), Ghent: Academia Press 1995.
231. Based on a number of individual cases (including among others kosher food, the ban on processions, the prayer before municipal council meetings and subsidies for church building), Van den Bergh makes the broad reach of his interpretation clear (Van den Bergh 1961, p. 85–88). He does criticize the role played by confessional parties in the Dutch system of government (Van den Bergh 1961, p. 90). We read more on the subject in his 1958 book *Hoofdlijnen van het Nederlandse Staatsrecht* (Outlines of Dutch constitutional law). To Van den Bergh the fundamental opposition in politics is between progressives and conservatives, which of course leaves room for more than two parties; they are simply always different mixes of the same opposition. In Van den Bergh's view that opposition is *provided by nature*, because it follows from 'the nature of human personality'; it is also necessary for the proper functioning of democracy. Confessional parties, by contrast, are grouped around statements of faith, with members often holding diametrically opposed ideas on important political problems. They have effectively organized themselves around the wrong, politically irrelevant, principles. In Van den Bergh's words, 'From the perspective of constitutional law, that is highly regrettable, because it means that the foundation on which democracy is built is extremely shaky.' See George van den Bergh, *Hoofdlijnen van het Nederlandse Staatsrecht, met nog een zestal staatsrechtelijke opstellen* (Outlines of Dutch constitutional law, with six extra papers on constitutional law), Haarlem: H.D. Tjeenk Willink and Zn 1958, p. 57–58. His student A.A. De Jonge adopts this criticism in part, as shown by his critical discussion of the role of confessional parties in the democratic crisis of the interbellum; see De Jonge 1968, p. 19–20; on Van den Bergh as his teacher, see p. 3. For a recent evaluation of the future for Christian politics in the Netherlands, see Ewout Klei and Remco van Mulligen, *Van God Los: Het einde van de christelijke politiek?* (Rid of God: The end of Christian politics?), Amsterdam: Nieuw Amsterdam 2014.
232. As also shown by the detailed bibliography, provided by N. Chr. E. van den Bergh-Marcus, in Van Poelje 1960; see p. 290–294.
233. Van den Bergh 1961, p. 82–83.

2 Alternatives and criticism

1. Introduction

In Germany militant democracy is an accepted constitutional principle. The 'eternity clause' makes it a central component of the German Constitution, the Grundgesetz. German jurists worked on the abstract idea of militant democracy to develop a legally workable doctrine.[1] In the first case in which a party was prohibited by the Federal Constitutional Court, the court indicated that the founders of the constitution had made a fundamental choice for a substantive interpretation of the concept of democracy: a 'militant democracy'.[2] The German Constitution is therefore not neutral when it comes to values.[3] Democracy is a 'set of values', which must be defended in practice against its enemies.[4] Militant democracy has been incorporated to varying degrees in other states, such as Italy, Israel and Spain, as well as France[5]; the president has the option of taking special measures if the institutions of the French Republic are threatened.[6] And perhaps even more importantly, in a large number of states parties really *are* banned.[7]

We have already seen, however, that despite this broad acceptance, a general, coherent theory is lacking.[8] The most important criticism of militant democracy has thus been the absence of such a theory. In thinking about militant democracy, utility prevails at the cost of a solid foundation in political philosophy. We have already seen that Loewenstein's 'war analogy' is not a useful one. In recognition of this absence, the work of other political philosophers, not always directly related to militant democracy, is often said to provide such a foundation.[9] More recently, other authors have also tried to fill this gap by devising more comprehensive, independent theories of militant democracy.

The following discussion first examines the political philosophers that are usually relied upon in the militant democracy debate. First of all, there is particular attention given to the work of Karl Popper. Not only is he is regularly linked with militant democracy, but his idea of democracy exhibits certain similarities with that of Van den Bergh. Carl Schmitt, John Stuart Mill and John Rawls are also discussed. Finally, I look at two recent and important attempts at establishing a theory of militant democracy: the work of political scientist Alexander Kirshner and the work of legal scholar Svetlana Tyulkina.

2. Alternative theories of militant democracy

Karl Popper

A good many discussions of militant democracy seek support in Karl Popper's *The Open Society and Its Enemies,* published in 1945. Karl Popper (1902-1994) is one of the most prominent liberals of the last century.[10] His classic defence of the open society rightly gave him an important place in overviews of liberal thinkers.[11] In discussions of militant democracy Popper is also never far away.[12] This is mainly due to his discussion of tolerance, which remarkably enough is somewhat hidden away in a note in *The Open Society and Its Enemies* that resulted in the maxim 'no tolerance for the intolerant'.

No tolerance for the intolerant

Let us begin with the famous note in *The Open Society and Its Enemies.* In this note (note 4, chapter 7, part 1, to be precise), Popper discusses a number of paradoxes. It is a short essay in itself. For us the main point is the 'paradox of tolerance' (unlimited tolerance leads to the disappearance of tolerance) and the 'paradox of democracy' (a majority can decide to elect a tyrant as their ruler). Popper's answer to the paradoxes is rather dissatisfactory. We could 'easily sidestep' them by realizing that there simply cannot be any tolerance for the intolerant, nor any democracy for the antidemocrats.[13] The famous passage in this respect is as follows:

> If we extend unlimited tolerance even to those who are intolerant, if we are not prepared to defend a tolerant society against the onslaught of the intolerant, then the tolerant will be destroyed, and tolerance with them. In this formulation, I do not imply, for instance, that we should always suppress the utterance of intolerant philosophies; as long as we can counter them by rational argument and keep them in check by public opinion, suppression would certainly be most unwise. But we should claim the *right* to suppress them if necessary even by force; *for it may easily turn out that they are not prepared to meet us on the level of rational argument, but begin by denouncing all argument*; they may forbid their followers to listen to rational argument, because it is deceptive, and teach them to answer arguments by the use of their fists or pistols. *We should therefore claim, in the name of tolerance, the right not to tolerate the intolerant.* We should claim that any movement preaching intolerance places itself outside the law, and we should consider incitement to

> intolerance and persecution as criminal, in the same way as we should consider incitement to murder, or to kidnapping, or to the revival of the slave trade, as criminal.[14] (my italicization, BR)

It is easy to see the rhetorical power of this passage, but more difficult to see the precise grounds on which 'the right not to tolerate the intolerant' can be claimed. In a democracy, in any case, it is not obvious that antidemocrats must be opposed, purely on the grounds that they do not listen to rational argumentation (as the use of the word 'therefore' implies). In order to oppose antidemocrats, we need another, more substantive definition of democracy; for instance, democracy is majority decision making *and* protection of fundamental rights. Only then is there a foundation, such as protection of fundamental rights, for acting against antidemocrats. The question is then, does Popper have a better-developed idea of democracy to offer?

Popper's concept of democracy

The Open Society and Its Enemies offers points of departure for a more detailed theory of democracy. In the note discussed above, we already see an emphatic focus on 'rational discussion'. This is characteristic of Popper's approach: the approach of a philosopher of science who turned to political philosophy.[15] That approach is a conscious choice.[16] It makes democracy the mirror image of the scientific community, both 'governed by the ideals of free inquiry'.[17] We also see that elsewhere in *The Open Society*:

> Only democracy provides an institutional framework that permits reform without violence, and so the *use of reason in political matters*.[18] (my italicization, BR)

This connection between democracy and science is potentially fruitful, as becomes clear when we link it with another well-known concept in Popper's work, 'piecemeal engineering':

> But the piecemeal method permits repeated experiments and continuous readjustments. In fact, it might lead to the happy situation where politicians begin to look out for their own mistakes instead of trying to explain them away and to prove that they have always been right. This—and not Utopian planning or historical prophecy—would mean the introduction of scientific method into politics, since the whole secret of scientific method is a readiness to learn from mistakes.[19]

In other words, he is describing democracy as a 'scientific form of government', a political system with the scientific method of trial and error at its heart.[20] For Popper, politicians should embrace this system. As the British political philosopher Bhikhu Parekh (born 1935) writes, 'For him democracy is the political expression and institutionalization of the scientific method,'[21] with 'free speech and free elections' as its 'most distinctive feature'.[22]

Here Popper's ideas overlap with Van den Bergh's militant democracy theory, where the essence of democracy is sought in its capacity for self-correction.[23] Popper comes closest to Van den Bergh when he describes the ability to learn from mistakes as a unique quality of democracies:

> Our society is far from perfect. But a discussion of the faults of our society is welcomed in all Western democracies; and practical steps to remedy matters are constantly being taken and others are being searched for, in all democracies—certainly, more than ever before, *and certainly more than in any other form of society*.[24] (my italicization, BR)

In Van den Bergh's work, after all, we read:

> Every democrat admits that democracy often leads to erroneous decisions. However, it offers more safeguards than any other system to ensure that these decisions, as soon as it becomes apparent that they are incorrect, are revised.[25]

Bryan Magee (born 1930), an interpreter and popularizer of Popper, works out this aspect in more detail. According to Magee, the explanation for democracies being more successful than authoritarian systems, at least when it comes to quality of life, lies in this self-critical attitude.[26]

Every form of government policy expresses an expectation of the future; that expectation is also an empirical claim.[27] Often those expectations turn out to be incorrect: because circumstances change or because the expected effects are different, or even absent. We must therefore see government policy as a continually tested hypothesis. In the words of Magee, 'A policy is a hypothesis which has to be tested against reality and corrected in the light of experience.'[28]

An authoritarian system is characterized by limited space for this kind of testing. Criticism of policy, in advance or in retrospect, is not necessarily appreciated,[29] thus robbing the system of what might be its most important source of progress: learning from mistakes.[30] Authoritarian thinking is thus irrational and unscientific. This contrasts with democracy, in which 'incompatible views are expressed and conflicting aims pursued', in which everyone can study problems independently and put forward proposals to solve them and in which everyone is free to criticize the solutions of others, in particular the government's proposed solutions.[31] It is, above all, a system in which criticism also leads to adaptation of government policy.[32]

Popper's ideal politician is therefore one who admits his own mistakes. Experience, however, shows that politicians and governors can become attached to their own proposals and solutions, even when these proposals have long failed to withstand the test of reality, as in the case of so many 'pet projects' and 'prestige works'. For that reason, Magee suggests, there must also be the opportunity to replace the *individuals* who determine the right policies at regular intervals and without violence.[33]

This element is also clearly present in Bhikhu Parekh's interpretation of Popper:

> In an open society the citizens resolve their differences through debate and discussion. Every citizen is respected as a potential source of ideas and arguments, and his right to speak and to be heard is fully safeguarded. Diversity of opinions is not only respected but also encouraged. The government's policies are not accepted uncritically but subjected to the test of reason and experience and amended in the light of criticism. Politicians show 'scientific readiness' to learn from experience and to 'look for their mistakes instead of trying to explain them away'.[34]

Popper, certainly in the interpretations of Magee and Parekh, offers a *further* elaboration on the idea of self-correction.

In the end, however, this is not Popper's concept of democracy, as acknowledged, for instance, by Parekh in so many words.[35] Popper himself sees the ability to replace a government not so much as the ultimate sanction for governors with too little inclination for self-reflection, but rather as a tool to prevent tyranny.[36] Popper sees tyranny as the polar opposite of democracy, what autocracy was to Loewenstein and dictatorship to Van den Bergh. A democracy stands for a government that can be 'removed without bloodshed', while tyranny offers no possibility of removing a government, other than through revolution.[37]

Popper gives his clearest definition in *The Open Society*:

> We can now describe, as the principle of a democratic polity, the proposal to create, develop, and protect, political institutions for the avoidance of tyranny.[38]

And, a little later, he compares this with democracy as majority decision making:

> The theory of democracy is not based upon the principle that the majority should rule; rather the various methods of democratic control, such as general elections and representative government, are to be considered as no more than well-tried and … reasonably effective institutional safeguards against tyranny, always open to improvement, and even providing methods for their own improvement.[39]

The essence of democracy lies in the prevention of tyranny.[40] Again we see how Popper stresses the (unique) opportunities democracy offers for improvement, the 'scientific' aspect of democracy, but it is subordinate; the prevention of tyranny comes first.

Popper and militant democracy

Can this explanation of democracy be extended to a theory of militant democracy? The Israeli legal scholar Gur Bligh thinks so. He places this idea of 'democracy as prevention of tyranny' in the context of a different remark by Popper on constitutions in *The Open Society*, where he writes that constitutional changes that endanger the 'democratic character' of the constitution should be prohibited.[41] Bligh presents this combination as a cautious first formulation of a militant democracy theory. And indeed, if we seek the essence of democracy in the prevention of tyranny, then it has a reason to act against those who threaten to erode its democratic character; after all, they bring its polar opposite, tyranny, back into the picture.

A different question is whether it is a tenable theory. For example, a definition of democracy as 'prevention of tyranny' raises a good many questions. Is it a tenable definition of democracy? Is democracy not a concept of legitimacy, meaning that the definition should contain something along the lines of 'self-government by the people' if we still want it to be democracy? Popper is aware of this tension. In a later essay he observes:

> I think I may call it a theory of 'democracy', even though it is emphatically not a theory of the 'rule of the people', but rather the rule of law that postulates the bloodless dismissal of the government by a majority vote.[42]

Popper thus explicitly cuts the connection between legitimacy and democracy. He even sees 'legitimacy' as a pernicious concept: 'The (in my opinion, vicious) principle of legitimacy plays a great part in European history.'[43] Popper distances citizens from the state. The people do not govern. The government governs; the people merely provide a check on the government.[44]

But there is yet another problem when it comes to militant democracy. Popper does not seem so convinced of the militant character of this notion of democracy, nor does he rule out the possibility of abolishing democracy by democratic means. In *The Open Society* we read:

> He who accepts the principle of democracy in this sense is therefore not bound to look upon the result of a democratic vote as an authoritative expression of what is right. Although he will accept a decision of the majority, for the sake of making the democratic institutions work, he will feel free to combat it by democratic means, and to work for its revision. *And should he live to see the day when the majority vote destroys the democratic institutions, then this sad experience will tell him only that there does not exist a foolproof method of avoiding tyranny.* But it need

> not weaken his decision to fight tyranny, nor will it expose his theory as inconsistent.[45] (my italicization, BR)

This sentiment resembles that of Hans Kelsen: if democracy is abolished, all that remains is hope, here in a different version: 'Alas, the battle against tyranny was unsuccessful.' That seems a remarkable change of course. The explanation might lie in Popper's later writing on democracy.

In 'The Open Society and the Democratic State', an essay published in 1964, Popper writes about the difference between the 'open society' on the one hand and 'democracy' on the other. The *open society* is a particular form of society plus the values which belong to it, such as: 'freedom, tolerance, justice', the freedom to choose one's own beliefs, and the 'pursuit of happiness'.[46] *Democracy*, on the other hand, is a 'set of institutions', including 'a constitution, civil and criminal law, legislative and executive organs, such as the government and the rules by which it is elected'.[47] The values from the former category are each ends in themselves, whereas this does not hold of the values in the latter category.[48]

This distinction explains why *The Open Society* is sometimes so difficult to read as a theory of militant democracy. To Popper democracy is a means, not an end. It is the best means, but the goal remains the open society. If democracy is abolished it is not the goal that is destroyed, but the most important means of achieving it. That does not mean that one must resign oneself to such a majority decision, for that is the other side of the coin: if democracy is only a means to an end, the majority decisions it produces do not enjoy automatic legitimacy or correctness, and that also applies to the decision to appoint a tyrant.[49] This last point is important, as it means that resistance in the name of the open society is justified. Popper is ambiguous as to the timing of that resistance. Sometimes he appears to suggest that one might only take up arms for the open society *after* democratic suicide;[50] at other times he appears to consider preventive action justified for the sake of protecting democracy.[51]

Popper thus does not oppose democratic suicide as a possible *institutional* consequence of majority rule, but rather the *claim to truth and legitimacy* of a majority that wants to abolish democracy; *that* claim need not be respected by citizens. Thus Popper creates space for resistance, which fits into his general scepticism towards power and governments, *including* democratic governments.[52] A strong will to live in an open society is what ultimately makes an open society militant. Democracy is merely the first, very important, line of defence; if that is removed, it is down to the citizens themselves, the *true* supporters of the open society.[53]

Popper as a militant democracy thinker

Is Popper's theory one of militant democracy? And is Popper a militant democracy thinker? The answer to both questions is yes, albeit only partially.

Popper's theory sets boundaries to democratic tolerance and thus contains an unmistakably militant element. It is not Kelsenian relativism. Aside from its militant character, his 'scientific democracy' is an idea that agrees closely with Van den Bergh's notion of self-correction. In fact, in Magee's interpretation it might even usefully supplement that idea. At the same time there are a number of gaps in the theory. For instance, the abolition of democracy is not explicitly excluded, and it is unclear at what point it is permissible to take action against antidemocrats; conflicting claims can be found in Popper's work. Furthermore, Popper does not see democracy as the *ultimate* goal, but merely as a means to an end, albeit an important one.

This is a clear difference from Van den Bergh. To Van den Bergh democracy is always the goal, never a means, which gave him a unique position in the social-democratic SDAP. Van den Bergh is also unambiguous when it comes to acting against antidemocrats.

Popper's theory is therefore best described as a theory of militant democracy within a broader defence of the open society. Democracy and the open society coincide in Popper's view, but they must be distinguished; that distinction, however, is often missed.[54] From a formal perspective democracy can be abolished; Popper argues against the idea that citizens must accept such a majority decision. They must then do all they can to restore democracy, the most important guarantee for an open society. One might argue that Popper sees intervention, even *before* it reaches such a point, as justified. Alongside statements to the contrary we *also* read, 'We need not tolerate even the threat of intolerance; and we must not tolerate it if the threat is getting serious.'[55]

This fragmented treatment of democracy in *The Open Society*, in fact, is understandable. A first explanation is simple: Popper did not write a book on militant democracy. His thinking touches on the problem, but it is not a sympathetic argument for, nor a considered position on, antidemocratic parties. It is a reaction to the rise of totalitarian ideologies, just as Hannah Arendt's *The Origins of Totalitarianism* (1951) was. Popper wanted to understand them, reduce their attraction and contrast them with 'the value and importance of *liberty* in the widest sense'.[56] To add to that, Popper saw *The Open Society* above all as a book about the influence of historicism, with Plato and Marx as the primary subjects.[57] The subordinate role of democracy as a theme in *The Open Society* is reflected in the attention to Popper's political philosophy. That attention, despite calls for closer study from Richard Robinson (1951),[58] Bryan Magee (1974)[59] and John Gray (1976),[60] among others, remains very limited.

Popper can hardly be blamed for developing an 'incomplete' theory of militant democracy, nor can his interpreters be accused of attempting to read a militant democracy theory in his work or expressly painting him as a defender of democracy, rather than the open society—since a fully-fledged theory of militant democracy is lacking.

Carl Schmitt

Another, somewhat uneasy, intellectual father of militant democracy is Carl Schmitt (1888-1985). For a short period he was an important jurist of the Third Reich (1933-1936), and he is not exactly known as a defender of democracy. Nevertheless, Gregory Fox and Georg Nolte describe his criticism of the procedural concept of democracy as the most influential in continental Europe.[61]

Early on, Schmitt opposed the 'relativist, equal treatment of all political ideas' in Germany.[62] In 1928 in his *Verfassungslehre* he states that the Reichstag can never decide to change the form of government of the German state into an absolute monarchy or a Soviet republic.[63] For Schmitt, there is a crucial distinction between the *pouvoir constituant* (of the people) and the *pouvoir constitué* (of the elected representatives) that is derived from it.[64] Schmitt's proposal in *Legalität und Legitimität*, published in 1932, is an extension of this argument: the substantive core of a constitution can never be set aside, regardless of any majority, on the basis of procedural rules.[65]

In Schmitt's view there is thus a distinction between the *constituent* power, which elects a particular constitutional order, and the *constituted* power, of the authorities *within* the (constituted) system. According to this distinction, a constitution therefore contains substantive and formal principles.[66] The substantive principles embody the identity of the constitution and spring from a fundamental choice by the people, the chosen constitutional order. The formal principles, such as decision-making procedures and institutions like the parliament, are an extension of this choice, designed to implement and realize the chosen constitutional order. This means that the principles from this last category have 'implicit limits': they are limited *by their nature* and can never abolish what they were designed for.[67]

According to Schmitt, the substantial choice encompassed by a constitution makes it a completely different document from regular laws.[68] A constitution that attempts to gloss over this fundamental choice, that does not acknowledge any specific colour or acts against its enemies, will eventually be used against itself.[69] Schmitt sketches a gloomy future for such a 'value-neutral constitution':

> The majority would be permitted to use legal means to close the door to legality, through which they themselves entered, and to treat partisan opponents like common criminals, who are perhaps reduced to kicking their boots against the locked door.[70]

Within that formal/substantive framework, the Weimar constitution appeared to be hung up on two very different thoughts:[71] Kelsenian value-neutrality on the one hand and substantive democracy theory on the other, or, in Schmitt's terminology, legalism and formalism on the one hand, and a substantial, material choice for a constitutional order on the other.[72]

For Schmitt such duality is impossible: a choice for values excludes value-neutrality.[73] A constitution cannot declare a choice for a constitutional order and at the same time view *all* alternative orders as equal. So in reality Weimar had two constitutions, contained in a single document. The only solution for Weimar, other than reform, was therefore a choice for a substantive *interpretation* of the constitution:

> As this constitution now stands, it is full of contradictions.... Now, if in the knowledge that the Weimar Constitution is two constitutions, one chooses between them, then the decision must fall for the principle of the second constitution and its attempt to establish a substantive order.[74]

Schmitt warns his readers to make their minds up fast:

> Otherwise, it will meet a quick end along with the fictions of neutral majority functionalism that is pitted against value and truth. Then, the truth will have its revenge.[75]

That revenge came quickly. At the end of 1932 Carl Schmitt was constitutional advisor to Chancellor Kurt von Schleicher (1882-1934).[76] Around the turn of the year 1932-1933 Von Schleicher made a final attempt at preventing power from falling into the hands of Hitler and the NSDAP.[77] He asked President Hindenburg to declare a state of emergency and ban the Nazi and Communist parties,[78] which in fact was Schmitt's plan, an idea he had long defended, even publically, that comes almost straight out of *Legalität und Legitimität*.[79] But Hindenburg refused. For him defending the constitution meant 'upholding the letter of that document'; anything else would mean breaking his constitutional oath, an idea that made him shudder.[80] Hindenburg wanted a more sustainable solution, rather than to use his authority regarding exceptional circumstances yet again.[81] On 30 January 1933 he therefore chose Franz von Papen's fatal idea 'to hedge' in Hitler: Hitler became chancellor of the Reich.[82] The 'legal door' Schmitt wrote about would, as we know now, soon be definitively closed.

How should we interpret Schmitt's ideas on a value-laden constitution? Is this a theory of militant democracy? A particular nuance is important here: the identity of the constitution does not necessarily need to be democratic as such; to Schmitt the issue is purely one of combatting *constitutional* self-destruction. In his interpretation of Schmitt, Marc de Wilde also rather speaks of 'anti-constitutional parties' and a 'militant constitution'.[83]

It would therefore be going too far to call Schmitt's work a theory of militant democracy. *In* a parliamentary democracy, however, there is no doubt as to Schmitt's position: he considers it 'absurd that a parliamentary democracy should offer an equal chance to all parties'.[84] Or, as the American philosopher Guy Oakes writes:

> In Schmitt's view, a decision to place the National Socialists on the same legal footing with parties committed to the Weimar Constitution would amount to a reductio ad absurdum of the Constitution itself.[85]

That was the Schmitt of *Legalität und Legitimität*. In a strange moment of opportunism he changed his mind and in 1933 became a member of the NSDAP and a prominent Nazi jurist,[86] as mentioned in chapter 1. Under the title *Der Führer schützt das Recht*, the re-invented Schmitt wrote a cold defence of the Night of the Long Knives, in which Von Schleicher and others were murdered as potential opponents of Hitler.[87] In 1936, however, Schmitt's views on Weimar were to prove fatal: enemies inside the party and in the academic world initiated a Gestapo investigation, after which he lost his government and party positions.[88] He was permitted to keep his university position, but after the war he also lost this due to his Nazi collaboration.[89]

In the light of this history, it is somewhat ironic that the crucial safeguard in the German Constitution, the unchangeable core (GG Art. 79 para. 3)[90] designed to ensure that such things can never happen again, is a legacy of Schmitt's ideas. Other thinkers can be referenced for militant democracy in a broad sense, but the unchanging core is Schmitt's invention.[91] His theory that changes to *the nature* of constitutions can only be limited would also play an important role in the development of ideas on what are currently called *unconstitutional constitutional amendments*: even constitutional changes that are 'valid' in principle can be declared unconstitutional.[92] Schmitt himself saw the idea of the unchanging core as a necessary condition of banning parties consistently from a legal perspective.[93] In a new afterword to *Legalität und Legitimität* in 1958 he writes:

> The essay encountered bitter resistance, specifically to its core thesis: *that the legality of a party can only be denied when the authority to make constitutional amendments is limited.*[94] (my italicization, BR)

The 'bitter resistance' to his ideas has disappeared, but Schmitt's contribution, understandably, remains only rarely acknowledged.[95]

John Stuart Mill

Another thinker who is associated with militant democracy is the British philosopher John Stuart Mill (1806-1873).[96] This connection rests on an excerpt from the final chapter of his book *On Liberty* (1859), in which he speaks about the applications of his 'harm principle': is it permissible for the state to intervene if someone sells himself as a slave? The passage reads as follows:

> The reason for not interfering, unless for the sake of others, with a person's voluntary acts, is consideration for his liberty. His voluntary

> choice is evidence that what he so chooses is desirable, or at the least endurable, to him, and his good is on the whole best provided for by allowing him to take his own means of pursuing it. *But by selling himself for a slave, he abdicates his liberty; he foregoes any future use of it beyond that single act.* He therefore defeats, in his own case, the very purpose which is the justification of allowing him to dispose of himself.... *The principle of freedom cannot require that he should be free not to be free.* It is not freedom, to be allowed to alienate his freedom.[97] (my italicization, BR)

The same goes for democratic states *mutatis mutandis*: like the individual, society does not have the 'freedom not to be free'.[98] The state cannot make future democratic decision making impossible with a single democratic decision. *Why* that is ruled out, however, remains unclear.

J.S. Mill himself does not use this analogy in the context of militant democracy, and although that does not detract from its rhetorical power, it remains more of a succinct illustration of the problem. It might contain the germ of a feasible militant democracy theory, but it is insufficiently worked out. To put it a different way, the actual argumentation has yet to begin, and those arguments are not to be found in J.S. Mill.

John Rawls

A fourth thinker from whom arguments for a militant democracy can be derived is the American political philosopher John Rawls (1921-2002). Rawls became widely known for *A Theory of Justice* (1971), the 'most philosophically impressive attempt' to formulate an all-encompassing political philosophy. [99] According to some his theory is also the 'most important legal philosophy of the twentieth century'.[100] Two concepts are central to his theory: the 'original position' and the two justice principles.

The original position can be seen as a means of making Rawls' abstract adage 'justice as fairness' more concrete.[101] In the original position citizens discuss what a just society would look like, or, better put, how the *institutional* framework of such a society would be constructed.[102] However, they work from behind a 'veil of ignorance': they know about politics, social sciences and economic theory; there is no limitation on general information, but their personal characteristics are excluded from the discussion.[103] No one has information on their own position in society, social status, intelligence, talents or limitations. Neither does anyone know what their philosophy of life will be, nor even their psychological traits, whether they will be risk-averse or not, optimistic or pessimistic; everything is unknown.[104] In short, under these conditions the banker, for instance, will be reluctant to reduce the tax rate to a minimum, and a healthy young (wo)man will not easily determine that from now on it is 'every man for himself' in healthcare. They do not know how they will emerge from behind the veil.

In these *fair* circumstances the individuals discuss the foundations of their polity, hence 'justice as fairness': 'the principles of justice follow from a fair starting situation'.[105]

It is unclear why there are *several* individuals in the original position. Since Rawls abstracts away from their personal traits, there are no issues on the basis of which they might differ in opinion (a steelworker from a banker, a Muslim from a Christian). They are essentially clones of one another who can be endlessly duplicated but without adding to the argument. One might just as well use a blindfolded person; the difference seems purely literary.[106]

But let us assume for a moment that several individuals together consider the institutions of a just society: what would they decide? According to Rawls they would arrive at two principles of justice:

1 'Each person is to have an equal right to the most extensive total system of equal basic liberties compatible with a similar system of liberty for all'.
2 'Social and economic inequalities are to be arranged so that they are both: a) to the greatest benefit of the least advantaged, consistent with the just savings principle, and b) attached to offices and positions open to all under conditions of fair equality of opportunity'.[107]

The first principle aims at equal liberty for everyone, so an unequal distribution is ruled out. Everyone enjoys the same (negative) liberties: freedom of expression, the right to fair process and voting rights.[108] The second principle is about social justice, about distribution; one might call it positive freedom.[109] Part 2b acknowledges that inequalities can spring from the positions people hold in society (salary, status, etc.), but that does not mean that those inequalities have to be erased (which would result in communism); the requirement is simply that citizens have an equal opportunity of attaining these positions.[110] Part 2a is called the 'difference principle': it is better if in a hypothetical society of five people one of them earns 100,000 euros and the four others 30,000 euros, than that each of the five earns 25,000 euros.[111] The idea is: inequality is allowable, but the least well-off must benefit from it; they must be better off in this social order than in one with greater social and economic equality.[112] When this is the case, opposition to this principle by the least well-off might be said to be more envy- than justice-related.[113]

The principles are not on an equal footing: the second is subordinate to the first. Rawls calls this the 'priority of liberty': 'a lesser or an unequal liberty cannot be exchanged for an improvement in economic well-being'.[114] In other words, 'abolishing elections for the sake of economic stability' by appealing to the 'difference principle' is unacceptable, even if it would advantage the least well-off.[115] Or, to give another example, freedom of expression cannot be limited in order to increase economic growth.[116] Are there no possible limits on freedom then? Yes, there are: liberties *can* (only) be restricted 'for the sake of freedom itself'.[117]

It is here that militant democrats find a point of departure.[118] Further on in *A Theory of Justice* Rawls writes the following on tolerance:

> The limitation of liberty is justified only when it is necessary for liberty itself, to prevent an invasion of freedom that would be still worse.[119]

A logical follow-up question would then be, does that mean that intolerant groups need not be tolerated? After all, they potentially violate liberty, so can they be opposed in the name of this same liberty? Is intolerance towards the intolerant 'necessary for liberty itself'? Under the heading 'Toleration of the intolerant' Rawls divides the question into three separate questions. In their militant-democratic interpretation of Rawls, Fox and Nolte build on the two questions they deem relevant for militant democracy. First, does an *intolerant* group have the right to complain about not being tolerated? And second, in what circumstances does a *tolerant* group have the right not to tolerate an intolerant group?[120]

The answer to the first question is simple for Rawls: 'A person's right to complain is limited to the principles he acknowledges himself'.[121] Rawls, however, also indicates that the lack of the right to complain (for the intolerant group) does not automatically mean that the tolerant group must suppress those who are intolerant.[122] Nevertheless, the tolerant group *does* have that right; the answer to the second question follows from the original position:

> This right follows readily enough since, as the original position is defined, each would agree to the right of self-preservation. Justice does not require that men must stand idly by while others destroy the basis of their existence.[123]

In the original position all 'contractants' acknowledge the right to self-preservation. They acknowledge not only the two principles of justice, but also the right to defend the just society once it is established.[124] That is logical: if we follow Rawls, it is the most just society, so the institutions that safeguard it must also be defended when threatened. The only question remaining is, *when* is it permissible to intervene? Can this be done before the intolerant group directly threatens the liberties of others?[125] Rawls' answer is:

> Thus just citizens should strive to preserve the constitution with all its equal liberties as long as liberty itself and their own freedom are not in danger. They can properly force the intolerant to respect the liberty of others, since a person can be required to respect the rights established by principles that he would acknowledge in the original position. But when the constitution itself is secure, there is no reason to deny freedom to the intolerant.[126]

Essentially, Rawls requires us to wait as long as possible. Only if the tolerant group really believes, with good reason, that its freedom and the institutions that safeguard it are in danger can it intervene and suppress the intolerant group.[127]

It only takes a small adjustment to formulate Rawls' theory of tolerance and intolerance in terms that belong more explicitly to militant democracy: a political party that proclaims that it will do away with fundamental freedoms can be banned. This is not a restriction of freedom, but rather an application of the first principle of justice (equal liberty), the realization of equal liberty as far as possible, which is thus safeguarded in the long term.[128] In choosing the moment of prohibition, one should wait as long as possible, show confidence in democracy and the rule of law, but intervene as soon as a real risk arises. A militant democracy theory based on Rawls' *A Theory of Justice* seems feasible in principle, but it is deeply embedded in a broader theory of justice; it *assumes* many points, such as the principles of justice, that are not directly necessary for a militant democracy theory. The disadvantage of this is that as a *theory of militant democracy* it is not only less elegant, but also more vulnerable to criticism (after all, you must *also* accept Rawls' theory of justice). This does not detract from the usefulness of Rawls' theory as a sparring partner for any militant democracy theory, since the theory offers a powerful warning against over-eagerness to intervene.

Kirshner's theory of militant democracy

An interesting attempt to formulate a theory of a militant democracy is *A Theory of Militant Democracy* by Alexander Kirshner. It is the first monograph exclusively devoted to the problem of militant democracy. Kirshner starts out from Loewenstein's central proposal: democrats must actively defend their democracy.[129] The question of *whether* a democracy can intervene in the case of an antidemocratic threat is not formally addressed in the book. It is taken as a given; the question is *when* and *how* to intervene. The book's subtitle, 'The Ethics of Combatting Political Extremism', in fact gives an indication of this. Political extremism (understood as antidemocratic ideas) must be challenged, but what standards ensure that that can be done in an ethical, just manner? Kirshner offers a framework of 'regulatory principles' to shape and delimit action against antidemocratic parties.[130]

What are those principles? First of all, there is the *participation principle*: all individuals have 'an equal claim on participation in democratic decision making'.[131] This participation encompasses more than just voting; it also pertains to being eligible for election, being able to speak and to associate freely with others.[132] Everyone thus has the following 'democratic rights': active and passive suffrage (i.e., respectively, the right to be elected and the right to vote in elections), freedom of expression and freedom of association. That applies to antidemocrats as well, but it does not make them immune to restrictive measures; it simply means that in principle the hypothetical situation of 'democratic apartheid', in which part of the electorate are permanently excluded, should be avoided.[133]

If the above is true (everyone has an equal claim to participation), as Kirshner assumes, then it follows that citizens should not restrict other citizens in pursuing their own interests rashly or without a valid reason.[134] This leads to a further principle: *limited intervention*. To Kirshner this principle is the answer to the question 'When should democrats go militant?' The aim of intervention must be exclusively to make it possible for other citizens to 'participate safely'.[135] Exclusion mechanisms (including party bans) can only be used when antidemocrats infringe on the rights of others, period; they cannot be applied to achieve a utopian 'ideal or fully realized democracy'.[136] The democratic rights of antidemocrats must also be respected for *as long as possible*.[137] The fact that they have legitimate interests in participation means that they cannot be excluded if they only have a narrow chance of success.[138] That means there must be space for antidemocrats who do *not* infringe on the rights of others, but who *can* oppose further democratic reforms or even perhaps represent a real threat to democracy at a later time.[139]

The third and final principle is that of *democratic responsibility*, the concept that limiting democratic participation comes at a cost in a democratic sense. If this concept is missing, Kirshner predicts that certain measures will be used rashly,[140] and if overly heavy-handed measures are used without sufficient consideration, it makes the government system less democratic and less legitimate.[141] Repressive measures have 'democratic costs'.[142] For instance, mistakes happen: there will be cases in which measures that restrict democracy are taken when there was no real violation of rights. There is also carelessness in measures against antidemocrats. If you ban a party, for instance, you might prevent a violation of rights, but at the same time you also make it impossible for the party to pursue their other, *legitimate* interests.[143] A ban on speech that explicitly calls for electoral violence might safeguard others' right to participation, but because such a ban is open to interpretation, it might lead to prevention of shocking but legitimate speech.[144] It is for democrats to 'manage' this 'paradox of militant democracy', according to Kirshner.[145] The principle of democratic responsibility can help by serving as a reminder of the democratic cost of repression.

Kirshner's theory is in a way a very American theory of militant democracy, as we can see firstly from the *rights* orientation of the defence of democracy. Kirshner defends democracy as a value or aim in itself,[146] but in the end that is not his fundamental point of departure, as it was for Van den Bergh, who takes the essence of democracy (self-correction) to derive the idea that the system does not technically have to allow its own abolition, thereby rendering action to prevent this not a betrayal of democracy's own principles. In Kirshner the point of departure is the right of every individual to participate and to promote his own interests, which offers an advantage. It makes militant democracy more concrete than Van den Bergh's or Popper's. Democracy is no longer an abstract system that may or may not be abolished.

A further American flavour is provided by the preoccupation with judicial review of legislation, or, to put it better, the linking of the problem of militant democracy with judicial review. Kirshner sees his theory as a convenient alternative for the protection of democracy by a judge. The role of judges is mainly in the margins of democracy, fine-tuning the rules of the democratic game through judicial review: is flag burning covered by freedom of expression, for instance?[147] For the bigger challenges, such as when a two-thirds majority has been established and wants to deprive part of the electorate of their right to vote, heavier artillery is required. Declaring laws unconstitutional in retrospect is, after all, probably pointless; the judges will be side-lined. Kirshner gives the example of the South African National Party. In 1951 this party sought to deprive all black voters in the Cape Province of the right to vote. The judge, however, declared the bill invalid on formal grounds: the required two-thirds majority was not achieved. The party then simply changed the structure of the Senate so that the law could be adopted anyway. The composition of the court was also immediately adjusted.[148] Kirshner sums it up as follows:

> If the South African example is not a wild aberration, if it is plausible that groups with sufficient political influence to pass seriously discriminatory legislation can overcome a judicial decision hindering their efforts, then we may conclude that in some cases safeguarding democracy will require more than invalidating suspect laws.[149]

That is understandable. Do we imagine that Adolf Hitler would have accepted a judgement that his infamous Enabling Act was 'unconstitutional'? No, probably not. It strikes me as highly unlikely that the NSDAP would respond along the lines of, 'Yes, voters, we were planning to abolish democracy, but well there's a hitch; we have to accept the judge's verdict.'[150] Kirshner has a point: in order to combat antidemocratic parties, it is probably necessary to act *before* they are in a position to implement antidemocratic legislation. Prevention is better than cure. We find a comparable viewpoint in Amitai Etzioni's work, when it comes to fragile new democracies:

> There are those who hold that democracies need not fear free elections because even if extremist parties gain a majority, the courts will uphold individual and minority rights. The record though—from Nazi Germany to generals' rule in Latin American—shows that such governments soon load the courts with their supporters or recast the constitutions to suit their purposes. True, when democracies are well-established, and anti-democratic parties are small and more of an annoyance or a gadfly than a genuine threat, they can be tolerated.

> However, when democracies are just being formed, such parties—especially if they are strong and the liberal forces weak—must be kept at bay, at least until the liberal forces have a chance to develop.[151]

Now for the more important question: how should we evaluate Kirshner's theory of militant democracy? An important point of criticism is the limited attention given to the question of justification. Kirshner's theory is, after all, not about *whether* it is permissible to act against antidemocrats, but about *when* and *how*. Like Loewenstein, Kirshner assumes that democratic self-defence is legitimate in principle, acknowledging himself that he gives little attention to this question.[152] He presents his theory as an unadorned set of regulatory principles, and in a certain sense it is. At its heart, however, it ultimately is *not*, and here the question of justification returns like a boomerang.

Kirshner's entire framework rests on the 'right to participate', described in the first regulatory principle: the principle of participation. If the right to participate is infringed on or threatened, it is permissible to intervene. This is what forms the justification within Kirshner's democracy theory, but in a theory of militant democracy, or a 'regulatory theory', one cannot get away with a justification of this kind. After all, it remains a theory on limiting democracy, and that requires a deeper justification for the limits set on democracy. The grounds for prohibition, or justification for intervention in a concrete case, are derived from this foundation. In Van den Bergh's work that foundation is self-correction (in one of the two proposed interpretations) and intervention is only acceptable when that principle is infringed upon. In Popper's work it might be found in 'prevention of tyranny', on the basis of which antidemocrats may be confronted. In Kirshner's work the foundation is the right to participate. The problem, however, is that the argumentation for this right to participate is left out of the study, leaving us with a number of questions.[153] What precisely is a 'right to participate'? It seems to be a precondition for, and part of, democracy, which is necessary if we want to use it as a justification to limit democracy. It must effectively be excluded from the normal democratic process, for otherwise it can be revoked by that same process. This, it seems, is how we have to interpret it. Kirshner indeed observes in passing:

> My own intuition is that a regime that has disenfranchised a quarter of its population is not fully democratic.... Yet my intuition makes sense only if I believe that opponents of democrats possess basic democratic interests and therefore a right to participate.[154]

And a little later:

> In the rest of this work, I will treat antidemocrats as if they possess the interests described above.[155]

So, regardless of any actual democracy, individuals *always* possess a right to participate if they have 'basic democratic interests'. For Kirshner you have these interests when you attach *some* importance to the outcome of *any* object of democratic decision making, from the regulation of smoking in cafés to the level of benefits or taxes, or the question of whether people are required to keep their dogs on a lead in the park. Kirshner argues that in that sense even the most hardened antidemocrats, besides their hostility towards the system, attach importance at least to a few *other* matters, and thus also have an interest in the outcome of the democratic process.[156] Kirshner thus views the 'ascetic antidemocrat' as a caricature. Since everyone has basic democratic interests to some extent, everyone has a right to participate; real antidemocrats, like everyone else, have a right to participate.

The rights therefore have a 'pre-democratic character' and in fact a 'pre-state character', tinging the theory with natural law. In any case the rights do *not* have a positive law character; they are not granted by a democratic state but are *already there*. That broadens the theory: the justification can also serve to legitimize opposing an undemocratic regime in order to establish democracy.[157] But that raises the burden of proof. On what basis should we assume that a *right* to participate follows from an *interest* in participation? And what if someone denies that right? That turns the theory on its head, making it essentially extremely abstract. We saw in chapter 1 that Milan Markovitch's theory suffered from the same shortcoming. Van den Bergh's theory in the second interpretation then appears better founded: the starting point is a real, existing democracy; an established democracy, once it is indeed established, does not have to allow its own abolition without putting up any resistance, or at least, this does not follow from its own logic.[158] In any case this lowers the burden of proof somewhat in comparison with postulating a (natural law) right to participate. Kirshner does not satisfy the burden of proof required by such a right, at least in this work.

Despite this omission, Kirshner's militant democracy theory should be commended. His regulatory principles are a useful supplement to the foundations of militant democracy, or the justification of interventions.

Svetlana Tyulkina: counterterrorism and religious extremism

Another recent study dedicated to militant democracy is Svetlana Tyulkina's *Militant Democracy: Undemocratic Political Parties and Beyond* (2015). Tyulkina offers a comparative overview of militant democracy as a legal concept.[159] Most of the book focuses on mapping the legal application of militant democracy in practice: how do different democracies implement 'militant democracy measures'? She, for instance, examines Germany, Spain, Turkey and the European Court of Human Rights in detail.[160] Interesting in her approach is that specific problems or aspects of militant democracy are linked to the study of a relevant country, giving this study an edge over Markus Thiel's comparative legal work on militant democracy.[161]

A discussion of 'soft measures' is thus linked with an analysis of militant democracy in India and Israel, addressing restrictions on freedom of expression in election campaigns (India)[162] and excluding parties from elections as an alternative to a general party ban (Israel).[163] In the same way Spain and Turkey are used in a discussion of possible extensions of militant democracy outside its traditional area of application, to combatting terrorism and the protection of secularism, respectively.[164]

The emphasis on legal comparison, however, means that Tyulkina gives little attention to the justification of militant democracy from the perspective of political philosophy. Tyulkina, like Kirshner, starts out from the assumption that Loewenstein was right: acting against antidemocrats is legitimate in principle.[165] But where Kirshner builds a theory as to the principles that must regulate such intervention, Tyulkina does not venture into theory formation; her aim is a discussion from a legal and comparative legal perspective. Her approach is based on the fact that militant democracy *exists*, and must therefore be studied.[166] As a result, she takes on the role of a sort of contemporary Loewenstein, with the same advantages (a useful overview of 'militant' legislation, jurisprudence and practice in a large number of countries) and disadvantages (little attention to justification from the perspective of political philosophy). It would not be too much of a stretch to suggest that Tyulkina in fact (significantly) updates Loewenstein's comparative legal work of 1937.

That would seem to suggest that Tyulkina's analysis has less to offer us here, although that is not entirely so. First of all, her overview offers a number of important observations in passing, including those on the transition to democracy in post-communist states[167] and the question of whether international law confers a duty of militant democracy (answer: not really).[168] She also offers a number of thoughts that are relevant for the more theoretical discussion of militant democracy.

First, following Sajó, she points to the topical nature of Loewenstein's analysis of emotionalism (instead of fascism alone, which is merely a variant of it).[169] Also in 'contemporary politics', according to Tyulkina (and Sajó), there is emotional manipulation of the electorate.[170] Rational decision making is replaced with 'identity politics' and the release of emotions among the 'masses'.[171]

That seems a fruitful idea, and although Tyulkina herself gives no examples, this type of political context might put one in mind of a case discussed elsewhere in her book: *Prabhoo vs. Kunte.* In 1996 the highest Indian court concluded that the local politician Yeshwant Prabhoo had rightly lost his seat; Prabhoo had led a campaign based on his Hindu religious identity, contravening Indian law.[172] The verdict quoted from a 'characteristic' speech from Prabhoo's campaign; the speaker is his 'spin doctor' Bal Thackeray:

> Hinduism will triumph in this election and we must become hon'ble recipients of this victory to ward off the danger on Hinduism, elect

> Ramesh Prabhoo to join with Chhagan Bhujbal who is already there. You will find Hindu temples underneath if all the mosques are dug out. Anybody who stands against the Hindus should be showed or worshipped with shoes. A candidate by the name Prabhoo should be led to victory in the name of religion.[173]

Political provocation and violence are not unusual in Indian elections.[174] The destruction of a mosque by Hindu extremists in 1992 led to a 'wave of communal violence' in which thousands were killed.[175] Likewise, Thackeray's speech served as an 'ethnic tinderbox'.[176]

To Tyulkina emotionalism in politics illustrates the need for militant democracy:

> 'Constitutional government, by its very nature, can appeal only to reason'. Realistically, the defence of democracy can be effectuated only through political and legislative means based on reason. Therefore, the concept of militant democracy should remain one of the safeguards democracies can resort to in offsetting emotionalism in politics.[177]

That means that Loewenstein's militant democracy is 'not an abstract or outdated theory'.[178] A justification is not given in much more detail. Tyulkina's work on this point remains very much restricted to Loewenstein's sharp but not extensively developed intuition that democracies must do *something* towards self-defence.

That gives it a strongly dogmatic character. No attention is given to the question of reconciling party bans with the essence of democracy; the problem is mentioned but not discussed.[179] We also read that 'Loewenstein … was perfectly aware of the available critiques of his solution',[180] but we are then left to make do with his 'war analogy', which is painted as 'simple' and 'straightforward'.[181] We saw earlier, though, that this analogy does not stand up to scrutiny. Other justifications are also mentioned, such as the 'intolerance of the intolerant', attributed to Popper, Locke and Rawls, and the idea of Sajó that 'the state's most natural characteristic is self-defence', and therefore that the same applies to a militant democracy.[182] In the end no definitive choice is made, and instead the following practical justification is offered:

> Keeping in mind the tragedies of the past, and in the absence of any realistic alternatives, militant democracy appears to be a justified concept so long as it is capable of excluding conceptually and institutionally the abuse of opportunities for restricting rights.[183]

In short, intervention to defend a democracy is acceptable; the important point is to ensure that *conceptual* and *institutional* abuse is avoided.

Another interesting thought lies in the possible extensions of the concept itself; according to Tyulkina this is the most important part of the book.[184]

Such an extension is possible because Tyulkina takes a broad definition of militant democracy to begin with. It is 'the capacity of liberal democracies to defend themselves against challenges to their continued existence by taking pre-emptive action against those who want to overturn or destroy democracy by abusing democratic institutions and procedures'.[185] It might be said that Tyulkina sees militant democracy as a sort of justification strategy, among others, that governments can call on to legitimize intervention. So certain characteristics are linked to it, such as its preventive tendencies, the continuation of democracy and the abuse of procedures by antidemocrats, but it does remain a broad definition[186]—making it possible to explore new applications of militant democracy.

The new applications that Tyulkina discusses are the fight against terrorism and approaches to religious extremism. When governments legitimize their treatment of these threats with an appeal to militant democracy, they are invoking the underlying justification of militant democracy, namely, that it is acceptable for a democracy to defend itself (so it is somewhat ironic that this very issue of militant democracy, its justification, is not worked out extensively in Tyulkina's work).

An appeal to the *rationale* of militant democracy when it comes to counterterrorism, according to Tyulkina, offers the advantage that the measures must explicitly remain within the normal constitutional order. Where thinking on counterterrorism could lead to measures that would better fit a sort of semi-'state of exception', as is currently the case in Australia according to Tyulkina, militant democracy offers a useful alternative.[187] With militant democracy as a leading principle, there is a continual reminder that the 'constitutional order and democracy at large' can also be protected in accordance with the 'fundamental principles of democracy'.[188] It ensures that judicial review of the executive power remains in place. No power shift takes place within the separation of powers, as would be the case in a state of exception.[189] In Tyulkina's view it is also a logical extension: militant democracy is designed as a barrier against emotionalism, and the tactics of terrorists, 'fear and intimidation', are 'a kind of politics of emotion',[190] or, in other words:

> Tolerance of emotionalism attributed to any actor, be it extreme political parties or terrorist movements, can be fatal for democracy, and there must be a mechanism present to subvert such activities.[191]

Of course, there are arguments to be made against this extension. It remains questionable, for example, whether the concept of militant democracy does not lose its distinctive meaning here. Does it not mix the territories of 'state security' and 'militant democracy' too much, while they are essentially two very different questions?[192]

The German political scientist Sabrina Engelmann expresses a particularly firm opinion in this respect, viewing the combination of counterterrorism and militant democracy as a conceptual mistake with potentially risky consequences.[193] Counterterrorism is about ensuring security, not defending democratic principles.[194] She sees it as follows: counterterrorism defends the state (any sort of state), whereas militant democracy defends a particular political system within that state.[195] Security is certainly a prerequisite for democracy.[196] It would be absurd to start trying to establish democracy in a failed state such as Somalia. Security, however, is a prerequisite for *all* states, democratic or not, and its defence is thus not something that is characteristic of the defence of democracy.[197]

According to Engelmann, counterterrorism measures should be continually evaluated and adjusted because the nature of the threat can change rapidly; militant democracy, on the other hand, works at a different pace, with more or less permanent mechanisms ensuring that the democratic process is not derailed, as in the case of the German eternity clause and the party ban.[198] One might say that, following this interpretation, counterterrorism measures, in terms of civil rights, are ideally severe but brief, whereas militant democracy is less invasive but more permanent. The risk is therefore that when counterterrorism is 'sold' as militant democracy, we end up with the harsh measures, intended to defend the state (counterterrorism) for the long term, that are meant for protecting democracy (militant democracy).[199]

A more pragmatic objection is the following: to what extent is the arsenal of militant democracy suited to standing up to terrorism? Banning a party that glorifies terrorism might be effective, but surely challenging terrorism also calls for (far-reaching) intelligence work, with more extensive powers of criminal prosecution for police and intelligence services? Tyulkina acknowledges this too.[200] Should we then include these measures in the arsenal of militant democracy? That would, however, be a remarkable stretch of the concept. Or do these measures require a *different* legitimization?

And so we come to a more principled objection: does this not mean that militant democracy, as a broad, abstract 'justification' for action, becomes some sort of interpretive football? If militant democracy as a concept is to be effective, and specifically have the *limiting* effect that Tyulkina intends, then it must be clearly delimited, and that requires unambiguous choices. Otherwise all kinds of policies (good and bad) will still be implemented, but now under the (legitimising) flag of militant democracy. There are signs that that is precisely what is currently happening.[201] Tyulkina also sees this, and offers two rules of thumb: 1) the necessity must be clear, and 2) there must be 'strict procedural guarantees'.[202] But are these unique aspects of militant democracy? Does counterterrorism *need* a militant democracy concept for that? A firm anchoring of counterterrorism within the constitutional order is an interesting (and attractive) perspective, but how that anchoring could work *through* militant democracy requires further elaboration.

According to Tyulkina, militant democracy is also relevant to the threat of religious extremism. In principle militant democracy can guard the boundaries of democracy against religious extremism.[203] When religion changes into a political ideology, this can form a serious threat to democracy.[204] The secular character of a state should prevent such developments and keep religion out of the domain of politics. A militant democracy *rationale* can be applied to protect these secular principles.[205] The advantage of applying militant democracy in this domain, according to Tyulkina, lies in the understanding that any action taken must be strictly necessary, at least under one of the two rules of thumb mentioned above.[206] Restraint is effectively embedded in the theory and practice of militant democracy. It is second nature, partly because of the idea that its measures are generally very invasive, and partly because people realize that we are not dealing with an exceptional situation; it is a defence of democracy *within* the boundaries of the constitutional order. Tyulkina gives Turkey as an example where this is not yet working properly in all respects: a realistic estimation of the threat (and with it the need for intervention) appears to be absent.[207]

Finally, a more general point: Tyulkina's approach fails to address the issue of justification. As mentioned, Tyulkina elaborates on Loewenstein and Sajó's work on emotionalism, but otherwise simply assumes that intervention against antidemocrats is justified. Perhaps there is something to be said for such a bold assumption from a comparative legal perspective: if one defines the legitimate expressions of militant democracy too narrowly, one might well excessively limit a comparative study. Nonetheless, in my view, the absence of a clearly worked-out justification also leads to problems in Tyulkina's work.

First, these problems are visible in the capacity for judgement that the study offers: based on her limited normative groundwork and broad definition, Tyulkina can only make suggestions where a well-supported choice would really have been preferable: is this concrete application, for instance, in Spain, a good example of a militant democracy or not? The conclusion of the Indian case study is that the approach is 'one possible response' to the threat, assuming 'potentially dangerous political movements'.[208] The example of militant democracy in Israel is described as an 'interesting variation'.[209] In the same category, we find the repeated observation that militant democracy is not a 'universal panacea', but that this should not discourage democracies from implementing the concept under certain circumstances.[210]

Secondly, the question of justification returns when it comes to abuse of the system. Tyulkina herself explicitly states that the risk of abuse inherent in militant democracy goes back to, and is increased by, the absence of a 'general legal theory and clear definition'.[211] At the same time, Tyulkina appears not to see that a better worked-out justification, with a precise definition of militant democracy, is exactly what is required as an important safeguard against abuse. In fact, she even states that she considers it imprudent to define militant democracy 'in precise and definite terms', because this would limit 'the meaning and application of the concept'.[212] However, the flipside of the coin is that those 'new applications' might turn out to be entirely wrong applications, or indeed abuse. Based on her broad definition, there are few applications of militant democracy that Tyulkina can exclude or recommend *a priori*, while her recommendation with respect to abuse is at heart never more than reliable, independent judicial review.[213]

To sum up, Tyulkina's comparative legal study demonstrates three things. First, Loewenstein's analysis of fascism, understood as an analysis of the political phenomenon of 'emotionalism', may be relevant today, a point that is also made by Sajó. Second, militant democracy could potentially be extended in law to 'new' adjacent areas of counterterrorism and religious extremism. This happens regularly and the problems often overlap, as in the case of extremist political parties with a terrorist branch, be it secret or open. Third, Tyulkina's study (unintentionally) shows that one cannot avoid dealing with the issue of justification in a theory of militant democracy. Her study thus confirms how pressing the lack of a (convincing) general theory, noted by Jan-Werner Müller, really is: a formulation and discussion of the justification are needed to further militant democracy as an independent theory of democracy.

3. Pragmatic criticism of militant democracy

The greatest point of criticism relates, as mentioned, to the absence of a properly worked-out theory of militant democracy. The political philosophers discussed often contribute useful insights and building blocks, but in the end only Kirshner's work represents an attempt at a coherent theory.

This absence is understandable. In part it may be due to the origins of militant democracy in Loewenstein's comparative legal work. In his wake authors have continued to think further about militant democracy.[214] A second explanation may lie in the diffuse nature of the practical applications of militant democracy,[215] which vary from requirements for internal party democracy (Spain) to party bans in Germany, and even include the president as protector of the constitution in France.[216] It does not appear fruitful to construct an abstract theory of militant democracy based on its various manifestations. Still, that is the approach often taken. This explanation therefore closely resembles the first: after all, working one's way up from a description to a general theory was the method employed by Loewenstein.

But even if we tackle this problem and succeed in formulating a general, coherent theory of militant democracy, there are two important points of criticism that must still be addressed. The first is the suspected ineffectiveness of militant democracy, discussed in the next section.

Pragmatic objections

An important objection to party bans is pragmatic in nature: banning does not work, or, worse still, it is counterproductive. The members reorganize; parties return, hardened and motivated, with different names. The ban on the Nederlandse Volks-Unie (Dutch Peoples Union) was largely symbolic in any case: the party has been active again since 1996 and has even participated in various municipal and provincial elections.[217] In 2015 the banning of political parties and organisations was discussed in the Dutch House of Representatives, in the context of religious extremism. Quite some doubts were raised about the effectiveness of bans. When antidemocratic organizations were discussed, GroenLinks (the GreenLeft) MP Linda Voortman stated that debate was probably a more prudent weapon against reprehensible ideas than prohibiting antidemocratic parties.[218] On behalf of D66 (the Social Liberal Party), Van Weyenberg put it even more firmly: 'Many conservatives think that the problem then disappears: you've prohibited it by law, so it no longer exists. But it is just like mould: the dark and the damp are perfect conditions for it to grow.'[219]

And yes, there is certainly something in that. One probably will not change the minds of determined party members with a party ban, and what is to prevent them from founding a new party? Of course, they might well have to jump through some hoops, but in the end those are merely administrative manoeuvres; no serious antidemocrat will be put off by that. Those in the know will not be confused by a new party colour, logo or slogan. The result: extremist parties will return doubly motivated and now able to exploit their newly acquired political martyrdom. And even if they do not return, it seems premature to talk of success: instead they will go underground, and in the darkness Van Weyenberg spoke of they will proliferate like mould. It all seems plausible enough, but is it true?

Research on the effectiveness of party bans runs into several difficulties. Although political science should be capable of tackling these difficulties, it has not yet succeeded in every respect.[220] The difficulties first of all lie in the number of available cases. Parties are not banned every day, nor even every year or decade. Research therefore necessarily tends to take the form of case studies rather than quantitative work. It is also difficult to ascertain how much effect should be attributed to a party ban next to other circumstances of a concrete case.[221] To add to that, national contexts can be so specific[222] that it is hard to generalize regarding anti-extremist 'strategies' (including party bans).[223] Finally, it is also difficult to say anything about the 'anticipatory effect' of a ban: the possibility of a ban might well already influence the behaviour of political actors.[224] In other words, how do you know what antidemocratic parties have *not* been founded?

Despite these problems, there are enough starting points in the literature. Empirical research on militant democracy in general, and specifically on party bans, is growing, and the first results are becoming available.[225] There is also a substantial body of relevant research on the effects of repression of extremists in a broader sense. The party ban is traditionally seen as the first and foremost repressive instrument; in fact, it is seen as the most invasive form, alongside other, lighter measures such as 'forfeiture of basic rights' and loyalty requirements for officials.[226] Finally, political scientists have also shone their light on the functioning of unprohibited extremist, antidemocratic parties in a democracy. A combination of these insights should be sufficient to enlighten us on whether the intuitive, pragmatic objections can stand up to scrutiny.

The pragmatic objections worked out in detail

Let us begin by working out the pragmatic objections in greater detail. Party bans are supposed to be ineffective because the party members can reorganize and start up a new party. The second objection points to the counterproductive effects of repression.[227] A formal party ban, or an informal party ban functioning as a 'cordon sanitaire', neutralizes tensions within the party: its members can then unite in their battle against 'the other', against the system. In the democratic game of give and take, it becomes necessary to moderate points of view; this need is absent in the case of a ban. In the absence of a realistic prospect of participation, parties can even maximize their support by persisting in their extremism. And giving extremists a 'musk of taboo' might also lend them notoriety, making them 'intrinsically more appealing to young people'.[228]

The fact that parties do indeed reorganize is apparent from the Czech experiences with repression of the extreme right. Since 2002 Dêlnická Strana (the Workers' Party) has been active on the extreme right, as one of the many loose extreme right-wing associations in the Czech Republic.[229] These organizations have generally fallen apart due to internal conflict, but the Workers' Party gained momentum due to collaboration with neo-Nazi militants. An important catalyst was the electoral success of the National Democratic Party of Germany in the adjacent German federal state of Saxony. An (unarmed) paramilitary organization was established to 'monitor crime' in areas with Roma settlements. In 2008 the Workers' Party organized a mass demonstration in the border town of Litvínov, which derailed when the 500 party members and sympathizers in attendance attempted to reach 'Janov', a part of town with a substantial Roma population.[230] Molotov cocktails, stones and fireworks were thrown at the police.[231] Later more weapons and even pitchforks were found.[232] Around 300 Roma men had armed themselves in turn to defend their neighbourhood.[233] It was a battlefield, labelled the 'Battle of Janov' by the Workers' Party.[234] Along with other incidents, this increased the visibility of the party.[235] In 2009 the party gained 1.07 percent of the vote in European Parliament elections, which had serious consequences because now it had the right to public funding.[236]

A first attempt at banning the party stalled in 2009 because the government did not have its evidence in order.[237] A second attempt followed in 2010, and this time the court agreed, finding a three-part foundation for banning the party. First, its aim was to propagate 'national, racial, ethnic and social intolerance' and as a result 'to limit the basic rights and freedoms' of specific groups of citizens.[238] Second, the party had an ambivalent relationship with political violence. In any case violence was not renounced, and the party even glorified acts of violence by its members and sympathizers.[239] Third, the party wanted to replace state organs with party organs, the most telling example being the foundation of their own paramilitary organization.[240]

Nevertheless, the ban was not an unqualified success. Even before the first legal case, leaders in the Workers' Party had already made preparations for a new start in the case of a ban.[241] They had taken over the administration of another small party and given it a new name, the Dêlnická strana sociální spravedlnosti (the Workers' Party of Social Justice). After the verdict in 2010 the administration and many of the members moved over to the new Workers' Party of Social Justice.[242] The Houdini-style trick had direct success. That summer the 'new' party received 1.14 percent of the vote in elections for the Czech Chamber of Deputies.[243] In the local elections in the autumn, however, the party did not achieve any notable result.[244]

So here we have a party that is banned but then continues under a different name and even (initially) encounters growing support, or at least gains more votes. The Czech political scientist Miroslav Mareš (born 1974) attributes this in part to an omission in Czech law: it is not possible to tackle the spreading of the prohibited party's propaganda. The new party can therefore take over all the symbols of the banned party; so voters know the message is still the same. The dividing line between the new party and the banned one thus becomes very vague indeed. Germany has laws preventing such a new beginning.[245] But aside from the question of whether the law needs sharpening, the Czech example shows that banned parties reorganize. A ban, after all, does not ban the individuals; they remain in place. This is clear not only in the Czech Republic. Parties have succeeded in reorganizing more or less immediately after a ban in Germany, France, Turkey and Belgium, too.[246] These examples cast doubt on the effectiveness of party bans, so it seems that there is some truth to the first pragmatic objection. The use of party bans against the extreme right in Germany and France has not weakened these organizations.[247] They actively develop strategies to prevent a ban, as well as to survive afterwards should it happen.

But perhaps more important is the fact that the organizations not only appear to survive, but that the core seems to harden in its viewpoints,[248] suggesting not only ineffectiveness but counterproductive effects, in line with the second pragmatic objection.

Repression of extremist factions runs into another complicating factor: stigma. Reintegration of former extremists into society can be hampered by the fact that, for instance, as in the Netherlands, there is little social tolerance for those associated with extreme right-wing ideas, unlike extreme left-wing ideas.[249] Membership might not increase (due to fear of stigma), but it is not significantly reduced either.

When it comes to excessive repression, the German political scientist Michael Minkenberg perceives the possibility that, in the absence of other means of expression, an organization may transform into an 'autonomous terrorist group'.[250] Comparable concerns are expressed by commentators in Belgium and Spain,[251] and Miroslav Mareš does not exclude the possibility that prohibited groups will resort to violence in the Czech situation, because the options for political representation have been cut off.[252]

The pragmatic objections tested

British political scientist Tim Bale challenges both pragmatic objections outlined above on the basis of comparative research on party bans in Turkey, Spain and Belgium.[253] These countries are not chosen at random: each has its own specific extremist threat.[254] If it can be demonstrated that party bans are not necessarily ineffective or counterproductive in three relatively different democracies, we can be more certain that prohibiting parties is not a bad idea *per se*.[255] Bale tests three hypotheses, two of which are relevant here: 1) a ban on a party considered dangerous aggravates the situation (making a ban counterproductive), and 2) party bans make no difference; the parties persist in their activities as before (so a ban is ineffectual).[256] Bale shows that neither hypothesis stands up in the cases of bans on Kurdish parties and the Islamist Refah Party in Turkey, the left-wing nationalist Batasuna in Spain or the right-wing nationalist Vlaams Blok in Belgium.[257] The threat did not become greater in any of these cases (first hypothesis), and the parties did not simply continue with business as usual (second hypothesis).

With respect to the Turkish situation, one may argue that new parties were always coming up to replace the banned parties (as in the Czech Republic), and certainly when it comes to the Kurdish parties, where the 'line of succession' is 'very direct'. However, as Bale emphasizes, that is just one part of the story: each of the successor parties in Turkey further moderated its viewpoints,[258] although one can, given the current developments (especially after the failed 2016 coup), question how profound such moderation is when it comes to the AK-party, which is the successor of the Refah Party.[259] The same applies to the Belgian situation: Vlaams Belang turned out to be more moderate than its banned predecessor, the Vlaams Blok,[260] as the aspiration for a corporatist (antidemocratic) state, for example, disappeared from the party programme.[261]

In Spain the expectation of commentators was that the banning of Batasuna would lead to 'intensification' and 'polarization': the 'left-wing nationalists' could then become 'democratic martyrs', leading to an increase in violence and aversion to democracy.[262] The threat of the ETA, with whom Batasuna maintained close connections, was also relevant.[263] Since 1968 this terrorist organization has waged a violent war for the independence of the Basque Country, resulting in 836 deaths and 2367 wounded.[264] In short, banning Batasuna was expected to be counterproductive. However, the opposite turned out to be the case: the ban was followed by one of the least violent periods to date.[265] Of course, that might be attributed to the success of the intelligence services, but then one would expect such success to be at least negated by the predicted negative effects of the ban.[266] Attendance in regional elections also increased, despite explicit calls from Batasuna not to vote.[267] Most important of all, a year after the ban, Batasuna leader Arnaldo Otegi initiated important first steps towards peace.[268] That is not to say that these developments are a direct result of the ban, Bale emphasizes, but it shows that the ban 'did not at least prevent what is widely regarded as a genuine opportunity for peace'.[269] That makes the assumption improbable that party bans will be counterproductive *per se*.[270] And to add to this: in May 2018 the ETA even announced that it dissolved itself completely.[271]

Bale asserts that both hypotheses can be shown to be false. Intuitive opinions on party bans are not supported by the facts. In each of the three democracies studied, party bans have not increased the threat; in other words, they were not counterproductive *per se* (first hypothesis). At the same time, the banned parties did not persist in their activities undaunted, so the bans were not ineffective *per se* (second hypothesis).[272]

Bale's conclusion is thus that party bans are not ineffective *per se*, and that the consequences that they do have are not counterproductive *per se*. What Bale shows is that party bans 'do not necessarily turn out badly'.[273]

Frank Buijs (1949-2007) and Meindert Fennema (born 1946) present the same picture: repression is effective, leading to weakening of extremist organizations.[274] 'Extremists' are individuals who not only criticize the democratic system, but who reject it and do not shrink from violence in doing so.[275] The weakening from repression has two causes. First, repression raises the risk associated with membership,[276] an effect that is increased when there are also negative consequences for a person's career linked with membership.[277] A party therefore finds it difficult to recruit candidates, which translates into a drop in the quality of the elected representatives of the people, who in turn reduce respect for the party.[278] In this way repression can be the start of a downward spiral, which shrinks the extremist party.

Dutch political scientists Buijs and Fennema also point out, like Bale, that repression leads to moderation.[279] But they are more sceptical than Bale on this point: at any rate, it leads to *outward* moderation. Buijs and Fennema therefore speak of 'more moderate presentation' and even 'concealing' instead of actually 'moderating viewpoints'.[280] In any case this does lead to an 'adaptation dilemma' *within* the organization: to what extent should the party adapt? In the case of far-reaching adaptation, the 'radicals' will complain of a 'loss of principles'; in the case of overly limited adaptation, the 'moderates' will turn their back on the party.[281] This weakens the party or organization, causing it to splinter.[282] Buijs and Fennema do, however, emphasize that it is necessary to guard against the *themes* of the extremist party becoming taboo, because that can seriously delay the public debate on certain issues, as in the case of policy on refugees and discussions on the integration of migrants.[283] Buijs and Fennema remain somewhat sceptical and therefore argue for a restrictive application of repression.[284]

The Dutch sociologist and political scientist Bart Tromp points out that a similar 'adaptation dilemma' appears in some sense even before any repression takes place.[285] Antidemocratic parties always have a choice between participation and violent resistance. If they choose participation, they are 'compelled to base their position of power in politics on their electoral support and on their parliamentary tactics and strategy'.[286] That ensures that they embrace a number of democratic ideological principles, such as the right to vote and majority decision making.[287] This is initially seen as purely functional, as a means to an end, but as time goes on, the means begins to take on the shape of an end. Maintaining the party organization, for example, becomes a goal in itself, leading to the gradual fading of the original ideological and antidemocratic goals into the background. Tromp mentions the development of the Western European social democrats as an example. Initially they saw democracy as a *means* of realizing their socialist ideal, but eventually this changed into defining democracy as the 'best possible' system and an *end* in itself.[288] As we have already seen, George van den Bergh played an important role in this process within the Dutch SDAP. Thus simply having a democracy, in its normal day-to-day functioning, can work as a 'disciplinary' influence on antidemocratic powers.[289] The American political scientist Nancy Rosenblum specifically links this process to the democratization of religious antidemocratic parties, in particular Islamic extremists.[290]

Tromp points out that this is a process that requires time and is one of internal 'ambiguities' and 'contradictions' between members who want to adapt and those who maintain their 'aversion' to (or contempt for) democracy.[291] Tromp's analysis thus seems compatible with that of Buijs and Fennema. A democracy cannot infinitely rely on its disciplinary influence. It takes time. If greater haste is required, repression can serve to intensify the 'adaptation dilemma', as there is more at stake, and thereby accelerate the process.[292] Moreover, recent research provides further nuances on the moderating influence coming purely from participation.[293]

Another nuance is introduced by the Italian political scientist Giovanni Capoccia. On the basis of a study of three successful cases of 'democratic survival'—Czechoslovakia, Finland and Belgium in the interbellum—he concludes that, although repression is always necessary, inclusive strategies can be an important, decisive addition.[294] An entirely inclusive strategy (Germany and Italy in the interbellum) is imprudent,[295] but the successful re-integration of extremists into the democratic system, winning back their loyalty, can reduce the risk of a revolution.[296] As we saw, this problem is present in the Netherlands, specifically with respect to extreme right-wing thinking: the stigma linked to it hampers re-integration. From Capoccia's perspective an inclusive strategy should attempt to remove these obstacles as far as possible.[297]

Positive side effects of party bans

We can also point to other positive side effects of party bans and prohibition legislation. A party ban might set a boundary on what is politically 'acceptable' and provide a powerful confirmation of the democratic system.[298] It offers a 'signposting of the constitutional boundaries of tolerance'.[299]

A preventive and deterrent influence is also attributed to legal control of party bans.[300] For instance, Svetlana Tyulkina believes that the European post-communist states had more faith in their budding democracies during their transition periods because of the presence of militant democracy as an emergency brake; if things were to go wrong, there was always the option of intervention.[301] At the same time, the mere presence of these provisions in the constitution was 'a clear message' to antidemocrats that they would not be met with unlimited tolerance.[302]

From a sociological perspective militant democracy could even have a 'didactic' and thus also 'democratizing' function. The supposed paradoxical character of a party ban in a democracy opens up a 'discursive field' in which the nature of democracy can be fundamentally questioned.[303] The democratic character of the state is suddenly the subject of discussion. Its 'public expression' has a 'didactic function' and contributes to a renewal of democratic culture.[304] Democracy is then found in the 'discursive field' *after* a party ban.[305]

Pragmatic objections: conclusions

This overview has considered the effectiveness of party bans, and in a broader sense of repression of political organizations, in the cases of left-wing, right-wing and religious extremist parties. What they share is their extremism: they not only criticize the democratic system; they also oppose it, if necessary with violence. They are truly antidemocratic parties.

The overview shows that neither pragmatic objection stands up to scrutiny: party bans are not ineffective *per se*, and if they are effective they are not necessarily counterproductive. Moreover, the consensus appears to be that combatting antidemocratic factions demands some form of repression, with party bans forming the main method. Repression of antidemocratic parties appears to weaken them and often to cause them to disappear. In other words, repression 'works'.[306] If new incarnations appear, they generally moderate their viewpoints. This can be a case of merely concealing their 'real' views, but such a move results in an 'adaptation dilemma', leading in turn to splits within, and weakening of, the party. Two points can be added to the picture. Democracy in itself has a disciplinary function: antidemocratic parties are made less antidemocratic simply through participation in the democratic process, although this is a slow process, requiring time to have any noticeable effect. Not all cases can wait, and sometimes repression can have an accelerating effect, intensifying dilemmas for antidemocrats.

The second nuance lies in the importance of a parallel inclusive approach. The chance of successfully warding off an antidemocratic threat appears to increase when an inclusive strategy is employed alongside repression. That means improving the reintroduction of antidemocrats. Without options for democratic re-integration former members remain on the margins of society.

The New York law professor Stephen Holmes describes how two paradigms compete for priority in the discussion on militant democracy: the 'toe in the door' and the 'safety valve'.[307] The toe-in-the-door scenario shows that tolerating antidemocrats is dangerous: it 'legitimates illegitimate aims' and paves the way to takeover of power.[308] Tolerance must therefore be ruled out. The metaphor of the safety valve states that antidemocrats must be admitted to the democratic system: there their sentiments can be channelled, whereas if they are excluded they will 'fester and perhaps explode'.[309]

Holmes states that democracies will have to choose one of the two metaphors, each of which reveals part of the truth: repression or concession.[310] The political science literature offers clarity and a reconciliation between the two competing metaphors, with the emphasis on repression. The idea that antidemocrats radicalize when banned, and not given a channel to express their views, seems plausible from a theoretical perspective, but it turns out not to be reflected much in reality. Nevertheless, we should not dismiss the 'safety valve' metaphor altogether: for an optimal result, we have seen that repression is best combined with inclusive strategies.

The conclusion is that the common pragmatic objections, all things considered, do not hold. Party bans are an important and quite often effective tool in democratic self-defence, an option a democracy should have in its armoury.

Militant democracy outside the Western European context and 'transitional constitutionalism'

Up until now we have discussed antidemocratic parties in European democracies (including Turkey). Does a look at the African continent have anything to teach us? This is completely different terrain. The young, often unstable African democracies, to the extent that they can already be called functioning democracies at all, have problems of their own. The constant presence of ethnic tensions can lead to a 'politicization' of ethnicity in 'multiparty systems': parties organize themselves along ethnic lines.[311] This increases conflict between different communities, and ethnic politics, when taken to the extreme, make democracy impossible: parties no longer stand for ideas or interests but for their own group identity, leaving nothing of the real political debate remaining.[312]

The vast majority of the sub-Saharan African states have the option of banning 'particularistic parties', that is, parties with an 'ethnic, racial or tribal basis' (forty of the forty-eight states).[313] Comparative research into party bans shows no clear positive or negative effect with respect to reduction in conflict. In their study of twelve party bans in six different sub-Saharan African states, German political scientists Matthias Basedau and Anika Moroff write:

> The results clearly show that particularistic party bans are not a universal remedy for inter-communal conflict.... This is not to say that particularistic party bans do not have any positive effects.[314]

And in the introduction to a special edition of *Democratization* on ethnic party bans in Africa, Basedau and the political scientists Bogaards and Hartmann come to a similar conclusion.[315] Incidentally, it is remarkable that in the African context 'reorganization' seems not to play a role. In her comparative study of African party bans, Moroff found only one party that persisted despite a ban.[316]

Although the 'African studies' seem to have little to tell us about the real effectiveness of party bans in (fragile) democracies, they can still teach us something else about them. Or to put it better, they can heighten our sensitivity to an inherent risk of party bans: opportunistic abuse by ruling parties. In the unstable, divided democracies of the African continent, this risk emphatically comes into the foreground. Studies by Bogaards, Hartmann, Basedau and Moroff emphasize that illegitimate repression in the African context is a real risk.[317]

Of course, in the consolidated European democracies, which are free of such ethnic divisions, this problem is of a completely different (and generally smaller) order. We should not forget, though, that even European history has its examples of illegitimate repression 'in the name of freedom' or 'protection of institutions': from the French revolutionaries (1793) to the violent opposition of Belgian governments to socialist parties (1880-1914).[318]

The risk of abuse can also be a concern in a more immediate sense. Militant democracy is also seen as a constitutional principle that can oversee the transition from undemocratic to democratic systems. This effect, for example, is suggested for Eastern European states with a communist history.[319] This is a matter of *transitional constitutionalism*.[320] In the transition to a democratic system, for example, it can be necessary to exclude leading members or sympathizers of the old regime from the still young democratic process.[321] An example is the verdict of the ECHR in *Zdanoka vs. Latvia*. Tatjana Zdanoka, a prominent former member of the Communist Party of Latvia, had her passive suffrage revoked for actions that included her party's attempt to overturn the restored independence of Latvia through a coup.[322] The ECHR upheld the verdict of the Latvian Constitutional Court, referring explicitly to Latvia's transition to democracy:

> While such a measure may scarcely be considered acceptable in the context of one political system, for example in a country which has an established framework of democratic institutions going back many decades

> or centuries, it may nonetheless be considered acceptable in Latvia in view of the historico-political context which led to its adoption and given the threat to the new democratic order posed by the resurgence of ideas which, if allowed to gain ground, might appear capable of restoring the former regime. The Court therefore accepts in the present case that the national authorities of Latvia, both legislative and judicial, are better placed to assess the difficulties faced in establishing and safeguarding the democratic order.[323]

Although the ECHR allows a certain leniency here towards a democracy in transition, we should nonetheless wonder whether the present risk of abuse, particularly in these young democracies (as we saw in Africa), does not make militant democracy (with party bans) unsuitable for periods of transition. One might reasonably argue that the problems of these Eastern European states are completely different from those of the African countries, in that they relate to a transition from authoritarian communism to democracy, not to a transition from tribal, ethnically divided colonies to democracies. In the latter situation the tensions and divisions are, after all, far more deeply embedded, whereas in the post-communist states it is mainly ideological principles that need casting off. The relatively small number of party bans imposed in post-communist democracies also seems to confirm a more careful application, certainly now that extremist parties are not particularly scarce in these countries.[324]

It would mean that a militant democracy *can* indeed set the transition from dictatorship to democracy on the right track, but that extra care is needed in communities divided along ethnic lines. Otherwise party bans can be misused as a tool to clamp down on competing tribes or ethnic groups.

4. Principled criticism of militant democracy

In addition to pragmatic criticism, there is principled criticism. Some critics do not point to alleged ineffectiveness or counterproductivity, but rather challenge the idea that it is possible to draw up a coherent theory of militant democracy. Much of this criticism comes from the perspective of political philosophy and works along the lines of the distinction between procedural and militant democracy.[325] One such objection would be that a militant democracy is not really a democracy, because it makes use of 'dictatorial means'. This was exactly the response to Van den Bergh in 1936.[326]

The critics of militant democracy appeal to the notion of procedural or relativist democracy. The most important legal philosopher to represent this view is Hans Kelsen. His views have been discussed in detail in contrast to Van den Bergh's inaugural lecture. Kelsen's point of departure is that a democracy is value-neutral: viewpoints are not tested on their content; only the votes are counted. The result is that a democracy can abolish itself. If it tries to resist and to remain in place against the will of the majority, it ceases to be a democracy. All that remains is hope that if democracy goes under, it will eventually rise again and return stronger than before. For Kelsen democracy is the political translation of a relativistic *Weltanschauung.*

The concept of procedural democracy is worked out by the Dutch constitutional jurist Theo Bellekom based on the 'marketplace of ideas' metaphor.[327] The metaphor comes from the American debate on freedom of speech. Democracy is seen as a 'game that consists of offering and exchanging ideas on a market accessible to everyone'.[328] The metaphor is thus an economic one, closely related to the classic formulation by Joseph Schumpeter, in which democracy is defined as an

> institutional arrangement for arriving at political decisions in which individuals acquire the power to decide by means of a competitive struggle for the people's vote.[329]

The right ideas will naturally float to the top, in competition with other ideas or through evaluation when they are implemented.[330] One has to trust the corrective effect of elections: less good ideas will be defeated by better ones, and those who propagate bad ideas are not re-elected.[331] The most important means against antidemocratic parties in this system are therefore argumentation and persuasiveness.[332]

Procedural democracy thus does not expect much of the constitutional structures in defence of the democracy. Defending democracy comes down to political will. Democrats might even find their will strengthened by the challenge of antidemocratic powers and the debate on radical alternatives to democracy.[333] The closest example to this model is the United States,[334] where in fact 'freedom of association' is not formally recognized in the constitution.[335] Nonetheless, political parties there enjoy far-reaching protection against party bans. There are laws that restrict freedom of association, but they are dysfunctional regulations from 'hot and cold wars'.[336] They have fallen into disuse since the 1960s, and the stringent test used by the Supreme Court in cases of fundamental freedoms makes a party ban particularly unlikely. It is a dead letter. There is also a strong tradition of 'a more or less absolutist understanding of freedom of expression and association'.[337]

It should be noted that certain aspects of the American system *de facto* work restrictively, such as the district system and resulting monopoly of the Democratic and Republican parties.[338] This makes the problem less urgent and allows for a little more leeway in other areas: the chance of an antidemocratic threat 'materializing' is relatively small. However, as discussed in the introduction, the election of political eccentric Donald Trump as president of the United States has shown that, *if* a party is taken over by an antidemocratic candidate, in a two-party system the threat is more acute—the road to power is much shorter than in a multiparty democracy (setting aside the question how democratic Trump's programme is, the point here is merely that he was an unconventional candidate that successfully evaded the informal restrictions of the American two-party system and was able to lead the Republican Party to become president).[339]

The traditional answer to procedural democracy has been discussed above. It is the argument of the 'substantive democrats': democracy is more than a purely formal decision-making process. It is a misunderstanding to reduce democracy to vote counting. The essence of democracy lies in certain fundamental values, freedom and equality,[340] or in the German case human dignity. The content, not the way in which it came into being, ultimately determines how democratic legislation is.[341] A good example of such an idea is Bonger's classic definition discussed above:

> Democracy is a form of government involving the self-government of a collectivity, in which a large proportion of its members participate either directly or indirectly, and where freedom of conscience and equality before the law are safeguarded, and the members are committed to this idea.[342]

Alongside self-government (the procedural aspect), Bonger emphasizes the importance of respect for two fundamental values: freedom of conscience and equality before the law (the substantive aspect). Without those values a democracy cannot really function, so the system can no longer be labelled as such.[343] We might then refer to it as a *value-laden* democracy.

Van den Bergh took Bonger's definition as a starting point for his argument, as we saw, but one might argue that he extended Bonger's concept of democracy. When Van den Bergh writes that to him the 'deepest essence of democracy' lies more in 'respect for the individuality of every human being' than in the 'majority principle', it is characteristic of the first interpretation of his work.[344] Van den Bergh thus leaves out the procedural aspect of democracy and in fact formulates something akin to the key principle behind the German substantive democracy: respect for human dignity.[345] The European Court of Human Rights also opted for a substantive interpretation of democracy in the Refah case.[346]

It should be clear why a militant democracy feels more at home with the notion of substantive democracy. If you want to act against antidemocratic parties, you must first articulate the values (and thus the justification) that form the basis for such action. In the procedural concept of democracy, and in a *fully* procedural democracy, there is no space for militant democracy. In fact, it turns out that even the democracy that appeared the most procedural on paper does not take that principle to its extremes: the United States legislated against a supposed communist, antidemocratic threat. In constitutions and constitutional practice, states generally show some signs of 'militancy'; perhaps one should therefore speak of 'varieties of militancy' rather than of the dichotomy between procedural and militant/substantive democracies.[347] In practice very few democracies are prepared to watch the ship go under with Hans Kelsen.

Nevertheless, the procedural democrats have a number of valid points to make in their criticism of the concept of substantive democracy. Is a substantive democracy not too far removed from a number of important associations or meanings of democracy? If democracy stands for certain values that it is intended to safeguard, such as respect for the individuality of every human being, or freedom and inequality, what remains of the original idea of *democracy*: government by the people? Does a substantive democracy not put too much emphasis on the rule of law, here in part meant in the sense of protection of fundamental, possibly inviolable, rights,[348] leaving room only for limited (delineated) democratic decision making? And, subsequently, trying to avoid that conclusion, by lumping all that together under 'democracy'? The procedural democrats also have a point when they note that democracy loses a great deal of its characteristic neutrality in this way. Furthermore, is a democracy really capable of governing itself properly if it excludes certain voices from the discussion? Does value-neutrality not safeguard precisely the fact that only the arguments count, so that (in theory) the best-argued government is guaranteed? Related to this is another possible criticism: does a substantive democracy not leave too little of the democratic process intact? What remains of the original ideal of government by the people?[349] Does it not take too many subjects out of the hands of the democratically legitimized legislator by declaring a number of values inviolable?

A militant democracy based on substantive democracy also has another specific weakness. What is regarded as the essence of democracy also forms the grounds for justification for acting against antidemocratic parties. For instance, a party might threaten freedom of conscience and equality before the law, which would then form the justification for repressive action. A substantive democracy theory therefore quickly provides a broad, but rather unclear, foundation. Van den Bergh saw freedom of conscience and equality before the law as inviolable principles. Incorporating these values in a banning provision will lead to all kinds of interpretation issues. Too much interpretive freedom on this issue is undesirable; such freedom also invites abuse of the party ban regulations. We have seen how real this risk is.

These are issues that a militant democracy theory cannot simply gloss over. It is not sufficient simply to reject a pure procedural concept of democracy, certainly not if it is simply to embrace a substantive democracy instead. In the next chapter, I will argue that the second interpretation of Van den Bergh, democracy as self-correction, succeeds in finding the right line between the procedural and substantive democracy concepts, making it possible to deal with the objections mentioned above.

Closely related to this criticism is the argumentation of the Groningen professor of constitutional law Douwe Elzinga.[350] In his work the adage of procedural democracy, 'the majority decides', is supported by a theory on the validity of law. His starting point is a *relativist concept of freedom and law*. In this concept of justice, the normative power of a law (its validity) is relative to the extent of acceptance.[351] The greater the consensus, the stronger the normative power; the smaller the consensus, the more limited is its validity. The law is then experienced as less 'law'; its 'independence' as a legal norm is reduced.[352]

This view shares some common ground with the 'doctrine of the sovereignty of law' proposed by the former Leiden professor of constitutional law Hugo Krabbe (1857-1936). The central concept in Krabbe's work is the 'sense of justice' ('rechtsgevoel'). To Krabbe, this sense of justice is 'the more or less living psychological power of the sense of justice which is constantly at work in the entire population';[353] more concretely, it is a 'general human tendency', such as a sense of ethics, beauty and religion.[354] It is 'the *real* power which decides on the validity of the law'.[355] To Krabbe justice is everything which—and exclusively that which—'is recognized as such by the people's sense of justice'.[356] Elzinga also connects the force of law to the extent of acceptance, albeit less radically than Krabbe.[357]

This connection is particularly felt in the problem of antidemocratic parties, because when antidemocratic parties acquire substantial support, the principles of democracy, seen from the perspective of the relativist concept of law, have by definition become controversial.[358] This means that the government's most important tool, the law, has lost legitimacy and validity. Elzinga gives a sharp formulation of the consequent paradox:

> The instruments law offers the government to defend liberal democracy are less legitimate in their use and application as the need for their use and application grows.[359]

That has the following consequences, specifically for party bans:

> In circumstances in which prohibiting a political party is really necessary to protect the democracy from downfall, the law is not ... or is barely capable of legitimizing a party ban anymore.[360]

It is here that Elzinga also explicitly discusses Van den Bergh's theory of militant democracy, and in particular the first interpretation: the value-laden principled democracy.[361] *Contra* Van den Bergh, Elzinga proposes that when an antidemocratic political party has a majority or even a near majority, 'no legal grounds whatsoever' can justify such a party being 'removed from the process of shaping the political will'.[362] The principle of democracy is infringed upon when minorities impose their will on majorities 'in the name of the "law"', without that law being experienced as normative any longer by a majority.[363] This brings Elzinga to the following observation:

> A minority uses the weapons of the law in the name of freedom to make an end to democracy; in essence this is no different from the minority which uses the weapons of the law to defend democracy.[364]

What remains, then? In any case not standing patiently by as a dictatorship is rolled out across the country. The 'principal unacceptability of the use of illegitimate or barely legitimate instruments' makes the defence of democracy a task for society.[365] In the absence of legitimate legal means it comes down to power:

> Society can bring all its weapons to bear (both figuratively and literally) to defend democracy. The 'homo homini lupus'—the civil war—which results will return liberal democracy to its origins.[366]

Nonetheless, Elzinga offers another way out, to prevent such an apocalyptic, Kelsenian scenario. The relativist concept of law, in contrast with the traditional procedural notion of democracy, leaves open the possibility of party bans in cases in which there is sufficient consensus as to the principles of the democracy. The relativist concept of law is not opposed to party bans in itself, but it is opposed to their application by minorities against majorities who no longer perceive a law to be normative. Elzinga therefore also writes:

> When it is not … the entire democratic system which is at stake, but the issue is political parties which expressly represent [political] minorities, the use of the legal remedy of banning a party in principle is not excluded.[367]

So party bans are not ruled out, but, Elzinga adds, the utmost restraint must be exercised.[368]

Elzinga thus succeeds in formulating a refined criticism of militant democracy through the lens of the relativist concept of freedom and law. Militant democracy faces a sharp dilemma. At the moment in which intervention is most necessary, its legal remedies (the party ban) are no longer justifiable. And when its legal means *are* legitimized by a firm consensus on democratic principles, their application seems premature and thus, one may argue, undemocratic. Elzinga therefore concludes that the problem of democratic self-defence cannot be properly solved in law; it will probably come down to society.[369]

Ghent constitutional law scholar Eva Brems points out similar obstacles. She formulates it as a problem of timing. The democratic dilemma (is it permissible for a democracy to take action against antidemocrats?) is intensified by this problem.[370] Even if you can justify militant action in principle, the right moment for intervention is not a given. Her analysis fits well with that of Elzinga:

> The threat of anti-democratic tendencies and hence the need to interfere increases as their support grows. Yet once anti-democratic views have the support of a substantial segment of the population, the democratic legitimacy of an interference diminishes.[371]

But when antidemocrats gain popularity, not only does that decrease the legitimacy of measures; their feasibility and effectiveness probably also suffer and one can expect public indignation and unrest.[372] At the same time, Brems also points out that early application can make the measures seem disproportionate.[373]

A coherent militant democracy theory must address this issue. After all, it seems that there is really never 'a good moment' for intervention by a militant democracy. It is either too early or too late.

But even if we assume that a good or acceptable moment exists, we may encounter another problem. There appear to be no *legal* criteria for choosing the right moment for intervention, and their absence would make the decision to intervene a purely political one.[374]

Another question is how relevant the militant democracy paradigm is in times of religiously inspired terrorism,[375] which concerns groups who do not attempt to acquire power within the democracy but who want to overthrow the state (and the democracy) from outside with violence.[376] Should we not therefore focus mainly on the 'preventive, security-oriented state' and violations of privacy, freedom of movement and property that the threat of religiously inspired terrorism brings with it?[377]

A closely related criticism focuses specifically on religious extremism. To what extent are the tools of a militant democracy suited to intervention against religious actors? Religious extremists appeal to freedom of religion and expression, but do not necessarily organize themselves into parties.[378] It is then often a case of (travelling) radical religious preachers, the so-called 'hate preachers'.[379] They are able to reach a considerable audience with their antidemocratic message. Nonetheless, they remain out of reach of militant democracy, and as long as they do not commit any crimes, no action can be taken against them. Arabists and experts on Islam commenting on the issue indicate that these preachers succeed in remaining precisely within the boundaries of freedom of expression, while those in the know understand what is written between the lines.[380]

One might also wonder whether we should give more prominence to the role of civil society in the defence of democracy, as discussed by Jan-Werner Müller in his *Constitutional Patriotism*.[381] Then we are not talking about democratic processes and debate, but, for example, about demonstrations and boycotts.[382] Such social resistance can symbolically confirm that democracy also protects minorities. Examples are the demonstrations against the extreme right in Germany and the ETA in Spain.[383] Such social resistance would be preferable to politicians, who will always be accused of political opportunism if they act against antidemocrats, and lawyers, who, because of their more distant, procedural logic, are probably not political enough to be able to intervene in antidemocratic challenges.[384]

Finally, let me address two more specific points of criticism. First, should the theory of militant democracy not also make demands on the internal party democracy, the organization of parties?[385] The German approach to militant democracy, for example, does that very explicitly in Article 21 of the Constitution: 'Ihre innere Ordnung muß demokratischen Grundsätzen entsprechen.' On this basis the Federal Constitutional Court requires among other things that party members must have a say, that the members must be equal and that there is the freedom to become a member, and indeed to cancel membership.[386] Second, one could see party bans as a sort of 'veiled supraconstitutionalism', establishing certain values above the constitutional level.[387] Is a supraconstitutional construct such as the German eternity clause not a better protective structure than a prohibition?

5. Alternatives and criticism: conclusions

Several alternative theories of militant democracy have been developed after Loewenstein and Van den Bergh. They are first and foremost militant interpretations of the work of four political philosophers: Mill, Schmitt, Popper and Rawls.

When it comes to *John Stuart Mill* we can be brief. In a different context, Mill formulates an intuition that lies at the foundation of militant democracy: in freedom one cannot definitively renounce one's freedom. This is no more than a starting point for working out a theory in more detail.

Carl Schmitt has more to offer. A distinction must be made between substantive principles (a fundamental choice by the people, the chosen constitutional order) and formal principles (decision-making procedures and institutions such as the parliament). The formal principles are extensions of the substantive principles, and are designed to implement and realize the chosen constitutional order. They can never undo that constitutional order. That can only be done by a fundamental choice of the people.

Schmitt's theory is more of a theory of the militant *constitution* or state; that state *can* be democratic, but it is not a requirement. The defence of democracy thus ultimately has a weakness: if a large proportion of the people are determined to get rid of democracy at some point, if they want to make a different fundamental choice, we are left empty-handed; there is no *positive* argument to be given for democracy. The only argument then is that this has been chosen and we have to live with it, because it is stated in the constitution. Whereas the second interpretation of Van den Bergh could justify intervention in such cases by pointing to the loss of the unique capacity of self-correction, in Schmitt's case the new fundamental choice is also the final choice.

Karl Popper and *John Rawls* then come closer to a theory of militant democracy. Popper makes a sharp distinction between the open society on the one hand (a system of values, and an end in itself) and democracy on the other (a set of tools and thus only a means to an end). To Popper the defence of democracy must therefore be seen in the broader context of the defence of the open society: in that defence democracy is an important safeguard and support. This means that Popper, despite some ambiguities, speaks out strongly against extensive tolerance of antidemocratic powers. The aim of democracy is to prevent tyranny (*that* is its function within the configuration of the open society) by allowing changes of government to occur without bloodshed. It is permissible to ban parties who want to abolish democracy and introduce tyranny, violence and chaos. Democrats must also claim the right to act against the intolerant and do so when the threat begins to manifest itself. Popper's view of democracy also offers starting points for the development of Van den Bergh's democracy as self-correction. Besides preventing tyranny, Popper strongly emphasizes the scientific character of democracy: *trial and error* and the unique willingness to learn from one's own mistakes. In the next chapter we will connect these aspects with the ideas of Van den Bergh.

In John Rawls' work the defence of democracy, or, better put, the defence against intolerance, springs directly from the original position, a thought experiment that abstracts away from one's personal characteristics to assess what makes a just society. According to Rawls, the 'contractants' in this original position should also conclude that there is a right to constitutional self-preservation: justice does not demand that citizens look on as the basis of their existence is destroyed. Or, in Rawls' terms: the principle of equal freedom for everyone can be restricted for the sake of safeguarding that same principle. The disadvantage of Rawls as a basis for democratic self-defence, to put it irreverently, is the extra 'baggage': there are several questionable assumptions, such as the two principles of justice, which are not necessary for a coherent theory of militant democracy. On the timing of intervention Rawls' views are largely the same as Popper's. There is a right to act against the intolerant. At the same time, Rawls indicates that it would be unreasonable to intervene in the absence of a substantial threat to the constitution. Rawls' formulation suggests later intervention than Popper's.

We have also discussed two recent attempts to come to a more detailed militant democracy theory. *Alexander Kirshner* builds his theory on a right to participate. Everyone has that right, even *before* there is a constitution, giving the theory a flavour of natural law that is not explicitly worked out but is assumed as a starting point. This weakness is compensated by two other regulatory principles that Kirshner distils from this right to participation: the principle of limited intervention and democratic responsibility. These are principles for regulating the application of the party ban. Limited intervention means that intervention against antidemocrats is only allowed if they (threaten to) violate the democratic right of others to participate. For example, a party proposes depriving part of the electorate of their right to vote. If participation rights are not at issue, antidemocrats must be tolerated, however disruptive, annoying or provocative they may be for the functioning of the democracy; democracy cannot, Kirshner stresses, be perfected by excluding antidemocrats. Democratic responsibility means that every intervention, even if it fulfils the principle of limited intervention, must still take into account 'democratic costs'. Prohibiting parties entails a cost in a democratic sense. For instance, it might turn out that a measure has been unfairly applied, but even if the application is just, it can damage democracy: the other *legitimate* interests represented by a banned party must find their political expression elsewhere. Democratic responsibility therefore calls for moderate and cautious use of bans.

In comparison with Rawls and Popper, Kirshner therefore places a double lock on action against antidemocrats. First, Kirshner is more concrete in his explanation of the moment at which action is acceptable (the participation principle): namely, when the participation of others is endangered and there is a threat of violation of their democratic rights. That is more precise than the 'threat of intolerance' (Popper) or the need to 'preserve the constitution' (Rawls). It is, however, a limitation based on Kirshner's contestable justification for intervention, namely, the right to democratic participation. Second, Kirshner also builds in a 'conscience test' for democrats (the democratic responsibility principle): intervention *always* comes at a cost in a democratic sense, so overly hasty action must always be prevented. We will return to the democratic conscience test later on, in conjunction with the theory of democracy as self-correction. Finally, Kirshner's theory points in the direction of a little observed feature of militant democracy. It might well be that this system forms a better safeguard than judicial review against laws that violate fundamental human rights. After all, if all goes well, antidemocratic parties who represent a danger never enter parliament at all, whereas in states in which it falls to judges to block the impure products of a (partially) antidemocratic legislator, they can be side-lined without much difficulty. Kirshner's example of South Africa shows this. Do we really believe that judicial review could have prevented Hitler from seizing power in Germany? That he would have gone along with the verdict that his Enabling Act was unconstitutional? Would that not mean that intervening much earlier is needed, so that antidemocrats could never have used the parliament as a springboard in the first place? There is much to be said for that. As Kirshner states:

> It would require a theological confidence in legal institutions to believe that once these antidemocrats are in a position to pass legislation that they will be deterred from their goals by a phalanx of robed lawyers.[388]

And then we are still assuming that the lawyers really would speak out against the new regime.[389]

Svetlana Tyulkina's work contains a broad range of interesting observations, not least on the common ground between militant democracy and transitional constitutionalism, counterterrorism and combatting of religious extremism. Militant democracy theory can make good use of these explorations of new terrain, and the same goes for some of her sharp legal observations. At the same time, Tyulkina offers no independent militant democracy theory; that was not the primary aim of her research, which offered a comparative overview of the legal concept of militant democracy. When it comes to the justification of militant democracy, we find no new insights in her work.

We then arrive at the points of criticism of militant democracy. One of the most important objections to the idea of militant democracy is a pragmatic one: party bans do not work or are counterproductive. That sounds plausible, but it turns out that this objection does not entirely stand up to scrutiny. Party bans are not ineffective *per se*, as is regularly assumed. Political science research shows that repression weakens the organization of extremists and can lead to moderation. Whether the antidemocrats are on the extreme left or right wing or are religiously inspired, it is wise for democracies to take action if the threat becomes serious. A complementary inclusive approach is, however, recommended. That means banning the party but offering the members the option of re-introduction into society. In addition to an inclusive approach of this kind, if a party is banned the issues it raised must not be excluded from discussion (and thus *de facto* banned). Otherwise the public debate is unnecessarily delayed, sometimes causing further damage. It also allows extremists to maintain, as Front National founder Jean-Marie Le Pen once claimed, that they are 'saying out loud what people are quietly thinking'.[390]

If it turns out that party bans work, that in itself is still not a compelling reason to implement one. Principled objections might be so weighty that a potentially effective method is rejected all the same. The most important of these objections have been discussed here. In the next chapter I elaborate on democracy as self-correction to formulate a fully-fledged militant democracy theory. The principled criticism will then be summarized point by point, so that we can test democracy as self-correction against it.

Notes

1. Müller 2012, p. 536.
2. Donald P. Kommers, 'The Jurisprudence of Free Speech in the United States and the Federal Republic of Germany', *Southern California Law Review* 1980, p. 657–695 (680); Müller 2012, p. 536.
3. Kommers 1980, p. 674.
4. Müller 2012, p. 536.
5. Klamt 2007, p. 154–155; Müller 2012, p. 536.
6. Müller 2012, p. 536.
7. Fox and Nolte 1995, p. 37, and Müller 2013b, p. 1263; see also the comprehensive overview in Bourne *forthcoming* 2018.
8. See Müller 2012, p. 536–537; Bligh 2013, p. 1326–1327; and Rosenblum 2007, p. 18, note 2.
9. Müller points to 'related discussions, on tolerance and state neutrality'. See Müller 2012, p. 537.

10. Popper's stance developed over time, from a social democrat in his youth to a liberal 'in the classic sense of the word'; see Bryan Magee, *Popper*, London: Woburn Press 1974, p. 83–84.
11. See, with respect to the Netherlands: Dirk Verhofstadt, *De Liberale Canon: Grondslagen van het liberalisme* (The liberal canon: foundations of liberalism), Antwerp: Uitgeverij Houtekiet 2015, p. 122–124; G.A. van der List, 'Karl Popper', p. 59–71, in P.B. Cliteur and G.A. van der List (eds.), *Filosofen van het hedendaags liberalisme* (Philosophers of contemporary liberalism), Kampen: Kok Agora 1990.
12. See, among others, Tyulkina 2015, p. 14; Molier 2014, note 2; Bligh 2013, p. 1329; Stefan Rummens and Koen Abts, 'Politiek extremisme en de weerbaarheid van de democratie' ('Political extremism and the militancy of democracy'), *Ethische Perspectieven* 2008, vol. 18 no. 4, p. 512–536 (512); Konrad Lachmayer and Gerhard Thallinger, 'Conference Report—Widening the Scope: Reflections on the Human Rights Law Session of the XVth Academy of European Law', *German Law Journal* 2004, vol. 5 no. 9, p. 1155–1169 (1164–1165); Thienel 2008, p. 65 and 69; Ami Pedahzur, *The Israeli Response to Jewish Extremism and Violence: Defending Democracy*, Manchester: Manchester University Press 2002, p. 2; Raphael Cohen-Almagor, 'Disqualification of Lists in Israel (1948-1984): Retrospect and Appraisal', *Law and Philosophy* 1994, vol. 13, p. 43–95 (54–55); J.C.P.M. Vis, *Politiek en democratie: een inleiding* (Politics and democracy: an introduction), Groningen: Wolters-Noordhoff 1988, p. 83.
13. See Popper 2013, p. 581–582 (note 4, chapter 7, part 1). I also follow this interpretation in Rijpkema 2012.
14. Popper 2013, p. 581–582.
15. See also Bryan Magee, *Popper*, London: Woburn Press, 1974, p. 74–78 and 83.
16. Popper 2013, p. xlii; nonetheless, Popper appears to make conflicting statements about it elsewhere. See John Gray, 'The Liberalism of Karl Popper', *Government and Opposition* 1976, vol. 11 no. 3, 337–355 (341).
17. Alan Ryan, 'Introduction', p. ix–xxii (xviii–xix), in Popper 2013. See also Magee 1974, p. 77–78, and John Gray, 'The Liberalism of Karl Popper', *Government and Opposition* 1976, vol. 11 no. 3, 337–355 (347–348).
18. Popper 2013, p. xliv.
19. Popper 2013, p. 153. See also Karl Popper, *Conjectures and Refutations*, New York: Routledge 2002 (henceforth Popper 2002a), p. 473: 'Principles of Liberalism may be described (at least today) as principles of assessing, and if necessary of modifying or changing, existing institutions, rather than of replacing existing institutions.'
20. That is not to say, though (as some of his critics suggest), that Popper was a technocrat; he did not support government by a scientific elite or by experts; see Alan Ryan, 'Introduction', p. ix–xxii, in Popper 2013, p. xviii.
21. Bhikhu Parekh, *Contemporary Political Thinkers*, Oxford: Martin Robertson 1982, p. 143. See also Van der List 1990, p. 65.
22. Parekh 1982, p. 143.
23. That becomes even clearer in the interpretation of Magee; see Magee 1974, p. 77–78.
24. Karl Popper, 'On Toleration', p. 314–328 (318), in Jeremy Shearmur and Piers Norris Turner (eds.), *After the Open Society: Selected Social and Political Writings*, London/New York: Routledge 2008 (henceforth Popper 2008a). See also Popper 2013, p. 120 (with a focus on improvement of the institutions themselves).
25. Van den Bergh 1936a, p. 9.
26. Magee 1974, p. 74–75.

27. Magee 1974, p. 75; Van der List 1990, p. 65.
28. Magee 1974, p. 75.
29. Magee 1974, p. 75–76 and 77.
30. See also Gray 1976, p. 349, and Van der List 1990, p. 64.
31. Magee 1974, p. 78.
32. Magee 1974, p. 78.
33. Magee 1974, p. 78.
34. Parekh 1982, p. 142.
35. Parekh 1982, p. 142–143. See also p. 149–153 for his criticism of Popper, who in his view pays too little attention to the 'nature and structure of political life'. Blinded by his rationalism, Popper, for example, pays no attention to 'diversity of values', the inherent disorder and unrest in the political arena (in contrast, for instance, with an academic conference), the point that 'rationality cannot be defined in "objective" and abstract terms' and, finally, the difference between 'theoretical problems' and 'political problems'. Parekh sums up the problem incisively as follows: 'He sees a society as if it were a community of scientists, the newspapers as if they were scientific periodicals, the sessions of a legislative assembly as if they were scientific congresses and the government as if it were engaged in conducting political experiments designed to falsify political proposals.' This interpretation strikes me as unfair and exaggerated. First, it unfairly places Popper among the technocrats (see also Ryan 2013, p. xviii). Moreover, Popper's science analogy also offers a vision of how democracy functions in optimal circumstances. He would not deny that those circumstances are rarely achieved (as witnessed by his scepticism regarding 'public opinion'), but the unique aspect of democracy is that it strives for that ideal and, yes, sometimes succeeds in realizing it in part. Parekh's criticism is reminiscent of those who use what might be termed the 'sociological theory' of Thomas Kuhn to argue against Popper, to show that his notion of science is incorrect. Here again it is assumed that Popper is describing reality, when he is merely demonstrating the ideal. On this criticism see also Van der List 1990, p. 69–70.
36. Of course, it could be seen as a sliding scale; in the end tyranny is nothing other than government by rulers *extremely* disinclined to self-reflection.
37. Popper 2013, p. 118.
38. Popper 2013, p. 118. Of course, one could interpret Popper's concept of tyranny more along the lines of self-correction, for example, by claiming that tyranny really means the absence of self-correction. This, however, would involve some stretch of interpretation: Popper does not state explicitly that this is the essence of tyranny, nor does he state a connection between his scientific explanation of democracy (which comes close to self-correction) and the ability to remove a government.
39. Popper 2013, p. 119.
40. See also Bligh 2013, p. 1329, and Thienel 2008, p. 65.
41. Bligh 2013, p. 1329. See Popper 2013, p. 368.
42. Karl Popper, 'On Democracy', p. 360–369 (364), in Shearmur and Turner 2008 (henceforth Popper 2008b); see also Popper 2013, p. 118.
43. Popper 2008b, p. 362.
44. See Karl Popper, 'The Open Society and the Democratic State', p. 231–248 (243), in Shearmur and Turner 2008 (henceforth Popper 2008c). See also Popper 2008b, p. 363.
45. Popper 2013, p. 119.
46. Popper 2008c, p. 240.
47. Popper 2008c, p. 240.

48. Popper 2008c, p. 240.
49. That is also clear from what Popper writes in 'On Democracy': 'When we say that the best solution known to us is a constitution that allows a majority vote to dismiss the government, then we do not say that the majority vote will always be right. We do not even say that it will usually be right.' See Popper 2008b, p. 364. In *The Open Society* too: 'He who accepts the principle of democracy … is … not bound to look upon the result of a democratic vote as an authoritative expression of what is right' (Popper 2013, p. 119). See also the interpretations in Magee 1974, p. 78–79, and Parekh 1982, p. 143, which link this with 'intolerance of the intolerant'.
50. See Popper 2013, p. 119: 'Although he will accept a decision of the majority, for the sake of making the democratic institutions work, he will feel free to combat it by democratic means, and to work for its revision. And should he live to see the day when the majority vote destroys the democratic institutions, then this sad experience will tell him only that there does not exist a foolproof method of avoiding tyranny.' The same applies to *Conjectures and Refutations*; see Popper 2002a, p. 472: 'We are democrats, not because the majority is always right, but because democratic traditions are the least evil ones of which we know. If the majority (or "public opinion") decides in favour of tyranny, a democrat need not therefore suppose that some fatal inconsistency in his views has been revealed. He will realize, rather, that the democratic tradition in his country was not strong enough.' This interpretation also appears to be followed by Robinson; see Richard Robinson, 'Dr. Popper's Defense of Democracy', *Philosophical Review* 1951, vol. 60 no. 4, p. 487–507 (506). For a different interpretation, see Magee 1974, p. 82–83.
51. In an essay on tolerance; see Popper 2008a, p. 315: 'To the question whether such a party [a party that secretly or openly strives for the end of democracy, BR] has a right to claim that it should be tolerated, the theories of democracy and of tolerance give, I believe, a clear answer. The answer is: no. We need not to tolerate even the threat of intolerance; and we must not tolerate it if the threat is getting serious.'
52. Popper 2008c, p. 242: 'The use of the one term "Democracy" for both a certain form of government and for certain social values and forms of social life, had led to a confusion, roughly speaking of means and ends—of political means and social and individual ends. As a consequence, necessarily imperfect political means are defended and extolled as if they were ends in themselves. But the truth is that all forms of government are imperfect, and even dangerous, and that democracy is no exception.' One might suggest that Popper sees himself, as a liberal, as necessarily sceptical with respect to any form of concentration of power; compare, for example, his remarks on public opinion in Popper 2002a, p. 470: 'Public opinion (whatever it may be) is very powerful. It may change governments, even non-democratic governments. Liberals ought to regard any such power with some degree of suspicion.'
53. Popper 2008c, p. 243–244; Popper 2002a, p. 472; and Popper 2013, p. 120.
54. See, for example, Tyulkina 2015, p. 14, and Bligh 2013, p. 1329, in which the 'open society' and 'democracy' are seen as interchangeable.
55. Popper 2008a, p. 315.
56. Magee 1974, p. 87.
57. See Robinson 1951, p. 488.
58. See Robinson 1951, p. 487.
59. See Magee 1974, p. 15 and 87.
60. Gray 1976, p. 338.
61. See Fox and Nolte 1995, p. 18–20.

62. Papier and Durner 2003, p. 345.
63. Schmitt 2008, p. 79–80; see also Papier and Durner 2003, p. 345.
64. Schmitt 2008, p. 128; for the connection with Schmitt's *Diktatur* from 1921, see De Wilde 2008, p. 95–96, and Ellian 2009, p. 202–204.
65. Carl Schmitt, *Legality and Legitimacy* (*Legalität und Legitimität*, 1932), Durham and London: Duke University Press 2004, among others, p. 58–60; see Fox and Nolte 1995, p. 19, Müller 2013b, p. 1257, Klamt 2012, p. 28–29; see also recently Invernizzi Accetti and Zuckerman 2017, p. 185.
66. Fox and Nolte 1995, p. 19.
67. Fox and Nolte 1995, p. 19; Papier and Durner 2003, p. 345. The notion of militant democracy developed by Gelijn Molier with respect to freedom of expression also goes back to this distinction; see Gelijn Molier, 'De vrijheid van meningsuiting: "it's politics all the way down"' ('Freedom of expression: "it's politics all the way down"'), p. 205–242 (239–240), in Afshin Ellian, Gelijn Molier and Tom Zwart (eds.), *Mag ik dit zeggen? Beschouwingen over de vrijheid van meningsuiting* (May I say this? Views on freedom of expression), The Hague: Boom Juridische Uitgevers 2011.
68. Schmitt 2004, p. 93.
69. See also David Dyzenhaus, 'Legal Theory in the Collapse of Weimar: Contemporary Lessons?', *American Political Science Review* 1997, vol. 91 no. 1, p. 121–134 (125), and Müller 2013b, p. 1257.
70. Schmitt 2004, p. 30.
71. Schmitt 2004, p. 46–47 and 93–94.
72. Schmitt 2004, p. 94. See also John McCormick, 'Identifying or Exploiting the Paradoxes of Constitutional Democracy? An Introduction to Carl Schmitt's Legality and Legitimacy', p. xiii–xlii (xxxi), in Schmitt 2004.
73. Schmitt 2004, p. 46; see also p. 27.
74. Schmitt 2004, p. 94.
75. Schmitt 2004, p. 94, and Ellian 2009, p. 208.
76. Bendersky 2014, p. 81.
77. Bendersky 2014, p. 81.
78. Bendersky 2014, p. 81. See also De Wilde 2008, p. 92–93 and 108, and Ellian 2009, p. 207.
79. Bendersky 2014, p. 81–82, and John McCormick, *Carl Schmitt's Critique of Liberalism: Against Politics as Technology*, Cambridge: Cambridge University Press 1997, p. 266.
80. Bendersky 2014, p. 82 and 80.
81. De Wilde 2008, p. 93.
82. Bendersky 2014, p. 82. Von Papen was really Hindenburg's first choice, but he felt compelled to choose Hitler on the basis of the election result of 6 November 1932, in which the NSDAP might have sustained a loss but remained the largest party in the Reichstag; see De Wilde 2008, p. 93 and note 4.
83. De Wilde 2008, p. 95–96; see also Fox and Nolte 1995, p. 20.
84. Dyzenhaus 1997, p. 125; see also Invernizzi Accetti and Zuckerman 2017, p. 186.
85. Oakes 1986, p. x.
86. See De Wilde 2008, p. 97–98; Schmitt's antisemitism, however, was in no way opportunistic, but rather a constant in his thinking: p. 112–114.
87. See McCormick 1997, p. 266–267.
88. Oakes 1986, p. xi, and McCormick 1997, p. 267.
89. Fox and Nolte 1995, p. 20.
90. Article 79 paragraph 3 of the Grundgesetz reads, 'Eine Änderung dieses Grundgesetzes, durch welche die Gliederung des Bundes in Länder, die

grundsätzliche Mitwirkung der Länder bei der Gesetzgebung oder die in den Artikeln 1 und 20 niedergelegten Grundsätze berührt werden, ist unzulässig.'

91. See Fox and Nolte 1995, p. 17, Klamt 2012, p. 29; see also Papier and Durner 2003, p. 345.
92. See Yaniv Rosnai, 'Unconstitutional Constitutional Amendments—The Migration and Success of a Constitutional Idea', *American Journal of Comparative Law* 2013, vol. 61, p. 657–719 (674–674 and 715).
93. It remains questionable whether that is true. One might easily place an unchanging core or 'eternity clause' alongside banning parties as two of the different defence mechanisms a government can employ, based on justification from one theory of militant democracy. Both mechanisms, after all, require a comparable justification, as acts (banning parties, making regulations unalterable) that at first sight appear highly undemocratic. *Which* mechanism is subsequently chosen is a question of confidence. Is an unchanging core sufficient when antidemocratic parties are on the point of tinkering with the constitution? Or does one have to ensure that they never reach that position (see chapter 3, point 6 under 'Criticism of militant democracy answered')?
94. Schmitt 2004, p. 96.
95. See Fox and Nolte 1995, p. 19, and Müller 2013b, p. 1261; see also McCormick 2004, p. 140 (note 1 in chapter 3). This regularly occurred with ideas that could in some way be linked with the traumatic Weimar period, even from less controversial thinkers; see Greenberg 2014, p. 16.
96. See, for example, Fox and Nolte 1995, p. 16–17; Bligh 2013, p. 1328–1329; Tyulkina 2015, p. 33; and François Ost, 'De sfinx aan de stadspoorten: enkele vragen om een debat te openen over anti-democratische partijen' ('The sphinx at the city gates: a few questions to open up the debate on antidemocratic parties'), p. 179–191 (183), in Adams and Popelier 2004.
97. J.S. Mill, 'On Liberty', p. 41–132 (121), in Alan Ryan (ed.), *Mill: Norton Critical Edition*, New York/London: W.W. Norton and Company, 1997.
98. See Bligh 2013, p. 1328.
99. Alan Ryan, *On Politics: A History of Political Thought from Herodotus to the Present*, London: Penguin 2012, p. 972 (henceforth Ryan 2012a); John Rawls, *A Theory of Justice*, Cambridge (M.A.): Harvard University Press 1999.
100. Thomas Mertens, *Mens and Mensenrechten: basisboek rechtsfilosofie* (Humans and human rights: a handbook of legal philosophy), Amsterdam: Boom 2012, p. 241.
101. See Leif Wenar, 'Rawls', p. 393–411 (396), in David Estlund (ed.), *The Oxford Handbook of Political Philosophy*, Oxford: Oxford University Press 2012; Ronald Tinnevelt, 'Rawls over de rechtvaardigheid van samenleving en wereld' ('Rawls on the justice of society and the world'), p. 449–477 (457), in Marin Terpstra (ed.), *Onenigheid en Gemeenschap: basisboek politieke filosofie* (Discord and society: a handbook of political philosophy), Amsterdam: Boom 2012; and Alan Ryan, *The Making of Modern Liberalism*, Princeton: Princeton University Press 2012, p. 506 (henceforth Ryan 2012b).
102. Wenar 2012, p. 397.
103. Rawls 1999, p. 119.
104. Rawls 1999, p. 118.
105. Tinnevelt 2012, p. 457.
106. R.A.V. van Haersolte, 'John Rawls', p. 209–228 (214), in P.B. Cliteur and M.A. Loth (eds.), *Rechtsfilosofen van de twintigste eeuw* (Legal philosophers of the twentieth century), Arnhem: Gouda Quint 1992.
107. Rawls 1999, p. 266. See also Tinnevelt 2012, p. 457–458, and Mertens 2012, p. 243.

108. Ryan 2012b, p. 512.
109. See also Mertens 2012, p. 243–244.
110. See Tinnevelt 2012, p. 258.
111. See Van Haersolte 1992, p. 217–218, and Mertens 2012, p. 243–244.
112. See Tinnevelt 2012, p. 458.
113. The flipside of the 'difference principle' could be called the 'envy principle', as Richard Epstein writes: 'the envy principle, ... holds that I am worse off solely because you have become better off'; see Richard Epstein, 'Forget the Envy-Principle', *Forbes* (online), 19 January 2010.
114. Rawls 1999, p. 132, 214–220 and 266; this priority entails realization of the first principle of equality of liberty before another principle (such as the second) can be thought of (see p. 214). See also Mertens 2012, p. 244.
115. Ryan 2012b, p. 512.
116. Mertens 2012, p. 245.
117. Mertens 2012, p. 244.
118. See, for example, Fox and Nolte 1995, p. 17–18; Bligh 2013, p. 1329–1330; Markus Thiel, 'Comparative Aspects', p. 380–424 (381), in Thiel 2009 (henceforth Thiel 2009b); and Issacharoff 2007, p. 1407–1411.
119. Rawls 1999, p. 188.
120. Rawls 1999, p. 190. Rawls also discusses a third question: if you have the right not to tolerate the intolerant, to what ends are you allowed to exercise that right? See also Fox and Nolte 1995, p. 17.
121. Rawls 1999, p. 190.
122. Rawls 1999, p. 191.
123. Rawls 1999, p. 192.
124. See also Fox and Nolte 1995, p. 18.
125. Rawls 1999, p. 192.
126. Rawls 1999, p. 192.
127. Rawls 1999, p. 193. See also Fox and Nolte 1995, p. 18.
128. Fox and Nolte 1995, p. 18.
129. Kirshner 2014, p. 3.
130. See Kirshner 2014, p. 27–28, 59 and 166.
131. Kirshner 2014, p. 27.
132. Kirshner 2014, p. 33.
133. Kirshner 2014, p. 46.
134. Kirshner 2014, p. 47.
135. Kirshner 2014, p. 47.
136. Kirshner 2014, p. 27. Compare also Stefan Rummens, 'Deliberation can be rough', p. 269–289 (288), in Afshin Ellian and Gelijn Molier (eds.), *Freedom of Speech under Attack*, The Hague: Eleven Publishing 2015: 'The existence of smaller extremist parties should not in itself be considered a threat to the political system. It is only when these become sufficiently strong to actually have a significant impact on the quality of policies and legislation that the most drastic measures could become appropriate.'
137. Kirshner 2014, p. 27.
138. Kirshner 2014, p. 85.
139. Kirshner 2014, p. 53.
140. Kirshner 2014, p. 28.
141. Kirshner 2014, p. 57.
142. Kirshner 2014, p. 55.
143. Kirshner 2014, p. 55–56.
144. Kirshner 2014, p. 56.
145. Kirshner 2014, p. 55.

146. Kirshner 2014, p. 35.
147. Kirshner 2014, p. 14.
148. Kirshner 2014, p. 12.
149. Kirshner 2014, p. 12. For a different view, see Peter Macklem, 'Militant democracy, legal pluralism, and the paradox of self-determination', *International Journal of Constitutional Law* 2006, vol. 4 no. 3, p. 488–516 (514). Macklem argues that antidemocratic parties should be allowed to come to power: 'The task of democratic institutions is to restrain the government of the day from acting in an unconstitutional manner.' Otherwise the restriction on rights is too far-reaching: 'Until it becomes policy, however, a radical political agenda—whether advanced by an individual or a political party—represents freedom of expression and association in action.' And: 'Political agendas should be scrutinized not ex ante but as close to the threshold between proposal and policy as possible.'
150. See also Kirshner 2014, p. 14.
151. Etzioni 2007.
152. Kirshner 2014, p. 28.
153. See also recently: Anthoula Malkopoulou, 'The Self-Limiting Theory of Militant Democracy' (review of Kirshner, *Militant Democracy*), *Rediscriptions* 2016, vol. 19 no. 1, p. 108–112 (111).
154. Kirshner 2014, p. 46.
155. Kirshner 2014, p. 47.
156. Kirshner 2014, p. 41.
157. See, for example, Kirshner 2014, p. 7–9 and 28–33.
158. The consequence is that in this approach the democracy must be present in the first place; in other words, before there is democracy, in Van den Bergh's view, at least in my interpretation, one does not *necessarily* have a 'right to democracy'; it does not necessarily legitimize a 'democratic revolution'. See also chapter 1, under 'Markovitch and the law of reaction'.
159. Tyulkina 2015, p. 1.
160. See Tyulkina 2015, p. 65–70 (Germany), p. 70–74 and 144–160 (Australia), p. 95–104 and 189–202 (ECHR), p. 110–115 (India), p. 110–119 (Israel), p. 125–139 (Spain) and p. 169–184 (Turkey).
161. Thiel 2009.
162. Tyulkina 2015, p. 110 and 114.
163. Tyulkina 2015, p. 119.
164. Tyulkina 2015, p. 125–139 (Spain) and p. 169–184 (Turkey).
165. See, for example, Tyulkina 2015, p. 219–220.
166. Tyulkina 2015, p. 21.
167. Tyulkina 2015, p. 48–51.
168. Tyulkina 2015, p. 51–54; see also Fox and Nolte 1995, p. 63–65 ('The duty not to abolish democratic rule does not necessarily entail a complementary duty to adopt self-protective measures. The Political Covenant, in language echoed by all other human rights treaties, requires state parties "to adopt such legislative or other measures *as may be necessary* to give effect" to this and other enumerated rights. This rule describes states' obligations at a very general level: if, in order to ensure the continuation of democratic rule, it is *necessary* to adopt measures of self-protection, then they must be adopted'; see p. 64). Rudolf Thienel is more resolute: on the basis of both the European Convention on Human Rights and EU law, member states are obliged to defend themselves against radical movements seeking the downfall of democracy; see Thienel 2008, p. 66–67; see also Klamt 2012, p. 351, with the nuance that the fundamental *idea* of militant democracy, and with it the defence of

democracy, is a duty based on the Convention and EU law, but that member states are *not* obliged to implement *specific* measures from the repertoire of militant democracy.

169. Tyulkina 2015, p. 13–14 and 34.
170. Tyulkina 2015, p. 34.
171. See the discussion of Sajó in chapter 1.
172. Tyulkina 2015, p. 112–113, and Issacharoff 2007, p. 1423–1429.
173. Tyulkina 2015, p. 112, and Issacharoff 2007, p. 1423.
174. Issacharoff 2007, p. 1424.
175. Issacharoff 2007, p. 1424
176. Issacharoff 2007, p. 1424.
177. Tyulkina 2015, p. 34.
178. Tyulkina 2015, p. 207; see also p. 34: 'Therefore, the argument that the concept of militant democracy as introduced by Loewenstein is irrelevant to our present context is inaccurate to say the least.'
179. Tyulkina 2015, p. 32. She indicates elsewhere that for her it is more a matter of giving an overview of a number of justifications in order to demonstrate that militant democracy is not just an 'isolated, old-fashioned, abstract idea from post-war Europe'; see p. 20–21.
180. Tyulkina 2015, p. 32, and worded differently on p. 27, and again on p. 209.
181. Tyulkina 2015, p. 32 and 27.
182. Tyulkina 2015, p. 32–33. See also p. 17–18, where Popper is remarkably introduced as a 'legal scholar'. John Stuart Mill is also briefly mentioned, p. 33 and note 40.
183. Tyulkina 2015, p. 38.
184. Tyulkina 2015, p. 217.
185. Tyulkina 2015, p. 15.
186. Tyulkina 2015, p. 35.
187. Tyulkina 2015, p. 157.
188. Tyulkina 2015, p. 157 and 217–218.
189. Tyulkina 2015, p. 158.
190. Tyulkina 2015, p. 217.
191. Tyulkina 2015, p. 217.
192. That is probably the case if one considers the distinction between 'legal' and 'illegal' power takeovers important, that is, non-violent and violent takeovers, as Van den Bergh puts it; in the same sense, see Vis 1988, p. 85. For comparable criticism (*contra* Sajó), in the context of the EU, see Klamt 2012, p. 391–392.
193. Sabrina Engelmann, 'Barking Up the Wrong Tree: Why Counterterrorism Cannot Be a Defense of Democracy', *Democracy and Security* 2012, vol. 8, p. 164–174 (171 and 172).
194. Engelmann 2012, p. 167. Engelmann gives another four arguments, some more convincing than others, for maintaining a separation between the concepts: terrorism has no *substantial* effect on democracy (p. 167–168, with an answer to the expected objections on p. 170), there is confusion as to the definition of democracy (p. 168), non-democratic states use the same counterterrorism legislation as democratic states (p. 168), and counterterrorism might protect the state but is in itself a threat to democracy (p. 168–169).
195. Engelmann 2012, p. 167.
196. Engelmann 2012, p. 167.
197. Engelmann 2012, p. 167.
198. Engelmann 2012, p. 170–171. Engelmann does not develop this so concretely.
199. Engelmann 2012, p. 171.
200. Tyulkina 2015, p. 217, see also Klamt 2012, p. 391–392.

201. See Michael G. Young, 'Kent Roach. The 9/11 Effect: Comparative Counter-Terrorism', *Terrorism and Political Violence* 2013, vol. 25 no. 5, p. 852–854 (853): 'This is not to say that the US was the only state to trample on human rights; certainly the UK, Australia, and Canada have crossed the line of legality on many occasions. Extraditions that resulted in torture (e.g., Omar Khadr in Canada), confessions taken without consent (e.g., Hicks in Pakistan/Australia), imprisonment without trial in the UK, and the practice of listing terror suspects without public evidence have all been carried out under the guise of national security, but in secret. Clearly, the apparent sanction of inhumane and illegal treatment of terror suspects continues to be commonplace under a militant democratic model emerging from the war on terror.'
202. Tyulkina 2015, p. 217.
203. Tyulkina 2015, p. 218.
204. Tyulkina 2015, p. 183.
205. Tyulkina 2015, p. 183.
206. Tyulkina 2015, p. 181.
207. Tyulkina 2015, p. 181–182 and 218–219. Tyulkina comes to a harsh judgement on Turkey (see p. 183). For a comparable view, see Andrew Maloney, 'Democracy, Political Parties and the Will of the People', p. 53–67 (63–64), in Claudio Michelon, Gregor Clunie, Christopher McCorkindale and Harris Psarras, *The Public in Law: Representations of the Political in Legal Discourse*, Farnham: Ashgate 2012. In contrast, Issacharoff is very positive; see Issacharoff 2007, p. 1446: 'Far from creating an insuperable barrier to an Islamic voice in Turkish politics, the dissolution of the Welfare Party appears to have sparked a realignment in which committed democratic voices from the self-proclaimed Islamic communities found a means of integration into mainstream Turkish political life.'
208. Tyulkina 2015, p. 115.
209. Tyulkina 2015, p. 118.
210. Tyulkina 2015, p. 31, 209 and 213; for other examples, see p. 119, 206 and 208.
211. Tyulkina 2015, p. 28–29.
212. Tyulkina 2015, p. 35.
213. Tyulkina 2015, p. 212.
214. Largely contributing descriptive (rather than normative) work. See also Capoccia 2013, p. 216: 'A significant portion of the recent work on the institutions and policies of militant democracy is of a descriptive nature.'
215. Müller 2012, p. 537
216. Müller 2012, p. 536–537. For Spain, see also Pfersmann 2004, p. 50.
217. *Kamerstukken II* (Dutch Parliamentary Papers II) 2014/2015, 29 279, 226, p. 14 (Letter from the ministers of the Interior and Kingdom Relations and of Social Affairs and Employment) (henceforth *Notitie antidemocratische groeperingen* [Memorandum on antidemocratic factions]).
218. *Kamerstukken II* (Dutch Parliamentary Papers II) 2014/2015, 29 279, 243, p. 6–7: 'I do not think you can prevent the ideas of the two clubs [Vereniging Martijn and Hizb ut-Tahrir, BR] from circulating by prohibiting those clubs. You do not solve it with a complete ban. I think that is precisely the way to ensure that movements go underground, perhaps substantially exacerbating the situation. We must ensure that we enter into debate. That is much better.'
219. *Kamerstukken II* (Dutch Parliamentary Papers II) 2014/2015, 29 279, 243, p. 29.
220. Giovanni Capoccia reaches the same conclusion in a recent overview; see Capoccia 2013, p. 215–216: 'Under what conditions are militant rules likely to be politically viable—that is, formally enacted and then applied

against extremists? ... As a field, comparative political science is not close to providing satisfactory answers to these questions.'

221. See, for example, Basedau and Moroff 2011, p. 209.
222. See, for instance, *in general*, on the important differences in context within seemingly comparable post-communist countries: Shlomo Avineri, 'On Problems of Transition in Postcommunist Societies', *Cardozo Law Review* 1997-1998, vol. 19, p. 1921–1936 (1921–1922).
223. See Giovanni Capoccia, 'Defending Democracy: Reactions to Political Extremism in Inter-war Europe', *European Journal of Political Research* 2001, vol. 39, p. 431–460 (452).
224. Bogaards, Basedau and Hartmann 2010, p. 611.
225. See Capoccia 2013, p. 216: 'In recent years, not unlike the recent resurgence of interest in militant democracy among comparative constitutional lawyers and theorists, the attention of political scientists has been drawn to the topic, and a comparative research agenda is beginning to emerge.'
226. See Elzinga 1982, p. 114, and Bellekom 1982, p. 117. For an overview of Germany's repressive repertoire, see Michael Minkenberg, 'Repression and Reaction: Militant Democracy and the Radical Right in Germany and France', *Patterns of Prejudice* 2006, vol. 40 no. 1, p. 25–44 (36–39).
227. The following reasons are derived from Rummens and Abts 2008, p. 528–529; see also 531.
228. Ronald J. Krotoszynski, Jr., 'A Comparative Perspective on the First Amendment: Free Speech, Militant Democracy, and the Primacy of Dignity as a Preferred Constitutional Value in Germany', *Tulane Law Review* 2003-2004, vol. 87, p. 1549–1609 (1599).
229. The following description is based on Miroslav Mareš, 'Czech Militant Democracy in Action. Dissolution of the Workers' Party and the Wider Context of This Act', *East European Politics and Societies* 2012, vol. 26 no. 1, p. 33–55 (37–38) (henceforth Mareš 2012a). See also Miroslav Mareš, 'Right-Wing Extremism in the Czech Republic', *Friedrich Ebert Stiftung*, September 2012, p. 3 (henceforth Mareš 2012b).
230. Mareš 2012a, p. 38; 'Anti-Minority Violence: Czech Police Stop Rioters from Attacking Roma Camp', *Der Spiegel* (online), 18 November 2008.
231. 'Anti-Minority Violence: Czech Police Stop Rioters from Attacking Roma Camp'.
232. 'Anti-Minority Violence: Czech Police Stop Rioters from Attacking Roma Camp'.
233. 'Anti-Minority Violence: Czech Police Stop Rioters from Attacking Roma Camp'.
234. Mareš 2012a, p. 38.
235. For this short history see Mareš 2012a, p. 38, and F. Casal Bertoa and I. van Biezen, 'Party Regulation and Party Politics in Post-communist Europe', *East European Politics* 2014, vol. 30 no. 3, 295–314 (300).
236. Mareš 2012a, p. 38; Mareš 2012b, p. 3.
237. Mareš 2012a, p. 42.
238. Mareš 2012a, p. 43.
239. Mareš 2012a, p. 44.
240. Mareš 2012a, p. 44.
241. Mareš 2012a, p. 45.
242. Mareš 2012a, p. 45.
243. Mareš 2012a, p. 45.
244. Mareš 2012a, p. 45.
245. Mareš 2012a, p. 45–46.

246. For Germany and France, see Minkenberg 2006, p. 41. For Turkey, see Tim Bale, 'Are Bans on Political Parties Bound to Turn Out Badly?', *Comparative European Politics* 2007, no. 5, p. 141–157 (146). For Belgium, see Bale 2007, p. 152–153. See also recently on Slovakia: Miroslav Mareš, 'How Does Militant Democracy Function in Combating Right-Wing Extremism? A Case Study of Slovakian Militant Democracy and the Rise of *Kotleba—People's Party Our Slovakia*', in Ellian and Rijpkema *forthcoming* 2018. In the case of Germany, on the other hand, one can point to the effective bans from the 1950s; see Elzinga 1982, p. 146, note 83.
247. Minkenberg 2006, p. 41.
248. Minkenberg 2006, p. 41; Rummens and Abts 2008, p. 533; see also Elzinga 1982, p. 146.
249. Froukje Demant, Marieke Slootman, Frank Buijs and Jean Tillie, *Teruggang en uittreding: processen van deradicalisering ontleed* (Decline and withdrawal: processes of deradicalization analysed, report commissioned by the Netherlands National Coordinator for Counterterrorism), Amsterdam: The Institute for Migration and Ethnic Studies (IMES) 2008, p. 59.
250. Minkenberg 2006, p. 41. See also Rensmann 2003, p. 1133–1134.
251. See Ost 2004, 188–189 (Belgium), and Tyulkina 2015, p. 136 (Spain).
252. Mareš 2012a, p. 45. This might also call to mind the violence that broke out in 1991 when the army intervened in the threatened election victory of the radical Islamic group, the Front Islamique du Salut, in Algeria, which introduced a long, violent civil war (Issacharoff 2007, p. 1450–1451, note 197). However, it is not a good example of militant democracy (in the proper sense), as Issacharoff writes (see p. 1450–1451). See also Klamt 2007, p. 153.
253. Bale 2007, p. 141–157.
254. Bale 2007, p. 143. They thus approach the three ideal types developed by Ami Pedahzur: 'militant democracy' (Turkey), 'defending democracy' (Spain), 'immunized democracy' (Belgium); see also p. 143. For criticism of Pedahzur's classification, see Angela. K. Bourne, 'The Proscription of Political Parties and "Militant Democracy"', *Journal of Comparative Law* 2012, vol. 7 no. 1, p. 196–213 (198) (henceforth Bourne 2012b).
255. Bale 2007, p. 143.
256. Bale 2007, p. 145; the third hypothesis is linked with the first: does a party ban not threaten the democratic development already achieved?
257. Bale 2007, p. 145–154. For a legal analysis of the ban on Batasuna, see Victor Ferreres Comella, 'The New Regulation of Political Parties in Spain, and the Decision to Outlaw Batasuna', p. 133–156, in Sajó 2004; see also Ayres 2004.
258. Bale 2007, p. 146. This is confirmed by Turkish lawyer Olgun Akbulut with respect to Refah and its successor, the AK-party (the policy is more liberal and references to Islamic law have disappeared), but it is called into doubt with respect to the Kurdish parties (where support for the PKK appears to have become more open); see Olgun Akbulut, 'Criteria Developed by the European Court of Human Rights on the Dissolution of Political Parties', *Fordham International Law Journal* 2010, vol. 34, p. 46–77 (76). On moderation in the successor to Refah, see also Issacharoff 2007, p. 1446.
259. See also Tim Bale, 'Will It All End in Tears? What Really Happens When Democracies Use Law to Ban Political Parties', p. 195–224 (197–207), in Ingrid van Biezen and Hans-Martien ten Napel (eds.), *Regulating Political Parties: European Democracies in Comparative Perspective*, Leiden: Leiden University Press 2014; the European Commission for Democracy Through Law (Venice Commission), *Turkey: opinion on the amendments to the Constitution adopted by the Grand National Assembly on 21 January 2017 and to be submitted to a*

national referendum on 16 April 2017, 10–11 March 2017 (110th Plenary Session); and, for instance, Robert Fisk, 'The 70,000 Post-coup Arrests Are Now at the Heart of the Turkish Government's Propaganda War', *The Independent* (online), 8 October 2016.

260. For the nuances of this ban, see Eva Brems, 'Belgium: The Vlaams Blok Political Party Convicted Indirectly of Racism', *International Journal of Constitutional Law* 2006, vol. 4 no. 4, p. 702–711.
261. Bale 2007, p. 153.
262. Bale 2007, p. 148 and 151.
263. Bale 2007, p. 151; see also Issacharoff 2007, p. 1432–1433, and on the links between Batasuna and ETA: Ayres 2004, p. 113; Tyulkina 2015, p. 129, 131 and 133; and Akbulut 2010, p. 74.
264. Tyulkina 2015, p. 129.
265. Bale 2007, p. 150.
266. Bale 2007, p. 150.
267. Bale 2007, p. 151.
268. Bale 2007, p. 151–152.
269. Bale 2007, p. 152.
270. Of course, one might argue against Bale that this does not prove all that much; perhaps the positive trend would have occurred anyway and might even have gone faster or better without a party ban. But this introduces additional uncertainty. Bale's reasoning is as follows: in comparison with time t1 (before the ban), at time t2 (after the ban) there was no increase in violence or aversion to democracy. The objection assumes the following: in comparison with t1, at t2 there may have been a development towards reduced violence in any case (uncertainty is introduced) which was curbed by the party ban, making the ban counterproductive after all. The additional uncertainty introduced makes the objection less plausible than Bale's argument. To add to that there is also a methodological point: we can never compare a time t2 with a party ban with a time t2 without a party ban. In other words, the subject of study makes experimental testing impossible. The only option is to collect as much data as possible from situations before and after party bans in democracies that differ as widely as possible; and that is what Bale attempts to do. It is also worth noting that the collection of sufficient data is problematic, due to the subject of study: parties are not banned on a regular basis. Another criticism might be the question of how long a period one should measure the effects for. Does a party ban count as productive if the situation has not worsened in, for example, three, five or ten years? In 2011 Otegi was found guilty of an attempt at reinstating Batasuna. Is that a worsening of the situation? At the same time, Otegi continues to renounce violence: 'Over the past decade, Otegi has been perhaps the most high-profile pro-independence Basque nationalist among those who have refused to condemn ETA. But recently he and many in his movement have publicly rejected violence—although not ETA itself—as the way to achieve Basque independence, saying it must be done peacefully and democratically.' See Daniel Woolls, 'Basque Separatist, Arnaldo Otegi, Convicted of Terrorism in Spain', *The Huffington Post* (online), 16 September 2011.
271. Sam Jones, 'Basque Separatist Group ETA Announces Dissolution', *The Guardian* (online), 2 May 2018.
272. Bale 2007, p. 155; see also Bale 2014, p. 217–218, concluding that, in general, his earlier findings remain valid.
273. Bale 2007, p. 145 and 154–155. See also Issacharoff 2007, p. 1452–1453. When it comes to the banning of the 'former ruling party' in a political transition, see

Peter Niesen, 'Banning the Former Ruling Party', *Constellations* 2012, vol. 19 no. 4, p. 540–561 (557).

274. F.J. Buijs and M. Fennema, 'Democratie, extremisme en radicalisme in Amsterdam' ('Democracy, extremism and radicalism in Amsterdam'), p. 120–147 (139), in Meindert Fennema, *Help! De elite verdwijnt: veertig jaar Nederlandse politiek* (Help! The elite are disappearing: forty years of Dutch politics), Amsterdam: Bert Bakker 2012; previously published as F.J. Buijs and M. Fennema, 'Democratie en extremisme in Amsterdam' ('Democracy and extremism in Amsterdam'), in Irene van Eerd and Bernie Hermes, *Pluriform Amsterdam*, Amsterdam: Vossiuspers 1998.
275. Buijs and Fennema 2012, p. 126: they should be distinguished from the 'radicals', who also criticize democracy but do not reject it and renounce 'subversive violence', a distinction also employed by Stefan Rummens and Koen Abts; see Rummens and Abts 2008, p. 531.
276. Buijs and Fennema 2012, p. 139. See also Demant, Slootman, Buijs and Tillie 2008, p. 61, on the social and political repression of the extreme right in the Netherlands.
277. Buijs and Fennema 2012, p. 139.
278. Buijs and Fennema 2012, p. 139.
279. Buijs and Fennema 2012, p. 139–140.
280. Buijs and Fennema 2012, p. 139–140. In this connection see also Elzinga 1982, p. 146.
281. The term 'adaptation dilemma' comes from Van Donselaar; see Buijs and Fennema 2012, p. 140. See also Rummens and Abts 2008, p. 530–532.
282. Buijs and Fennema 2012, p. 140.
283. Buijs and Fennema 2012, p. 141. Another danger that they point out is linked to the concealing of views: there is a risk of a discrepancy arising between the views a party expresses and its real ideas. These 'cautious' views may well be more dangerous than the 'harsh expressions of extremism'. Who is to say whether we should take the 'stage views' at face value or whether we should look for the suspected underlying ideas? If judges have to decide on this point, freedom of expression may be increasingly restricted. After all, any apparently innocent or acceptable expressions might potentially conceal the suspected extremist ideology. Buijs and Fennema therefore suggest that the 'logical end point of this cat-and-mouse game between democrats and extremists', with regard to the extreme-right CD party, would be the slogan 'Vote CD, you know why!' (see p. 142–143).
284. Buijs and Fennema 2012, see p. 141–147, in particular p. 144.
285. Tromp 1991, p. 87–89.
286. Tromp 1991, p. 88.
287. Tromp 1991, p. 88.
288. Tromp 1991, p. 88.
289. See also Paul Harvey, 'Militant Democracy and the European Convention on Human Rights', *European Law Review* 2004, vol. 29 no. 3, p. 407–420 (410). See also Michael Herzog, 'Can Hamas Be Tamed?', *Foreign Affairs* 2006, vol. 85, p. 83–94.
290. Rosenblum 2007, p. 73–75. See Issacharoff 2007, p. 1446–1447.
291. Tromp 1991, p. 88.
292. Rosenblum points to the accelerating effect of repression in the Turkish case; see Rosenblum 2007, p. 74. Moderation in the case of the Tunisian extremist, Islamist party *Ennahda* in fact appears to have been caused by exclusion and repression; see Francesco Cavatorta and Fabio Merone, 'Moderation through Exclusion? The Journey of the Tunisian Ennahda

from Fundamentalist to Conservative Party', *Democratization* 2013, vol. 20 no. 5, p. 857–875 (871).

293. See Tjitske Akkerman and Matthijs Rooduijn, 'Pariahs or Partners? Inclusion and Exclusion of Radical Right Parties and the Effects on Their Policy Positions', *Political Studies* June 2014, p. 1–18 (online). Akkerman and Rooduijn concentrate on the radical (non-extreme) right wing and observe that parties that are tolerated and participate in the democratic game actually exhibit radicalization of their views rather than moderation or continuation. Along the same lines, see Michael Minkenberg, 'From Pariah to Policy-Maker? The Radical Right in Europe, West and East: Between Margin and Mainstream', *Journal of Contemporary European Studies* 2013, vol. 21 no. 1, p. 5–24 (19, no moderation), and Daniele Albertazzi, 'Reconciling "Voice" and "Exit": Swiss and Italian Populists in Power', *Politics* 2009, vol. 29 no. 1, p. 1–10 (6 and 8, an extreme party succeeds in playing a dual role and no moderation is achieved). Earlier research, on the other hand, appears to confirm moderating effects from participation; see William M. Downs, Carrie L. Manning and Richard N. Engstrom, 'Revisiting the "Moderating Effects of Incumbency": A Comparative Study of Government Participation and Political Extremism', *Journal of Contemporary European Studies* 2009, vol. 17 no. 2, p. 151–169.
294. Capoccia 2001, p. 451.
295. Capoccia 2001, p. 449.
296. Capoccia 2001, p. 451–452.
297. See also Stefan Rummens and Koen Abts, 'Defending Democracy: The Concentric Containment of Political Extremism', *Political Studies* 2010, vol. 58, p. 649–665 (659–660).
298. Judith Wise, 'Dissent and Militant Democracy: The German Constitution and the Banning of the Free German Workers Party', *University of Chicago Law School Roundtable* 1998, vol. 5, p. 301–343 (337).
299. Rummens and Abts 2008, p. 527.
300. Rummens and Abts 2008, p. 527.
301. Tyulkina 2015, p. 104; see also p. 207.
302. Tyulkina 2015, p. 104.
303. Wise 1998, p. 337.
304. Wise 1998, p. 336–337.
305. Wise 1998, p. 337.
306. This is also the conclusion of Stefan Rummens and Koen Abts on the basis of the consensus in the empirical political science literature; see Rummens and Abts 2010, p. 659. The fact that repression and exclusion can be effective with religiously inspired extremist parties is demonstrated by the development of the Tunisian Ennahda Party; see the case study in Cavatorta and Merone 2013.
307. Holmes 2006, p. 590–591.
308. Holmes 2006, p. 591.
309. Holmes 2006. p. 591.
310. Holmes 2006, p. 591.
311. Basedau and Moroff 2011, p. 206.
312. See Fernand Thange, *Multiculturalisme kritisch bekeken* (A critical look at multiculturalism), Antwerp/Apeldoorn: Garant 2010, p. 291 (note 242), and Basedau and Moroff 2011, p. 207. Or as Roger Scruton writes, 'In a place where tribal or religious loyalties take precedence, democratic elections, if they occur at all, occur only once.' See Roger Scruton, 'The Nation-State and Democracy', p. 75–87 (81), in Mark Dooley (ed.), *The Roger Scruton Reader*, New York: Continuum 2011.

313. Bogaards, Basedau and Hartmann 2010, p. 599–617 (600 and 606).
314. Basedau and Moroff 2011, p. 217–218.
315. Bogaards, Basedau and Hartmann 2010, p. 611: 'The contributions reveal that the effectiveness of party bans for managing ethnic conflict is generally limited and context-dependent.'
316. Anika Moroff, 'Party Bans in Africa—An Empirical Overview', *Democratization* 2010, vol. 17 no. 4, p. 618–641 (631–633).
317. Bogaards, Basedau and Hartmann 2010, p. 611–612, and Basedau and Moroff 2011, p. 217. See also, in a different context, Niesen 2012, p. 556–557. Harvey refers to a number of ECHR member states, such as Russia and the republics in the Caucasus, that form 'illiberal democracies' or 'semi-authoritarian regimes'. In these states abuse of 'democracy-protecting' measures in the name of the 'transition process' is not unlikely; see Harvey 2004, p. 410–411.
318. See Ost 2004, p. 180.
319. See, for example, Sajó 2004, p. 209–230, and also Bourne 2012a, p. 1065–1066, Tyulkina 2015, p. 50, and Fox and Nolte 1995, p. 67–68.
320. See Harald Eberhard, Konrad Lachmayer and Gerhard Thallinger, 'Approaching Transitional Constitutionalism', p. 9–24, in Harald Eberhard, Konrad Lachmayer and Gerhard Thallinger, *Transitional Constitutionalism: Proceedings of the 2nd Vienna Workshop on International Constitutional Law*, Nomos/facultas.wuv 2007. On the connection between transitional constitutionalism and militant democracy in the Eastern European context and with respect to freedom of expression, see Uladzislau Belavusau, 'Hate Speech and Constitutional Democracy in Eastern Europe: Transitional and Militant? (Czech Republic, Hungary and Poland)', *Israel Law Review* 2014, vol. 47 no. 1, p. 27–61 (in particular p. 58–61).
321. Eberhard, Lachmayer and Thallinger 2007, p. 16.
322. ECHR 16 March 2006, 58278/00 (Zdanoka/Latvia). This case is discussed in the context of the *Lithuanian* transition in Vaidotas A. Vaicaitis, 'Role of (sic) Lithuanian Constitutional Court during (sic) Period of "Transitional Democracy"', p. 89–102 (94–95), in Eberhard, Lachmayer and Thallinger 2007.
323. ECHR *Zdanoka*, §133–134; see also Vaicaitis 2007, p. 95. Tatjana Zdanoka was a member of the European Parliament for the Greens-European Free Alliance from 2004 to 2018. She is not excluded from *these* elections, and in March 2014 she acted as 'observer' of the referendum on the Ukrainian Crimean peninsula; see Damien McGuinness, '"Russian Agent" Row Hits Latvia Election', BBC (online), 10 April 2014, and her personal page on the European Parliament website: http://www.europarl.europa.eu/meps/nl/28619/TATJANA_ZDANOKA_home.html.
324. Tyulkina 2015, p. 51 and 91–92.
325. On the battle of meaning inherent in the concept of democracy, see Maurice Adams, 'De verbeelding van de politieke democratie door het recht: inleidende beschouwing' ('The representation of the political democracy by the law: introductory discussion'), p. 3–37 (3–8), in Adams and Popelier 2004. On the importance of the opposition between the two concepts of democracy in the discussion of militant democracy, see Navot 2008, p. 746.
326. See chapter 1 of this book, under 'Reception of Van den Bergh's inaugural lecture'. It seems that we can also place Langemeijer's reaction in this category in any case (as arising from a procedural concept of democracy); for the rest, his criticism will be briefly discussed in chapter 3; see the answer to point 2 under 'Criticism of militant democracy answered'.
327. Bellekom 1982, p. 118. See also Ost 2004, p. 182–183.
328. Bellekom 1982, p. 118.

329. Joseph Schumpeter, *Capitalism, Socialism and Democracy*, London/New York: Routledge 2010, p. 241; see Fox and Nolte 1995, p. 14.
330. Bellekom 1982, p. 118.
331. Bellekom 1982, p. 118.
332. Bellekom 1982. p. 118.
333. Fox and Nolte 1995, p. 15–16.
334. Bligh 2013, p. 1327. See Fox and Nolte 1995, p. 25, and Bligh 2008 for a nuanced view; 'American exceptionalism' when it comes to freedom of expression (more or less unrestricted protection) does not naturally extend one-on-one to freedom of association.
335. Freedom of association was first recognized as an independent right by the Supreme Court in *NAACP vs. Alabama* (1958); see the critical views of Thomas I. Emerson, 'Freedom of Association and Freedom of Expression', *Yale Law Journal* 1964, vol. 74 no. 1, p. 1–35.
336. See Fox and Nolte 1995, p. 25. This relates to the Smith Act (1940), with a ban on membership of factions that want to overturn the government by force; the Internal Security Act (1950), which implemented a duty for parties labelled 'subversive' to be registered; and the Communist Control Act (1954), which revoked the fundamental rights of the Communist Party of the United States, and any successors it might have. See also Bellekom 1982, p. 127–130.
337. Kent Roach, 'Anti-Terrorism and Militant Democracy', p. 171–207 (180), in Sajó 2004.
338. Bligh 2008, p. 1390, 1396 and 1413; Issacharoff 2007, p. 1420–1421; Navot 2008, p. 747.
339. See on this 'capture': Müller 2017, p. 12–13. On a different note it could be added that in the United States (perhaps in contrast to Europe) religiously inspired antidemocrats are a smaller, even non-existent, problem. See Holmes 2006, p. 589: 'There is no political wing of al-Qaeda fielding candidates in congressional or local elections and crying out to be banned by militant democracy. There may be sleeper cells inside the U.S., but there is no fifth column and, therefore, no McCarthy-style witch hunts and persecutions. In Europe, where terrorist plots have been incubated in immigrant neighborhoods, the situation is somewhat different and, perhaps, more worrying for democracy.'
340. Bellekom 1982, p. 117; see also Adams 2004, p. 29–30 and 36.
341. Stefan Sottiaux, 'Democratie en grondrechten: de inhoudelijke en procedurele democratiemodellen van Dworkin en Habermas' ('Democracy and fundamental rights: the substantive and procedural models of Dworkin and Habermas'), p. 39–64 (43), in Adams and Popelier 2004. See also Eva Brems, 'State Regulation of Xenophobia versus Individual Freedoms: The European View', *Journal of Human Rights* 2002, vol. 1 no. 4, p. 481–500 (482): 'Democracy and the rule of law also entail substantive requirements for rule making: the rules have to respect and protect the fundamental rights and freedoms of the citizens.' See also Ost 2004, p. 182–183.
342. Bonger 1934, p. 17. For the individual components, see p. 10–17.
343. On how a more procedural democracy can spill over into a more substantive democracy, see J.J.A. Thomassen, 'Democratie, problemen en spanningsvelden' ('Democracy, problems and areas of tension'), p. 15–33 (20–21), in Thomassen 1991. See also Adams 2004, p. 36.
344. Van den Bergh 1936a, p. 8. It might of course be argued *contra* Van den Bergh that respect for 'every human being' is expressed in the majority principle; every vote counts equally. See, for example, Waldron 1999, p. 249–250.

345. The first paragraph of Article 1 Grundgesetz reads: 'Die Würde des Menschen ist unantastbar. Sie zu achten und zu schützen ist Verpflichtung aller staatlichen Gewalt.'
346. Pieter Vanden Heede 2004, p. 216–217.
347. Müller 2013b, p. 1262–1263. In that sense see also Pfersmann 2004, p. 53: 'militant democracy—as a legal structure—is on a scale of degree with other forms of democracy, in other words, that democracies are always *more* or *less* militant.' An attempt at a more nuanced dichotomy can be found in Fox and Nolte's distinction between tolerant and militant variants of the formal and substantive democracy. A substantive democracy that rarely employs its defence mechanisms, for example, is a tolerant substantive democracy (France, Canada and India); a procedural democracy that, despite a strong (constitutional) affinity with the procedural model, has created several laws against antidemocrats, is then a militant procedural democracy (US); see Fox and Nolte 1995, p. 21–22, 24–26 and 27–32. For detailed criticism of this classification, see Thiel 2009b, p. 384–395, and Bourne 2012b, p. 198–201.
348. There are certainly other facets to the concept of the 'rule of law'; all Dutch standard constitutional handbooks in any case include the notion of 'fundamental rights' and their protection; see the overview in W.J.M. Voermans and J.H. Gerards, with M.L. van Emmerik and H.-M.Th.D. ten Napel, *Juridische betekenis en reikwijdte van het begrip 'rechtsstaat' in de legisprudentie and jurisprudentie van de Raad van State* (Legal significance and scope of the concept of 'constitutional state' in the legisprudence and jurisprudence of the Council of State), The Hague: Council of State 2011, p. 31–32 and 84–94. Kortmann's concept of the constitutional state is particularly interesting because he is the only one to complete the incorporation of democracy into the constitutional state by describing democracy as a *component of* the constitutional state; see Voermans et al. 2011, p. 32 and 92–93.
349. For a recent criticism in this direction, see James Allan, *Democracy in Decline: Steps in the Wrong Direction*, Montreal: McGill-Queen's University Press 2014; in particular on morally charged definitions of democracy, see p. ix–xi.
350. Elzinga 1982, p. 143–147.
351. Elzinga 1982, p. 143.
352. Elzinga 1982, p. 143.
353. Hugo Krabbe, *'Ongezonde Lectuur'* ('Unhealthy reading'), Groningen: J.M. Wolters 1913, p. 27.
354. See Hugo Krabbe, *De Moderne Staatsidee* (The modern idea of the state), The Hague: Martinus Nijhoff 1915, p. 42. See also Emanuel Margolis, 'Soviet Views on the Relationship between National and International Law', *International and Comparative Law Quarterly* 1955, vol. 4 no. 1, p. 117–118. See also Carla Zoethout, 'Hugo Krabbe over recht, staat en staatsrecht' ('Hugo Krabbe on law, state and constitutional law'), *Recht en Kritiek* 1991, vol. 17 no. 4, p. 468–481 (473).
355. Krabbe 1913 p. 26.
356. Elzinga and De Lange 2006, p. 190.
357. See also Elzinga's criticism of the sense of justice in Krabbe's work, in D.J. Elzinga, 'Leven en werk van Hugo Krabbe (1857-1936)' ('Life and work of Hugo Krabbe [1857-1936]'), p. 55–73 (69), in D.J. Elzinga, *De staat van het recht: opstellen over staatsrecht en politiek* (The state of the law: essays on constitutional law and politics), Zwolle: W.E.J. Tjeenk Willink 1990. The discussion of Krabbe here is an abridged passage from the more detailed account in Bastiaan Rijpkema, 'Dierenrechten als politiek-filosofisch probleem' ('Animal rights as a problem of political philosophy'), p. 131–151

(141–144), in Bastiaan Rijpkema and Machteld Zee (eds.), *Bij de beesten af! Over dierenrecht en onrecht* (Brutish! On animal rights and injustice), Bert Bakker 2013.

358. Elzinga 1982, p. 143.
359. Elzinga 1982, p. 143.
360. Elzinga 1982, p. 143.
361. Elzinga 1982, p. 144.
362. Elzinga 1982, p. 144.
363. Elzinga 1982, p. 145.
364. Elzinga 1982, p. 145.
365. Elzinga 1982, p. 145.
366. Elzinga 1982, p. 145.
367. Elzinga 1982, p. 145–146.
368. Elzinga 1982, p. 146.
369. Elzinga 1982, p. 145.
370. Brems 2002, p. 482. It should also be noted that when Brems speaks about antidemocrats she mainly means racist parties. Brems thus employs a broad definition of substantive democracy (in accordance with the first interpretation of Van den Bergh; the principled democracy).
371. Brems 2002, p. 482–483.
372. Brems 2002, p. 483. See also Vanden Heede 2004, p. 231. Systematic empirical research would be welcome here: party bans can work, as we saw, but what is the effect of timing (early or late) on the success of such a ban?
373. Brems 2002, p. 483. Cf. also Fox and Nolte 1995, p. 69–70: 'Bans on parties with substantial followings, may cause unrest; bans on parties with little support serve as instruments of repression.'
374. See Vanden Heede 2004, p. 231.
375. Also called 'theoterrorism' by Paul Cliteur to emphasize the specific character of religiously inspired terrorism. See, for example, Paul Cliteur, 'The Rudi Carrell Affair and Its Significance for the Tension between Theoterrorism and Religious Satire', *Ancilla Iuris* 2013, p. 15–41.
376. Müller 2012, p. 538.
377. See Müller 2013b, p. 1255, and Andras Sajó, 'From Militant Democracy to the Preventive State', *Cardozo Law Review* 2006, vol. 27 no. 5, p. 2255–2294 (2269–2270).
378. Müller 2013b, p. 1256.
379. See, for example, Pim van den Dool, 'Haatprediker Abu Hamza krijgt levenslang in VS' ('Hate preacher Abu Hamza receives life sentence in the US'), *NRC Handelsblad*, 9 January 2015, and 'Imamdeskundige: "Moskeeën onderschatten risico's rondreizende predikers"' ('Imam expert: "Mosques underestimate risks of travelling preachers"'), *Eindhovens Dagblad*, 22 January 2015.
380. See, for example, the commentary of the expert on Islam Mohamed Ajouaou of the VU University Amsterdam: 'They underestimate the ideological side of these people's stories. From a religious perspective they may not be so far from the mainstream, but not everyone reads between the lines. Sometimes there are explicit calls for hate or violence, and sometimes it is much more implicit' ('Mosques Underestimate Risks of Travelling Preachers', *Eindhovens Dagblad*, 22 January 2015). Similarly, see the Tilburg Arabist and expert on Islam Jan-Jaap de Ruiter on the Saudi-Arabian preacher Al-Qarni: 'These kinds of preachers are wise enough to remain just within the boundaries of our freedom of expression. He brushes against jihadism and what he says could be interpreted as encouraging violence, even if he would never directly call for it

himself' ('Criticism of Hate Preacher Al-Qarni Rises: "I don't understand why the mosque does this"', *Omroep Brabant* [online], 29 April 2015).

381. Jan-Werner Müller, *Constitutional Patriotism*, Princeton/Oxford: Princeton University Press 2007, p. 115.
382. Müller 2007 p. 115.
383. Müller 2007 p. 115.
384. Müller 2007, p. 114–115.
385. See, for example, Aukje van Roessel, 'Zelfcorrectie' ('Self-Correction'), *De Groene Amsterdammer*, 8 April 2015, and for a few of these points of criticism also Issacharoff 2007, p. 1260.
386. Issacharoff 2007, p. 1260.
387. Van der Woude 2009, p. 54.
388. Kirshner 2014, p. 165.
389. The fact that this cannot be assumed is shown by the position of the Dutch Supreme Court during World War II; see Corjo Jansen, with collaboration from Derk Venema, *De Hoge Raad en de Tweede Wereldoorlog: Recht en rechtsbeoefening in de jaren 1930-1950* (The Supreme Court and World War II: law and legal practice in the years 1930-1950), Amsterdam: Boom 2011 (in particular p. 323–332).
390. Buijs and Fennema 2012, p. 142.

3 Democracy as self-correction

1. Introduction

It is time to bring together the lines of thought from the previous two chapters. Van den Bergh was the first to develop and formulate a fully-fledged theory of militant democracy. On the one hand there is the 'principled democracy', in which particular values are considered a criterion for admission to the democratic process. For Van den Bergh those principles are freedom of conscience and equality before the law. Parties failing to acknowledge these principles are excluded from democratic participation. On the other hand we find in his inaugural lecture the idea of 'democracy as self-correction': democracy is characterized by the unique feature of enabling the people to correct their own mistakes, an idea also proposed by the French jurist Milan Markovitch. Democracy then only guards the outmost boundaries: decisions must be revocable. The framework must remain intact; within it everything is possible. There will always be the next elections, always a next moment at which the people can express their views.

In the previous chapter we discussed the pragmatic objections to party bans: a ban might not work or might be counterproductive, because it leads to a hardening of views and an attractive status of martyrdom, causing an escalation of action. Political science research shows that these objections cannot be fully maintained.

The objections originating from the perspective of political philosophy, however, still stand, so in this chapter we return to Van den Bergh. All the alternatives discussed raised problems. On the basis of Van den Bergh's foundation this chapter attempts to develop a comprehensive theory of militant democracy, making use of Popper's ideas. The new theory will then be tested against the points of criticism mentioned above.

2. A theory of militant democracy: democracy as self-correction

In reaction to the concept of procedural democracy, after World War II a different notion of democracy gained dominance. This take on democracy, in part, lets go of the will of the people. Of course, citizens can still make a great many decisions, but we must conclude that in operating as the people they are not competent, at least not in all areas. This calls for measures, and they can be found in the notion of substantive democracy, a concept that can be summed up as: yes, the will of the majority, but not if you want to change X or Y, with X and Y being fundamental and inviolable principles. They form basic rights and represent exceptions to the democratic process, with a judge generally overseeing compliance through judicial review.[1]

In Van den Bergh's speech we find points of departure for a concept of substantive democracy of this kind. In certain places he says that fundamental principles such as freedom of conscience and equality before the law must be accepted before a party can be admitted to the democratic arena. This is what I have previously termed 'principled democracy'. Parties who do not respect certain principles can be banned. It is important to realize that this provides a broad basis for bans. Parties can be banned if they fail to honour particular fundamental principles. That means a party can quite easily become eligible for prohibition, also saddling the judge with all kinds of problems of interpretation, such as when *exactly* it is the case that a party denies people freedom of conscience. The broader the grounds for prohibition, the greater the interpretation problems.

We must therefore turn to the second interpretation, democracy as self-correction. Under this definition democracy is a way for the people to govern themselves through self-correction: it means the people making their own decisions, as well as retaining the option of changing their minds. 'Democracy as self-correction' remains very close to the concept of procedural democracy, to majority decision making; it does not, however, seek the essence of democracy there, but rather in the self-corrective capacity of democracy. It is an interpretation that lies somewhere between procedural and substantive democracy, one that incorporates the advantages of substantive democracy without allowing too much leeway in establishing grounds for prohibition.

The idea of democracy as self-correction

Democracy as self-correction asserts that the unique characteristic of democracy is the revocable nature of decisions; decisions can always be reversed. Democracy means being able to reverse your steps.[2] Popper's scientific interpretation of democracy is an extension of that, as we have already seen. The combination of both ideas therefore appears particularly fruitful. Democracy as self-correction could then be described as follows.

A properly functioning democracy has a good deal in common with science (in its ideal form): policies are tested like hypotheses on reality, and correction can subsequently take place. Democracy allows for the expression of the most varied viewpoints. Anyone can put forward solutions and express criticism of those proposed by others, in particular those of the government. Ideally that leads to policy adjustments, and if that does not happen, eventually those who have not been receptive to criticism can be voted out within a reasonable period. The people can thus govern themselves through continual correction.

How different the situation is in an authoritarian system. Free criticism of policy is not a given under such a system, nor is there any guarantee that the government will really change its policy. Such a system deprives itself of the most important source of progress in exchange for assumed efficiency or simply for the sake of power. Those in authority make mistakes in their policies that could have been avoided through criticism before they were implemented.[3] They also persist in their mistakes, even after they have long been visible in practice, because retrospective criticism of the effects is not permitted.[4] The 'perpetual search for, and admission of, error' is least present in authoritarian systems.[5]

This picture is supported by the ideas of a number of lawyers and legal philosophers. Their theories each bring a particular aspect into focus of democratic self-correction in the context of defending democracy. First of all, there is the German jurist and legal philosopher Günter Frankenberg, who writes about the 'learning sovereign'. In Frankenberg's view the sovereign is not just the person who has 'the last word', as in the traditional description, but 'the one who learns while speaking the last word'.[6] This *learning* aspect is what turns a sovereign into a democratic sovereign. And a democratic sovereign must therefore design mechanisms that ensure that his horizon always remains open to new information. In terms of democratic self-correction, the framework must be kept in place, to enable self-correction. In the words of Frankenberg:

> The sovereign is like a learning god going to elementary school—constantly dependent on new information, forced to take necessary precautions so that the horizon remains open for new information. Thus learning has a self-critical and at the same time normative meaning, which radically separates the democratic from the pre-democratic or anti-democratic sovereign.[7]

We encounter a related idea in the work of Samuel Issacharoff, professor of constitutional law at New York University. A government can never pass a decision on the 'structure of the political process' that cannot be reversed by future majorities, not even with the support of a parliamentary majority at the time of the initial decision.[8] His theory thus has common ground with Van den Bergh's: at heart it is about safeguarding *revocability*: only decisions that a future majority can revoke are permitted (and of course that means *almost* all decisions). Based on this reasoning, for example, having elections cannot be abolished: that could not be undone via a democratic route. Issacharoff mentions the Refah case as an example:

> A decision to expand the role of religion in the public sphere (as with support to church schools) remains within the realm of a reversible political decision, while a removal of nonbelievers from the political process does not. In this sense, the strongest justification for the holding of the *Refah Partisi* case turned on the party's efforts to restore a version of the Ottoman millet system, in which each religious community would minister to its own affairs while the dominant Sunni majority alone would attend to the affairs of state. Making political power unaccountable to large segments of the population is just the sort of impediment to reversibility that threatens ongoing democratic governance.[9]

Another important element of democracy as self-correction is the emphasis on the *temporary* nature of decisions. Arguing against Hans Kelsen's relativist view of democracy, the Austrian lawyer and judge Rudolf Thienel demands attention for the temporary nature of decisions and the majorities that support them.[10] In Thienel's work we find a powerful formulation of this principle, which also lies at the foundation of democracy as self-correction:

> Democratic participation enables the citizen to participate in the creation of those rules which bind him—without, of course, underestimating the many fictions involved in this concept. But if we accept this idea, it is completely unconvincing, that an accidental majority, which is the result of a special historical and political situation, should be able to erase the basis for democratic participation not only for itself, but also for future generations and for future majorities.[11]

The learning sovereign, the revocability of decisions and the temporary nature of majorities all emphasize part of what democracy as self-correction is. Democracy as self-correction sees democracy as a system that offers more safeguards than any other to ensure that incorrect decisions can be reversed (revocability), that progressive insight is incorporated (learning), on the understanding that no decision should be seen as definitive (temporality). Democracy as self-correction builds on the insights of Van den Bergh and Popper, finding background support in the ideas of other legal scholars and legal philosophers. What characterizes *democratic* sovereignty, according to Frankenberg, is the willingness and perpetual opportunity to learn from mistakes. Democracy is unique in this respect, and that makes it worth defending.

Self-correction as a unique characteristic

Let us examine this claim more closely. Is self-correction really a unique characteristic of democracy?

To begin with, one might ask how this differs from government by an enlightened despot. Surely an enlightened despot could also apply self-correction? Is that not the same? I do not think so. First, it must be noted, of course, that the aspect of self-correction by the *people* is absent in the case of an enlightened despot. The people do not correct their own mistakes, but have to hope that the enlightened despot will be guided by progressive insight. However, one could still claim that *even* when governed by despotic self-correction the aspect of reversing decisions remains intact. It is simply not the people who reverse a decision but the enlightened despot. The answer to this lies in the word 'hope': one can only *hope* that an enlightened despot will reach new insights.[12] Democracy, by contrast, offers more safeguards than any other system to ensure that incorrect decisions really are reversed, making it unique in this respect. As we have already seen, in a democracy the most varied insights can be formulated by all citizens, an unimaginably large store of resources.

Then again, an enlightened despot *might* set up an ingenious advice mechanism, with advisors from all corners of the country, ensuring that he is always aware of new, possibly better insights. Yes, that is also a possibility. But in the end also such a system 1) does not allow anyone to determine whether the enlightened despot really makes sufficient use of these insights, and 2) there is no way of appointing someone more receptive to new insights if the current despot is insufficiently doing so. In other words, self-correction is *possible*, but there is no *guarantee*. With its periodic elections, democracy *does* offer a strong guarantee.

Two objections

There are two obvious objections. First, does democracy as self-correction not paint an overly rose-tinted picture of democracy in practice? Second, does democracy as self-correction, with its emphasis on progressive insight and in the analogy with the scientific community, not exhibit technocratic tendencies? In other words, are we not handing over democracy to experts?

With respect to the first objection: continual self-correction, incorporating progressive insight, will only ever be realized to a limited extent. That is not to say that the image is too rose-tinted. The only thing democracy as self-correction asserts is that, in providing the possibility of regular changes of government and the opportunity to express criticism, it creates the conditions for social progress like no other system. Democracy as self-correction sees every citizen as a potential source of ideas *and* not only accepts but encourages diversity of opinions, as we saw in Bhikhu Parekh's interpretation of Popper.

Nevertheless, no one will deny that the incorporation of new insights can take a long, sometimes outrageously long, time. In practice it is clear that in a considerable number of cases we actually do come close to the ideal. In the Netherlands, for example, this is shown in recent cases such as electronic tags for detainees,[13] organ donation[14] and pension plans.[15] Continual criticism of these plans was expressed from within and outside parliament, leading to their being rejected or adjusted, sometimes at an early stage. That is not to say that the perfect solutions have been found, but the process of improvement has unmistakeably been set in motion. This picture also accommodates internet consultation, which is now increasingly used for laws that may lead to particularly profound changes.[16] It is a form of institutionalization of criticism. Popper gives the controversial example of the Vietnam War. Would it have been conceivable in a system other than democracy to give the sharpest criticism free rein, through the main newspapers and most important television stations, and that as a result the government would change its policy to make withdrawal of troops its new goal?[17] And if the changes do not sufficiently address the criticism, or if reality proves the plans wrong, in a democracy there is always the option of replacing an unresponsive government with people who will implement the necessary changes.

Let us now turn to the suspected technocratic tendencies. This is an objection that is generally also made against Popper's political philosophy.[18] Such criticism is probably based on a serious misinterpretation of *The Open Society*. Yes, Popper writes about the analogy between democracy and science, an idea also used by proponents of democracy as self-correction, but as political philosopher Alan Ryan writes, it makes no sense to deduce from that that Popper would support government by a scientific elite:

> Because he believed adamantly in the logical distinctness of facts and values, he had no doubt that the role of experts, such as it was, was to tell us how to achieve what we had a mind to; it was up to us to decide what it was we wanted to achieve. Anything more was the kind of concession to the pretensions of philosopher-kings that he would not tolerate.[19]

Indeed, if Popper does anything in *The Open Society* it is to argue against the philosophy of Plato, who was perhaps the first technocrat.

Something similar applies to democracy as self-correction: it is the citizens who set priorities and decide the direction of policy; support by and criticism from experts is welcomed, but is not the deciding factor. Democracy as self-correction, after all, means that the people *themselves* govern through self-correction, thus maintaining a strong claim to legitimacy. In Popper's preferred definition of democracy, 'prevention of tyranny', this relationship between democracy and legitimacy is in fact explicitly severed, leading to his being wrongly suspected of technocracy.[20]

Of course, experts can exert a significant influence, simply because of their specialist knowledge, but in the end they are kept in check by the fundamental principle of democracy: 'one person, one vote'. It is no coincidence that experts find themselves able to exert excessive influence where this principle is not fully observed, as in the case of a number of supranational organs. Democracy as self-correction stands for nothing less than *self-government* through self-correction. The claim of technocracy therefore does not apply to democracy as self-correction.

The difference between democracy as self-correction and substantive democracy

I previously distinguished three concepts of democracy. A *procedural democracy* looks for the essence of democracy in (neutral) majority decision making and does not recognize any justification for a ban on antidemocratic parties; all ideas are equal. In the case of *democracy as self-correction*, a ban is permitted when the self-corrective capacity of the democracy is threatened. A *substantive democracy* looks to majority decision making plus a number of fundamental rights or principles for the definition of democracy; a ban in this view is possible if a party turns against certain fundamental rights.

Both democracy as self-correction and substantive democracy can serve as foundations for militant democracy. I believe that democracy as self-correction has the best credentials. First, it offers a justification from the perspective of political philosophy for the defence of democracy, one that is absent from the concept of procedural democracy. Of course, substantive democracy offers this too, but with two significant drawbacks. First, one might wonder whether we are still talking about democracy at all in a substantive democracy, as the concept is 'loaded' with all sorts of values, which, although commendable in themselves, nevertheless arguably have little to do with democracy as self-government by the people. Does the concept of substantive democracy not drift too far from this 'original' meaning?[21] Is this still government by the people?

If we assume that this definition does indeed involve self-government by the people, this raises another question; the second drawback: does substantive democracy not give the democratic debate too little latitude? Should one not have to convince parties in debate, even parties with whom one is very much in disagreement, rather than banning them? It seems to me that a democracy should strive as far as possible for this ideal if it wishes to be called a democracy. A broad foundation for banning parties, however, calls this into doubt in a substantive democracy. Democracy as self-correction does better by following procedural democracy closely, with a narrow justification for the prohibition of antidemocratic parties.[22] Democracy as self-correction also offers the best guarantee against abuse: where a justification for a ban is too broad, there is a risk of too wide an interpretation (in the best case) and abuse of power (in the worst case).

Self-correction as a justification for a ban

The justification for action therefore lies in erosion of the democracy's self-corrective capacity. Only if parties threaten to damage this, can we legitimately call them antidemocratic parties and ban them. A democracy is not acting undemocratically or inconsistently in doing this: its essence, after all, lies in the permanent revocability of its decisions. The thought experiment discussed above can be used to illustrate this. If we try to imagine all possible decisions in a democracy, *one* decision immediately stands out: the irrevocable decision to abolish democracy. This means the loss of the framework that makes that decision-making process possible in the first place. This is the justification for acting against antidemocrats, but we are not quite there yet.

A concrete legal banning ground for banning a party must follow from this justification. This will undoubtedly be narrower than one based on specific inviolable principles, as in the theory of substantive democracy. Nonetheless the justification in itself must be worked out before it can serve as a legal banning ground. After all, the purely formal decision to abolish democracy is not the only conceivable decision that would render self-correction impossible. Even Hitler's Enabling Act did not say, 'We hereby abolish democracy'; abolition was a consequence of the changes that the act made to the democratic system. We should therefore consider changes that seriously endanger the self-corrective capacity of the democracy and the revocability of decisions. Do severe restrictions on freedom of expression amount to the abolition of democracy? Has a democracy come to its end when alternative parties are excluded from participation in elections? In short, grounds for prohibition must include the necessary conditions for self-correction. Grounds for prohibition that include only the literal decision to abolish democracy would be purely for show. The question, therefore, is, *when* can you say that a decision leads to the abolition of democracy? In terms of democracy as self-correction, that means asking, when is the self-corrective capacity of democracy damaged? And what party aims are thus unlawful and justify a ban?

What counts as damage to self-corrective capacity?

How do we work out the justification to form the concrete legal grounds for a ban? Van den Bergh develops no clear criteria for this in his inaugural lecture.

If we are to ensure the beginnings of self-government, it seems that the minimum needed is: the guarantee of passive and active suffrage (that is, respectively the right to be elected and the right to vote), in combination with periodical, free elections by secret ballot. From the perspective of democracy as self-correction, we might call the right to vote and elections *the principle of evaluation.* Parties that threaten this principle, by abolishing the right to vote or fundamentally changing the way elections are held, are eligible for a ban. 'Fundamental changes', of course, do not refer to changes in the length of parliamentary terms from four to three or five years, for example, but *would* apply to a change to twenty years. It is impossible to formulate hard rules; constitutional law and political philosophy are not mathematics. In the end, the judge will have to interpret the proposed changes. It is clear, though, that a proposal to have elections every twenty years would render evaluation effectively non-existent.

If the articles on the right to vote and elections are removed from a democratic constitution, it would no longer be democratic. In Popper's ideal of scientific democracy, the right to vote and regular elections are the ultimate sanction for ministers who are insufficiently sensitive to criticism: they are voted out and replaced. After all, there is always the risk that they will identify too much with their solutions and become insensitive to criticism.

The principle of evaluation makes it possible for new ideas to gain primacy at set times. In practice that will often mean a change of the people in charge, but that is not the core point. The point is that there is an institutionalized moment at which that which does not work can be rejected and new ideas can be embraced. In the ideal situation, of course, a government and a parliament are constantly working on self-correction, but what is unique in a democracy is the very fact that it offers a hard guarantee of that self-correction: voting in elections. At that point ideas (and their proponents) are evaluated.

The principle of evaluation speaks for itself, but are there other principles that are required to safeguard democratic self-correction? How can we make the political philosophical justification, 'democracy as self-correction', more concrete? And especially, how can we transform the justification for intervention into a workable legal provision? We do not find an answer to that question in the discussions of political philosophers on democracy. It is therefore prudent that we look to two highly regarded judicial institutions. How do the German Federal Constitutional Court, the Bundesverfassungsgericht, and the European Court for Human Rights in Strasbourg flesh out the concept of democracy? With the help of their interpretations we can explore the boundaries of the self-corrective capacity. This brings the limits of democratic tolerance into the picture.

The Bundesverfassungsgericht on democracy

A judicial institution that has expressly had to consider the meaning of democracy is the Bundesverfassungsgericht (BVerfG), the highest court in Germany. The second part of Article 21 of the German Constitution, the Grundgesetz, includes explicit grounds for prohibition:

> Parties that, by reason of their aims or the behaviour of their adherents, seek to undermine or abolish the free democratic basic order [freiheitliche demokratische Grundordnung] or to endanger the existence of the

> Federal Republic of Germany shall be unconstitutional [verfassungswidrig]. The Federal Constitutional Court shall rule on the question of unconstitutionality.[23]

In 1952 the Socialistische Reichspartei Deutschlands (SRP), in fact a successor of the NSDAP, was banned on the basis of this provision.[24] This was the first party ban in the young post-war German democracy.

Two concepts are important in this context: *Verfassungswidrigkeit* and *Verfassungsfeindlichkeit*. The Bundestag, Bundesrat and Bundesregierung can submit a request to the BVerfG to have a party declared *verfassungswidrig* (unconstitutional); the BVerfG has the exclusive power to decide these cases,[25] potentially leading to a ban.[26] *Verfassungsfeindlich* (anti-constitutional), on the other hand, is a less serious designation. It is not a legal judgement, and no judicial authority is involved. Every year the Ministry of the Interior and the individual federal states draw up a *Verfassungsschutzbericht* in which they discuss the activities and oversight of organizations that are considered anti-constitutional.[27] The 2013 Verfassungsschutzbericht, for instance, covered the right-wing extremists of the Nationaldemokratische Partei Deutschlands (NPD), the left-wing extremists of the Deutsche Kommunistische Partei (DKP), and parties such as the Islamic extremists of Hizb ut-Tahrir (not a political party).[28] Although the designation itself does not mean a ban, the ease with which a party or faction can be labelled 'verfassungsfeindlich' does lead to criticism. It can, after all, prevent opinions that in themselves are legitimate from being expressed out of fear of being placed on 'the list'. The Verfassungsschutzbericht may then have a 'chilling effect' and could narrow the debate.[29] And indeed there were (successful) appeals against being mentioned in it.[30] In these legal proceedings the BVerfG demonstrated that it was sensitive to the risks of the chilling effect.[31]

Back to Verfassungswidrigkeit and the actual party ban. When it comes to Verfassungswidrigkeit, the BVerfG has confirmed that it can also act against non-violent parties. However, that is only possible when the party resists the 'most fundamental principles of the liberal constitutional state'.[32] For our purposes it is interesting to look at which elements the BVerfG includes under the 'freiheitliche demokratische Grundordnung' when making its judgement. They are:

- respect for human rights, in particular the right to life and self-development;
- popular sovereignty;
- separation of powers;
- accountability of government;
- legality of the administration;
- independence of judicial authorities;
- the multiparty principle;
- the right to opposition.[33]

Both the SRP and the Kommunistische Partei Deutschlands (KPD), banned four years later, gave the impression that they aimed to erode these principles. In the case of the SRP, closer study of the party programme and party activities, among other points, revealed that the party's aim was to establish a dictatorship.[34] The party was also organized 'on dictatorial lines', and having a Nazi background was seen as a strong recommendation for attaining a high position within the party.[35] This endangered at least respect for human rights, the sovereignty of the people, separation of powers, government accountability, independence of judicial authorities and the multiparty and opposition principles. Essentially they ticked almost every box. The KPD was also banned for its 'fundamental attitude' of wanting to establish a 'proletarian dictatorship'.[36] In this judgement the BVerfG also explicitly indicated that a party's goals alone could be sufficient for a ban.[37] However, that must be coupled with an attitude that is actually *combatively* antidemocratic; merely contemplating alternative state systems is not enough.[38] Militant democracy is thus a separate line in the defence of the state and can be clearly distinguished from the protection of public order, which is only at issue at a later stage, and which can be tackled by means of the state of exception.[39]

In 2017 the BVerfG updated this framework in a high-profile party ban case against the extreme-right Nationaldemokratische Partei Deutschlands (NPD).[40] In addition to actively opposing the free democratic basic order, under Germany's new militant democracy framework, it must now also have *some* potential to actually threaten this order.[41] In the case of the NPD this potential was lacking according to the BVerfG, so even though the party actively opposed the free democratic basic order, it was not banned.[42]

For the BVerfG the 'freiheitliche demokratische Grundordnung' is more restricted than the constitutional order.[43] Nevertheless, the list of fundamental principles is already quite extensive. It certainly does not protect democracy *alone*. Perhaps it does not set the entire constitutional order in stone, but substantial parts of the 'rule of law' are enshrined—in other words: the majority principle *plus* a number of fundamental values. For the protection of the self-corrective capacity of the democracy that is not necessary. It should also be kept in mind that this more extensive basis for prohibition is already the result of a judicial interpretation of an overly *vague* basis for prohibition in the first place; the only concrete criterion the judge is offered in the Grundgesetz (Art. 21II), after all, is the 'freiheitliche demokratische Grundordnung'.

But what elements should we take from this interpretation? Candidates are separation of powers, government accountability, the multiparty principle and the right to opposition. Respect for human rights, independent judicial authorities and legality of the administration are important values, but are more constitutional than democratic in nature. In other words, a liberal democracy encompasses these values, but they are not needed for the self-corrective mechanism. We can also skip the remaining principle of popular sovereignty. This element is implied by 'democracy as self-correction', which, after all, means self-government by the people by means of self-correction. It would be rather circular reasoning if, in answer to the question 'What constitutes erosion of the self-corrective mechanism?' we were to reply, 'Erosion of popular sovereignty.'

Separation of powers constitutes a more interesting component. This classic constitutional concept aims to keep executive, legislative and judicial powers separate. Here the important question is, do the other powers threaten to eclipse the legislature? This immediately brings the relationship between legislator and judge into the picture; as the Dutch saying goes, 'the judge must not sit in the legislator's chair'. An instrument such as judicial review of legislation carries that risk.[44] This is a legitimate problem and relevant to the self-corrective mechanism. If elected representatives of the people are regularly overruled by unelected judges, the people are seriously impeded in applying self-government by self-correction. This grates all the more when judges pass judgement on the basis of a constitution that cannot be changed, or is very hard to change.[45] This gives the judge, rather than the legislator, the last word. Since the judge is unelected, self-correction is impossible in such a system. In practice, it tends not to come to that. The legislator can have the last word by changing the constitution, albeit in some cases with great difficulty.[46] The judge in turn can employ some interpretive restraint.[47] However, this does not offer certainty, and all that does not change the fact that far-reaching extension of judicial powers represents a substantial threat to the functioning of self-correction, and with it to democracy. Germany is an interesting case in this respect: the German combination of review with a, in part, formally, unchangeable constitution gives judges, not the representatives of the people, the last word unconditionally. That is difficult to reconcile with the concept of democracy as self-correction.

We can conclude that separation of powers, as a stand-alone principle, does not belong to the core of 'democracy as self-correction'. If the judicial authorities were to override the legislator so extensively that meaningful self-correction is impossible, then it would probably be more consistent to see this as an erosion of the principle of evaluation we outlined earlier: after all, it deprives citizens of the power to evaluate government policy, or it might be said that the periodical free elections by secret ballot that implement the principle of evaluation are meaningless in such a hypothetical situation: people can vote, but it does not make any difference. In other words, it is not necessary to postulate an *extra* principle of separation of powers. The principle of evaluation assumes that neither the judge nor the executive can have the last word.

Let us turn to *government accountability*. The government is created to execute the laws of the representatives of the people. How these laws are executed by the administration and who oversees their execution (normally: parliament and the judge) are not cast in stone. That is not to say that there is a better system than the classic triad of administration, parliament and judiciary, or even that a better system could be conceivable. I merely wish to assert that a government, and with it accountability of the government, are not essential for the self-corrective capacity of democracy. Of course, democracy, as well as the self-corrective capacity, probably functions better with it, but democracy, in theory at least, can exist without it.

Should we adopt the *multiparty principle*? At face value self-correction appears to benefit from having competition between multiple parties. This principle is even recognized in international law: participation of multiple parties is a minimum requirement for elections being considered genuinely democratic.[48] In the absence of at least two parties, there is no real freedom of choice and little possibility of correction. It would not be possible, for example, to vote for a party that, contrary to the ruling party, wants to reverse a particular decision. But does this mean that there must be *parties* per se? No, probably not. It is conceivable, and according to some people even preferable, to have a democracy without parties. Citizens then vote for their individual representatives, who subsequently work towards compromise in parliament without party discipline or coercion. The Dutch Constitution does not even formally recognize the existence of political parties. The multi*party* principle is a product of German democracy, which is grafted onto the existence of political parties and which protects them in the Constitution (Art. 21 para. 1 GG).[49]

At its core, however, it is not about those two or more parties but about preventing what might be called 'exclusion of political competition'. Whether we are talking about reducing democracy to a one-party state such as North Korea (in a democracy with parties) or about restricting passive suffrage (the right to be elected) to a select group of citizens (in a democracy without parties), it is always a case of excluding other voices, and thus possible choices. Those voices are essential to the capacity for self-correction.

So we do need to count a 'principle of political competition' as part of the core of the self-corrective mechanism. Anyone should be allowed to stand for election, and given the predominance of party democracies, we should add the freedom of association. Abolition of these freedoms must be seen as an erosion of the self-corrective capacity. Abolition or effective abolition is, of course, different from restrictions on reasonable grounds. Here, too, we must appeal to the prudence of the judge. A party, for example, that strives to raise the legal requirements to establish an association does not directly damage the essence of self-correction. The same applies to the legal ban on criminal associations or reasonable rises in the electoral threshold.[50] A recent judgement by the Bundesverfassungsgericht on the German electoral threshold in the elections to the European Parliament shows that judges should be capable of distinguishing intolerable damage to the core of the principle from more acceptable, reasonable restrictions.[51]

That leaves *the right to opposition.* Here I will be brief. The main significance of this principle is found in connection with the presence of a government. The right to act in opposition means that it is possible, as a party or a representative of the people, to resist government policy, and thus to act and plead against the majority in parliament who support that policy. I established above that democracy as self-correction does not essentially assume the presence of a government, so in this sense this derived principle also belongs to the periphery and not the core of the self-corrective mechanism. Of course, it must be possible for a parliamentary minority to oppose a parliamentary majority, but this is also already implied by the principle of evaluation (of policies).

The principle of political competition

What can we learn from the BVerfG's interpretation of the 'free democratic basic order'? A large number of components are on the margins of, or even outside, the core of what we consider necessary for the functioning of democratic self-correction. The BVerfG's interpretation nevertheless highlights an important condition for self-correction: the *principle of political competition*, based on the multiparty principle. Exclusion of political competition must be made impossible. In a one-party state or a state with exclusive passive suffrage (an 'elected aristocracy'), democracy as self-correction is out of the question. One might even call it the antidemocratic measure par excellence: those excluded from passive (or indeed active) suffrage, after all, are definitively deprived of the opportunity to do anything about this decision (such as reversing it). They can only be freed from their democratic isolation by others.[52] An example is the aim of the banned Turkish party Refah Partisi (Welfare Party), to exclude non-believers, broadly defined as non-Sunni Muslims, from the political process.[53] This goes against the principle of political competition and with it the self-corrective mechanism.

We have already established that self-correction needs the principle of evaluation. We can now add the principle of political competition, usually effectuated by the freedom of association and passive suffrage (the right to be elected).

The ECHR on democracy

A judicial institution that regularly passes judgement on the legal interpretation of the concept of democracy is the European Court of Human Rights (ECHR). This court passes judgement on human rights in forty-seven member states on the basis of the European Convention on Human Rights. In the Refah case the ECHR proclaimed that the actions of political parties in a democracy must fulfil two requirements: 1) their methods must be 'legal and democratic', and 2) their goal must be in accordance with 'fundamental democratic principles'.[54] All other changes or adjustments to the state structure are permissible.[55] In fact, these are the same dual grounds for prohibition as Van den Bergh proposed for a new Political Parties Act.[56]

The Refah case could rightly be called a landmark decision. In 2003 the Grand Chamber of the ECHR approved the ban of the Turkish party Refah Partisi. Dissolving the country's largest party, that also participated in government *and* provided the prime minister, is by any standard a 'radical intervention in democratic political life'.[57] In its defence before the ECHR, the Turkish state appealed explicitly to the idea of militant democracy.[58]

Refah was gradually advancing, winning 22 percent of votes in national elections in 1995, and then 35 percent a year later in local elections.[59] This made Refah the strongest party in parliament, with 158 of the 450 seats.[60] Opinion polls predicted even larger election gains and a two-thirds majority in national elections four years later.[61] In 1997 the Turkish Public Prosecutor asked the Constitutional Court to dissolve the party because of its hostility towards the secular character of the Turkish state.[62] Turkish history and 'specific features of Islam' have led the Turkish constitution to give extra weight to this principle.[63] In 1998 the party was disbanded by the Turkish Constitutional Court.[64]

In the past the ECHR had, without exception, ruled *against* the Turkish state when it came to party bans,[65] but in 2003 it considered the ban of Refah as being in accordance with the Convention. Refah did not fulfil either of the requirements imposed by the court: 1) the party refused to renounce violence and even defended it in covert terms,[66] and 2) working towards the introduction of legal pluralism and sharia goes against the 'fundamental principles of democracy'.[67] According to the ECHR (the Grand Chamber confirmed the previous judgement in this respect), the irreconcilability could primarily be found in the following aspects of sharia: its criminal law, the law of criminal procedure, the legal status of women and the far-reaching imposition of religious rules in public and private spheres.[68]

It is not my intention here to fully dissect the Refah case. That has been done elsewhere, for instance, through consideration of the extent to which the judgement is limited to the Turkish context.[69] The aim is to learn from the way in which the ECHR spells out the concept of democracy in legal terms; what falls under the 'fundamental democratic principles'?

The aspects that the ECHR considers problematic in sharia law make it clear that fundamental democratic principles should be more broadly interpreted than democracy in a strict sense; we are talking about democratic *and* constitutional principles. A good deal, however, remains unclear. It is not explained how that broad interpretation of democracy looks precisely. Where in German jurisprudence we see an extensive list of separate elements, the *specific* content of democracy in the Refah case is left hanging. The ECHR considers certain aspects of sharia not to be in accordance with fundamental democratic principles. The question is, why not? What exactly is covered by the umbrella concept of 'fundamental democratic principles' that cannot be reconciled with the components of sharia mentioned?

Of course, we can imagine various possible answers, but simply pronouncing them irreconcilable is dissatisfying.[70] The Germans would do better with their definition, which is properly worked out in jurisprudence.

It is therefore perhaps no coincidence that a German judge wrote a 'concurring opinion' on the case, in which he maps out this issue.[71] He supports the judgement, but calls attention to a specific issue: the double requirement formulated by the ECHR for the functioning of political parties. Judge Georg Ress considers them too general and dogmatically formulated.[72] The imprecise nature of the formulation risks the possibility of party bans becoming far too broadly interpreted after the Refah case. Ress calls attention to the statement referred to by the ECHR in formulating the requirements (in §98). In Ress' words:

> So the very general sentences of paragraph 98 of the judgment need some further clarification and limitation in the light of the principle of proportionality and in the light of the judgments which are quoted at the end of that paragraph. I have no doubt that the aims for which the applicant party and its prominent leaders stood and which they advocated rather vigorously are not in conformity with basic rules of democracy and justify the dissolution. The only point I wanted to make is that the Court's observation in paragraph 98 of the judgment must be read in the light of the other quoted judgments and within the interpretation that was given in these judgments, in particular *United Communist Party of Turkey and Others*, and not be taken for a general dictum, as its wording might appear to suggest.[73]

In its judgement *United Communist Party of Turkey* the ECHR does indeed examine what a democracy entails in more detail. The court found a violation of Article 11 (the freedom of assembly and association) of the Convention: a Turkish communist party was banned before it even got under way,[74] which was too drastic.[75] On reading the judgement, the fundamental role that the ECHR attributes to freedom of expression in a democracy particularly stands out. The court words it as follows:

> Democracy is without doubt a fundamental feature of the European public order.... That is apparent, firstly, from the Preamble to the Convention, which establishes a very clear connection between the Convention and democracy by stating that the maintenance and further realisation of human rights and fundamental freedoms are best ensured on the one hand by an *effective political democracy and on the other by a common understanding and observance of human rights*.... The Court has identified certain provisions of the Convention as being characteristic of democratic society. Thus in its very first judgment it held that in a 'democratic society within the meaning of the Preamble and the other clauses of the convention', proceedings before the judiciary should be

> conducted in the presence of the parties and in public and that that fundamental principle was upheld in article 6 of the Convention.... In a field closer to the one concerned in the instant case, the Court has on many occasions stated, for example, that *freedom of expression constitutes one of the essential foundations of a democratic society and one of the basic conditions for its progress and each individual's self-fulfillment* ..., whereas in the Mathieu-Mohin and Clerfayt judgment cited above it noted the prime importance of *Article 3 of Protocol No. 1*, which enshrines a characteristic principle of an effective political democracy.[76] (my italicization, BR)

Although the ECHR does not give a full definition of democracy, it is nonetheless one of the most detailed discussions by the ECHR on democracy.[77] The impression the Refah case gave is immediately confirmed: the ECHR's view of democracy is broad, with constitutional overtones. The model that the court uses is that of a 'liberal democracy'.[78] What is more important is how the ECHR interprets that concept 'legally' in *United Communist Party of Turkey*.

Fortunately, the court gives us a number of footholds; there are provisions that the court considers particularly 'characteristic of democratic society', one of which is Article 10 of the Convention, freedom of expression. According to the court, this freedom is 'one of the essential foundations of a democratic society' and a basic requirement for the functioning of democracy. Certainly freedom of expression is also important for 'self-fulfillment' (a more individualistic interpretation of freedom of expression), but the ECHR particularly emphasizes its value to democracy. It also refers to Article 3 of the Convention First Protocol, which guarantees the right to periodical free elections by secret ballot. The court also brings in Article 6 of the Convention, the right to a fair trial, under its interpretation of democracy; here again we clearly see the strong constitutional colouring.

The emphasis on freedom of expression as a condition for democracy deserves attention. In the jurisprudence of the Bundesverfassungsgericht, freedom of expression is also connected with democracy in a way that resembles the ECHR interpretation.[79] The Dutch Supreme Court, in accordance with the ECHR, also points to the importance of an open debate in society.[80] In the United States, too, this 'instrumental defence' of freedom of expression has a long tradition. Its most important representative is found in the work of American philosopher Alexander Meiklejohn (1872-1964).[81] Under this view the First Amendment is primarily intended to support democratic self-government.

It is not difficult to see the significance of freedom of expression for self-correction. The idea of democracy as self-correction, after all, rests on the presence of policy alternatives. The principles of evaluation and political competition have already made way for the presentation of these alternatives; the playing field is as broad as possible. Now the 'players' (individuals, whether united in parties or not) must have the opportunity to express their alternative vision. Freedom of expression is thus an indispensable link in the chain of 'democracy as self-correction'. The elections can be entirely free and every political movement well represented, but without free discussion of proposals, self-government by self-correction is an illusion. *Freedom of expression* should be added to the core elements of democracy as self-correction.

Three remarks on Refah and subsequent jurisprudence

Before we make up the balance, there are three matters in Strasbourg jurisprudence that demand our attention. First, we have a lesson that has already been discussed in part: the testing of religious party programmes. This needs to happen much more clearly, at least more so than in the Refah case. It must be clearly stated *which* of a religious party's ideas are irreconcilable with *which* values and why those values are among the 'fundamental democratic principles'.

These values cannot simply be declaimed and then served up in a mishmash of democratic and constitutional elements. This requires a clear theory of the essence of democracy. The apodictic character of the judgement leads to suspicions that this is lacking. Democracy as self-correction attempts to assist precisely here, clearly demarcating the core that we should protect.

The European Court of Human Rights actually bit off more than it can chew in the Refah case. Why state that sharia as such is irreconcilable with democracy and human rights?[82] This puts the court on theological terrain, an area in which it should not be involved at all,[83] and playing into the critics' hands: after almost fifteen centuries of Islamic theology one can always come up with an interpretation of sharia to prove the opposite.[84] It would have been more sensible for the court to restrict its positions to the familiar territory of constitutional law and Convention interpretation. The aim would then not be to establish whether or not sharia as such is compatible with 'fundamental democratic principles', but whether a party's *concrete* proposals can stand that test. For example, if Refah's interpretation of sharia were inevitably to lead to the abolition of freedom of expression, then that, and not sharia, should be the reason to conclude that it is irreconcilable with democracy. To be sure, the conclusion can probably remain the same, but the argumentation must be clearer. Otherwise the court opens itself up to predictable but no less justifiable criticism.[85] It would also contribute to a clearer, more constructive delimitation of democratic tolerance. Sharia itself should not be branded undemocratic; instead an indication should be given of which points of a specific interpretation of sharia clash with democratic values. Such an approach could also substantially contribute to the development of a democratic Islam within the boundaries of the European liberal democracy.[86] Nevertheless, more recent ECHR jurisprudence similarly assumes that democracy and any form of sharia are irreconcilable in principle.[87]

The second point is that an important aspect of the Refah case was the real threat posed by the party. It was the largest party in national and local elections, and trends showed that support was more likely to rise than fall. The court notes:

> The Court accordingly considers that at the time of its dissolution Refah had the real potential to seize political power without being restricted by the compromises inherent in a coalition. If Refah had proposed a programme contrary to democratic principles, its monopoly of political power would have enabled it to establish the model of society envisaged in that programme.[88]

It then states:

> While it can be concluded, in the present case, that Refah's policies were dangerous for the rights and freedoms guaranteed by the Convention, *the real chances that Refah would implement its programme after gaining power made that danger more tangible and more immediate.* That being the case, the Court cannot criticise the national courts for not acting earlier, at the risk of intervening prematurely and before the danger concerned had taken shape and become real. *Nor can it criticise them for not waiting, at the risk of putting the political regime and civil peace in jeopardy, for Refah to seize power and swing into action, for example by tabling bills in Parliament, in order to implement its plans.*
>
> In short, the Court considers that in electing to intervene at the time when they did in the present case the national authorities did not go beyond the margin of appreciation left to them under the Convention.[89] (my italicization, BR)

The latter quote invites us to deduce, by contrast, that in the absence of a real, acute threat, a party or association cannot simply be banned. The court appears to maintain the possibility that if intervention occurs too early the 'margin of appreciation' would indeed be exceeded, leading to a violation of Article 11 ECHR.

That conclusion seems unjustified. As Dutch jurist Marloes van Noorloos shows, in two cases on the radical Islamic association Hizb ut-Tahrir, the level of the threat played no role whatsoever.[90] Both the German and the Russian bans, in 2012 and 2013 respectively, were approved by the ECHR with reference to Article 17 of the Convention (prohibition of abuse of rights). In both cases it was established that the association (not a political party) was opposed to 'fundamental democratic principles', and that was sufficient. An estimation of their support or potential support played no part in the test. The intention to use rights enshrined in the Convention *against* those same rights made an appeal to those rights impossible. In the words of the court (in the Russian case):

> In view of the above considerations, the Court finds that the dissemination of the political ideas of Hizb ut-Tahrir by the applicants clearly constitutes an activity falling within the scope of Article 17 of the Convention. The applicants are essentially seeking to use Articles 9, 10 and 11 to provide a basis under the Convention for a right to engage in activities contrary to the text and spirit of the Convention. That right, if granted, would contribute to the destruction of the rights and freedoms set forth in the Convention and referred to above.[91]

In the cases against Hizb ut-Tahrir, the abuse clause of Article 17 is expressly mentioned.[92] It is remarkable that in the Refah case no special attention is given to this article. Refah's appeal was rejected on the grounds that the ban constituted a legitimate restriction of Article 11. In the cases against Hizb ut-Tahrir, however, the court does not review the grounds for restriction: Article 17 means that Article 11 does not apply at all.

Could this explain the lack of a 'threat test'? If the court makes its evaluation based on the grounds for limiting freedom of association given in Article 11, an assessment takes place, and within that assessment the chance of realizing the party programme plays a role. After all, the court has to assess whether the restriction is '*necessary* in a democratic society'. However, when Article 17 blocks an appeal to a right enshrined in the Convention, the actual threat plays no role: the party or association simply forfeits its right of association and thus enjoys no protection against a ban according to the Convention. It is then, of course, important to decide at what point the aims of a party are *so* opposed to the Convention that Article 17 is activated (and Article 11 excluded), and when a party can in principle rightfully appeal to Article 11 (under which the exercise of this right, in certain circumstances, can be limited). Clearly Hizb ut-Tahrir falls into the former category and Refah into the latter. In the first category the actual threat plays no role, whereas in the second category this factor is taken into consideration. The ECHR thus really uses two lines in its defence against antidemocratic parties and associations, a first fundamental test (Art. 17), followed by a more refined, interpretive test for the remaining cases (Art. 11).

If this interpretation is correct, the Hizb ut-Tahrir cases, by contrast with what we assumed with Van Noorloos, do *not* constitute a correction of the Refah case.[93] The way in which Article 17 functions in the area of *hate speech* also appears to point in this direction. If the expression of an opinion is fundamentally at odds with the values of the Convention, Article 17 blocks an appeal to Article 10 and no substantive review takes place.[94] This would concern issues such as Holocaust denial or labelling Jews as the source of problems in Russia.[95] Belgian constitutional lawyer Pieter Vanden Heede also stressed, even before the Hizb ut-Tahrir cases, that there are two ways in which the ECHR assesses party bans: Articles 11 and 17. Vanden Heede advises against use of Article 17 for the very reason that it does not allow for examination of the actual risk represented by a party.[96]

It also appears that there is much to be said for the 'two-line' explanation. This allows for a good explanation of the difference in attention to threat levels. The distinction between the two 'lines of defence', however, remains problematic. Additional research, including a closer comparison between Refah and the Hizb ut-Tahrir cases, in part in the light of hate speech jurisprudence, might point us in the direction of useful criteria. Is it, for example, a question of non-categorical exclusion of violence? In Refah *too* the party's stances on violence were ambiguous, to say the least.[97] The difficulties in the application of Article 17 in hate speech jurisprudence (under Article 10, freedom of expression) suggest that a clear-cut distinction will not be easy to devise.[98]

On the basis of the Hizb ut-Tahrir cases we can in any case conclude, as the third and final point, that the ECHR has made the double-edged sword of Article 11 and 17 of the Convention particularly sharp. We saw in *United Communist Party of Turkey* that the ECHR is keen to allow plenty of space for discussion and robust debate. At the same time, this *also* means that those who wish to simply destroy such debate can make no further claim on those rights.

The three principles of democracy as self-correction

Both the BVerfG and the ECHR have had to think about the question of how to flesh out abstract concepts as, respectively, the 'freiheitliche demokratische Grundordnung' and the 'fundamental democratic principles'. These are, after all, concepts against which party goals must be assessed, and the consequences of that assessment can be far-reaching. Both courts understandably wrestle with the question of how such abstract concepts can be translated into legally workable criteria. I do not attempt to pass judgement on the extent to which they have achieved this, as too few judgements have been investigated and a more detailed study of their jurisprudence is beyond the scope of this work. The separate elements contributed by the two institutions serve as inspiration for a further interpretation of the concept of 'democracy as self-correction'. They are the sorely needed starting points for the question of which principles we can point to as necessary for democracy as self-correction.

Previously we established that a *principle of evaluation* is indispensable; without it there is no democracy. Active suffrage and elections normally realize this principle. Based on our closer investigations, we can now add two further principles.

First, we can distil the *principle of political competition* from the German multiparty principle. In the language of competition law, monopolies must be made impossible. Political competition must be safeguarded.

There are two safeguards to ensure this. In a democracy without parties, passive suffrage ensures that new challengers can always arise. Passive suffrage therefore cannot be restricted to a select group. For a party democracy (practically *all* democracies), the guarantee of political competition should additionally be sought in the freedom of association, or the freedom to establish political parties. One party should never be able to *de facto* transplant the state. That would mean the end of political competition; alternative policy options can no longer be proposed outside the party. This is why one-party states can never be democracies.

On the basis of the ECHR jurisprudence we can add a second necessary principle: *freedom of expression*. The ECHR emphasizes that democracy cannot exist without freedom of expression; the same applies to the narrower concept of 'democracy as self-correction'. Freedom of expression lays the foundation for putting forward alternative visions, for criticism and changes of course. Parties can form freely, citizens can stand for election and they can regularly evaluate the alternatives in elections, but it must also be possible to put forward all these alternative visions, from ideas on the good life to the right level of welfare benefits. Freedom of expression ensures that this is possible.

That results in the following overview. The self-corrective mechanism at least requires:

- the principle of evaluation
- the principle of political competition
- freedom of expression

If a party threatens to abolish one of the above values and principles or to damage its core, the self-corrective mechanism is directly endangered. The list outlines the *minimum* requirements. Within the theory of democracy as self-correction such aims can be labelled antidemocratic, making the party eligible for prohibition. The judge has a legally workable standard. He knows to which principles, and by extension fundamental rights, he should pay attention.

Protection of these principles preserves the core of self-correction, whereby regrettable and bad decisions, such as tinkering with *other* fundamental rights (not in the realm of these principles), can be reversed. That is not to say that this summary is definitive. Perhaps there are other values or principles that need to be added to the list in order to maintain self-correction. I think, however, that we have the core in sight with the list as it stands. However, the fact that it is not definitive is not to say that the *judge* should not have a limited list. Political theory, legal scholarship and the legislator must discuss the elements of a correct definition, and this choice must then be laid down in law by the legislator. The discussion ends there; the judge must then be able to work with a limited set of criteria; one cannot reasonably ask more of him regarding such a sensitive and political subject.

Procedural safeguards I: judicial supervision

The narrow grounds for prohibition in the theory of democracy as self-correction in itself offers an important safeguard against abuse. A ban is only possible when the self-corrective mechanism is damaged. The limited list prevents the judge from (unwillingly) having to enter political territory. If the judge strays onto political terrain, he becomes part of a battle from which he can only emerge with less authority. The judge's decision must therefore be as apolitical as possible. It does not help if he himself has to define what 'fundamental democratic principles' are. Whatever the judgement in such a situation will be, he will always carry with him the suspicion that his choice of values was at least politically *inspired*. And even if he manages to avoid this, with broad grounds for prohibition he will inevitably stumble upon almost insoluble problems of interpretation, which will also eventually erode his authority. As early as 1936 Van den Bergh pointed out the impossible task of the judge in such a situation:

> The [Dutch] legislator clearly did not comprehend the difficulty of the task with which he burdened the judge. This can only arouse greater surprise as it becomes clear that the legislator was in fact aware of this, that he had even designed regulations for *political* associations, for political parties. In this respect the history of the law is unambiguous. Many members of the [Parliament] have actually thought specifically of political associations.
>
> Our current law thus prohibits the political party whose aim conflicts with public morality [goede zeden]. And the judge must make a decision free from any 'political' consideration! Where can he find support, where clear criteria?[99]

Making a judgement 'free from any political consideration' does indeed appear impossible when the grounds for prohibition are vague, let alone in cases of the judge acting in bad faith, using such grounds *intentionally* to allow his political considerations to have an influence. A narrow, closely defined foundation for a ban can offer a safeguard against interpretation problems that undermine authority as well as politically inspired judgements.

I turn now to additional *procedural* safeguards. Given the invasive character of a party ban, the call for such safeguards is justified.[100] That is also the line taken by the European Commission for Democracy through Law, or the Venice Commission, in a report on party bans.[101] In addition to a more general reservation (it must be a measure of 'last resort'), this advisory body of the Council of Europe (and with it the ECHR) emphasizes the procedural safeguards that party bans should come with.[102] Or as Kirshner states, a party ban brings 'democratic costs' with it, compromising democracy.

How should we translate this concept, termed 'democratic responsibility' by Kirshner, into extra safeguards?

Van den Bergh proposes to leave the judgement on banning political parties exclusively to a Supreme Court, which can only make that decision by unanimous vote.[103] The Prosecutor General is then the official with the authority to demand a ban. The reasoning here is that this benefits independence, as the Prosecutor General is appointed for life.[104]

Bellekom, too, argues for exclusively authorizing a Supreme Court to decide on party bans,[105] as does the Venice Commission, which in the first instance thinks of letting a Constitutional Court decide.[106] Elzinga, however, rightly points to an important disadvantage of this construct: appeal and judgement in different institutions are excluded.[107] One might argue that Van den Bergh in part pre-empts this problem by requiring a unanimous decision. Nonetheless, the safeguards of a judgement in multiple courts are greater. The fact that this would mean a lower court initially considering the issue, seen in that light, is not so problematic: ultimately the Supreme Court can weigh in. The limited experience and development of the law when it comes to party bans are also an extra argument for a judgement by *multiple* institutions: jurisprudence in this area is limited, in the Netherlands and elsewhere. Take, for example, the radically different interpretations that the Dutch district and appeals court gave to the banning provision in Article 20, Book 2 of the Dutch Civil Code in the case of the paedophile association Vereniging Martijn (to be sure, an association, not a political party).[108] It was no excessive luxury that the Supreme Court could draw on their interpretations before giving a definitive judgement, deciding to ban the association.[109]

Procedural safeguards II: the European dimension of militant democracy

Another option, of course, is to look to the international level for the court that has to pass judgement on such precarious matters. There is something to be said for that. These institutions, after all, are placed at a distance from local, national politics and should therefore, in theory, be able to function as neutral arbitrators. Issacharoff, for example, writes:

> Requiring … a source of review independent of the executive provides a check on the misuse of this dangerous power. Perhaps the clearest example is the use of international tribunals, such as the European Court of Justice [sic], to review party prohibitions. Such crossnational bodies are removed from any immediate accountability to domestic political processes and are unlikely to respond narrowly to partisan or sectional interests.[110]

A disadvantage of such an approach is that a democracy effectively places itself under permanent external supervision. The most important decisions on national democracy are then, after all, made by an international organ. A democracy thus no longer has the final say over the defence of its institutions. Aside from the (un)desirability, it is important to note that, of course, a capable and in principle neutral organ that can fulfil this function is not available everywhere. In fact, an organ with the standing of the ECHR probably exists only in Europe.[111] One might also wonder whether the advantage of this assumed detached neutrality is not outweighed by the disadvantage of insensitivity and lack of knowledge of the local, national political situation. Even if that lack of knowledge can be remedied, such an institution faces a dilemma. On the one hand, it seems impossible to come to a correct judgement in a concrete case without doing something about that lack of knowledge and 'deeply analysing the political environment of a particular country'.[112] How else can one truly assess the risk, for example? On the other hand, such in-depth research can easily lead to the accusation that the overarching organization has entered 'the domain reserved for national authorities'.[113] The role that this kind of international organ can fulfil is therefore likely to be largely supplementary. The European Court of Human Rights employs a critical standard, but via the 'margin of appreciation' nevertheless allows the member states some latitude.[114]

At the same time, the European dimension of militant democracy is already a reality in a different respect. In addition to the ECHR, the European Union also applies a (currently modest) form of 'supranational democracy-protection' and has the authority to do so based on its treaty obligations.[115] In the case of the EU, however, it is not a question of supervising the execution of militant democracy, but rather of its own 'militant democracy measures', which can be effectuated against member states with the aim of protecting democracy there. Of course, the most prominent is the 'nuclear option' in Article 7 of the Treaty of Lisbon: if a state significantly breaks with fundamental European values, a state's membership can be suspended.[116] The Article 7 procedure was triggered by the European Commission with regard to Poland in December 2017 for worries over the independence of the country's judiciary.[117] Other, less far-reaching, ad hoc sanctions have already been imposed, for instance, in the Haider affair, which (partially) led to Article 7 in its present form.[118] When it became clear that the radical right-wing party of Jörg Haider (1950-2008) would participate in government in Austria in 2000, the fourteen other EU member states all decided to suspend diplomatic contacts with the country.[119] It was a combined initiative on the part of the other EU member states, without a basis in treaties, taken before the new Austrian government was actually able to realize any concrete plans, and it only lasted for a few months.[120] It made the sanctions, as Müller writes, look 'somewhat ridiculous', and the whole affair 'in some ways deeply traumatized European elites'.[121] The principle behind it, however, was highly significant: by imposing sanctions on a member state, they punished that state for the fact that a radical right-wing party came so far as to participate in government. It gave a clear signal that the EU, or at least the individual member states, are watching and that vigilance or even active intervention to protect democracy can be expected.[122] Other EU worries focused on Hungary and Romania, and there, too, there have been interventions in different ways, for instance, through proceedings started by the European Commission in the European Court of Justice.[123]

The fact that the EU acts as a border guard for the national democracies is really not that surprising. The EU, along with the ECHR, is an expression of the post-war European 'constitutionalist ethos': a mindset inspired by the trauma of the interbellum, characterized by a serious mistrust of national sovereignty and parliamentary decision making.[124] The European democracies delegated their power in part to unelected institutions, national and supranational, to 'lock in' their liberal democracies, thus protecting themselves against a 'return to authoritarianism'.[125] The establishment of the ECHR can also be explained as resulting from the desire of the damaged European democracies to 'consolidate democracy' through self-restriction by international law, locking in the 'political status quo against their non-democratic opponents'.[126] As Jan-Werner Müller describes:

> Distrust of unrestrained popular sovereignty—and even the unconstrained parliamentary sovereignty that a German constitutional lawyer once called 'parliamentary absolutism'—is in the very DNA of postwar European politics.[127]

Müller is in favour of European oversight of democracy in member states, but he does not want to base it solely on a rationale of 'never again'. He gives a principled argument for EU intervention in national democracies: via the European Council, each member state, including potentially *undemocratic* member states, decides on the 'lives of all Europeans'.[128] Strictly speaking there are no 'purely domestic matters' in the EU, according to Müller.[129]

In Müller's view an EU intervention must fulfil three requirements: 1) there must be a 'track record of violating liberal-democratic principles', 2) intervention must not take place if restoration can be enforced nationally (for instance, by the courts), and 3) the case must involve radical deviations from 'shared understandings' on democracy.[130] Moreover, Müller proposes expanding both the EU infrastructure and the arsenal of measures. An independent organ should oversee democracy in the member states and, keeping the requirements mentioned in mind, should be able to impose sanctions less far-reaching than Article 7 of the Lisbon Treaty *without* having to vote on this in the European Council.[131] Other protective mechanisms simply remain in place.[132]

Nevertheless, there is something ironic about the idea that the EU should act as protector of democracy in the member states. It seems realistic to expect that the legitimacy of the EU in this area will at least be contested. Critics will argue that the EU itself has a primarily negative effect on democracy in its various member states.[133]

Here we encounter a paradox. The EU is increasingly political, and this development is expressed, among other things, in a European party system. From a democratic point of view that is a commendable development.[134] In terms of legitimacy, too, it could be very significant: the EU then shifts, to put it coarsely, from a less democratic supranational system to a more federal democratic constellation. That should ensure that interventions in national democracies can be justified more convincingly; there would be less force to the argument 'Take a look at how undemocratic you are yourself.' At the same time, however, and here we come to the paradox, this politicization means that the EU is less effective as an independent arbiter.[135] It is one of the reasons why, for example, Müller proposes an independent supervisory organ, removed from European politics. The question then is whether such an organ, embedded in an increasingly political union, would be able to maintain that role. The counterintuitive conclusion might then be that the EU can only function as an arbiter as long as it is supranational, and that all further politicization, in the absence of a federal EU, will hinder it functioning as an arbiter.

However, another development is possible within the European dimension of militant democracy, namely, the situation in which instead of the European Court of Justice supervising the democracies of the member states, the opposite happens and national courts oppose what they see as EU erosions of their national democracies. Certainly in member states with an unchangeable constitutional core in an 'eternity clause' (such as Germany), we can legitimately ask to what extent European integration can be reconciled with the democratic principles protected 'for eternity' by this core. This gives us the interesting situation in which the battle over the future of the European democracies appears to be fought out between two 'counter-majoritarian' institutions par excellence: the (national) constitutional courts versus the European Court.[136] The German Bundesverfassungsgericht is unmistakeably at the forefront in this development, although other national courts seem to move in that direction too, particularly the Czech court.[137]

The highest German court explicitly retains the right to review all EU developments for their (ir)reconcilability with the German Constitution.[138] This led to a series of much-discussed and criticized judgements on the Treaties of Maastricht and Lisbon, and more recently on the government bond buy-back programme.[139] In the case of the Lisbon Treaty, the German Constitutional Court even directly stated that the eternity clause made it impossible for Germany to become part of a European federal state.[140] British legal scholar Michael Wilkinson describes the situation as follows:

> If it is legitimate to institutionalise the protection of democracy against itself—key to the idea of 'militant democracy'—then Karlsruhe's actions appear nothing short of heroic. Taking fundamental rights and democratic guarantees off the table of parliamentary deliberation is intended to prevent the Bundestag from committing suicide by

> transferring powers to a democratically unaccountable body such as the EU.... Karlsruhe has even been cast by some in the unlikely role of Rebel, or protagonist of democratic Resistance. Although this attribution seems far-fetched ..., there is a kernel of truth to it. The German Court is unwilling to delegate the task of guarding democratic sovereignty to the institutions of the EU in general and the European Court of Justice in particular.[141]

The question is how this competence battle will develop, on this and other issues, now that the German Court is behaving more assertively,[142] while the European Court refuses to give in. The European Court approved the buyback programme, despite German constitutional objections.[143] Moreover, it is difficult to explain the prejudicial question of the Bundesverfassungsgericht in this case as a sign of deference.[144] Even if the Bundesverfassungsgericht conforms to the supranational order, there are still in principle twenty-seven other national courts, of which, according to the German Court, currently at least ten are taking a similar course.[145]

Seen in this light, the European dimension of militant democracy will only become more important. Remarkably enough, that will probably happen along the lines of two opposing developments, with on the one hand a further development of supranational oversight of national democracies, but on the other hand also resistance from national courts in the name of the national democracies, against supranationalism.

Democracy as self-correction is, in principle, set up as a *self-supporting* system: the defence of democracy is organized at the national level. The orderly execution of this process is promoted by two 'national' safeguards: judicial supervision (discussed earlier) and the procedures around submitting requests for party bans (to be discussed below). At the same time, we observed in chapter 2 that there is a real chance of abuse of party bans in young and unstable democracies. It is not inconceivable that in these cases a militant democracy might benefit from supplementary *negative* supervision of party bans. The ECHR offers this kind of negative control: a party ban reaches the ECHR after a complaint regarding infringement of individual rights (in this case the right of association). The court thus functions as a restricted judge in the final instance. It does not impose party bans and can only overturn unfair bans. Of course, it is a problem that precisely in the places where such supranational oversight would be most desirable, as for example in the African democracies, a suitable organ is not yet available.

Procedural safeguards III: the request for a party ban

Another question is, who can submit a request for a party ban? In Germany the *Bundestag*, *Bundesrat* and *Bundesregierung* can ask the BVerfG to ban a party. Müller's intuition with respect to European politics also seems relevant here, in the national context: it is probably better to create distance between the organs involved in 'oversight of democracy' and politicians. Of course, there is already a distance between courts and politicians, but one can attempt to create such distance (in part) between politicians and the organ requesting the ban. The Dutch model is an interesting example. Under the current Dutch party ban regime, the organ making the request is the Public Prosecution Service (Art. 20, Book 2, para. 1 of the Civil Code). Despite the minister of justice having the authority to issue instructions (Art. 127 of the Judiciary Organization Act), the Public Prosecution Service is positioned at some distance from politicians, guaranteeing the apolitical character of the process as far as possible.[146]

Now in this system two problems seem likely: 1) there is a party that is widely believed (in the House of Representatives too) to represent a serious threat to the self-corrective mechanism, but the Public Prosecution Service takes no action; and 2) there are serious doubts as to whether a party can be labelled antidemocratic, but the Public Prosecution Service nonetheless begins proceedings for a ban. In both cases the minister of justice's authority to instruct offers a solution. The minister in turn is accountable to the House of Representatives, so the House can challenge him regarding both procrastination (the first problem) and overzealous behaviour (the second problem) on the part of the Public Prosecution Service. The rule of confidence (to remain in office, a minister needs the support of a parliamentary majority) ensures that the minister will have to listen eventually. This structure appears preferable to a situation in which the House of Representatives must *always* vote on such a request, or a construction whereby the government directly decides on initiating ban proceedings. This would politicize the process from the start. Of course, a determined government can still get its way through the authority to instruct (and it, in turn, can be instructed to use that authority by the House of Representatives that can dismiss a government on the basis of the rule of confidence). But in the Dutch system at least *some* distance is built in: after all, the process is executed by the Public Prosecution Service, which does have (some) room for its own assessment.[147] The Dutch system, therefore, with the 'ban requesting agency' placed at a certain distance from day-to-day politics, seems favourable, provided that the government can instruct that agency, with the parliament acting as a final check.

The design of party bans

The banned extreme right-wing Czech Workers' Party became the Workers' Party for Social Justice. Not long afterwards they participated in elections as a 'new' party and achieved a good result in party terms. As outlined above, the ringleaders of the banned party had anticipated a ban and already had the new party ready and waiting like an empty shell; the members of the banned party were immediately able to move to the new party. When it comes to Turkey, one could even speak of a '"spare party" system': parties that feared a ban regularly had a 'new' party ready and waiting.[148] In Spain, too, the banned Batasuna attempted to return to politics 'under a different guise' after 2003.[149] But in Spain, on the basis of the Batasuna ban, this was impossible. Two successors of Batasuna were never registered, and two others were declared illegal.[150]

In other words, one party ban is not the same as another. A militant democracy theory must also cover the consequences of a ban, by which is meant: the 'chosen' *legal* consequences of a party ban, which can be determined by the legislator. The *actual* effects of a party ban on the organization of factions and (de)radicalization, of course, cannot be chosen.

For example, take the consequences of a party ban in the Netherlands. In the Netherlands a party can be banned and dissolved on the basis of Article 20, Book 2 of the Civil Code. This happened to the Nationaal-Socialistische Beweging (the collaborating National Socialist Movement, NSB) in 1945, the Nationaal Europese Sociale Beweging (the National European Socialist Movement, founded by a former Waffen-SS commander, NSEB) in 1956, and the Centrumpartij '86 (the Center Party '86, a racist political party, CP'86) in 1998.[151] If a party is banned, this means that the legal entity must also be dissolved (Art. 20, Book 2, para, 1). To be banned, its *operations* must be in conflict with public order. If only its *aims* are in conflict with public order, the party can only be disbanded (Art. 20, Book 2, para. 2) and must then receive the opportunity to adjust its aims.[152]

The consequences are threefold.[153] First, there are the civil law consequences of the dissolution: after settlement the legal entity ceases to exist. There are also the penal consequences of the ban. Article 140 paragraph 2 of the Dutch Penal Code makes participation in the continuation of a banned organization a punishable offence.[154] A third category is formed by what could be termed electoral consequences, which primarily follow from the Electoral Code: the party's name is removed from the register, and this is published in the *Staatscourant* (Government Gazette). From this moment on, it is impossible to participate in elections under the same name or any name exhibiting close similarities.[155] The right to party funding also lapses, as does the right to space in the allotted 'broadcasting time for political parties'.[156]

Viewed from the theory of militant democracy, a party ban must achieve a minimum of two things. First, it must become impossible to participate in elections as a party. That is the main aim. Access to parliament should be blocked. Second, effectiveness of the ban should also be safeguarded by cutting off the route for possible successors, thus avoiding the described Czech situation.

This can be achieved in various ways. András Sajó makes the following proposal:

> A more potent restriction occurs when the outlawed party's leader is prevented from being a founder in another party, or, as I would recommend, if a new party's formation may be denied if a dissolved party's leaders or founders act as founders or leaders in the new party.[157]

The variation mentioned is in place in Turkey: members of a banned party are excluded from politics for five years.[158] Sajó's proposal differs only cosmetically from this. Antidemocrats become political outcasts, lacking certain political rights. The foundation of a new party can be directly refused if a former leader is involved (independent of the party programme).[159] This is a far-reaching restriction on the (individual) right to freedom of association, while it is not directly clear why such a restriction is necessary for defending democracy. The measure thus misses its mark. In this respect the Dutch system is preferable: *only* the re-establishment of the same or a similar party (a *de facto* successor party) is banned—and for everyone. That is what is needed in protecting democracy, and at the same time the former founders' and leaders' freedom of association stay intact. This also fits better with the previously mentioned inclusive approach and the avoidance of political stigma. The former leaders of an antidemocratic party must be offered the opportunity to return to democratic life within the limits of democratic tolerance. Finally, it is not difficult to see how a ban based on the leader as an individual can still be circumvented by successor parties: a banned leader can easily appoint an intermediary as the formal founder of a successor party. It is even a construct found at a high level: after Tayyip Erdogan's AK party win in the Turkish national elections of 2002, it was not the founder Erdogan who became prime minister, but his fellow party member Abdullah Gül. Erdogan was excluded from participation in the elections and was not allowed to become head of government because of a conviction for 'inciting religious or ethnic hatred and violence'. The Turkish press, however, soon saw through this construct and spoke of Gül as the official prime minister and Erdogan as *de facto* prime minister.[160]

Other measures are conceivable. For instance, in Germany the dissemination of propaganda and symbols of banned parties has been criminalized, with the explicit aim of preventing their resurrection.[161] Israel has a similar stipulation, although it specifically refers to symbols of *terrorist* organizations: expressing sympathy for such an organization, including waving a flag, is a criminal offence.[162] It resembles the proposal of Dutch MP and CDA (Christian Democratic Appeal) leader Sybrand Buma in 2014: glorification of terrorism must be criminalized.[163] The Israeli ban on propaganda only applies if the banned party can be labelled a terrorist organization; in Germany that is not necessary.

The desirability of such measures, however, is debatable: a party ban then no longer covers only freedom of association, but also extends to freedom of expression. In this sense the same criticism applies as regarding Sajó's proposal to effectively deprive former party leaders of their right to association: it is not precise enough. In other words, it seems not directly necessary to restrict freedom of expression in order to combat antidemocratic parties.[164] However, here we are talking about the defence against antidemocratic parties. Whether freedom of expression must be restricted in the interest of the fight against terrorism when it comes to 'terrorist opinions' (as in the proposal of Dutch CDA MP Sybrand Buma and in the German system)[165] is a different question.[166]

Members of parliament and party bans: two models

What should happen to MPs from a banned party? It seems logical that one of the legal consequences of a party ban should be that members lose their seats in parliament. At the same time this corrodes their 'free mandate'—being accountable only to their voters, not their party.

There are different ways to deal with this problem. A first approach to the seats of a banned party lets MPs keep their seats. We might call it the 'unconditional model'. In the Netherlands this is the case. When a party already in parliament is banned, the MPs keep their seats.[167] That is the consequence of the Dutch Constitution (from 1848): parties are not recognized as such. MPs have a free mandate: only in exceptional circumstances can membership of parliament be ended.[168] Those exceptional circumstances do not include leaving a party, nor do they include the banning of a party.

The Dutch Constitution therefore assumes that all members of parliament have acquired their seats independently. This is a fiction: in 2012 Raymond de Roon (PVV), for instance, was elected with 347 votes and Steven van Weyenberg (D66) with 989.[169] For comparison, in order to achieve the electoral quota (the number of votes needed for one seat) 62,828 votes were required.[170] There are few points in which the Dutch Constitution is so at odds with reality. Certainly, the Constitution was written before there were modern political parties, but even in the many revisions of the Constitution a provision on parties has never been adopted.

In any case, the consequence of this system is that members of parliament from banned parties keep their seats. In the worst case that means that members of parliament from a banned party remain members of the House of Representatives for almost four years. One might argue that we simply have to wait it out; there is little chance of their being voted in again. Nonetheless, antidemocrats maintain their platform under this model, whereas a party ban aims to prevent this very scenario. The fact that it only affects a few individuals does not necessarily matter. Even individuals can generate a good deal of attention with the assistance of parliamentary instruments. Dutch political practice shows that a parliamentary question is asked easily, perhaps too easily. In other words, underestimating the impact of antidemocratic MPs keeping their seats fails to appreciate that parliament is not just 'a forum for the recording of preferences', but can also be a platform for the 'mobilization of political forces'.[171] In addition, often an appeal can be made to funding and political immunity.[172] Moreover, antidemocratic members of parliament can also hinder the functioning of this institution if they are present in large enough numbers, thus in part creating the problem they proclaim to be the solution to: in short, the strategy of the NSDAP in Weimar Germany.[173] The Netherlands is not alone in this choice. Spain, too, is a prominent example of a system in which the representatives of the people are permitted to keep their seats. When Batasuna was banned, its seven members of parliament from the autonomous Basque region along with dozens of local representatives simply remained in their seats.[174]

A different model, a 'conditional model', can be found in Germany and Turkey, where a strong relationship exists between the MPs' seats and the fate of the banned party. On paper the German regulation does not differ much from the Dutch situation: Article 38 of the Grundgesetz (GG) gives the representatives of the people a free mandate, originating from its voters, not its party.[175] Nevertheless, the Bundesverfassungsgericht judged that it follows 'compellingly' from GG Article 21 that members of parliament from a banned party should lose their seats.[176] Otherwise, as the BVerfG reasoned, they would still be capable of realizing their antidemocratic aims.[177] The Turkish Constitutional Court also has the authority to revoke the seats of members of parliament from banned parties, but it can choose which MPs lose their seats and which do not. In the case against Refah, 'the five most prominent and responsible' party members, including Necmettin Erbakan, lost their seats.[178] At that point the party was the largest in parliament, with 158 of 450 seats.[179]

There is much to be said for the conditional model of how the German and Turkish systems deal with the MPs of banned parties. They deprive the uprooted antidemocratic members of parliament of an effective launch platform for a new political movement, and, even more importantly, they directly cut off the possible implementation of the banned party's programme. This also prevents antidemocratic MPs from hindering the operations of parliament. Nonetheless, there are also arguments to opt for the 'unconditional model'. In Elzinga's view, it offers some compensation for 'abruptly cutting off the option of political communication'.[180] The acute consequences of the party ban are dampened; a 'safety valve' remains in place. In addition, a link between membership of parliament and membership of the party, however limited, would, on the whole, erode the free mandate, tying MPs more closely to their parties. The question is whether such watering down of the free mandate, and strengthening of the position of political parties, is really the way to go. The free mandate places a check on overly strict parliamentary party discipline and overall party power.[181] And, at least in the Netherlands, the first cracks in the independent position of parliamentarians are already beginning to show, given discussions on 'seat robbery', and the subsequently introduced new measures to restrict some parliamentary privileges of MPs who 'stole' their seats.[182]

Two nuances can be made on the respective unconditional and conditional approaches. First, the unconditional model. As it stands now, in the Netherlands it is still the voter, not the judge, who decides on the fate of the MPs of banned parties.[183] In a 1987 parliamentary debate this was still termed a 'good practice', by Minister Korthals Altes.[184] Nevertheless, the Dutch unconditional model has a serious weakness that can be remedied without radical change. Under the current arrangement, members of parliament keep their seats not only after a party ban, but *also* when they are convicted of the criminal continuation of their banned party.[185] An MP's seat in parliament cannot be revoked, not even if he attempts to join former party members in breathing new life into the banned party.

The possibility of losing membership of parliament would in these cases draw a clear line under the past of the MPs, marking the preconditions for a new, independent existence as a member of parliament. The banned party belongs to the past; the MP receives a new chance if he accepts the ban. In the best case it can encourage self-reflection; the door to the old party is definitively closed, in parliament too. It would be unreasonable to resolutely cling to the free mandate in this very specific case. The exception can be properly justified, and the infringement of the free mandate is small. The MP's new chance is linked to an ultimate boundary. It is an intermediary solution, without representing a fundamental change to the unconditional model.[186] This would be a sensible nuance, creating a 'nuanced unconditional model'.[187] From the perspective of a militant democracy, such a nuanced unconditional model represents the minimum of what would be required for defending democracy.

A second nuance regards the conditional model and can be found in Turkey. In Germany, the strongest conditional model, the 'banned' MPs *automatically* lose their seats; in Turkey, as we have seen, MPs *can* lose their seats when their party is banned; the judge has the option to expel only certain MPs. In this way only those members who disproportionately added to the antidemocratic character of the party can lose their seats, as happened to 5 of the total of 158 Turkish Refah MPs. This Turkish version, a 'nuanced conditional model', arguably offers opportunities for a more context-sensitive approach, in contrast with the 'all-or-nothing' decision as in Germany.

3. Criticism of militant democracy answered

The outlines of democracy as self-correction are now clear: the principle of self-correction serves as a justification for democratic self-defence, the three supporting principles (evaluation, political competition and freedom of expression) provide narrow grounds for prohibition, there are extra procedural safeguards for careful application, and finally there is a strict design for party bans. I have also formulated an answer to the pragmatic points of criticism, which turned out not to stand up to scrutiny. The principled criticism rooted in political philosophy, however, remains standing.

This criticism touches the core of the idea of militant democracy and democracy as self-correction. The most important point of criticism in the literature was the lack of a coherent theory that would further work out a justification for, and the design of, party bans. The theory of democracy as self-correction as such hopes to fill this gap. Now we turn to the tenability of its various component parts. These objections will be discussed point by point below, based on the theory as developed above, therewith further elucidating the theory of democracy as self-correction.

A militant democracy is undemocratic: banning parties cannot be justified, while a variant justified by a theory of substantive democracy places too many restrictions on the democratic process

Whether it is undemocratic depends on the chosen view of democracy. Within the procedural theory of democracy, militant democracy is seen as undemocratic, but not necessarily under substantive democracy. Substantive democracy involves majority decision making plus protection of fundamental rights. Fitting in with substantive democracy, however, does not make a militant democracy immune to criticism from 'proceduralists'; they still have some ammunition. Does a militant democracy following the pattern of a substantive democracy not hand over too many issues to the rule of law, for example? What is left of the original ideal of government by the people? Is the democratic legislator's freedom for decision making not too restricted? In short, are we not largely exchanging 'democracy' for the 'rule of law', while calling it a 'substantive democracy' in order not having to explicitly acknowledge this shift? The theory of substantive democracy cannot save militant democracy from this accusation, except by acknowledging that the original meaning of democracy really *has* disappeared into the background.

Democracy as self-correction allays this criticism by treading a line between the two poles of procedural and substantive democracy, remaining very close to the procedural idea of democracy, but without crossing the line to 'value-neutral' relativism.

Democracy as self-correction leaves as much as possible to the democratic process. That means that issues that are very important but that do not belong to the core of self-correction must be defended in democratic debate. Democracy as self-correction, however, guarantees that any bad decisions can always be reversed. Democracy as self-correction can temper the objections of proceduralists, without removing all defence mechanisms and rendering democracy defenceless.

Action against antidemocrats might be justified, but in practice a legitimate moment for intervention cannot be identified

Intervention by a militant democracy is always badly timed. It may be too early, in which case the party is still small, making intervention look premature and undemocratic. Or it may be too late, in which case the party will already have substantial support, again making intervention undemocratic. Elzinga bases his criticism on his relativist concept of freedom and law, an idea that is implicitly present in Brems' work. In the end both points of criticism come down to the same issue: whether intervention is justified in theory or not, in practice it will really always come too soon or too late.

As far as the relativist concept of freedom and law is concerned: the idea of democracy as self-correction is opposed to it. The legitimacy of intervention in democracy as self-correction is not based on current agreement with a norm, but on the preservation of the framework that makes expression of that agreement possible. This comes from the idea that agreement today may not entail agreement tomorrow. Thus democracy as self-correction emphasizes the *temporary* nature of agreement.[188] Under a relativist concept of law, the entire state structure is permanently incidental. This concept, therefore, in the end, does not sufficiently take into account the whimsical nature of agreement with norms.

In fact, democracy as self-correction can also supplement the relativist concept of law. Democratic self-correction (elections, parliamentary debate), after all, is the most accurate available thermometer of agreement with norms. The only thing democracy as self-correction demands is that that thermometer is kept intact, so that we can still ascertain how people see particular norms in the future and subsequently adjust those norms in an orderly democratic fashion.[189] Within these *very* broad boundaries (only leaving the thermometer itself untouched) a wide range of styles of government and associated norms are possible. That seems to be a justifiable 'institutionalization' of the relativist concept of law. It is also an answer to the previously discussed criticism of Gerard Langemeijer.[190]

Both Elzinga and Brems consider the timing of measures to be problematic. The following can be said in response. First, the lack of the *perfect* moment for intervention does not mean that an *acceptable* moment is inconceivable. Compare the terms of parliament discussed above: the perfect term cannot be determined, but that does not mean that there is nothing to be said about acceptable terms.

Antidemocrats who want to combat or abolish the self-corrective capacity of democracy are acting in conflict with the essence of democracy. They thus place themselves outside the order of what a democracy that wants to remain loyal to its core values must tolerate. The limits of democratic tolerance have been reached. That means that the right to intervene against antidemocratic parties has also been triggered. It is activated as soon as an antidemocratic party reveals its antidemocratic aims. For clarity, the only criterion is its *aims*, so a party that qualifies for a ban may well be (formally) non-violent. That is what Van den Bergh argued, and it is in agreement with the interpretation of the Bundesverfassungsgericht on militant democracy: non-violent parties are also eligible for a ban. It is not needed to prove that they incite violence or that party members are guilty of crimes.

The fact that the right to intervene arises at that moment, however, does not mean that the guillotine must fall at that moment. From Van den Bergh's inaugural lecture we have deduced an *opportunity principle*, a warning to wait as long as possible: a party must first be opposed in the democratic arena. Only when the expected danger to democracy becomes greater than the infringement of democracy represented by a ban is it an opportune moment to ban a party. The ban of the Turkish communist party took place *before* it had become active, and was thus rightly rejected by the ECHR in *United Communist Party of Turkey*: this threat could still have been tackled through democratic debate.

Popper, Rawls and Kirshner, too, indicate that one should wait as long as possible to intervene for reasons of democracy; intervention entails democratic 'costs'. Popper appears to be willing to intervene earlier than Rawls, and certainly earlier than Kirshner.[191] On the other hand, it could be argued that minorities, which are often the *first* victims of antidemocratic tendencies, might reasonably demand relatively early intervention.[192] As a rule of thumb the moment must come somewhere between the extremes of the ban of the Turkish communist party (too early) and the military intervention in Algeria against the Front Islamique du Salut (too late). It is then down to government ministers and judges together to determine the *acceptable* moment for a party ban and, in Kirshner's terms, to control the democratic costs.[193]

Finally, it can be observed that the focus of democracy as self-correction offers protection against premature intervention. It is, after all, a question of banned *parties*. The expression of antidemocratic views is not covered by the theory; that is the territory of freedom of expression. Only from the moment that antidemocrats begin to organize themselves into parties do they become eligible for a ban; in other words, only freedom of association can be restricted. This is also how the German system functions, for example.[194] The moment of intervention is put off in democracy as self-correction out of reasons of principle, giving as much freedom of expression as possible. Moreover, antidemocratic parties, because of their level of organization, probably represent a more pressing threat to democracy than individual antidemocratic politicians who make use of their right to freedom of expression.[195]

Even if an acceptable moment for intervention can be defined, the absence of legal criteria means that it will always be a political decision

The right to intervene arises at the moment that a party threatens the self-corrective capacity of democracy. Another question is, when should one make use of that right and actually intervene? The previous point of criticism assumed that the precise moment of intervention would be impossible to decide. We have rejected that argument: there is an acceptable moment for intervention.

Nevertheless, we lack hard legal criteria to judge whether a party ban has really been declared at that 'acceptable' moment. The chosen moment might be acceptable from the perspective of political philosophy, but there will always be a hint of politics about it, simply because it involves banning a *political party*.[196] The answer to this problem, however, should not be sought in the development of legal criteria for timing, which probably cannot be more sharply formulated than the opportunity principle discussed earlier: when the danger outweighs the infringement of democracy represented by a ban.

A supplementary solution, however, can be found in procedural safeguards. The suspected political character can in part be remedied by placing the institution that puts forward the ban on a distance from the government (and politics). But it does not offer absolute certainty; we need only remind ourselves of the Dutch system, where the minister still ultimately has the authority to instruct the Public Prosecution Department. In the end it will come down to an 'independent and competent judiciary', and this does not differ much from other situations in which we consider it legitimate for governments to 'restrict our rights and freedoms'.[197] It is the task of legislators, legal philosophers and jurists to think through these kinds of hard cases *in advance* and to specify the legal framework as far as possible, but this is the limit; the rest is left to the discretion of the judge.[198]

Should opposition to antidemocrats not be left to society? For example, demonstrations can symbolically confirm democratic values

Partly, yes. Democracy as self-correction also makes demands on the individuals who populate the institutions of a democracy: they must act in the spirit of democracy as self-correction, exhibiting a democratic ethos. That means that government ministers should straightforwardly emphasize the value of democracy, especially at times when democracy is threatened. This can be extended to the society as a whole; it can thus be expected of democrats in general. An understanding of why democracy is unique can contribute to such a widely shared democratic ethos. It is with good reason that we have described the quest for a justification for militant democracy as a quest for the essence of democracy, a *positive* defence of democracy, not 'the worst form of government except for all the others'. The German Constitution even contains a stipulation that specifically encourages citizens to exhibit resistance as a last resort. In GG Article 20 para 4 we read:

> All Germans shall have the right to resist any person seeking to abolish this constitutional order, if no other remedy is available.[199]

In the final instance, the defence of democracy falls back on its citizens. Popper might have formulated it this way.

However, as the German jurist Markus Thiel (born 1973) argues, it is somewhat 'risky' to put one's faith exclusively in civil resistance to the dismantling of democracy.[200] Fanatical antidemocrats in particular might be very prominently present in the public debate in a divided democracy.[201] The black and white solutions that they suggest may be irresistible at a democratic low point.[202] In short, we come to Loewenstein's analysis: particularly in times of crisis it becomes easy to manoeuvre against democracy, gaining a large group of supporters. Democratically minded powers in new democracies, moreover, are, as Etzioni argues, often not yet sufficiently developed to stand up to well-organized antidemocrats.[203] History also shows that civil resistance does not always get off the ground, or fails to materialize in time: the fact that someone does not actively support antidemocrats does not mean that he would also actively combat them. So yes, there is certainly a role for 'civil society', but no, it is not enough.

Should we not also pay attention to parties' internal democracy?

From a democratic perspective, demands on a party's internal democracy are particularly intrusive. They allow the state to penetrate 'deep into the heart of all political organizations'.[204] At the same time it remains unclear why a party without a democratic organizational structure should be penalized purely for that reason if it otherwise exhibits no antidemocratic aims. Of course, an undemocratic organization could be a 'warning sign' of what might happen if the party came to power, but it seems unrealistic to assume that this risk would only be evident in the party's organizational structure in such a case. All kinds of (extra) interpretational problems are created, and the relationship between state and parties is muddied when the state becomes actively involved with internal party democracy.[205] Moreover, regardless of its internal organization, a party must otherwise adhere to all 'external' democratic rules. In the Netherlands that means, among other things, that its members of parliament vote without consultation or compulsion and that they keep their seat if they break with their party; the free mandate, as discussed earlier.

Requirements regarding the internal organization of a political party are an extra restriction on the freedom of association. This restriction does not appear to be justifiable without further argument. Parties can and must be judged on their aims. Dissatisfaction with party organization can be expressed through the regular channels: cancellation of membership or an election defeat.[206]

Is an eternity clause not really a better protection mechanism than a party ban?

These two protection mechanisms need not be mutually exclusive. A party ban actively defends certain values, whereas an eternity clause *passively* establishes those values, but the two can be based on the same justification. In principle there is therefore no objection to a system in which both protective structures are in place. Democracy as self-correction, however, expressly focuses on party bans, an *active* defence of democracy. The reason is that I do not expect eternity clauses to be particularly effective. As discussed earlier, it is difficult to imagine that an antidemocratic party with sufficient support would be held back by a constitutional court, and still more difficult to imagine that such a party would be put off by a clause that claims to be eternal (spontaneously or under the direction of the judge). In my view, one would have to intervene much sooner, before antidemocratic parties attain a position from which they could really tamper with the constitution. When it comes to effectiveness, I would thus want to use something like the following hierarchy, from more to less effective: party bans, constitutional testing, eternity clauses. To be sure, eternity clauses are not useless, but a more active defence is also required.[207]

Is militant democracy cut out for dealing with new, twenty-first-century problems?

Imagine that the above points of criticism can indeed be allayed. What should we think about: 1) religiously inspired terrorism, 2) civil rights in the 'security state', and 3) radical preachers? These are certainly important problems. At the same time, they do not really detract from the relevance of militant democracy, just as, for instance, environmental problems do not detract from the relevance of good education. The risk of democratic suicide is inherent in democracy, and the problem will thus remain relevant as long as there are democracies. According to some it goes back to Plato,[208] with infamous historic examples from Weimar to Algeria. Moreover, the theory of militant democracy has a universal quality. That does not mean that every country in any phase is suitable for democracy. It does mean that as soon as a democracy has been established somewhere, the question of the limits of democratic tolerance becomes relevant, and that question is often all the more urgent in young democracies. It would also be evidence of a historically unjustifiable conceit to think that the self-abolition of democracy in Europe is a thing of the past. In fact, it is probably to be recommended that this quest be undertaken in times of presumed peace. Van den Bergh did it in a time when an antidemocratic party (the NSB) was in parliament, and he was accused by many of writing a political speech against a specific party, whether or not in service of his own party, the SDAP. Something similar occurred in Spain: the law that first made party bans possible was seen as the anti-Batasuna law.[209] So yes, it is also necessary to consider the twenty-first-century problems listed, but that does not detract from the importance of the quest for the right way of dealing with antidemocrats.

When it comes to *religiously inspired terrorism*, it is important to understand that antidemocratic parties often have an informal terrorist branch, as in the case of ETA in relation to Batasuna in Spain and the IRA to the Irish Sinn Féin. Acting against such a terrorist branch is uncontroversial from the perspective of political philosophy, but what should be done about the radical religious sister party that disseminates the same ideas in an apparently legal manner? This is where militant democracy comes into the picture in combatting religiously inspired terrorism.

Then we have the problem of *radical preachers.* By operating with casual ties to organizations and making use of freedom of expression, they are able to propound their antidemocratic message, slipping through the net of militant democracy. Democracy as self-correction protects democracy by building a dam against abuse of democratic processes. Parliament and the switches of the legislative apparatus must remain unattainable to antidemocrats. That is the limit: at the moment when antidemocratic forces become *organized.* It is a form of self-restriction on the part of militant democracy. That means that radical preachers cannot be confronted on the basis of militant democracy, while at the same time their horizon is restricted: as soon as a step is made in the direction of realization of their ideology, at least via a democratic route, they will find militant democracy on their tracks.

This does not prevent antidemocratic propaganda of so-called 'hate preachers' presenting a serious problem for liberal democracy, certainly when followers are called on to reject the democracy, with or without violence.[210] If the antidemocratic texts are coupled with calls for violence, this problem is more the territory of security and should be approached from that perspective, with the use of criminal law and if necessary the intelligence services.[211] In this respect it is of course problematic that they rarely *openly* appeal for violence. The question is to what extent criminal law can be led by the religious context within which some appeals must be seen, since some appeals only gain meaning when they are understood in that context.[212] Whatever the answer, militant democracy only comes into the picture when antidemocrats organize and enter the territory of freedom of association.

Finally, *civil rights in the 'security-orientated state'*. A discussion of the security state falls outside the reach of militant democracy. It concerns issues such as the tension between protection of privacy on the one hand and effectively dealing with terrorism on the other. Can internet service providers, for example, be obliged to systematically retain the internet and telephone data of all citizens (including those who are not suspects)?[213] The Dutch court said no to such a law, to the dissatisfaction of the minister of justice.[214] This and similar dilemmas will primarily have to be solved within the theory of counterterrorism, not militant democracy. Intervention within the theory of militant democracy is of a completely different (and far more restricted) order: it is a matter of a specific right (freedom of association) of specific individuals (members and founders of a party hostile to democracy), which can be restricted in very specific circumstances (erosion of the principle of self-correction), to protect democracy (not the *state*, as in counterterrorism).[215]

Notes

1. On the development of judicial review of legislation after World War II, see Tim Koopmans, 'Some Comparative Comments on Judicial Review', p. 45–49, in E.J.H. Schrage (ed.), *Judicial Review*, Nijmegen: Paul Scholten Instituut/Ars Aequi Libri 2002; on this trend see also Müller 2013a, p. 142–143.
2. For this formulation I am indebted to Sebastien Valkenburg.
3. Magee 1974, p. 76.
4. Magee 1974, p. 76.
5. Magee 1974, p. 77.
6. Günter Frankenberg, 'The Learning Sovereign', p. 114–132 (115), in Sajó 2004.
7. Frankenberg 2004, p. 115. Although the possibility is open, Frankenberg does not use this as a justification for acting against parties who wish to reduce the 'horizon' or even permanently darken it; for his view on militant democracy, see p. 131–132.
8. Issacharoff 2007, p. 1465.
9. Issacharoff 2007, p. 1465. For comparable reasoning on 'disenfranchisement', see Kirshner 2014, p. 50, and for a Dutch example, see Buijs and Fennema 2012, p. 143: 'In a democratic society it is permissible to propose abolition of the compulsory teaching of Frisian in schools in Friesland, but it is not permissible to propose depriving the Frisians of their right to vote.'
10. Thienel 2008, p. 64.
11. Thienel 2008, p. 64.
12. As Frankenberg notes with respect to the 'learning sovereign': Frankenberg 2004, p. 115.
13. Annemarie Kas, 'Senaat verwerpt enkelband van Teeven na "genadeloze" kritiek' ('Senate votes down Teeven's electronic tag after "merciless" criticism'), *NRC Handelsblad*, 24 September 2014.
14. 'D66 geeft nabestaande grotere rol in orgaanwet' ('D66 gives next of kin greater role in Organ Donation Act'), *De Volkskrant* (online), 8 January 2014.
15. 'Klijnsma loodst pensioenwet door Eerste Kamer' ('Klijnsma steers Pensions Act through Senate'), *De Volkskrant* (online), 17 December 2014.
16. See 'No. 9a (Internetconsultatie)', in the strategy for legislation of the Ministry of Security and Justice, available via https://www.kcwj.nl/kennisbank/draaiboek-voor-de-regelgeving/hoofdstuk-2-formele-wetten-op-voorstel-van-de-regering-n-19.
17. Herbert Marcuse and Karl Popper, *Sociale hervorming of sociale revolutie? Een confrontatie* (Revolution oder Reform? Herbert Marcuse und Karl Popper. Eine Konfrontation, 1971), Baarn: Het Wereldvenster 1971, p. 23; in English translation, 'Karl Popper, "On Reason and the Open Society"', in Shearmur and Turner 2008.
18. Ryan 2013, p. xviii-xix.
19. Ryan 2013, p. xix.
20. See criticism of this point in T.E. Burke, *The Philosophy of Karl Popper*, Manchester: Manchester University Press 1983, p. 178: If we imagine a system in which a group with hereditary rights has all the power (a House of Lords with no House of Commons, for example) but which *does* have its own procedure for voting out and replacing an existing government according to its

own logic, then this system would fall under Popper's definition of democracy despite having almost nothing in common with the concept of democracy as we normally understand and use it.

21. See also Allan 2014, p. ix–xi.
22. Translated in the terms of Mark Chou (Chou 2013, p. 64–65, 74–75 and 78), it could be formulated as follows: democracy as self-correction attempts to find a stable position between 'too much democracy' on the one hand (no restrictions on 'ideas and perspectives': the procedural democracy, *in extremis*) and on the other hand 'too little democracy' (very extensive restrictions, often in response to 'too much democracy': the substantive democracy, *in extremis*). Chou states that a democracy will always swing back and forth between these two poles, and that this pendulum swing, this dynamic, can in some cases lead to democratic suicide ('democide', a rather weak, linguistically incorrect play on words), be it through 'too much democracy', or 'too little democracy'. Democracy as self-correction attempts to call a halt to this dynamic by choosing a point of equilibrium at which there is sufficient substantive democracy 'injected' into the system to make sure the democracy does not fail due to too much democracy, but without restricting the democracy too much (and thus falling prey to too little democracy). In fact, Chou is not an advocate of militant democracy, appearing to consider it too closely associated with too little democracy; see Chou 2013, p. 12, 53, 68, 72.
23. This English translation is available at https://www.gesetze-im-internet.de/englisch_gg/.The German original reads, 'Parteien, die nach ihren Zielen oder nach dem Verhalten ihrer Anhänger darauf ausgehen, die freiheitliche demokratische Grundordnung zu beeinträchtigen oder zu beseitigen oder den Bestand der Bundesrepublik Deutschland zu gefährden, sind verfassungswidrig. Über die Frage der Verfassungswidrigkeit entscheidet das Bundesverfassungsgericht.'
24. Bundesverfassungsgericht 23 October 1952, *E* 2, 1 (SRP-Verbot); see Elzinga 1982, p. 141.
25. Nieuwenhuis 2003, p. 201, and Bellekom 1982, p. 131.
26. See Elzinga 1982, p. 140–141.
27. Bellekom 1982, p. 144, note 60.
28. See *Verfassungsshutzbericht* 2013, Berlin: Bundesministerium des Innern, p. 91 (NPD), 173 (KPD) and 239 (HuT).
29. Martin Oppenheimer, 'Social Control Mechanisms in a Modern Welfare State: The Case of the Federal Republic of Germany', *Critical Sociology* 1977, vol. 7 no. 1, p. 65–68 (65). This effect is also assumed when it comes to the loyalty requirements (and associated screening) of civil servants; see G. Brinkmann, 'Militant Democracy and Radicals in the West German Civil Service', *Modern Law Review* 1983, vol. 46, p. 584–600 (600).
30. In 2005 the right-wing newspaper *Junge Freiheit* successfully contested its mention in the *Verfassungsshutzbericht* of Nordrhein-Westfalen; see '"Junge Freiheit" vor Bundesverfassungsgericht erfolgreich', *Frankfurter Allgemeine Zeitung*, 28 June 2005.
31. See '"Junge Freiheit" vor Bundesverfassungsgericht erfolgreich': 'Durch die Erwähnung im Verfassungsschutzbericht würden die Wirkungsmöglichkeiten der 1986 gegründeten "Junge Freiheit" nachteilig beeinflußt, betonten die Bundesverfassungsrichter. Potentielle Leser könnten davon abgehalten werden, die Zeitung zu erwerben. Es sei auch "nicht unwahrscheinlich", daß Inserenten, Journalisten oder Leserbriefschreiber deshalb die Zeitung boykottieren.'
32. Nieuwenhuis 2003, p. 202; see also Bellekom 1982, p. 130–131.

33. See *BVerfG* SRP-Verbot, 23 October 1952, *E* 2, 1, p. 12–13. This overview is derived from Nieuwenhuis 2003, p. 202, Elzinga 1982, p. 140, David P. Currie, *The Constitution of the Federal Republic of Germany*, Chicago: University of Chicago Press 1994, p. 216, and Papier and Durner 2003, p. 356. For an English translation, and different rendering, of the full passage, see Pfersmann 2004, p. 52–53, note 15.
34. Nieuwenhuis 2003, p. 202.
35. Currie 1994, p. 216.
36. Nieuwenhuis 2003, p. 202. See Bundesverfassungsgericht 17 August 1956, *E* 5, 85 (KPD-Verbot).
37. Elzinga 1982, p. 140; see a detailed discussion in Tyulkina 2015, p. 76.
38. See Bovend'Eert and Burkens 2012, p. 91.
39. See Papier and Durner 2003, p. 357.
40. BVerfG 17 January 2017, 2 BvB 1/13 (*NPD II*); Gelijn Molier and Bastiaan Rijpkema, 'Germany's New Militant Democracy Regime: National Democratic Party II and the German Federal Constitutional Court's "Potentiality" Criterion for Party Bans', *European Constitutional Law Review* 2018, vol. 14 no. 2, p. 394–409; Afshin Ellian, Gelijn Molier and Bastiaan Rijpkema, 'Weerbare democratie en het probleem van timing: de zaak tegen de NPD' (Militant democracy and the problem of timing: the case against the NPD), *Nederlands Juristenblad*, vol. 92 no. 24, p. 1650–1660. Earlier, in 2003 the Bundesverfassungsgericht also refused to ban the extreme right-wing NPD, the primary reason being that too many infiltrators participated in the party to establish with any certainty what the party's *own* direction would have been. The infiltrators had entered the party for the sake of collecting evidence for the legal case in hand. For all this see: Claudia E. Haupt, 'The Scope of Democratic Public Discourse: Defending Democracy, Tolerating Intolerance, and the Problem of Neo-Nazi Demonstrations in Germany', *Florida Journal of International Law* 2008, vol. 20 no. 2, p. 169–217 (175–181); Rensmann 2003, who believes that the NPD judgement has substantially raised the threshold for banning political parties in Germany (see p. 1134); BVerfG 18 March 2003, 2 BVB 1/01 (NPD I), §52.
41. See in more detail: Molier and Rijpkema 2018; Ellian, Molier and Rijpkema 2017.
42. The new BVerfG approach also created some new complications, since now there is a category of parties that actively oppose the free democratic order but are not banned (for their lack of potential). These parties still enjoy the same protection as regular parties, on the basis of the 'party privilege', and they receive state subsidies. A constitutional amendment was adopted in response to the latter complication (state subsidies) in 2017, creating the possibility of cutting subsidies for this category; see Molier and Rijpkema 2018.
43. Nieuwenhuis 2003, p. 202.
44. See, for example, the objections in Jeremy Waldron, *Law and Disagreement*, Oxford: Oxford University Press 1999.
45. Erik Jurgens also points this out; see E.C.M. Jurgens, 'Over de illusie dat rechterlijke toetsing van de wet aan onze huidige Grondwet zinvol is' ('On the illusion that judicial review of the law with respect to our current constitution is worthwhile'), p. 117–123 (122), in Paul Cliteur, Hans Franken and Wim Voermans (eds.), *Naar een Europese Grondwet* (Towards a European Constitution), The Hague: Boom Juridische Uitgevers 2004: 'In the case of such an important judicial power, namely the power to strike down decisions of the legislator which have sometimes been accepted by a majority (as in the case of the social laws in Roosevelt's "New Deal" in the 1930s)—and to do so on

the basis of constitutional texts two centuries old—it is appropriate to ask whether the balance of power has not been seriously disrupted. To whom are the judges accountable for such political decisions, decisions which can hardly be corrected by the legislator due to the large relative majorities needed for changes to the constitution?'

46. Another option is the Canadian 'notwithstanding clause', whereby the parliament has the option *in extremis* of overriding the judge's interpretation; the legislator thus has the final word. For a discussion see Jeffrey Goldsworthy, *Parliamentary Sovereignty: Contemporary Debates*, Cambridge: Cambridge University Press 2010, p. 202–224, and Jerfi Uzman, *Constitutionele remedies bij schending van grondrechten: Over effectieve rechtsbescherming, rechterlijk abstineren en de dialoog tussen rechter en wetgever* (Constitutional remedies in the case of violation of fundamental rights: On effective protection of rights, judicial abstention and the dialogue between judge and legislator, diss. Leiden), Deventer: Kluwer 2013, p. 521–595.
47. In the United States there is also extensive debate between advocates of judicial restraint on the one hand and advocates of judicial activism on the other; for a brief discussion of this topic with sources, see Paul Cliteur, 'Naar een Europese Grondwet: een Colloquium metajuridicum' ('Towards a European Constitution: a Colloquium metajuridicum'), p. 1–22 (16), in Cliteur, Franken and Voermans 2004.
48. Gregory Fox, 'The Right to Political Participation in International Law', *Yale Journal of International Law* 1992, vol. 17, p. 539–607 (555–560 and 606). The idea of an international 'right to democracy' (or political participation) can ultimately be traced back (in part) to a proposal by Loewenstein in the context of the *Universal Declaration of Human Rights*; see Rensmann 2011, p. 988–989.
49. See Nieuwenhuis 2003, p. 201.
50. In contrast with Nieuwenhuis, besides the multiparty principle (or system), Elzinga 1982, p. 140, also distils from German jurisprudence the principle of 'equal opportunities for all political parties'. Here that is treated as part of the first principle, that of multiple parties. When there are multiple political parties, for example, but all parties except one are severely restricted in their operations, this is a *de facto* violation of the multiparty principle that will be easily recognized by the judge. The 'principle of political competition' described below, derived from the multiparty principle, in fact removes the need for this.
51. Bundesverfassungsgericht 26 February 2014, 2 BvE 2/13, §53 and 54: 'Differenzierungen im Wahlrecht können vielmehr auch durch Gründe gerechtfertigt werden, die durch die Verfassung legitimiert und von einem Gewicht sind, das der Wahlrechtsgleichheit die Waage halten kann. . . . Hierzu zählen insbesondere die mit der Wahl verfolgten Ziele. Dazu gehört die Sicherung des Charakters der Wahl als eines Integrationsvorgangs bei der politischen Willensbildung des Volkes . . . und, damit zusammenhängend, die Sicherung der Funktionsfähigkeit der zu wählenden Volksvertretung.'
52. On this and the different position this issue holds in Kirshner's theory, see Kirshner 2014, p. 50.
53. See Issacharoff 2007, p. 1465.
54. ECHR 13 February 2003, 41340/98, 41342/98 and 41344/98, *NJ* 2005, 73, incl. note E.A. Alkema (Refah Partisi/Turkey), §97–98. See Hans-Martien ten Napel, 'Het EHRM en de "waarlijk democratische regeringsvorm"' ('The ECHR and the "true shape of democratic government"'), *NJCM-Bulletin* 2007, vol. 32 no. 8, p. 1090–1106 (1103). On these two demands in ECHR jurisprudence, see also Marloes van Noorloos, 'Extreme Speech in a Religious Context: A Legal

Theoretical Perspective on the Case Law of the European Court of Human Rights', p. 163–183 (172–176), in Ellian and Molier 2015. For the previous history of Refah in Turkey (where it was no less than the fifteenth banned party since the beginning of the current republic), see Tyulkina 2015, p. 173–177 (with the number of party bans on p. 174).

55. Ten Napel 2007, p. 1103.
56. See Van den Bergh 1936a, p. 29.
57. Kevin Boyle, 'Human Rights, Religion and Democracy: The Refah Party Case', *Essex Human Rights Review* 2004, vol. 1 no. 1, p. 1–16 (1–2).
58. Boyle 2004, p. 2 (note 3).
59. Mustafa Koçak and Esin Örücü, 'Dissolution of Political Parties in the Name of Democracy: Cases from Turkey and the European Court of Human Rights', *European Public Law* 2003, vol. 9 no. 3, p. 399–424 (415).
60. See Tardi 2004, p. 103.
61. ECHR *Rehaf Partisi,* §107. The court, of course, notes that polls are not entirely reliable, but they confirm the trend shown by real elections.
62. Koçak and Örücü 2003, p. 415.
63. Koçak and Örücü 2003, p. 415–416, and Tyulkina 2015, p, 175–176.
64. Koçak and Örücü 2003, p. 416.
65. Tyulkina 2015, p. 180 and 190.
66. ECHR *Refah Partisi,* §129–131.
67. ECHR *Refah Partisi*, §116–127, in particular §123. Both requirements were discussed in the context of the third and final condition for a permitted restriction of Article 11 of the Convention: being 'necessary in a democratic society' (see §68 onwards).
68. ECHR *Refah Partisi*, §123.
69. See, for example, Paul van Sasse van IJsselt, 'Sharia en de democratische paradox; terugkeer van de crisistoon' ('Sharia and the democratic paradox: return of the crisis tone'), *Nederlands Juristenblad* 2006, vol. 81 no. 34, p. 1952–1953 (1952).
70. See also Boyle 2004, p. 12–14, and Van Noorloos 2015, p. 174.
71. On this 'concurring opinion' see also the interpretation of Van Noorloos 2015, p. 180–181.
72. Boyle 2004, p. 8, agrees.
73. ECHR *Refah Partisi,* concurring opinion of Judge Ress, joined by judge Rozakis.
74. ECHR 30 January 1998, 133/1996/752/951 (United Communist Party of Turkey/Turkey), §61. An appeal to Article 17 was also incapable of justifying the ban (see §60): the party programme did not express a wish to erode rights enshrined in the Convention.
75. See also Tyulkina 2015, p. 100, and for a detailed discussion p. 98–100.
76. ECHR *United Communist Party of Turkey,* §45. When it comes to the importance of freedom of expression, we find comparable reasoning in ECHR 7 December 1976 (Handyside/United Kingdom): 'The Court's supervisory functions oblige it to pay the utmost attention to the principles characterising a "democratic society". Freedom of expression constitutes one of the essential foundations of such a society, one of the basic conditions for its progress and for the development of every man.' See A.J. Nieuwenhuis, 'Tussen grondrechtelijke vrijheid en parlementaire onschendbaarheid: de vrijheid van meningsuiting van de parlementariër' ('Between constitutional freedom and parliamentary inviolability: the parliamentarian's freedom of expression'), *Tijdschrift voor Constitutioneel Recht* 2010, vol. 1 no. 1, p. 4–23 (5–6 and note 11).
77. See Boyle 2004, p. 7. The court also refers consistently in later cases to ECHR *United Communist Party of Turkey*; see Tyulkina 2015, p. 100.

78. See also Boyle 2004, p. 8.
79. Winfried Brugger, 'The Treatment of Hate Speech in German Constitutional Law (Part II)', *German Law Journal* 2003, vol. 4 no. 1, p. 1–44 (32): 'If, as the Federal Constitutional Court consistently claims, free speech is constitutive for the speaker and necessary for open debate, democracy, and stable society, then this right should be protected accordingly.' See also Nieuwenhuis 2010, p. 5.
80. Nieuwenhuis 2010, p. 6.
81. A. Meiklejohn, *Free Speech and Its Relation to Self-Government*, New York: Harper Brothers 1948. On Meiklejohn, see E. Barendt, *Freedom of Speech*, Oxford: Oxford University Press 1985, p. 20–21, Wojciech Sadurski, *Freedom of Speech and Its Limits*, Dordrecht: Kluwer Academic 1999, p. 20–21, and Nieuwenhuis 2010, p. 6.
82. ECHR *Refah Partisi*, §123. See Boyle 2004, p. 12: 'The stridency of the European Court's assessment of Islamic law and shariah is regrettable. In effect the Court seems to say that shariah, *tout court*, is incompatible with universal rights, or at least European ideas of democracy and rights.'
83. On the competence of the court in this area, for example, Christian Moe passes harsh judgement in '*Refah* Revisited: Strasbourg's Construction of Islam', p. 235–271 (270–271), in W. Cole Durham, Jr., Rik Torfs, David M. Kirkham and Christine Scott, *Islam, Europe and Emerging Legal Issues*, Farnham: Ashgate 2012.
84. Boyle 2004, p. 12. For detailed discussion see Moe 2012, p. 253–255 (and 235–236). It is probably superfluous to say that this is not a question of *whether* a *correct*, authentic interpretation of sharia is possible (the 'true sharia'); the point is merely the empirical observation that different interpretations are employed by different believers.
85. An example of such criticism is Boyle 2004, p. 12–14, who goes beyond this to link it with 'islamophobia'. See also Issacharoff 2007, p. 1446: 'The condemnation of all sharia likely was far too sweeping and almost certainly applied a different standard to Islamic religious belief than would have been applied to any Christian faith,' and Tyulkina 2015, p. 194: 'However, none of these arguments could justify the Court's provocative statement that Sharia and democracy are per se not compatible, and that the presence of the former in politics excludes any possibility of coexistence with the latter'; see also p. 199.
86. Christian Moe broadens the function of more precise argumentation: it could be an 'invitation to constructive debate with Muslims', a debate in greater detail and on precisely the subjects that cause friction (Moe mentions women's rights). This would also be a debate in which the court *would* have 'considerable moral authority'; see Moe 2012, p. 271; see also p. 255.
87. Tyulkina 2015, p. 194; see also Moe 2012, p. 235, and note 1.
88. ECHR *Refah Partisi*, §110.
89. ECHR *Refah Partisi*, §110.
90. Van Noorloos 2015, p 181.
91. ECHR 14 March 2013, 26261/05 and 26377/06 (Kasymakhunov and Saybatalov/Russia), §113. In the German case the judgement was as follows: 'Having regard to the above, the Court considers that the first applicant attempts to deflect Article 11 of the Convention from its real purpose by employing this right for ends which are clearly contrary to the values of the Convention, notably the commitment to the peaceful settlement of international conflicts and to the sanctity of human life. Consequently, the Court finds that, by reason of Article 17 of the Convention, the first applicant may not benefit from the protection afforded by Article 11 of the Convention'; see ECHR 12 June 2012, 31098/08 (Hizb ut-Tahrir/Germany), §74.

92. As Van Noorloos also writes elsewhere in her contribution; see Van Noorloos 2015, p. 175–176.
93. This interpretation of Article 17 of the Convention is also supported in Vanden Heede 2004, p. 229: 'a thorough, concrete investigation is out of the question'; and Tyulkina 2015, p. 96–97.
94. Antoine Buyse, 'Dangerous Expressions: The ECHR, Violence and Free Speech', *International and Comparative Law Quarterly* 2014, vol. 63 no. 2, p. 491–503 (495).
95. Buyse 2014, p. 494.
96. Vanden Heede 2004, p. 229. Sajó argues for solving the question of party bans via Article 17 of the Convention; see Sajó 2004, p. 225.
97. See, for example, ECHR *Refah Partisi*, §131, Van Noorloos 2015, p. 175, and Sajó 2004, p. 222.
98. Cases are too easily dismissed if Article 17 is chosen (Sottiaux) and there is a lack of criteria for deciding whether Article 17 or Article 11 applies (Buyse). See Stefan Sottiaux, '"Bad Tendencies" in the ECHR's "Hate Speech" Jurisprudence', *European Constitutional Law Review* 2011, vol. 7 no. 1, p. 40–63 (62–63), and Buyse 2014, p. 495–496. See also (for a more positive view) Jan-Peter Loof, 'Restricting Free Speech in Times of Terror: An ECHR Perspective', p. 185–216 (215–216), in Ellian and Molier 2015.
99. Van den Bergh 1936a, p. 14.
100. See also Issacharoff 2007, 1467. One could also argue that, instead of creating extra procedural safeguards, it should not be a (unaccountable) judge who decides in the first place; for such an argument and an interesting alternative (reviving the ancient Greek practice of ostracism, albeit in a modern fashion), see Anthoula Malkopoulou, 'Ostracism and Democratic Self-defense in Athens', *Constellations* 2017, vol. 24, p. 623–636 (in particular: 632–634).
101. *Guidelines on Prohibition of Political Parties and Analogous Measures*, European Commission for Democracy through Law (Venice Commission), adopted 10-11 December 1999, Strasbourg 2000, available via http://www.venice.coe.int/webforms/documents/default.aspx?pdffile=CDL-INF%282000%29001-e. This study was requested in 1998 after a large increase in the number of party ban cases in the ECHR; on this and on the report in general, see Tyulkina 2015, p. 102–104.
102. Tyulkina 2015, p. 103.
103. Van den Bergh 1936a, p. 28–29.
104. See Article 2 paragraph 1 of the Act on the legal status of judicial officials (Wet rechtspositie rechterlijke ambtenaren); see Elzinga 1982, p. 153, note 99.
105. Bellekom 1982, p. 140. Bellekom also considers the appointment of a special constitutional court (such as a department of the Council of State) an option for this issue; in his view it would provide good leverage in the debate on constitutional testing.
106. Guidelines on Prohibition of Political Parties and Analogous Measures, p. 5 (guideline 7); see also Tyulkina 2015, p. 103.
107. Elzinga 1982, p. 153, note 99.
108. See Gelijn Molier, 'De Vereniging Martijn mag toch bestaan: over de scheiding van recht en moraal' ('The Vereniging Martijn may exist after all: on the separation of law and morality'), *Nederlands Juristenblad* 2013, p. 1502–1509, with a comparison between district court and appeals court on p. 1508–1509; Tymen van der Ploeg, 'Hoe moeilijk is het om een vereniging te verbieden? Deel 2: de zaak Martijn' ('How difficult is it to ban an association? Part 2: the Martijn case'), *Nederlands Juristenblad* 2013, p. 2808–2810 (2810).

109. Supreme Court of the Netherlands 18 April 2014, AB 2014/38 (concl. A-G L. Timmermans) incl. note G. Molier and J.G. Brouwer (Vereniging Martijn).
110. Issacharoff 2007, p. 1454 (we can assume from the context of Issacharoff's argument that he means the European Court of Human Rights and not the Court of Justice of the European Union). For a comparable theory, see Gregory Fox and Georg Nolte, 'A Defense of the "Intolerant Democracies" Thesis', p. 445–448 (447), in Gregory Fox and Brad Roth, *Democratic Governance and International Law*, Cambridge: Cambridge University Press 2000: 'By encouraging international bodies to review the propriety of bans there will at least be an opportunity for the numbers of bans to be reduced.'
111. On the unique position of the European Court of Human Rights, see Rick Lawson, 'Overvloed en onbehagen: de Universele Verklaring en de Europese bescherming van de mensenrechten' ('Abundance and unease: the Universal Declaration and European protection of human rights'), *Internationale Spectator* 2008, vol. 62 no. 12, p. 659–662.
112. Tyulkina 2015, p. 102, with respect to the ECHR.
113. Tyulkina 2015, p. 102.
114. See Andrew Legg, *The Margin of Appreciation in Human Rights Law: Deference and Proportionality*, Oxford: Oxford University Press 2012, p. 92–93. See, for example, the judgement on the ban of the Spanish Batasuna: ECHR 20 June 2009, 25803/04 and 25817/04 (Herri Batasuna/Spain), §74–75; in fact, the court also functioned in this way in the previously discussed Refah case. Another illustrative case is ECHR *Zdanoka* (on revoking suffrage), §134: 'The Court therefore accepts in the present case that the national authorities of Latvia, both legislative and judicial, are better placed to assess the difficulties faced in establishing and safeguarding the democratic order. Those authorities should therefore be left sufficient latitude to assess the needs of their society in building confidence in the new democratic institutions, including the national parliament, and to answer the question whether the impugned measure is still needed for these purposes, provided that the Court has found nothing arbitrary or disproportionate in such an assessment.'
115. For a detailed discussion see Jan-Werner Müller, 'Safeguarding Democracy inside the EU', *Transatlantic Academy Paper Series 2012-2013*, no. 3, 20 February 2013 (henceforth Müller 2013c), Klamt 2012, in particular p. 300–452, and Müller 2013a; see also Rensmann 2003, p. 1135–1136, and Papier and Durner 2003, p. 370.
116. See Müller 2013a, p. 146, and Klamt 2012, p. 311–321; on p. 321 he states, 'Alles in allem bringt die Vorschrift des Art. 7 EUV den Gedanken der Streitbaren Demokratie auf der Ebene der Europaischen Union deutlich zum Ausdruck.'
117. 'Rule of Law: European Commission Acts to Defend Judicial Independence in Poland', *European Commission Press Release*, 20 December 2017, http://europa.eu/rapid/press-release_IP-17-5367_en.htm; Daniel Boffey and Christian Davies, 'Poland May Be Stripped of EU Voting Rights over Judicial Independence', *The Guardian* (online), 19 July 2017; Laurent Pech and Kim Lane Scheppele, 'Poland and the European Commission, Part III: Requiem for the Rule of Law', *Verfassungsblog*, 3 March 2017.
118. Wojciech Sadurski, *Constitutionalism and the Enlargement of Europe*, Oxford: Oxford University Press 2012, p. 84–86 and 91–92; Müller 2013c, p. 5 and 17.
119. Sadurski 2012, p. 84. For a critical discussion of the sanctions, see Müller 2013a, p. 139 and 144–145; see also Müller 2007, p. 113–114. Klamt 2012, p. 323–326, is equally critical, nonetheless seeing the *Haider* case as 'Refah for the EU' when it comes to militant democracy; the idea first gained practical relevance at a supranational level (see p. 325 and 326). See also Thomas Chris-

tiansen and Christine Reh, *Constitutionalizing the European Union*, Basingstoke: Palgrave Macmillan 2009, p. 156.

120. Sadurski 2012, p. 85; Müller 2013c, p. 13.
121. Müller 2013c, p. 5.
122. See Sadurski, p. 85: 'Rather, they should be seen as a general ideological statement about the limits of what is, politically and ideologically, acceptable in the EU: what are the limits of the diversity, on the eve of a monumental increase of the diversity within the Union' (the expansion with the accession of ten new member states in 2004, BR).
123. Müller 2013a, p. 139–141.
124. Müller 2014, p. 251.
125. Müller 2014, p. 252.
126. Andrew Moravcsik, 'The Origins of Human Rights Regimes: Democratic Delegation in Postwar Europe', *International Organization* 2000, vol. 54 no. 2, p. 217–252 (243–244): 'We have seen that the origins of the ECHR, the most successful international human rights adjudication and enforcement regime in the world today, lies not in coercive power politics or socialization to idealistic norms, as contemporary international relations theories predict. Instead its origins lie in self-interested efforts by newly established (or reestablished) democracies to employ international commitments to consolidate democracy—"locking in" the domestic political status quo against their nondemocratic opponents.' And more generally: 'By placing interpretation in the hands of independent authorities managed in part by foreign governments—in other words, by alienating sovereignty to an international body—governments seek to establish reliable judicial constraints on future nondemocratic governments or on democratically elected governments that may seek (as in interwar Italy and Germany) to subvert democracy from within' (p. 228). See also Müller 2014, p. 252.
127. Müller 2013a, p. 143.
128. Müller 2013a, p. 143.
129. Müller 2013a, p. 143.
130. Müller 2013a, p. 145.
131. Müller 2013a, p. 147–148. Cf. also Müller 2007, p. 119, where Müller is considerably more reserved: 'Clearly, the EU excludes the nondemocratic, but below the level of clear-cut deviance from democratic principles it is not obvious what the Union could do.'
132. Müller 2013a, p. 149; besides Article 7 of the Lisbon Treaty, these are, for example, the treaty infringement proceedings, the protection of civil rights in concrete cases by the EU court and politicians challenging one another.
133. Müller 2013a, p. 138, also foresees this, but he is not convinced by it; see p. 141–142; for a similar criticism see Peter Mair, *Ruling the Void: The Hollowing of Western Democracy*, London: Verso Books 2013, p. 99–142.
134. Müller 2013a, p. 147. The fact that this will be a difficult process can be explained based on the EU not originally having been intended as *democratic*, or only in the sense that it functioned as a (partial) supranational protective check on the derailing of national democracies. Cf. also Müller 2014, p. 252: 'In short, "Europe", rather than evolving into a powerful federal state, as some enthusiasts for a pan-European polity had hoped after the war, was supposed further to constrain national democracies, not to supersede them. Even more than at the national level, no particular value was placed on political participation. In fact, popular participation was limited as much as possible: interdependence was to be created and "deepened" by benevolent elites cooperating across national borders; it was not based on anything like movements

from below. Whatever elites achieved would of course eventually require some acceptance by the peoples of Europe; but here the main idea was that the practical benefits of integration would be so obvious (and obviously desirable) that at least something like tacit consent on the part of the peoples of Europe could be presumed over time.'

135. Müller 2013a, p. 147.
136. Franz Mayer, 'Rebels without a Cause? A Critical Analysis of the German Constitutional Court's OMT Reference', *German Law Journal* 2014, vol.15 no. 2, p. 112–146 (141).
137. See Mayer 2014, p. 133–134.
138. Jürgen Bast, 'Don't Act beyond Your Powers: The Perils and Pitfalls of the German Constitutional Court's Ultra Vires Review', *German Law Journal* 2014, vol. 15 no. 2, p. 168–181 (168–169); see also Mayer 2014, p. 116, and Michael Wilkinson, 'From Karlsruhe, with Love? Questioning the Constitutionality of Unconventional Monetary Policy' (October 2014), LSE Law—Policy Briefing Paper No. 6, p. 3.
139. Michael A. Wilkinson, 'Authoritarian Liberalism in the European Constitutional Imagination: Second Time as Farce?', *European Law Journal* 2015, vol. 21 no. 3, p. 313–339 (335–336). See, for example, the criticism in Mayer 2014, p. 115–117, and Klaus Garditz, 'Beyond Symbolism: Towards a Constitutional *Actio Popularis* in EU Affairs? A Commentary on the OMT Decision of the Federal Constitutional Court', *German Law Journal* 2014, vol. 15 no. 2, p. 183–201, and with respect to Lisbon in particular, Daniel Halberstam and Christoph Möllers, 'The German Constitutional Court Says "Ja zu Deutschland"', *German Law Journal* 2009, vol. 10 no. 8, p. 1242–1258.
140. Gábor Halmai, 'Unconstitutional Constitutional Amendments: Constitutional Courts as Guardians of the Constitution?', *Constellations* 2012, vol. 19 no. 2, p. 182–203 (185). See also Wilkinson 2015, p. 335–336.
141. Wilkinson 2015, p. 333. Alongside possible positive effects on German democracy, Germany's 'militant attitude' may have had negative effects on the democracies in other member states, seen from the broader perspective of the EU since the euro crisis; for detailed discussion see Wilkinson 2015, p. 334–336.
142. See also Wilkinson 2014, p. 3 (with respect to the buy-back programme); a similar increase in assertiveness, according to Wilkinson, was also already visible in the Lisbon judgement: 'And beyond a reflection of the political and economic difficulties faced in other parts of the Eurozone, which can be traced at least in part to the design flaws of EMU itself, the shift in tone from the Maastricht Urteil to the Lisbon and OMT decisions suggests another point of significance, discernible in the difference between a "not yet" and a "never" with regard to the development of a democratic supranationalism. Sovereign statehood now is sacrosanct, even if incongruously protected by individual fundamental rights and constitutional courts' (Wilkinson 2015, p. 335–336).
143. Sebastian Jost, 'Europas Richter urteilen über Draghis Milliarden-Plan', *Die Welt* (online), 16 June 2015.
144. See Mayer 2014, p. 111–112: 'But looking closer, it turns out that this reference to the ECJ is, in fact, the right thing done in the wrong way at the wrong time. The one thing it is not is a surrender, as some initial media comments suggested.' And Garditz 2014, p. 199: 'The BVerfG's referral to the ECJ for a preliminary ruling is accompanied by a message that the BVerfG is determined to enter into an open conflict with the ECJ by additionally activating the constitutional identity control, should the latter qualify the OMT Decision as being in conformity with EU primary law. Uttering barely concealed threats is

a questionable method of communication between the courts that keeps the elaborate and apocryphal machinery of European inter-court-cooperation working. The ECJ, for the first time, has to decide on a referral that is furnished with an announcement that the referring court reserves a right to later disregard what it views as an unsuitable decision.' An example of the misinterpretation Mayer is talking about is *NRC Handelsblad's* take on the case; see 'Europees Hof keurt opkoopprogramma ECB goed' ('European Court approves ECB buy-back programme'), *NRC Handelsblad* (online), 16 June 2015: 'The German Bundesverfassungsgericht (Constitutional Court) in Karlsruhe considered the case and largely agreed with the complainants in February 2014. But at the same time the German courts left the final judgement on the case to the European Court in Luxemburg, an unusual step by which the German Constitutional Court in fact relinquishes the authority to decide on monetary policy to the European level.' In Germany this was better interpreted; see Jost 2015: 'Allerdings ist der EuGH (European Court of Justice, BR) bei seinem Urteil nicht an die Empfehlungen des Gutachters gebunden. Und selbst wenn aus Luxemburg ein milder Richterspruch kommt, ist die Sache für die EZB noch nicht ausgestanden. Das Bundesverfassungsgericht hat sich nämlich eine Art letztes Wort vorbehalten, sollten die EuGH-Richter den Bedenken aus Karlsruhe nicht ausreichend Rechnung tragen.' Nevertheless, there are also signals that the BVerfG will in time be reconciled with a new hierarchy; see Halmai 2012, p. 186.

145. See Mayer 2014, p. 133–134, who believes that the court has seriously overestimated the number of national courts following a comparable course.
146. On the minister's authority to instruct, see G.J.M. Corstens, *Het Nederlandse strafprocesrecht* (Dutch criminal procedure law, revised by M.J. Borgers), Deventer: Kluwer 2011, p. 99–101, and C.A.J.M. Kortmann, *Constitutioneel Recht* (Constitutional Law, revised by P.P.T. Bovend'Eert, J.L.W. Broeksteeg, B.P. Vermeulen and C.N.J. Kortmann), Deventer: Kluwer 2012, p. 255. The current arrangement by Article 127 of the Judiciary Organization Act is the result of a debate in the 1990s; the position of the Public Prosecution Service with respect to the minister of justice at the time was considerably less clear, and the Public Prosecution Service in any case regularly had a great deal of independence; see P.B. Cliteur, 'Indien verantwoordelijk dan bevoegd? De constitutionele positie van het Openbaar Ministerie' ('If responsible then competent? The constitutional position of the Public Prosecution Service'), p. 124–137 (125–126), in M.C. Burkens, E.C.M. Jurgens, A.K. Koekkoek and J.J. Vis (eds.), *Gelet op de Grondwet* (A view on the constitution), Deventer: Kluwer 1998.
147. Of course a disadvantage is that in this system in principle a simple majority can decide to submit a request. The alternative, a special procedure in which the House of Representatives must express itself with a two-thirds majority, on the other hand, would make the discussion on the party ban a very political affair. In my view the Dutch arrangement is preferable. It should be noted that a judge would still *always* examine a ban; the only issue here is the submission of a request.
148. Tyulkina 2015, p. 171.
149. Bourne 2012b, p. 204.
150. Bourne 2012b, p. 204–206.
151. G. Leenknegt, 'Commentaar op artikel 8 van de Grondwet' (Commentary on article 8 of the constitution), in E.M.H. Hirsch Ballin and G. Leenknegt (eds.), *Artikelsgewijs commentaar op de Grondwet* (Commentary on the constitution), online edition 2017 (www.Nederlandrechtsstaat.nl); Bourne

forthcoming 2018 ; Gelijn Molier, 'Het verbod van een politieke partij: een anomalie in een democratie?' ('The ban of a political party: an anomaly in a democracy?'), *Nederlands Juristenblad* 2016, no. 34, p. 2438–2446.

152. It is also questionable whether in the Netherlands a *purely* antidemocratic party could be banned according to current law; Van den Bergh thought so in 1936, but in 2009 Van der Woude is more cautious: until now 'punishable forms of discrimination and encouragement of hate' always played a role. Nevertheless, he leaves the possibility open (due to the pairing of 'public order' with 'fundamental principles of the organization of our society' and 'foundations of the legal system' in jurisprudence); see Van der Woude 2009, p. 23 (and on the pairing mentioned, see p. 20). In fact, the old regulation, that is, *before* 1976, set down in the Association and Assembly act (Wet vereniging en vergadering) of 1855, on which Van den Bergh also based his arguments, allowed for the possibility of *preventive* oversight by the Crown (in actual fact the minister): an association could be denied the status of a legal entity if this was in the 'general interest'; see E.C.M. Jurgens, 'De "erkenning" van het COC' ('The "recognition" of the COC'), *Nederlands Juristenblad* 1969, vol. 44, p. 76–78, and Elzinga and De Lange 2006, p. 357. It was thus possible for the minister in 1970 to refuse the status of a legal entity to the homosexual interest association COC; on this case see the note by Jurgens on the rejection of the appeal: KB 24 June 1970, AA 1971, 253.
153. This overview is based on the *Notitie antidemocratische groeperingen* (Memorandum on antidemocratic factions), p. 7–8, and Van der Woude 2009, p. 18–19.
154. Germany has a comparable regulation in Article 84 of the *Strafgesetzbuch*. See Sajó 2004, p. 226 and note 21.
155. For a detailed discussion see *Notitie antidemocratische groeperingen* (Memorandum on antidemocratic factions), p. 7.
156. See *Notitie antidemocratische groeperingen* (Memorandum on antidemocratic factions), p. 7. The legal basis for this can be found in the Political Parties Funding Act (Wet op de financiering politieke partijen, Art. 1 sub b) and the Media Act (Mediawet 2008, Art. 1.1); both acts recognize only parties with a registered designation in the sense of the Electoral Code (Kieswet) as political parties.
157. Sajó 2004, p. 223.
158. Tyulkina 2015, p. 172.
159. For a detailed discussion of the disadvantages, see Kirshner 2014, p. 53–55. See also Issacharoff 2007, p. 1446. In fact, Sajó also emphasizes that the chosen method must restrict fundamental rights *as little as possible* (see Sajó 2004, p. 229–230), but in this case he clearly makes a different assessment. For a nuanced argument in favour of a form of 'political expulsion', see Malkopoulou 2017.
160. For all this see Tardi 2004, p. 107–108.
161. The ban is set down in Articles 86a and 86 of the German *Strafgesetzbuch*; see Andreas Stegbauer, 'The Ban of Right-Wing Extremist Symbols According to Section 86a of the German Criminal Code', *German Law Journal* 2007, vol. 8 no. 2, p. 173–184 (174): 'Section 86a StGB, by reference to Section 86 (1), nos. 1, 2 and 4 StGB ties into the ban of unconstitutional parties and other organizations *in order to protect the democratic rule of law by preventing the revival of those associations and their aims*' (my italicization, BR).
162. See Navot 2008, p. 753–754.
163. 'Buma onder vuur om "gedachtepolitie" tegen verheerlijking terrorisme' ('Buma under fire over "thought police" against glorification of terrorism'), *De Volkskrant* (online), 4 September 2014.

164. In fact, Sajó also indicates that he is opposed to restricting freedom of expression, because he does not consider it necessary for a militant democracy; see Sajó 2004, p. 228–229. It is also interesting that in Israel the opposite reasoning is used. Limiting freedom of association or suffrage is seen as more serious than restriction of freedom of expression. There it *is* possible to prosecute someone on the basis of the support he expresses for a terrorist organization, but it seems *not* to be possible to deny someone access to the Knesset, the Israeli parliament, on the basis of the same expression of support; see Navot 2008, p. 754.
165. See 'Germany Bans Support for ISIS', *The New York Times*, 12 September 2014.
166. Another question that could be connected with the issue of party bans is whether membership of an unconstitutional party or having anticonstitutional sympathies should lead to exclusion from roles in the civil service. See Brinkmann 1983 and Tyulkina 2015, p. 78–79.
167. See Elzinga 1982, p. 162, *Notitie antidemocratische partijen* (Memorandum on antidemocratic parties), p. 7, and Van der Woude 2009, p. 19.
168. Elzinga 1982, p. 162.
169. See *Uitslag van de verkiezing van de leden van de Tweede Kamer van 12 september 2012* (Result of the election of members of the House of Representatives of 12 September 2012), The Hague: Kiesraad 2012, p. 20 and 21.
170. *Uitslag van de verkiezing van de leden van de Tweede Kamer van 12 september 2012* (Result of the election of members of the House of Representatives of 12 September 2012), p. 14. The unrounded electoral threshold for a seat was 62,828 35/150 votes.
171. Issacharoff 2007, p. 1410. Issacharoff seems to take a broader view: the elections too, or even *primarily*, especially the 'electoral arena', offer this kind of platform.
172. Issacharoff 2007, p. 1410.
173. Issacharoff 2007, p. 1410.
174. See Ayres 2004, p. 111.
175. Elzinga 1982, p. 141 and note 73. Article 38 GG reads as follows: 'Die Abgeordneten des Deutschen Bundestages werden in allgemeiner, unmittelbarer, freier, gleicher und geheimer Wahl gewählt. Sie sind Vertreter des ganzen Volkes, an Aufträge und Weisungen nicht gebunden und nur ihrem Gewissen unterworfen.'
176. Elzinga 1982, p. 141 and note 73 (also for criticism in the German literature); see also p. 163. The complete text of Article 21 GG at that time read:
    1. Die Parteien wirken bei der politischen Willensbildung des Volkes mit. Ihre Gründung ist frei. Ihre innere Ordnung muß demokratischen Grundsätzen entsprechen. Sie müssen über die Herkunft und Verwendung ihrer Mittel sowie über ihr Vermögen öffentlich Rechenschaft geben.
    2. Parteien, die nach ihren Zielen oder nach dem Verhalten ihrer Anhänger darauf ausgehen, die freiheitliche demokratische Grundordnung zu beeinträchtigen oder zu beseitigen oder den Bestand der Bundesrepublik Deutschland zu gefährden, sind verfassungswidrig. Über die Frage der Verfassungswidrigkeit entscheidet das Bundesverfassungsgericht.
    3. Das Nähere regeln Bundesgesetze.

    We have already seen the idea that political parties play a central role in the formation of the will of the people (as stated in the first paragraph of GG Art. 21) in the work of Hans Kelsen; see Kelsen 2002, p. 93; Sajó mentions this; see Sajó 2012, p. 564.
177. Currie 1994, p. 216.
178. Nieuwenhuis 2003, p. 208.

179. Tardi 2004, p. 103.
180. Elzinga 1982, p. 163.
181. For the pros and cons of party discipline, and a less negative perspective on this phenomenon, see J.J.A. Thomassen and R.B. Andeweg, 'Fractiediscipline. Vooroordelen en misverstanden.' ('Party discipline. Prejudices and misunderstandings.'), p. 154–175, in G. Voerman (ed.), *Jaarboek Documentatiecentrum Nederlandse Politieke Partijen 2005* (Yearbook of the Documentation Centre for Dutch Political Parties 2005), Groningen: Documentatiecentrum Nederlandse Politieke Partijen 2007. A memorandum by Minister Thom de Graaf also reveals government concerns about overly concordant parties and invisible members of parliament without a mandate; see Thomassen and Andeweg 2007, p. 155. See also Andreas Kinneging, *Geografie van goed en kwaad* (Geography of good and evil), Houten/Antwerp: Spectrum 2005, p. 290–294. Kinneging points in particular to the disadvantageous consequences of party discipline in combination with detailed coalition agreements. This leads to 'osmosis' between government and parliament, preventing the latter from properly fulfilling its checking function. Kinneging appears to accept the dominant position of parties, on the other hand, when he writes, 'The latter [party discipline, BR] will not disappear, as long as members of parliament are elected via a political party and are dependent on that party for re-election. That is not a serious problem either. On the contrary, the voter votes for a party and so recognizable party viewpoints must be expressed in parliament. Moreover, party discipline can be very much associated with dualism. After all, in itself it is separate from the relationship between government and parliament, but it remains dangerous, because it makes it much easier for the government to make itself master of parliament' (see p. 294).
182. 'Kamer verdeeld over aanpak "zetelroof"' ('House of Representatives divided over approach to "seat robbery"'), *NU.nl* (online), 25 November 2014; for a detailed overview of the 'seat robbery' phenomenon, debate and the proposed measures in the Netherlands, see Geerten Waling, *Zetelroof: fractiediscipline en afsplitsingen in de Tweede Kamer 1917-2017* ('Seat robbery: party discipline and party ruptures in the House of Representatives 1917-2017'), Uitgeverij Vantilt 2017. See also Jip Stam, 'Leve de onafhankelijke geesten. Waarom het individuele mandaat van parlementariërs de democratie weerbaarder maakt' ('Long live the independent minds. Why the free mandate of MPs makes democracy more militant'), in *Liberale Reflecties* (Liberal Reflections) 2017, vol. 58 no. 1, p. 15–22, arguing that the free mandate in itself serves as an extra safeguard against antidemocratic parties, giving individual MPs the power to resist antidemocratic tendencies in their party.
183. *Notitie antidemocratische partijen* (Memorandum on antidemocratic parties), p. 7; Van der Woude 2009, p. 19.
184. *Kamerstukken I* (Dutch Parliamentary Papers I) 1986/87, 17 476, 57b, p. 5.
185. See Elzinga 1982, p. 163. Based on Article 54 paragraph 2 of the Dutch Constitution, it is possible to exclude an individual from suffrage if he commits a crime and receives a sentence of at least a year. The core question then is, which offences does the law recognize as justifying exclusion? Unfortunately, these are not clearly listed, for example, in the Penal Code (for an overview see D.J. Elzinga, H.R.B.M. Kummeling and J. Schipper-Spanninga, *Het Nederlandse kiesrecht* [The Dutch right to vote], Deventer: Kluwer 2012, p. 87–88.)· For each offence, where applicable, it is indicated whether suspension of suffrage is a possibility, and that does *not* apply to Article 140 paragraph 2 of the Dutch Penal Code, the ban on continuation of a banned party. A conviction for this crime cannot 'in any way whatsoever have consequences' for

membership of parliament (Elzinga 1982, p. 163; see also Elzinga, Kummeling and Schipper-Spanninga 2012, p. 88). Which offences are included, then? Examples include a terrorist attack with the aim of destroying the constitutional form of government or illegally changing it; see Article 94 (in conjunction with 83 and 83a) in conjunction with 106 paragraph 2 and 28 paragraph 3 of the Dutch Penal Code. A sworn MP whose suffrage is revoked has to end his membership; see Elzinga 1982, p. 162. Certainly in this case this measure with respect to membership of parliament is largely symbolic. For an offence of this nature the punishment would probably be a prison sentence of several years, making it impossible for the member of parliament to return in time. The loss of suffrage, however, does have an effect when it comes to blocking possible parliamentary ambitions *after* serving the sentence. For other offences that justify expulsion, such as election fraud in the sense of Article 129 of the Dutch Penal Code, the expulsion can directly affect membership of parliament: the maximum prison sentence, after all, is only eighteen months, so the MP might be able to return to parliament in time. The duration of the expulsion is determined by Article 31 of the Penal Code: on the basis of paragraph 2, in the case of a temporary prison sentence, this leads to suspension for the duration of the prison sentence plus a minimum of two years and a maximum of five. The seat that becomes vacant in such a case is filled by another candidate from the same list, list group or combination of lists. In the case of a banned party, the seat thus remains empty (unless this party is in a list group or combination). For the details of this arrangement, see Elzinga, Kummeling and Schipper-Spanninga 2012, p. 219–223, in particular p. 221; in this connection, with respect to expulsion, see also p. 88–89.

186. Article 140 paragraph 2 of the Dutch Penal Code and Article 54 paragraph 2 of the Constitution do not need to be changed. The maximum prison sentence of a year is (just) sufficient (Art. 54 para. 2 of the Constitution). That is not unusually low; see, for example, the possible loss of suffrage (and thus membership of parliament) for election fraud (a maximum prison sentence of eighteen months): Article 129 in conjunction with 130 paragraph 2 and 28 paragraph 3 of the Dutch Penal Code. During the parliamentary debate on the new exclusion regime in the 1980s the issues of suffrage and banned continuation were briefly discussed, on the initiative of the PvdA, but the government turned down the suggestion (with the agreement of parliament). The argument was that far from *all* cases in which criminal behaviour had taken place in the sense of Article 140 of the Penal Code *also* involved behaviour for which exclusion from suffrage would be justified. That is not a very strong argument; the very fact that the exclusion *can* (and does not have to) be declared gives the judge sufficient freedom *not* to declare expulsion for a conviction for the continuation of a criminal organization but to do so for the continuation of a banned political party. See *Kamerstukken II* (Dutch Parliamentary Papers II) 1985/1986, 18 973, 7, p. 12–13, and on that see Elzinga, Kummeling and Schipper-Spanninga 2012, p. 88–89.

187. In the 1930s another system was proposed in the Netherlands in which 'revolutionary' representatives could have their membership of parliament revoked through a special procedure (see Elzinga 1982, p. 163). This was different from a party ban, focusing instead on the representatives of the people themselves and only on those who call for use of illegal methods to abolish democracy; it could be said that it relates to the members of parliament of *violent* parties. This kind of system, as Elzinga rightly states, however, suffers from a major disadvantage: the procedure could be abused to ban a party *de facto* by removing all its members of parliament (see Elzinga 1982, p. 163). The (rejected) idea

came in part from the De Wilde government commission (see *Verslag van de Staatscommissie, ingesteld bij Koninklijk Besluit van 24 januari 1936, No. 41, aan welke is opgedragen de voorbereiding van eene partieele herziening van de Grondwet* (Report by the government commission set up by Royal Decree on 24 January 1936, No. 41, tasked with preparation of a partial revision of the Constitution, henceforth Verslag Staatscommissie-De Wilde), The Hague: Algemeene Landsdrukkerij 1936, p. 10–12, with the following remark on p. 10: 'In recent years, however, in broader circles in our country the conviction has formed that it should not be tolerated that a representative of the people should recommend or promote illegal methods for the realization of his political ideas. The Committee shares this conviction, and is of the opinion that it must be possible to declare a member of the representation of the people who is guilty of this to have lost his membership. This is, after all, the only proper manner of provision.' See in particular p. 11, with respect to the seat of the revolutionary representative of the people that became open: 'In contrast with the solution of the government commission of 1934, which was tied to the boundaries stated in the Constitution, in the thinking of the Committee the place which became open would not be filled if a member was declared to have had his membership revoked. The measure of declaring membership revoked would lose its main impact if the political group to which the lapsed member belonged could then fill the empty seat with its members and continue to express its illegal aims.' Interestingly, George van den Bergh was also a member of the government commission, but, like the Leiden professor of law Roelof Kranenburg, among others, he provided a dissenting opinion: 'By removing a member or a number of members, it is possible to create an artificial majority in parliament, even for a revision of the Constitution. . . . The stipulation proposed by the Committee may therefore in certain circumstances in fact facilitate revolutionary aims.' For the objections of George van den Bergh, Willem Alberda, Dolf Joekes and Roelof Kranenburg, see Verslag Staatscommissie-De Wilde, p. 37–39 (the objections also involved the Council of State, which was not seen as neutral in this matter).

188. The Refah judgement could also be explained in this way (see Maloney 2012, p. 64): 'With regard to the forming of a "popular will", the Strasbourg Court argued that in order to secure the *continued* right of all Turkish citizens to participate in such a process, the Turkish authorities possessed both the right and the responsibility to legally dissolve a temporarily popular vehicle for the articulation and aggregation of preference on the grounds that its ideology and popularity posed a dual threat to democratic governance' (my italicization, BR). In fact Maloney considers the application of this principle in the Refah case to be incorrect because, in his view, the fundamental threat to democracy was absent.
189. Cf. also Fox and Nolte 2000, p. 446: 'There is certainly intrinsic value for future voters [in a restriction of electoral choices *in the present*, BR], who may be denied any opportunity to change their government save through extra-constitutional means.'
190. For this see chapter 1, under 'The reception of Van den Bergh's inaugural lecture'. Langemeijer writes in response to Van den Bergh: 'In other words, it may be true that the claim on the authority of the democratically made decision to abolish democracy, seen from a democratic point of view, is weaker than that of any other majority decision—after all, it lacks provision for the changing of opinion, which subjection of the minority makes so much more a requirement of reason—but it has a claim nevertheless, because its rejection would mean allowing the possible will of a future

majority to prevail over the established will of today's majority' (Langemeijer 1936, p. 884). This response, however, fails to recognize the special character of the decision to abolish democracy; what the future majority asks *in this case* is not simply that its own will prevail above the present will; it *merely* wishes to preserve the possibility of *also* having its future will expressed by democratic means.

191. The fact that Popper saw the American 'McCarthyism' as rather less problematic than other critics might be considered to confirm this; see Ryan 2013, p. xviii.
192. Frankenberg 2004, p. 132.
193. A ban of a small splinter group with little potential for growth probably costs more than it achieves in a democratic sense: the infringement of democracy (the ban) is 'greater' than the damage prevented. If a party has the potential to become a serious challenge to democracy (as in the case of Refah), the 'costs' of the infringement pale in comparison with the 'gain' of preventing serious damage to the three principles of self-correction.
194. Dieter Grimm, 'Freedom of Speech in a Globalized World', p. 11–22 (14), in Ivan Hare and James Weinstein (eds.), *Extreme Speech and Democracy*, Oxford: Oxford University Press 2010; it should be added that this applies as long as it is not a matter of support to parties or terrorist groups already banned.
195. See Rummens 2015, p. 288, and Sajó 2004, p. 228–229; see also recently Malkopoulou and Norman 2017, p. 445. Remarkably enough, Israel here opts for the opposite approach: support to terrorist organizations (and with it the spread of antidemocratic ideas in many cases) justifies restriction of freedom of expression, but (probably) not exclusion from participation in elections; see Navot 2008, p. 754.
196. The broad discussion and the accusations made with respect to the Spanish ban of Batasuna are illustrative in this respect. Here in fact it was not particularly beneficial that the law appeared specially written for this party; see Tyulkina 2015, p. 138, and on the debate in general, p. 135–138.
197. Tyulkina 2015, p. 212.
198. I would want to suggest that this answer, combined with the answers to critiques one and two above, could constitute a preliminary reply to Invernizzi Accetti and Zuckerman's recent criticism of militant democracy's 'inherent arbitrariness' (see Ivernizzi Accetti and Zuckerman 2017, p. 190). Arbitrariness is not *by definition* part of militant democracy, but a consequence of an underdeveloped justification and subsequent vague banning grounds (i.e., not stating which parties *exactly* can be banned) in some current militant democracy theories—see the critique of Kirshner 2014 and Tyulkina 2015 above. Instead of an 'all or nothing' dichotomous question, I would contend that the question of arbitrariness is rather a matter of degree, and subsequently of how misuse of militant democracy measures can be prevented *as much as possible* (a premise we, after all, also accept when it comes to the potential misuse of, for instance, the far-reaching state repression in penal law). I would argue that, as developed above, the answer to this question is in: 1) an explicit justification (clearly delimiting what counts as a legitimate use of militant democracy and what does not), 2) narrow legal grounds for banning political parties, and 3) procedural safeguards.
199. This English translation is available at https://www.gesetze-im-internet.de/englisch_gg/. The German original reads, 'Gegen jeden, der es unternimmt, diese Ordnung zu beseitigen, haben alle Deutschen das Recht zum Widerstand, wenn andere Abhilfe nicht möglich ist.'
200. Thiel 2009b, p. 418–419.
201. See Thiel 2009b, p. 419.

202. Thiel 2009b, p. 419.
203. See Etzioni 2007.
204. Issacharoff 2007, p. 1460.
205. See also Issacharoff 2007, p. 1461.
206. Issacharoff 2007, p. 1462. This might turn out differently if a party were to discriminate amongst its members for certain electable positions; see, for example, ECHR 10 July 2012, 58369/10 (Political Reformed Party/Netherlands).
207. As an extra advantage of party bans, Van der Woude points to their greater flexibility above supraconstitutionality: such bans are linked to court judgements on what can be viewed in the current moment to constitute erosion of fundamental principles. Court judgements can develop over time and with society (see Van der Woude 2009, p. 54–55). However, I would not see this as such an advantage: one of the most important aims of democracy as self-correction is to ensure that the judge has little flexibility, by giving him grounds for a ban that are as clear as possible, so that he is not drawn into a political battle.
208. Pfersmann 2004, p. 47.
209. See Tyulkina 2015, p. 138.
210. As a radical preacher in North Brabant did in April 2015, in fact without appealing for violence: 'Democracy forces us to accept different rules and moral values: that our daughters marry without permission from their parents, that men are permitted to marry men, women to marry women, that people can say what they want, that they can swear, democracy allows it all.' Instead he said people should 'follow the laws of Allah and the Koran'. See 'Preker in moskee Helmond roept op tot afkeren van democratie' ('Preacher in Helmond mosque calls for rejection of democracy'), *Eindhovens Dagblad*, 29 April 2015. In that sense popular Dutch language use is unfortunate: is it simply 'hate' that 'hate preachers' spread, or is it just as often (also) an antidemocratic ideology? That is different from 'hate'. The joint 2015 report of the Dutch General Intelligence and Security Service (AIVD) and the National Coordinator for Security and Counterterrorism (NCTV): *Salafisme in Nederland: diversiteit en dynamiek* (Salafism in the Netherlands: diversity and dynamic), The Hague 2015, (at p. 10), gives the example of a preacher who calls on people via the internet not to vote in local council elections because it would be a form of apostasy.
211. See, for example, Amos N. Guiora, *Freedom from Religion: Rights and National Security*, Oxford: Oxford University Press 2009.
212. In a recent Dutch criminal case concerning the threat of bodily harm, the judge explicitly interpreted a 'call to Allah' to 'pull out' and 'cut off' the tongues of specific persons, in the religious Islamic context, to be not only a request to Allah, but also an encouragement to violence against these persons by fellow believers; see District Court The Hague, 26-10-2016, ECLI:NL:RBDHA:2016:12789.
213. See Annick Diesfeldt and Fanny de Graaf, 'Dataretentie: een kwestie van alles of niets?' ('Data retention: a question of all or nothing?'), *Nederlands Juristenblad* 2015, no. 12, p. 740–747.
214. 'Stand van zaken ten aanzien van buiten werking stelling bewaarplicht telecommunicatiegegevens' ('State of affairs with respect to shutdown of retention requirement of telecommunications data'), 21 July 2015 (letter from the minister of justice to the House of Representatives). Available via http://www.tweedekamer.nl/kamerstukken/brieven_regering/detail?id=2015Z14266anddid=2015D28749.
215. As mentioned previously, Tyulkina argues that this specific starting point of militant democracy can ensure that counterterrorism *also* remains within the boundaries of the 'constitutional order'; see the discussion of Tyulkina in chapter 2.

Conclusion

1. Popper and Marcuse

In 1971 a German broadcaster attempted to organize a confrontation between the 'grand old men' of two influential philosophical currents: Karl Popper and Herbert Marcuse.[1] It was a confrontation between social reform and social revolution. Marcuse had acquired worldwide fame as the theoretician of international left-wing protest.[2] One of his well-known claims was that students would fulfil a crucial role in the social revolution. They would function as 'catalysts', 'preparing the way for the revolutionary movement'.[3] At university the 'frameworks' for the society of the future are formed. The development of 'critical thinking' in these places is therefore a decisive factor.[4] We still hear an echo of this in today's student protests. Popper and Marcuse had previously met only fleetingly, never having a chance for discussion.[5] No meeting took place this time either; the interviewer met them in their homes and collected their answers.

This confrontation by proxy boiled down to the question of whether a violent revolution can be justified for the sake of social progress. It was precisely the point of contention that divided the SDAP in the interbellum. George van den Bergh took a clear standpoint in the discussion, and in his inaugural lecture he sharply criticized a doctoral dissertation in which his fellow party member Van den Tempel defended such a socialist revolution as justified under certain circumstances. Van den Bergh, along with Bonger and others, thus set the SDAP firmly on the path of democracy. Democracy must always be an end, not a means—for socialists too.

Marcuse, however, had no doubts on the subject: in his view an end to suppression in the 'late capitalist society' could only be made by radical change to that society, by revolution.[6] Marcuse also assumes this could involve violence, albeit in covert terms.[7] Popper considers this stance, when it comes to the supposed suppression, 'immensely exaggerated', and given the implicit legitimation of violence probably as dangerous too.[8] At the end of the conversation, the interviewer nevertheless puts it to Popper once more:

> In conclusion, professor, once more the question of revolution: is it unthinkable to you that we should use violence to implement what we have come to know is better?[9]

Popper's answer is crystal clear. Even if we 'know' better, in a democracy revolution is out of the question.[10] Democracy offers the possibility of change without violence,[11] and the non-violent path is always preferable to the violent, first because 'revolutionary ideals and their supporters' almost always fall prey to such a revolution.[12] The English revolution gave us Cromwell, the French revolution led to Robespierre and Napoleon, and the Russian revolution led to Stalin.[13] Second, non-violent, democratic changes have the advantage that they take place in an atmosphere of public criticism: 'They enable us to be alert to unintended and undesirable consequences of our measures and to adjust them in good time, if such consequences present themselves'.[14] According to Popper, democracy thus offers a framework that makes continual reform possible. No radical overthrow of democracy can match that.[15] Those who overturn democracy are responsible not only for the victims of revolution but also for destroying the framework in which it is possible to tackle 'social abuses'.[16]

Here the thinking of Popper and Van den Bergh coincides. Van den Bergh not only resisted shortcuts to a socialist utopia in the 1930s; he also drew attention to a unique quality of democracy, namely, that decisions are revocable. Democracy offers a framework for continual improvement, the framework Popper speaks of. We can revoke every decision in a democracy. The only decision to which that does not apply is the decision to throw the entire framework overboard; institutionalized self-correction is then definitively lost and can no longer be restored by democratic means. That justifies resistance against those who seek to end democracy. It is the starting point of the militant democracy theory of 'democracy as self-correction' developed in this book: democracy as the ability to redo your steps.

2. The theory of democracy as self-correction

Democracy as self-correction attempts to offer a coherent theory for resisting extremists. The justification for acting against antidemocrats is sought in the protection of the self-corrective capacity of democracy, a unique quality of democracy that Van den Bergh pointed out in 1936. A democracy is characterized by its capacity for self-correction, the permanent revocability of *all* decisions, even more than by value-neutrality or protection of fundamental rights. The people govern themselves by continual self-correction. The chosen policy can always be adjusted in response to criticism, unexpected consequences or unforeseen circumstances. Democracy offers safeguards for this that no other system can. It invites criticism and encourages diversity of opinions. It is, in Popper's terms, the form of government that comes closest to the scientific method. This probably contributes to, or is even the deciding factor in, its success, for instance, in terms of living standards. When the self-corrective capacity comes under threat, democracy is allowed to defend itself.

This justification for intervention assumes an already existing democracy: it is not inconsistent for an established democracy to act against antidemocratic parties; it does not constitute betrayal of democratic values. That is a limited claim: it is not a justification for the *establishment* of a democracy, that is, the battle for democracy within a non-democratic state, or to put it another way, a democratic revolution. Democracy as self-correction thus stays away from contestable (natural law) principles necessary to support such a broad argument for democracy *outside* a democracy. Democracy as self-correction merely asks the question, must an *existing* democracy tolerate antidemocratic forces? The answer is no.

The self-corrective capacity of democracy is supported by three principles: those of evaluation, political competition and freedom of expression. Without these principles there is no self-government by means of self-correction. The principle of *evaluation* is safeguarded by active suffrage and free, periodical elections by secret ballot. This ensures that evaluation of policy is compelled to take place with some regularity, providing a sanction for unresponsive ministers. If they do not streamline their policy with new priorities and knowledge, they can be voted out. This safeguards the continuation of the process of self-correction. *Political competition* is made possible by passive suffrage and freedom of association. A principle of evaluation, of course, is meaningless if there are no alternatives for unresponsive ministers. Political competition gives content to the principle of evaluation. Strong political competition also ensures that an abundance of policy alternatives are devised for competition. *Freedom of expression* completes the trio. Alternative policy and criticism of government policy must not only be devised but also disseminated. Freedom of expression allows a democracy to draw on an incredible reservoir of ideas, unthinkable in any other system. Every citizen is seen as a potential source of useful alternatives and criticism.

A democracy does not have to tolerate a serious threat to these principles. This gives us narrow grounds for prohibition, in contrast with militant democracy theories that seek refuge in substantive democracy. A substantive democracy, with its conflation of democracy and rule of law, after all, can easily result in broad grounds for banning a party: threats to the rule of law (including rights not directly related to democracy) become threats to *democracy*. We have already seen this in the first interpretation of Van den Bergh: principled democracy, which protects not only the democratic process, but also freedom of conscience and equality before the law. These are undoubtedly important values, but they lead to parties too easily becoming eligible for prohibition. If the core of democracy (viewed here as self-government by self-correction) is not seriously threatened, antidemocratic parties must be confronted in *debate*. The narrow definition thus offers the first and most important safeguard against abuse. This is the basis of democracy as self-correction.

A party ban is irrefutably a heavy-handed intervention in a democracy. A second question is thus, when can it be used? Van den Bergh, Popper,

Rawls and Kirshner have broadly similar views here. A ban is a serious infringement of democracy. In Kirshner's terms, it brings 'democratic costs' with it, *even* in the case of a ban of a splinter group. From Van den Bergh's speech we therefore derived an *opportunity principle*: intervention is permissible but not obligatory. Within the theory of democracy as self-correction the right to intervene arises as soon as an antidemocratic threat manifests itself, but in principle reticence is called for. As a rule of thumb, one should wait until the danger is greater than the democratic costs of a ban. That is in any case *not* the moment when the votes are counted and an antidemocratic party or coalition, already with a substantial number of seats, can push through to a majority (roughly the scenario with FIS in Algeria). *Neither* is it the moment when an antidemocratic party is founded (as in the case of the *United Communist Party of Turkey*). In the first case it is too late, making it questionable whether a ban will be effective; in the second case it is too early and the democratic cost of a ban is probably higher than the danger of allowing the party to continue to exist. In the end it is down to the competent authorities to choose the acceptable moment between these extremes; it is then up to the judge to provide a check on them. Together they are responsible for protecting democracy, as well as minimizing the democratic costs. Democracy as self-correction aims to protect democracy without unnecessarily restricting it.

That brings us to another issue that a militant-democracy theory should attend to: *procedural safeguards*. Van den Bergh also talked about this in his inaugural lecture. How do you ensure that a party ban is carefully applied? There are in any case three possible procedural safeguards: review by multiple courts, supranational oversight and an apolitical institution to request party bans. First, of course, it comes down to a motivated, non-political judgement from an independent judge, aided by grounds for prohibition that are legally workable because they are narrow. A judicial process involving multiple institutions is preferable to a German system with only one court, albeit a highly authoritative one, that passes judgement on party bans. The jurisprudence on party bans is limited (and fortunately so, in view of its invasive character), but at the same time very different judicial opinions can exist regarding the concrete application of such an invasive measure. It can therefore do no harm if an institution such as the Supreme Court pronounces judgement in the final instance, benefiting from the arguments produced by the previous institutions.

A second safeguard is supranational oversight of democracy. Both the European Court of Human Rights and the European Union ensure that the future of militant democracy to a significant extent lies at the European level. The ECHR acts as the last resort for bans on political parties in the forty-seven member states of the Council of Europe, thus fulfilling a complex role. The court must first develop a theory of democracy to encompass the democratic traditions of all member states, for which the European Convention on Human Rights is of course the starting point.

In testing cases against this theory of democracy, it must then take into account the peculiarities of the specific member state at issue. Can the ECHR, for example, judge the extent to which an Islamist party represents a threat to secularism in Turkey, and with it a threat to democracy? Or, to what extent is excluding a politician from politics in Latvia justified by the transition from communism to democracy? In the cases studied here, the ECHR appears to be an adept tightrope walker, assuming a modest but critical role. Where the facts are clear, it does not shrink from drawing a line (as in the case of the *United Communist Party of Turkey*); at the same time, the court takes into account local circumstances and does not substitute its judgement for that of local authorities (as shown in the cases of *Refah*, *Batasuna* and *Zdanoka*). Although democracy as self-correction is (in principle) meant as a self-sufficient system, young democracies sensitive to abuse may benefit from the extra check on abuse that a supranational organ such as the ECHR can offer.

Whereas the role of the ECHR is complex, we can only see that of the European Union as paradoxical. On the one hand, we see a gradual increase in oversight of democracy, ranging from ad hoc sanctions in the Haider case to the current 'nuclear option': if a member state severely damages its democracy, its membership rights can be suspended on the basis of Article 7 of the Lisbon Treaty. These are not party bans, nor are they a form of direct oversight of the imposition of party bans (as is the case with the ECHR); EU oversight is (currently) more distant. Jan-Werner Müller, however, argues that EU oversight should be sharpened. He claims that the EU, at least in part, must be seen as a post-war instrument for reining in the power of majorities and parliaments, as explained by the 'lessons from Weimar'. If this is a component of the EU rationale, we should not be surprised that the EU also involves itself in national democracies. At the same time, Müller offers an additional, principled argument: every member state decides via the European Council, theoretically including *undemocratic* member states, on the lives of all European citizens. Although this trend is unmistakable, we also see a development in the other direction: that is to say, national courts (potentially) resisting further European integration 'in the name' of militant democracy. Further integration is seen as undermining democracy. The German Bundesverfassungsgericht leads the way in this, armed with a Constitution in which the German democracy is enshrined for eternity. In a series of pronouncements, including statements on the treaties of Maastricht and Lisbon, and more recently the euro crisis bond buy-back programme, the BVerfG has clearly flexed its muscles. As a rule its judgements are remarkably fiercely criticized, but so far the court has made no move towards retreat. And even if the BVerfG retreats, there are still twenty-seven other national courts.[17]

It also does not look like it will quickly become clear which development will gain the upper hand in the EU, but with the ECHR and the EU, militant democracy will undoubtedly gain an increasingly European dimension.

Then we come to the final safeguard: distance between the political arena and the organ responsible for submitting requests for a ban. In the Netherlands such a request is submitted by the Public Prosecution Department. Of course, this distance is to some extent hypothetical. In the end politics in the form of parliament and the government ultimately can get its way, via the minister of justice's authority to give instructions to the Prosecution Department, but an organ placed at a distance at least has the possibility of coming to its own judgement in the first instance. This interplay of forces can soften the potentially political character of ban proceedings. The German model, in which the government and parliament, among others, can submit such a request, is therefore undesirable since it adds a political flavour to the proceedings, right from the start.

Banned parties often try a sort of Houdini trick. The best example might be the Czech Workers' Party: its successor party was ready and waiting for members and administration to step in.[18] But other problems can also frustrate the effectiveness of a ban. In order to prevent these problems, we can formulate rules of thumb with respect to the design of a party ban: 1) a ban must *really* be a ban, 2) 'successor parties' must be liable to punishment, and 3) 'banned' members of parliament must lose their seats, at least if they work towards the re-establishment of the banned party. With respect to the first point, participation in elections as the same party must be impossible, and the continuation of the party must be a penal offence. These are the minimum consequences necessary to effectively call a measure a ban. The second point means that groups that present themselves as new parties but are really continuations of the old party must fall under the same ban. Collaborating on re-establishment must be a punishable offence. With respect to the third point, regarding 'banned members of parliament', two models compete for priority: the 'unconditional model', that is, unconditionally respecting the free mandate of MPs, and the 'conditional model', in which 'banned MPs' lose their seats when their party is banned; making their seats, to a certain extent, dependent on the fate of their party. In democracies that are firmly based on the free mandate of elected MPs, such as the Dutch system, revoking a seat in conjunction with a party ban would mean a fundamental change to the system. In countries such as Germany, where parties have a constitutionally recognized position in forming the will of the people, and also in Turkey, loss of a seat is seen as a logical consequence of a party ban: without it members of parliament can continue to abuse the parliamentary platform for their antidemocratic goals. There is much to be said for the German and Turkish approach. In any case, however, one could argue that *at least* collaborating towards the continuation of the banned party should be made impossible; that should lead to loss of the seat. This clearly draws a line, demarcating the conditions for a 'second chance' as a member of parliament. This issue of 'what to do with the seats of a banned party' might be viewed as a marginal issue without serious practical consequences, but that changes if we think of the Constitutional Court of Turkey having to decide what should happen to the seats of the largest parliamentary party, the 158 (out of 450) seats of the Refah Party.

Whereas a legislator *can* shape a party ban to a large extent, and can thus decide what happens to the seats of a banned party; he naturally cannot 'design' all actual effects of measures taken against antidemocrats. He can only consult empirical research. Studies into these effects show that the traditional objections to party bans (as 'ineffective' or 'counterproductive') do not stand up to scrutiny *and* that there are success stories. The parties that have taken the places of banned parties in Turkey and Belgium are less antidemocratic, and after the ban of Batasuna in Spain the party leader made the first steps towards peace, as clearly shown in the work of British political scientist Tim Bale. Political science further shows that the effectiveness of a ban can be increased by making the 'second chance' more concrete for former party members. The stigma of membership of antidemocratic groups, in the Netherlands specifically extreme right-wing groups, impedes a departure from their former party environment and re-entry into society. The starting point of this kind of inclusive approach is that the party or group is banned but that former members should be embraced. It is also important to avoid the stigma extending to the political issues that interested the banned party. This approach reduces not only the 'democratic cost' (the interests are still politically represented, despite the party ban), but also the potential breeding ground for re-launching the party.

Those are the main points of the theory of militant democracy developed here: democracy as self-correction. The theory rests on four pillars that any theory of militant democracy should include: the *justification*, *grounds for a ban*, *procedural safeguards* and attention to the *design*, and thus the consequences, of party bans.

Any democracy, either procedural or substantive in theory, in the end has mechanisms to defend itself.[19] That applies as much to the American procedural democracy as to the very substantive German democracy. Antidemocratic parties *are* banned, or excluded in other ways, with the advantage that in a militant democracy this takes place in public and must therefore be explicitly justified. The question is how. Democracy as self-correction aims to provide an answer.

Notes

1. Franz Stark, 'Woord na' (Afterword), p. 43–47 (43), in Marcuse and Popper 1971.
2. Stark 1971, p. 43.
3. Marcuse and Popper 1971, p. 17.
4. Marcuse and Popper 1971, p. 18.
5. Stark 1971, p. 43.
6. Marcuse and Popper 1971, p. 5 and 19.
7. Marcuse and Popper 1971, p. 21, Marcuse: 'Look, I do not think that this problem [violence against the prevailing system, BR] can be posed in a television interview intended for everyone; it can only be discussed with those involved,

within the circle of those who participate, and it must be attuned to particular situations. On the problem of violence in general I can only repeat what I have already said: that in the existing society violence is simply institutionalized to an immense degree, and the core problem is in the first instance who initiates the violence. I think that one can in any case say that in the period of incipient counter-revolution violence in the first instance comes from the existing society and that in this respect the opposition is confronted with the question of counter-violence, the violence of the defence, but certainly not to the violence of aggression.'

8. See Marcuse and Popper 1971, p. 23–24 (with respect to the suspected suppression) and p. 28 (with respect to the violence).
9. Marcuse and Popper 1971, p. 40.
10. In fact Popper would also argue that we could not know what is better in an *objective* sense; see Marcuse and Popper 1971, p. 35. For more detail on this, see the discussion of Van den Tempel's *Democratische vrijheid en socialistisch recht* (Democratic freedom and socialist justice) in chapter 1.
11. Marcuse and Popper 1971, p. 40.
12. Marcuse and Popper 1971, p. 40; see also p. 28.
13. Marcuse and Popper 1971, p. 40.
14. Marcuse and Popper 1971, p. 40.
15. Marcuse and Popper 1971, p. 40. Elsewhere in the interview Popper emphasized his definition of democracy, as we saw earlier, namely, the possibility of non-violent transfer of power; see Marcuse and Popper, p. 27.
16. Marcuse and Popper 1971, p. 28.
17. Of course, not all these courts have the same opportunities for review as the Bundesverfassungsgericht.
18. See Mareš 2012a, p. 45.
19. See Bligh 2008, p. 1440: 'Ultimately, the lesson may be that every democracy, whatever its free speech ethos, has to develop defense mechanisms that protect it from forces of anti-liberalism and intolerance. These mechanisms may be explicit and direct or implicit and unacknowledged. Whatever the case, the existence of these barriers should be recognized and their justifications and effects should be examined.' See also Issacharoff 2007, p. 1467.

Epilogue

Institutions are like fortresses.
They must be well designed *and* manned.[1]
Karl Popper, *The Open Society and Its Enemies*, 1945

Have we reached our goal? Is it sufficient for the defence of democracy here and elsewhere to cut off the path for antidemocrats and demarcate the outer limits of democratic tolerance? Perhaps. But a militant democracy probably also requires something from the individuals who populate its institutions, those who actually operate the controls. In *The Open Society* Popper emphasizes that even the best-designed institutions are dependent on the individuals who run them and who must apply their rules.[2] In other words, a democracy must also exhibit a 'willingness to preserve democratic institutions'.[3]

This attitude could be called a 'democratic ethos'. The democratic ethos in a democracy is of course broader than militant democracy alone, encompassing the entirety of a 'more or less sustainable pattern of thinking and acting', or a 'political culture'.[4] The question, therefore, is what is the specific emphasis of democracy as self-correction, and militant democracy in general, *within* that democratic ethos? What should we, in the light of democracy as self-correction, specifically underline within our democratic ethos? What components deserve extra attention?

In the context of this book it was not possible to address this issue earlier; it is a subject that would justify a separate study. Nevertheless, I would like to discuss it here, because it represents an important addition to the more institutional approach in this book.

I would like to argue that democracy as self-correction, within a broader democratic ethos, lays the emphasis on at least two points. Note that we now leave the traditional territory of militant democracy, understood as the *institutional* defence of democracy. What follows is therefore rather a perspective, an outline of what it might mean to embrace the theory of militant democracy developed here in a *political and cultural* sense. In short, what do democracy as self-correction and militant democracy in general demand of democrats?

The first point of emphasis of democracy as self-correction touches not so much on the defence of democracy as on its maintenance. It follows from what democracy as self-correction sees as the essence of democracy: the capacity for self-correction. Self-correction has a political and cultural side as well as an institutional aspect: it requires a particular attitude among participants in the democratic debate, and more specifically, about how we deal with 'mistakes' in politics.

We looked above at Popper's ideal politician. Popper looks forward to the 'happy situation' in which politicians search for their mistakes themselves and do not try 'to prove that they have always been right'.[5] In a lecture on tolerance in 1981 he even goes a step further:

> If I dream of a democratic Utopia, it will be one in which a parliamentary candidate can hope to attract votes by the boast that he discovered during the last year thirty-one mistakes made by himself and has managed to correct thirteen of them; while his competitor discovered only twenty-seven, even though he admittedly also corrected thirteen of them.[6]

So, according to Popper, mistakes must be actively sought out. A change of opinion should be exemplary of progressive insight, and it should be possible to win elections this way.

It looks like Popper's 'happy situation' will not easily be realized. For example, in the Netherlands when a minister is called to account, we often see a parliamentary debate in which the opposition parties take turns at trying to tackle him. For the minister involved it is a case of walking a fine line to save his own skin; then we can return, not much the wiser, to the order of the day. In a study of the accountability of ministers, constitutional jurist Robert Visser concludes that the 'accountability phase' in the House of Representatives is sometimes skipped, while this is an ideal moment to learn from mistakes; instead those present move directly to the phase of 'political judgement and political conclusion'.[7] Will the minister stay or go? That is apparently what we want to know. This dynamic took on a new dimension at the start of 2015 when the minister of justice of the day, Ivo Opstelten, and his state secretary Fred Teeven came under pressure when a fifteen-year-old (financial) deal with a drug criminal resurfaced: they resigned *before* they had explained their handling of the matter in the House of Representatives,[8] preferring to avoid the public castigation. Thus citizens and politicians hold one another hostage: citizens demand flawless politicians and politicians feign flawlessness by failing to admit their mistakes,[9] or by resorting to 'mistakes were made' (but not necessarily by *me*): what political commentator William Schneider calls the 'past exonerative tense'.[10] Anyone can 'admit' someone else's mistakes.

The Opstelten and Teeven episode could be seen as part of a broader culture, at least in the Netherlands, of settling scores, inside and outside politics: above all a culprit must be found for any mistake, and that culprit must be punished.[11] This leads to rigidity and conformism.[12] It is what Popper describes as the 'old ethic' in science and other domains, particularly in the judiciary: mistakes are unforgivable, can never be admitted, and if they emerge they lead to unanimous disgust,[13] but mistakes are inevitable, and we make a great many of them. We should therefore radically change our attitude to mistakes, writes Popper.[14]

That is not to say that mistakes should be without political consequences, but that the automatic link between 'mistakes' and 'resignation' should be viewed critically. However, do note that this is not about dubious expense claims or even serious criminal acts, which are separate issues, in which political ethics should be strict.[15] This is simply about embracing progressive insight, while acknowledging that a previous judgement was erroneous: '*political* mistakes' in other words. The rare individual who changes his mind is seen as 'performing a U-turn'. Changes of viewpoint are seen as a sign not that one has learnt but that one was wrong before. It is disastrous for a 'learning sovereign', disastrous for democracy as self-correction.

It is interesting to note an argument by Dutch historian and publicist Rutger Bregman in this context, who in addition to a right to freedom of expression also claims a right to change one's mind.[16] It is, after all, surprising that in politics, the very place where the most opinions are expressed, they seem to change the least.[17] Keeping Bertrand Russell in mind, we should see changes of opinion for what they really are: a sign of 'intellectual courage'.[18]

Democracy as self-correction similarly demands an open attitude to mistakes and less hesitation when it comes to changes of opinion. That is acting in the spirit of democracy as self-correction. Only then can the self-learning potential of democracy be fully enjoyed. That is not at all an easy culture change. The realization that an attitude of acknowledging and correcting mistakes is a unique characteristic of democracy might help in this respect. Popper's ideal is nevertheless hard to realize, as is best illustrated by Popper himself. The philosopher of falsifiability and (embracing) radical criticism accepted nothing less than the 'total acceptance of his own thought'.[19] Admitting mistakes was not on the cards for him; any hint of criticism was mercilessly torpedoed. Among Popper's students at the London School of Economics his main work of political philosophy was therefore generally known as *The Open Society—by One of Its Enemies.*[20]

The second element I would like to address under the term 'democratic ethos' is more important and urgent for militant democracy. This is about the political and cultural, non-institutional defence of democracy.[21] The attacks on, for instance, *Charlie Hebdo* in Paris and on a meeting on freedom of expression in Copenhagen showed again in a shocking manner that terrorism does not always mean random violence; it can also be directed at a specific democratic value: freedom of expression.[22] I say *again*, because it has long been clear that terrorism is (also) directed at freedom of expression, as in the case of the fatwa against Salman Rushdie, the Danish cartoon riots and the uproar after the YouTube short film *The Innocence of Muslims.*[23] But there are also less well-known examples, such as the French performance of a play by Voltaire that because of its 265-year-old criticism of Islam was only able to go ahead with heavy police protection.[24] After plans for publication were cancelled by Random House out of fear for repercussions, the novel *Jewel of Medina* was also 'postponed' by its new British publisher after an incident in which a firebomb was placed in their office letterbox.[25] British historian Tom Holland's documentary on the origin of Islam could not be shown after threats to the presenter.[26] Even a university lecture by the former pope discussing the 'historical and philosophical differences between Islam and Christianity' was followed by apologies and an official amendment after threats and violent protests.[27]

It is not always about *religious* extremism.[28] Self-censorship is encouraged by violence and the threat of violence from various groups and individuals. Bart-Jan Spruyt, chairman of the Dutch conservative Edmund Burke Foundation, claims to have been threatened by left-wing radicals,[29] and historian and publicist Zihni Özdil by the Turkish community in the Netherlands.[30] Spruyt has withdrawn from the debate, whereas Özdil remained and became an MP for GroenLinks (GreenLeft) in 2017.[31] A radio interview with writer Robert Vuijsje on the filming of his novel *Alleen maar nette mensen* (Only decent people, about the multicultural Dutch society) had to be called off because his safety could not be guaranteed after threats.[32] Singer Anouk received many serious threats after criticizing the controversial Dutch tradition of 'Zwarte Piet' (Black Pete, the companion of Saint Nicholas).[33]

In 2009 the commissioner for human rights of the Council of Europe Thomas Hammarberg wrote the following in his report about freedom of expression and extremism in the Netherlands:

> Freedom of expression has been under pressure in the Netherlands after the paralyzing impact of the politically and religiously motivated violence that led to the death of Theo van Gogh and the death threats against former MP Ayaan Hirsi Ali and other politicians. Protective security measures for politicians are a new reality in the Netherlands. The government realises that the number and gravity of incidents where freedom of expression has been impeded by (the threat of) violence appear to have increased. The Commissioner is concerned that the debate on freedom of expression is influenced by fears of terrorism, as well as a fear of growing self-censorship in cultural and social life.[34]

Professor of international relations and terrorism expert Rob de Wijk observed ten years ago that freedom of expression was already 'a thing of the past': 'We must accept that we can no longer say everything.'[35] After the *Charlie Hebdo* attack in 2015 Dutch political scientist and extremism researcher Cas Mudde wrote the following:

> Already several years ago I met Dutch public intellectuals who told me, in confidence, that they had stopped criticizing Islam(ism) in public because of violent threats to them and their family. Even the

> 'fearless' US comedian Stephen Colbert would not show the (in)famous Mohammed cartoons, or other images deemed offensive to Muslims, instead putting up a (funny) image of 'technical disturbances'. While making fun of his fear of a violent response, he never seriously problematized it and, in the end, censored himself. Even the few brave souls that do dare to satirize Islam(ism), often get censored by the media or their employers – South Park's notorious 'Mohammed episode' has been censored multiple times by Comedy Central![36]

Other authors also point to what could be called a 'culture of self-censorship'.[37]

Now a policy maker, governor or minister might of course think, yes, but they can always tread a bit more carefully for a while. An example of this approach can be seen when Dutch prime minister Balkenende called for greater reticence among the 'high-profile critics who populate our news magazines' after the murder of Theo van Gogh,[38] or when Minister of Justice Piet-Hein Donner at the same time played with the idea of resurrecting a dead letter from the Dutch Penal Code: blasphemy.[39] Commentators also suggest a similar approach with some regularity.[40] A second possible reaction is to label the issue a security problem, making it exclusively a case for the police and counterterrorism.

I believe that neither reaction is sensible. Certainly with respect to the former response, that has already been well explained by others. Negotiating with extremists is probably not a good idea, simply because, given the plethora of cases in which offence is taken, it is difficult to work out *how* precisely one should tread more carefully. Cartoons, novels, documentaries, critique of traditions and even classic theatre performances? Nor can we rule out the possibility that concessions will increase rather than reduce the threat of violence. In other words, rather than being 'pacified', the individuals involved might be 'encouraged by all that willingness to please'.[41] As early as 1994 Ronald Dworkin wrote:

> When we compromise on freedom because we think our immediate goals more important, we are likely to find that the power to exploit the compromise is not in our own hands after all, but in those of fanatical priests armed with fatwas and fanatical moralists with their own brand of hate.[42]

There is added value in examining this problem through the lens of militant democracy. The threat of violence from extremists against freedom of expression already implicitly restricts that freedom. *Actual* freedom of expression does not always coincide with *legal* freedom of expression.[43] That is important for democracy in general and for democracy as self-correction in particular. When the problem is exclusively approached from the perspective of counterterrorism, this wrongly remains out of the picture.

Freedom of expression is one of the three principles on which democracy as self-correction rests. They are the three principles that should be defended to keep democracy standing and preserve it for the future. Acting in the *spirit* of democracy as self-correction therefore also means developing a sensitivity to the more subtle erosion of those principles, in this case freedom of expression.

Government officials should convert this sensitivity into a principled defence of those freedoms.[44] That is *not* advising columnists to speak with reserve or avoid particular topics, *nor* is it making 'informal' requests that people do not make use of their freedom of expression for a while. Take the example of the famous phone call from Dutch minister Hans van den Broek in 1987 to prevent the broadcast of a fragment in the news programme *Achter het Nieuws* (Behind the News), because a parody of Ayatollah Khomeini had been received unfavourably in Iran.[45] These are the responses of a government that says, you have the freedom, but please do not use it. That is, in the end, actively contributing to the erosion of freedom. It resembles the remarkable signs that can be seen around a park in the southern part of Amsterdam,[46] picturing a woman making a call on her smartphone, with the caption 'Use it' above and 'Lose it' below. The message: keep your phone in your pocket around here. The local authorities seem to have given up on (effective) law enforcement in the area.

Montesquieu wrote in *De l'Esprit des Lois*: 'Liberty is the right to do everything the laws permit.'[47] This quote conceals a number of subtleties, which, according to some, even confused great thinkers such as Isaiah Berlin.[48] But at *face value* this is what it is all about. It should be a guide to politicians. Ministers should stand up for the rights of citizens to do what the law permits them to do, from criticism of religion in theatre performances to criticizing Dutch traditions. They should prevent actual and legal freedom of expression from diverging. After all, democratic self-correction takes place by the grace of diversity of opinions.

Is it all doom and gloom then? No, things *can* work out well.[49] Let me give a fairly recent example. In December 2014 there was a threat of 9/11-style attacks on cinemas showing the American film *The Interview*, a badly received comedy depicting a conspiracy to murder the president of North Korea.[50] Shortly beforehand Sony had already been the victim of a cyber-attack.[51] Sony decided to call off the première in New York and cancel the planned release at the last minute; cinemas had already taken the film off their programmes.[52] There were enraged responses in Hollywood at the cancellation, and some time later Sony decided to show the film on the internet and in a few cinemas after all.[53] In what was termed 'one of the most difficult and damaging episodes' in the recent history of Hollywood, President Obama remained unrelenting.[54] During his end-of-year press conference he addressed the journalists present in great constitutional clarity.[55] It is exclusively the American legislator who draws the boundaries of freedom of expression, not dictators, terrorists or extremists:

> We cannot have a society in which some dictator someplace can start imposing censorship here in the United States. Because if somebody is able to intimidate folks out of releasing a satirical movie, imagine what

> they start doing when they see a documentary that they don't like, or news reports that they don't like. Or even worse, imagine if producers and distributors and others start engaging in self-censorship because they don't want to offend the sensibilities of somebody whose sensibilities probably need to be offended. So that's not who we are. That's not what America is about.[56]

That is how an answer in the spirit of democracy as self-correction should look. A militant democracy also demands militant democrats.

Notes

1. Popper 2013, p. 120.
2. Popper 2013, p. 120. See a comparable formulation in Karl Popper, *The Poverty of Historicism*, London: Routledge 2002 (henceforth Popper 2002b), p. 60.
3. Burke 1983, p. 179.
4. Frank Hendriks, *Vitale democratie: theorie van democratie in actie* (Vital democracy: theory of democracy in action), Amsterdam: Amsterdam University Press 2006, p. 47.
5. Popper 2013, p. 153.
6. Popper 2008a, p. 328. For an overview of what Popper sees as old, authoritarian ethics (mistakes are a sin) and new, anti-authoritarian ethics (learning from mistakes), see p. 325–328.
7. Robert Visser, *In dienst van het algemeen belang: Ministeriële verantwoordelijkheid en parlementair vertrouwen* (Serving the general interest: Ministerial accountability and parliamentary confidence, diss. Leiden), Amsterdam: Boom 2008, p. 292–293.
8. Annemarie Kas, 'Deal met drugscrimineel die na 15 jaar bewindslieden de kop kostte' ('Deal with drug criminal that cost the ministers their heads after 15 years'), *NRC Handelsblad*, 10 March 2015.
9. See Tom-Jan Meeus, 'De hang naar foutloosheid die zich tegen politici keert' ('The predilection for flawlessness which backfires on politicians'), *NRC Handelsblad*, 21 December 2013. See also Ruud Koole, 'Hijgende vragen, vlotte babbels: de symbiose van politiek en media' ('Gasping questions, smooth chatter: the symbiosis of politics and media'), p. 101–114 (110–111), in Jo Bardoel, Chris Vos, Frank van Vree and Huub Wijfjes, *Journalistieke cultuur in Nederland* (Journalistic culture in the Netherlands), Amsterdam: Amsterdam University Press 2009, where Koole states that, in addition to media reporting, politicians themselves are *also* responsible for the negative image of politics, in part because of their limited willingness to admit to mistakes. He mentions decision making around the Betuweroute railway line as an example.
10. Carol Tavris and Elliot Aronson, *Mistakes Were Made (but not by me): Why We Justify Foolish Beliefs, Bad Decisions, and Hurtful Acts*, Orlando: Harcourt 2007, p. 3. For a brief history of the 'past exonerative tense', see 'A Political Sidestep', *National Public Radio*, 17 March 2007, available via http://www.npr.org/templates/story/story.php?storyId=8972606.
11. See the recent plea of Jeroen den Uyl and Has Bakker, 'Geef ook politici de kans om van fouten te leren' ('Give politicians a chance to learn from mistakes too'), *Trouw*, 24 April 2015.
12. Den Uyl and Bakker 2015.
13. Popper 2008a, p. 326.

14. Popper 2008a, p. 327.
15. Nevertheless, here too there is a call for a more nuanced view. Political commentator Tom-Jan Meeus points out that Ruud Lubbers drove into a post while under the influence of alcohol and later became prime minister, something that is inconceivable today. Have we not gone too far in our strictness? 'The assumed need for flawless politicians has turned into a predilection for governors who are almost completely inhuman. What citizens do, politicians should refrain from,' according to Meeus (see Meeus 2013). Leiden researcher into corruption Patrick Overeem argues for more moderate treatment of problems with expense claims: 'As a governor either you have to be squeaky clean or you will be sent away tarred and feathered. If someone declares too many taxi rides, you could come up with an appropriate sanction, such as a yellow card or a suspension. A career does not immediately need to be destroyed by it'; see 'Die fles champagne, mag ik die nu declareren of niet?' ('That bottle of champagne, can I claim for it or not?'), *De Volkskrant*, 28 July 2015. In this connection see also the call for more forgiveness from Christian Union member of parliament Gert-Jan Segers: 'If someone admits, I've done something stupid, I'm sorry, I'll pay back the excessive sums I took, then I can imagine that there is space for a second chance. Someone who put his entire life and soul into politics has now lost his job. His career has come to a standstill. It is a harsh result. You mustn't cover up what went wrong. But if you admit your mistakes, you should also get a chance to make reparations'; see 'Is er dan geen ruimte meer voor genade?' ('Is there no space left for clemency?'), *De Volkskrant*, 4 April 2015.
16. Rutger Bregman, 'Vrijheid van meningsverandering' ('Freedom to change one's mind'), *De Correspondent* (online), 24 October 2013.
17. Bregman 2013, Bregman also adds journalism.
18. Bregman 2013.
19. Stephen Thornton, 'Karl Popper', *Stanford Encyclopedia of Philosophy* (online), edition: summer 2014, http://plato.stanford.edu/archives/sum2014/entries/popper/.
20. Ryan 2013, p. xxi.
21. See also Cliteur and Rijpkema 2012, p. 246–255, and Paul Cliteur, 'De actuele betekenis van "weerbare democratie"' ('The current meaning of "militant democracy"'), p. 155–205 (163–164 and 166–175), in (afterword to) Van den Bergh 2014.
22. Afshin Ellian places this, when it comes to religiously inspired terrorism, in a broader struggle between the radical method of Western philosophy and religion; fundamentalists resist the notion that *everything* can be investigated, and 'they are prepared to kill for it'; see Afshin Ellian, 'Alles wat heilig is bevragen' ('Investigate everything that is holy'), p. 91–105 (103–104), in Suzanne Metselaar and Allard den Dulk (eds.), *Hoe denkers denken: filosoferen als ambacht* (How philosophers think: philosophizing as a craft), Amsterdam: Athenaeum–Polak and Van Gennep 2012; in this context see also Afshin Ellian, *Sociale cohesie en islamitisch terrorisme* (Social cohesion and Islamic terrorism, inaugural lecture, Leiden), p. 15.
23. For an overview see Paul Cliteur, Tom Herrenberg and Bastiaan Rijpkema, 'The New Censorship: A Case-Study of the Extrajudicial Restraints on Free Speech', p. 291–318 (318), in Ellian and Molier 2015.
24. See Nicolas Cronk, 'Introduction', p. 1–15 (6), in Nicolas Cronk, *The Cambridge Companion to Voltaire*, Cambridge: Cambridge University Press 2009. 'Blame It on Voltaire: Muslims Ask French to Cancel 1741 Play', *The Wall Street Journal*, 6 March 2006, and Hervé Loichemol, 'Une fatwa contre Voltaire?', *Le Monde*, 14 February 2006.

25. 'British Firm to Publish Controversial Novel', *The Washington Post*, 4 September 2008, and 'Publication of Controversial Muhammad Novel Delayed', *The Guardian* (online), 10 October 2008.
26. 'Channel 4 Cancels Islam Documentary Screening After Presenter Threatened', *The Telegraph* (online), 11 September 2012.
27. 'Pope Benedict XVI in His Own Words', BBC (online), 11 February 2013; 'Radical Muslim Who Made Death Threats against Pope Escapes Prosecution', *Daily Mail* (online), 26 September 2006; and Daniel Mandel, 'Preemptive Appeasement', *The Weekly Standard*, 20 September 2007.
28. See also Molier 2011, p. 206–207.
29. 'Bedreigd, of bang het te worden; 1 jaar moord Van Gogh' ('Threatened or afraid of being threatened; 1 year after Van Gogh's murder'), *Trouw*, 29 October 2005. This was about two death threats: during a debate at the University of Amsterdam Spruyt was interrupted by someone who thought he should be shot dead (2003); during a debate in Utrecht a connection was made with Volkert van der Graaf, who was convicted of murdering Dutch politician Pim Fortuyn (2004); see *Kamerstukken II* (Dutch Parliamentary Papers II) 2003/2004, 29 200 VII, 58, p. 8. A VPRO radio interview with Spruyt on 29 June 2004 regarding the threat can still be heard at http://www.vpro.nl/speel.POMS_VPRO_346995.html.
30. 'Zihni Özdil wil Nederland verbeteren' ('Zihni Özdil wants to improve the Netherlands'), *Vrij Nederland*, 13 June 2014.
31. See 'Z (Zihni) Özdil MA', on: https://www.parlement.com/id/vk9dd4pr7xyl/z_zihni_ozdil.
32. 'Robert Vuijsje met de dood bedreigd wegens "Alleen maar nette mensen"' ('Robert Vuijsje threatened with death due to "Only decent people"'), NRC *Handelsblad* (online), 15 October 2012.
33. 'Anouk nodigde dreigers thuis uit' ('Anouk invited those threatening her home'), *Omroep West* (online), 26-11-2013.
34. *Report by the Commissioner for Human Rights, Mr. Thomas Hammarberg, on his visit to the Netherlands*, 21-25 September 2008, Straatsburg, 11 March 2009. For an interview with Hammarberg, see 'Bescherm Kamerlid' ('Protect MP'), *De Pers*, 12 March 2009.
35. 'Bedreigd, of bang het te worden; 1 jaar moord Van Gogh' ('Threatened or afraid of being threatened; 1 year after Van Gogh's murder'), *Trouw*, 29 October 2005.
36. Cas Mudde, 'No, We Are NOT All Charlie (and That's a Problem)', *Open Democracy* (online), 7 January 2015. Mudde also points to the somewhat different, if no less relevant, issue of self-censorship out of fear of 'professional sanctions': 'many treat issues related to Jews and Israel much more sensitively than other groups and states, out of fear of professional sanctions (think about the recent Salaita case in the United States).'
37. See among others 'We laten onze eigen mensen in de steek' ('We are leaving our own people in the lurch'), *NRC Handelsblad*, 24 January 2015 (British political philosopher Larry Siedentop: 'The importance of public debate cannot be emphasized enough. Yes, there is a danger of self-censorship and skirting around sensitive subjects, but liberalism merits a robust defence. Not offending for the sake of offending. If difficult questions are addressed in a civilized manner, in public, it can do a load of good.'); August Hans den Boef, 'Intimidatie jihadisten leidt tot zelfcensuur' ('Intimidation by jihadists leads to self-censorship'), *De Volkskrant*, 12 January 2015; Kenan Malik, 'Met zelfcensuur help je minderheden juist niet' ('You won't help minorities by self-censorship'), *De Volkskrant*, 10 January 2015 ('Instead they have helped

to create a new culture of censorship. That is partly a matter of fear, of not wanting to take the kinds of risks which the editors of Charlie Hebdo did not shrink from and for which they have now paid such a high price.'); 'Public Debate Warns of Self-censorship in the Arts', *The Independent*, 16 March 2015 ('Jude Kelly, artistic director of the Southbank Centre, Munira Mirza, deputy mayor for education and culture, and Shami Chakrabarti, director of human rights organisation Liberty were among those who called the rise of self-censorship "chilling" and "catastrophic" for British culture.'). The latest *Freedom of Thought Report* by the International Humanist and Ethical Union also mentions the self-censorship experienced by opinion formers in the Netherlands; see *Freedom of Thought 2014: A Global Report on Discrimination against Humanists, Atheists, and the Non-religious; Their Human Rights and Legal Status*, International Humanist and Ethical Union 2014, available via http://freethoughtreport.com/download-the-report/.

38. 'Kabinet verdeeld over godslastering' ('Cabinet divided on blasphemy'), *Trouw*, 15 November 2004.
39. 'Kabinet verdeeld over godslastering' ('Cabinet divided on blasphemy'), *Trouw*, 15 November 2004. Since 1 March 2014 this dead letter has been defunct and the Netherlands no longer has a formal ban on blasphemy; for detailed treatment see Mirjam van Schaik and Jasper Doomen, 'De toekomst van godslastering' ('The future of blasphemy'), *Nederlands Juristenblad* 2014, no. 30, p. 2110–2116.
40. As, for instance: 'If we are not protective of free speech and do not recognize its limitations, that is risky for the quality of society and for the democratic system. We can also blow up democracy in the guise of that same free speech (Doekle Terpstra, '"Nee" tegen kwade boodschap Wilders' ['"No" to Wilders' malicious message'], *Trouw*, 30 November 2007)'; 'Chaos is the primary aim of the terrorists. Chaos in Iraq, in Spain, in France, in the Netherlands. Terror seeks to break order and sow fear. In this tense atmosphere a couple of ultra-right-wing polemicists are putting all their energy into teaching Islam a lesson. They want to compel Islam to enlightenment right now. . . . They do not discuss matters, they block the debate, beat and humiliate. They provoke aggression and that is precisely what we do not need. It is inevitable, there must be a Dutch version of Islam for this country. That can only be achieved with long discussion and debate. And patience. But my colleagues want to cast a 1400-year-old tradition which has been shaped by countless wars into a Dutch form overnight. That is impossible. Something else is going on. The direction taken by the right-wing columnists is a path to confrontation. They speak with mouths full of hate. Their tone has elements of the hard language of the Muslim fundamentalists, Hezbollah' (Kader Abdolah, 'De angst' ('The fear') *De Volkskrant*, 29 March 2004). And more recently, Peter Buwalda, 'Gewoon een beetje rustig aan doen met de Profeet' ('Just tread carefully with the Prophet'), *De Volkskrant*, 9 January 2015, and Annette Jansen, 'Zelfcensuur, wen er maar aan' ('Self-censorship, get used to it'), *Trouw*, 24 January 2015.
41. Paul Cliteur, *Het monotheïstisch dilemma, of De theologie van het terrorisme* (The monotheistic dilemma, or The theology of terrorism), Amsterdam/Antwerp: De Arbeiderspers 2010, p. 97–98. In this sense see also Malik 2015.
42. Ronald Dworkin, 'A New Map of Censorship', *Index on Censorship* 2006 (original in 1994), vol. 35 no. 1, p. 130–133 (132–133).
43. See Paul Cliteur, *The Secular Outlook: In Defense of Moral and Political Secularism*, Malden: Wiley-Blackwell 2010, p. 133–134; Paul Cliteur, 'Van Rushdie tot Jones: over geweld en uitingsvrijheid' ('From Rushdie to Jones: on violence

and publishing freedom'), p. 67–87 (86), in Ellian and Molier 2011; Cliteur, Herrenberg and Rijpkema 2015.

44. On a principled defence of this kind, see also Paul Cliteur, 'Salman Rushdie en de rechtsstaat in de 21ste eeuw' ('Salman Rushdie and the constitutional state in the 21st century'), p. 25–41 (35), Sadik Harchouchi and Juliët Jonkers (eds.), *Leve de rechtsstaat! Reflecties op de rechtsstaat in een dynamische samenleving* (Long live the constitutional state! Reflections on the constitutional state in a dynamic society), The Hague: Boom Lemma Uitgevers 2010.
45. The matter is discussed in detail in Cliteur 2013.
46. See Xandra van Gelder, 'Onbegrijpelijke borden rond het Sarphatipark' ('Incomprehensible signs around the Sarphatipark'), *Het Parool*, 11 February 2014.
47. Montesquieu, *The Spirit of the Laws* (*De l'esprit des lois*), Cambridge: Cambridge University Press 1989, p. 155 (book 11, chapter 3).
48. See Jacob T. Levy, 'Montesquieu's Constitutional Legacies', p. 115–138 (123), in Rebecca Kingston (ed.), *Montesquieu and His Legacy,* State University of New York (SUNY) Press 2009.
49. See for example 'Saudi-Arabië houdt Wilders al sinds 2006 in de gaten' ('Saudi Arabia has kept an eye on Wilders since 2006'), *Trouw*, 22 June 2015. The *Saudileaks* published by *Wikileaks* contained a report of a conversation from 2012 between the then Dutch ambassador Ron Strikker and a Saudi government official. The subject: Geert Wilders. Despite objections from his interlocutor, Strikker explains that 'the Netherlands does not agree with Wilders, but the laws in the Netherlands protect freedom of expression.' The diplomat gave the only correct answer: *within* the bounds of freedom of expression Wilders can express his opinion, like anyone else, even if we are very much in disagreement with that opinion. A more *prominent* example was the unyielding Danish prime minister Anders Fogh Rasmussen at the time of the Danish cartoon riots; see Cliteur 2014, p. 186.
50. 'Sony Cancels The Interview Release amid Threats', BBC (online), 18 December 2014.
51. 'The Interview: A Guide to the Cyber Attack on Hollywood', BBC (online), 29 December 2014.
52. 'The Interview: A Guide to the Cyber Attack on Hollywood'.
53. 'The Interview: A Guide to the Cyber Attack on Hollywood'.
54. 'The Interview: A Guide to the Cyber Attack on Hollywood'.
55. Obama was not always so clear, for instance, not in the 'Terry Jones affair'; see Cliteur, Herrenberg and Rijpkema 2015, p. 308–309.
56. Remarks by the President in Year-End Press Conference, 19 December 2014, available via https://www.whitehouse.gov/the-press-office/2014/12/19/remarks-president-year-end-press-conference; see also, with an image of the press conference, http://edition.cnn.com/2014/12/19/politics/fbi-north-korea-responsible-sony/.

Bibliography

Abdolah, Kader, 'De angst' ('The fear'), *De Volkskrant*, 29 March 2004.

Adams, Maurice, 'De verbeelding van de politieke democratie door het recht: inleidende beschouwing' ('The representation of political democracy by the law: introductory discussion'), p. 3–37, in Maurice Adams and Patricia Popelier (eds.), *Recht en democratie: de democratische verbeelding in het recht* (Law and democracy: the democratic illusion of law), Antwerp: Intersentia 2004.

Akbulut, Olgun, 'Criteria Developed by the European Court of Human Rights on the Dissolution of Political Parties', *Fordham International Law Journal* 2010, vol. 34, p. 46–77.

Akkerman, Tjitske, and Matthijs Rooduijn, 'Pariahs or Partners? Inclusion and Exclusion of Radical Right Parties and the Effects on Their Policy Positions', *Political Studies* June 2014 (online), p. 1–18.

Alberda, J.W., 'Democratie: beginsel, middel en doel. Geen gelegenheidspolitiek' ('Democracy: principle, means and end. No opportunity politics'), *Het Volk*, 21 April 1936.

Albertazzi, Daniele, 'Reconciling "Voice" and "Exit": Swiss and Italian Populists in Power', *Politics* 2009, vol. 29 no. 1, p. 1–10.

Allan, James, *Democracy in Decline: Steps in the Wrong Direction*, Montreal: McGill-Queen's University Press 2014.

Anderson, Perry, *Spectrum: From Right to Left in the World of Ideas*, London/New York: Verso 2005.

Avineri, Shlomo, 'On Problems of Transition in Postcommunist Societies', *Cardozo Law Review* 1997-1998, vol. 19, p. 1921–1936.

Ayres, Thomas, 'Batasuna Banned: The Dissolution of Political Parties under the European Convention of Human Rights', *Boston College International and Comparative Law Review* 2004, vol. 27, p. 99–113.

Bale, Tim, 'Are Bans on Political Parties Bound to Turn Out Badly?', *Comparative European Politics* 2007, no. 5, p. 141–157.

Bale, Tim, 'Will It All End in Tears? What Really Happens When Democracies Use Law to Ban Political Parties', p. 195–224, in Ingrid van Biezen and Hans-Martien ten Napel (eds.), *Regulating Political Parties: European Democracies in Comparative Perspective*, Leiden: Leiden University Press 2014.

Ball, Terence, 'James Mill', in Edward N. Zalta (ed.), *The Stanford Encyclopedia of Philosophy*, edition: summer 2014, http://plato.stanford.edu/archives/sum2014/entries/james-mill/.

Barendt, Eric, *Freedom of Speech*, Oxford: Oxford University Press 1985.

Basedau, Matthias, and Anika Moroff, 'Parties in Chains: Do Ethnic Party Bans in Africa Promote Peace?', *Party Politics* 2011, vol. 17 no. 2, p. 205–222.

Bast, Jürgen, 'Don't Act beyond Your Powers: The Perils and Pitfalls of the German Constitutional Court's Ultra Vires Review', *German Law Journal* 2014, vol. 15 no. 2, p. 168–181.

Bayer, Lily, and Maïa de la Baume, 'European Parliament Report Calls for Sanctions Procedure against Hungary', *Politico.com*, 12 April 2018.

Belavusau, Uladzislau, 'Hate Speech and Constitutional Democracy in Eastern Europe: Transitional and Militant? (Czech Republic, Hungary and Poland)', *Israel Law Review* 2014, vol. 47 no. 1, p. 27–61.

Bellekom, Th. L., 'Partijverboden' ('Party bans'), p. 113–146, in A.W. Heringa, R.E. de Winter and W.J. Witteveen, *Staatkundig Jaarboek 1982-1983* (Political almanac 1982-1983), Leiden 1982.

Bendersky, Joseph W., *A Concise History of Nazi Germany*, Lanham: Rowman and Littlefield 2014.

Berlin, Isaiah, 'The Bent Twig: A Note on Nationalism', *Foreign Affairs* 1972, vol. 51 no. 1, p. 11–30.

Blaas, P.B.M., *Henk Hoetink (1900-1963), een intellectuele biografie* (Henk Hoetink [1900-1963], an intellectual biography), Hilversum: Uitgeverij Verloren 2010, p. 84–87.

Bligh, Gur, 'Defending Democracy: A New Understanding of the Party-Banning Phenomenon', *Vanderbilt Journal of Transnational Law* 2013, vol. 46 no. 5, p. 1321–1379.

Bligh, Gur, 'Extremism in the Electoral Arena: Challenging the Myth of American Exceptionalism', *Brigham Young University Law Review* 2008, p. 1367–1440.

Boef, August Hans den, 'Intimidatie jihadisten leidt tot zelfcensuur' ('Intimidation by jihadists leads to self-censorship'), *De Volkskrant*, 12 January 2015.

Boffey, Daniel, and Christian Davies, 'Poland May be Stripped of EU Voting Rights over Judicial Independence', *The Guardian* (online), 19 July 2017.

Bogaards, Matthijs, Matthias Basedau and Christof Hartmann, 'Ethnic Party Bans in Africa: An Introduction', *Democratization* 2010, vol. 17 no. 4, p. 599–617.

Bonger, W.A., *Problemen der Demokratie: een sociologische en psychologische studie* (Problems of democracy: a sociological and psychological study), Groningen/Batavia: P. Noordhoff N.V. 1934.

Boomsma, Diederik, 'Ortega's filosofie van de "vitale rede"' ('Ortega's philosophy of the "vital reason"'), p. 7–22, in José Ortega y Gasset, *De opstand van de massamens* (The revolt of the masses), Rotterdam: Lemniscaat 2015.

Bourne, Angela K., 'Democratization and the Illegalization of Political Parties in Europe', *Democratization* 2012, vol. 19 no. 6, p. 1065–1085 (Bourne 2012a).

Bourne, Angela K., 'Militant Democracy and the Banning of Political Parties in Democratic States: Why Some Do and Why Some Don't', in Afshin Ellian and Bastiaan Rijpkema (eds.), *Militant Democracy: Political Science, Law and Philosophy*, New York: Springer *forthcoming* 2018.

Bourne, Angela. K., 'The Proscription of Political Parties and "Militant Democracy"', *Journal of Comparative Law* 2012, vol. 7 no. 1, p. 196–213 (Bourne 2012b).

Bovend'Eert, P.P.T., and H.R.B.M. Kummeling, *Het Nederlandse Parlement* (The Dutch Parliament), Deventer: Kluwer 2010.

Bovend'Eert, P.P.T., and M.C. Burkens, 'De Bondsrepubliek Duitsland' ('The Federal Republic of Germany'), p. 61–118, in L.F.M. Besselink, P.P.T. Bovend'Eert,

J.L.W. Broeksteeg and R. de Lange, *Staatsrecht van landen van de Europese Unie* (Constitutional law of the countries of the European Union), Deventer: Kluwer 2012.

Boyd Rayward, W., 'H.G. Wells's World Brain: A Critical Re-Assessment', *Journal of the American Society for Information Science* 1999, vol. 50 no. 7, p. 557–573.

Boyle, Kevin, 'Human Rights, Religion and Democracy: The Refah Party Case', *Essex Human Rights Review* 2004, vol. 1 no. 1, p. 1–16.

Bregman, Rutger, 'Vrijheid van meningsverandering' ('Freedom to change one's mind'), *De Correspondent* (online), 24 October 2013.

Brems, Eva, 'Belgium: The Vlaams Blok Political Party Convicted Indirectly of Racism', *International Journal of Constitutional Law* 2006, vol. 4 no. 4, p. 702–711.

Brems, Eva, 'State Regulation of Xenophobia versus Individual Freedoms: The European View', *Journal of Human Rights* 2002, vol. 1 no. 4, p. 481–500.

Brinkmann, G., 'Militant Democracy and Radicals in the West German Civil Service', *Modern Law Review* 1983, vol. 46, p. 584–600.

Brugger, Winfried, 'The Treatment of Hate Speech in German Constitutional Law (Part II)', *German Law Journal* 2003, vol. 4 no. 1, p. 1–44.

Buck, Robert J., *Thrasybulus and the Athenian Democracy*, Stuttgart: Franz Steiner Verlag 1998.

Buijs, F.J., and M. Fennema, 'Democratie, extremisme en radicalisme in Amsterdam' ('Democracy, extremism and radicalism in Amsterdam'), p. 120–147, in Meindert Fennema, *Help! De elite verdwijnt: veertig jaar Nederlandse politiek* (Help! The elite are disappearing: forty years of Dutch politics), Amsterdam: Bert Bakker 2012.

Burke, Edmund, *Reflections on the Revolution in France*, New Haven/London: Yale University Press 2003.

Burke, T.E., *The Philosophy of Karl Popper*, Manchester: Manchester University Press 1983.

Buwalda, Peter, 'Gewoon een beetje rustig aan doen met de Profeet' ('Just tread carefully with the Prophet'), *De Volkskrant*, 9 January 2015.

Buyse, Antoine, 'Dangerous Expressions: The ECHR, Violence and Free Speech', *International and Comparative Law Quarterly* 2014, vol. 63 no. 2, p. 491–503.

Capoccia, Giovanni, 'Defending Democracy: Reactions to Political Extremism in Inter-war Europe', *European Journal of Political Research* 2001, vol. 39, p. 431–460.

Capoccia, Giovanni, 'Militant Democracy: The Institutional Bases of Democratic Self-Preservation', *Annual Review of Law and Social Science* 2013, vol. 9, p. 207–226.

Casal Bertoa, F., and I. van Biezen, 'Party Regulation and Party Politics in Post-communist Europe', *East European Politics* 2014, vol. 30 no. 3, p. 295–314.

Cavatorta, Francesco, and Fabio Merone, 'Moderation through Exclusion? The Journey of the Tunisian Ennahda from Fundamentalist to Conservative Party', *Democratization* 2013, vol. 20 no. 5, p. 857–875.

Chou, Mark, *Theorising Democide: Why and How Democracies Fail*, Basingstoke: Palgrave Macmillan 2013.

Christiansen, Thomas, and Christine Reh, *Constitutionalizing the European Union*, Basingstoke: Palgrave Macmillan 2009, p. 156.

Cliteur, Paul, *Darwin, dier en recht* (Darwin, animals and justice), Amsterdam: Boom 2001.

Cliteur, Paul, 'De actuele betekenis van "weerbare democratie"' ('The current meaning of "militant democracy"'), p. 155–205, in *Wat te doen met antidemocratische partijen? De oratie van George van den Bergh uit 1936* (What to do with antidemocratic parties? The inaugural lecture of George van den Bergh of 1936), Amsterdam: Elsevier Boeken 2014.

Cliteur, Paul, *Het monotheïstisch dilemma, of De theologie van het terrorisme* (The monotheistic dilemma, or The theology of terrorism), Amsterdam/Antwerp: De Arbeiderspers 2010.

Cliteur, Paul, 'Indien verantwoordelijk dan bevoegd? De constitutionele positie van het Openbaar Ministerie' ('If responsible then competent? The constitutional position of the Public Prosecution Service'), p. 124–137, in M.C. Burkens, E.C.M. Jurgens, A.K. Koekkoek and J.J. Vis (eds.), *Gelet op de Grondwet* (A view on the constitution), Deventer: Kluwer 1998.

Cliteur, Paul, 'Naar een Europese Grondwet: een Colloquium metajuridicum' ('Towards a European Constitution: a Colloquium metajuridicum'), p. 1–22, in Paul Cliteur, Hans Franken and Wim Voermans (eds.), *Naar een Europese Grondwet* (Towards a European Constitution), The Hague: Boom Juridische Uitgevers 2004.

Cliteur, Paul, 'Salman Rushdie en de rechtsstaat in de 21ste eeuw' ('Salman Rushdie and the constitutional state in the 21st century'), p. 25–41, in Sadik Harchouchi and Juliët Jonkers (eds.), *Leve de rechtsstaat! Reflecties op de rechtsstaat in een dynamische samenleving* (Long live the constitutional state! Reflections on the constitutional state in a dynamic society), The Hague: Boom Lemma Uitgevers 2010.

Cliteur, Paul, 'The Rudi Carrell Affair and Its Significance for the Tension between Theoterrorism and Religious Satire', *Ancilla Iuris* 2013, p. 15–41.

Cliteur, Paul, *The Secular Outlook: In Defense of Moral and Political Secularism*, Malden: Wiley-Blackwell 2010.

Cliteur, Paul, 'Van Rushdie tot Jones: over geweld en uitingsvrijheid' ('From Rushdie to Jones: on violence and publishing freedom'), in Afshin Ellian, Gelijn Molier and Tom Zwart (eds.), *Mag ik dit zeggen? Beschouwingen over de vrijheid van meningsuiting* (May I say this? Views on freedom of expression), The Hague: Boom Juridische Uitgevers 2011.

Cliteur, Paul, and Afshin Ellian, *Legaliteit en legitimiteit: de grondslagen van het recht* (Legality and legitimacy: the foundations of law), Leiden: Leiden University Press 2016.

Cliteur, Paul, Tom Herrenberg and Bastiaan Rijpkema, 'The New Censorship: A Case-Study of the Extrajudicial Restraints on Free Speech', p. 291–318, in Afshin Ellian and Gelijn Molier (eds.), *Freedom of Speech under Attack*, The Hague: Eleven Publishing 2015.

Cliteur, Paul, and Bastiaan Rijpkema, 'The Foundations of Militant Democracy', p. 227–272, in Afshin Ellian and Gelijn Molier, *The State of Exception and Militant Democracy in a Time of Terror*, Dordrecht: Republic of Letters Publishing 2012.

Cohen-Almagor, Raphael, 'Disqualification of Lists in Israel (1948-1984): Retrospect and Appraisal', *Law and Philosophy* 1994, vol. 13, p. 43–95.

Colliot-Thélène, Catherine, 'Carl Schmitt versus Max Weber: Juridical Rationality and Economic Rationality', p. 138–154, in Chantal Mouffe (ed.), *The Challenge of Carl Schmitt*, London/New York: Verso 1999.

Cornelisse, Louis, 'Met wc-rol was politieke baas BVD allang tevreden' ('Political boss of the BVD had long been satisfied with toilet roll'), *Trouw*, 6 September 1995.

Corstens, G.J.M., *Het Nederlandse strafprocesrecht* (Dutch criminal procedure law, revised by M.J. Borgers), Deventer: Kluwer 2011.

Coupland, Philip, 'H.G. Wells's "Liberal Fascism"', *Journal of Contemporary History* 2000, vol. 35 no. 4, p. 541–558.

Cronk, Nicolas, 'Introduction', p. 1–15, in Nicolas Cronk, *The Cambridge Companion to Voltaire*, Cambridge: Cambridge University Press 2009.

Currie, David P., *The Constitution of the Federal Republic of Germany*, Chicago: University of Chicago Press 1994.

Dahl, Robert A., *On Democracy*, New Haven: Yale University Press 2000.

De Lange, R., N. Efthymiou and F. van Tienen, *Risico's voor de democratie: een juridische verkenning van het gevaar-criterium in het democratisch verdedigingsrepertoire in vijf landen: Duitsland, Frankrijk, Spanje, het Verenigd Koninkrijk en de Verenigde Staten* (Risks for democracy: a legal exploration of the 'threat'-criterion in the democratic defense repertoire of five countries: Germany, France, Spain, the United Kingdom, and the United States), Rotterdam: Erasmus Universiteit Rotterdam 2016.

De wil van het volk? Erosie van de democratische rechtsstaat in Europa (The will of the people? Erosion of democracy under the rule of law in Europe) (no. 104), *Advisory Council on International Affairs (AIV)*, June 2017, The Hague; an English translation of the report is available at https://aiv-advice.nl/download/efa5b666-1301-45ef-8702-360939cb4b6a.pdf.

Demant, Froukje, Marieke Slootman, Frank Buijs and Jean Tillie, *Teruggang en uittreding: processen van deradicalisering ontleed* (Decline and withdrawal: processes of deradicalization analysed, report commissioned by the Netherlands National Coordinator for Counterterrorism), Amsterdam: The Institute for Migration and Ethnic Studies (IMES) 2008.

Dennett, Daniel, *Intuition Pumps and Other Tools for Thinking*, New York: W.W. Norton 2014.

Diesfeldt, Annick, and Fanny de Graaf, 'Dataretentie: een kwestie van alles of niets?' ('Data retention: a question of all or nothing?'), *Nederlands Juristenblad* 2015, no. 12, p. 740–747.

Dool, Pim van den, 'Haatprediker Abu Hamza krijgt levenslang in VS' ('Hate preacher Abu Hamza receives life sentence in the US'), *NRC Handelsblad* (online), 9 January 2015.

Downs, William M., Carrie L. Manning and Richard N. Engstrom, 'Revisiting the "Moderating Effects of Incumbency": A Comparative Study of Government Participation and Political Extremism', *Journal of Contemporary European Studies* 2009, vol. 17 no. 2, p. 151–169.

Drees, Willem, letter to George van den Bergh, 2 October 1936, in the personal archive of George van den Bergh, owned by Van den Bergh's heirs.

Duggan, Christopher, *A Concise History of Italy*, Cambridge: Cambridge University Press 2014.

Dworkin, Ronald, 'A New Map of Censorship', *Index on Censorship* 2006 (original in 1994), vol. 35 no. 1, p. 130–133.

Dyzenhaus, David, 'Legal Theory in the Collapse of Weimar: Contemporary Lessons?', *American Political Science Review* 1997, vol. 91 no. 1, p. 121–134.

Earle, Edward Mead, 'H.G. Wells, British Patriot in Search of a World State', *World Politics 1950*, vol. 2 no. 2, p. 181–208.

Eberhard, Harald, Konrad Lachmayer and Gerhard Thallinger, 'Approaching Transitional Constitutionalism', p. 9–24, in Harald Eberhard, Konrad Lachmayer and Gerhard Thallinger, *Transitional Constitutionalism: Proceedings of the 2nd Vienna Workshop on International Constitutional Law*, Nomos/facultas.wuv 2007.

Eligür, Banu, *The Mobilization of Political Islam in Turkey*, Cambridge: Cambridge University Press 2010.

Ellian, Afshin, 'Alles wat heilig is bevragen' ('Investigate everything that is holy'), p. 91–105, in Suzanne Metselaar and Allard den Dulk (eds.), *Hoe denkers denken: filosoferen als ambacht* (How philosophers think: philosophizing as a craft), Amsterdam: Athenaeum–Polak and Van Gennep 2012.

Ellian, Afshin, 'De staat van uitzondering' ('The state of exception'), p. 177–213, in Gelijn Molier and Timo Slootweg (eds.), *Soevereiniteit en recht: Rechtsfilosofische beschouwingen* (Sovereignty and justice: Legal philosophical views), The Hague: Boom Juridische Uitgevers 2009.

Ellian, Afshin, 'Op de grens van vrijheid: ketterij in de vrije samenleving' ('On the boundary of freedom: heresy in free society'), p. 89–115, in Afshin Ellian, Gelijn Molier and Tom Zwart (eds.), *Mag ik dit zeggen? Beschouwingen over de vrijheid van meningsuiting* (May I say this? Views on freedom of expression), The Hague: Boom Juridische Uitgevers 2011.

Ellian, Afshin, *Sociale cohesie en islamitisch terrorisme* (Social cohesion and Islamic terrorism, inaugural lecture, Leiden), 2006.

Ellian, Afshin, Gelijn Molier and Bastiaan Rijpkema, 'Weerbare democratie en het probleem van timing: de zaak tegen de NPD' (Militant democracy and the problem of timing: the case against the NPD), *Nederlands Juristenblad* 2017, vol. 92 no. 24, p. 1650–1660.

Ellian, Afshin, and Bastiaan Rijpkema (eds.), *Militant Democracy: Political Science, Law and Philosophy*, New York: Springer *forthcoming* 2018.

Elzinga, D.J., *De Politieke Partij en het Constitutionele Recht* (The political party and constitutional law, diss. Utrecht), Nijmegen: Ars Aequi Libri 1982.

Elzinga, D.J., 'Leven en werk van Hugo Krabbe (1857-1936)' ('Life and work of Hugo Krabbe [1857-1936]'), p. 55–73, in D.J. Elzinga, *De staat van het recht: opstellen over staatsrecht en politiek* (The state of the law: essays on constitutional law and politics), Zwolle: W.E.J. Tjeenk Willink 1990.

Elzinga, D.J., and R. de Lange, *Van der Pot. Handboek van het Nederlandse Staatsrecht* (Van der Pot. Handbook of Dutch Constitutional Law), Deventer: Kluwer 2006.

Elzinga, D.J., H.R.B.M. Kummeling and J. Schipper-Spanninga, *Het Nederlandse kiesrecht* (The Dutch right to vote), Deventer: Kluwer 2012.

Emerson, Thomas I., 'Freedom of Association and Freedom of Expression', *Yale Law Journal* 1964, vol. 74 no. 1, p. 1–35.

Engelmann, Sabrina, 'Barking Up the Wrong Tree: Why Counterterrorism Cannot Be a Defense of Democracy', *Democracy and Security* 2012, vol. 8, p. 164–174.

Epstein, Richard, 'Forget the Envy-Principle', *Forbes* (online), 19 January 2010.

Ermakoff, Ivan, *Ruling Oneself Out: A Theory of Collective Abdications*, Durham and London: Duke University Press 2008.

Ermakoff, Ivan, 'Frail Democracy', in Afshin Ellian and Bastiaan Rijpkema (eds.), *Militant Democracy: Political Science, Law and Philosophy*, New York: Springer *forthcoming* 2018.

Eskes, J.A.O., *Repressie van Politieke Bewegingen in Nederland: een juridisch-historische studie over het Nederlandse publiekrechtelijke verenigingsrecht gedurende het tijdvak 1798-1988* (Repression of Political Movements in the Netherlands: a legal historical study of Dutch right of association in public law during the period 1798-1988, diss. Utrecht), Zwolle: W.E.J. Tjeenk Willink/NISER 1988.

Eskes, J.A.O., 'Verbied partij voordat die de democratie ontwricht' ('Ban party before it disrupts democracy'), *Trouw*, 11 August 2011.

Etzioni, Amitai, 'Democracy Is Not a Suicide Pact', *The National Interest* (online), 7 January 2007, the introduction of which appeared in *The National Interest* 2007, no. 90, p. 13.

Ferreres Comella, Victor, 'The New Regulation of Political Parties in Spain, and the Decision to Outlaw Batasuna', p. 133–156, in András Sajó (ed.), *Militant Democracy*, Utrecht: Eleven Publishing 2004.

Fisk, Robert, 'The 70,000 Post-coup Arrests Are Now at the Heart of the Turkish Government's Propaganda War', *The Independent* (online), 8 October 2016.

Fox, Gregory, 'The Right to Political Participation in International Law', *Yale Journal of International Law* 1992, vol. 17, p. 539–607.

Fox, Gregory, and Georg Nolte, 'A Defense of the "Intolerant Democracies" Thesis', p. 445–448, in Gregory Fox and Brad Roth (eds.), *Democratic Governance and International Law*, Cambridge: Cambridge University Press 2000.

Fox, Gregory H., and George Nolte, 'Intolerant Democracies', *Harvard International Law Journal* 1995, vol. 36 no. 1, p. 1–70.

Frankenberg, Günter, 'The Learning Sovereign', p. 114–132, in András Sajó (ed.), *Militant Democracy*, Utrecht: Eleven Publishing 2004.

Freedom of Thought 2014: A Global Report on Discrimination against Humanists, Atheists, and the Non-religious; Their Human Rights and Legal Status, International Humanist and Ethical Union 2014.

Garditz, Klaus, 'Beyond Symbolism: Towards a Constitutional *Actio Popularis* in EU Affairs? A Commentary on the OMT Decision of the Federal Constitutional Court', *German Law Journal* 2014, vol. 15 no. 2, p. 183–201.

Gelder, Xandra van, 'Onbegrijpelijke borden rond het Sarphatipark' ('Incomprehensible signs around the Sarphatipark'), *Het Parool*, 11 February 2014.

Gentile, Giovanni, 'The Philosophic Basis of Fascism', *Foreign Affairs* 1928, vol. 6 no. 2, p. 290–304.

Gibbons, Tom, 'Modernism and Reactionary Politics', *Journal of Modern Literature* 1974, vol. 3 no. 5, p. 1140–1157.

Goes van Naters, Marinus van der, letter to George van den Bergh, with attachment, 6 October 1936, in the personal archive of George van den Bergh, owned by Van den Bergh's heirs.

Goes van Naters, Marinus van der, *Socialistische Staatsvernieuwing* (Socialist state revival), Arnhem: Van Loghun Slaterus Uitgevers-maatschappij N.V. 1937.

Goldsworthy, Jeffrey, *Parliamentary Sovereignty: Contemporary Debates*, Cambridge: Cambridge University Press 2010.

Gray, John, 'The Liberalism of Karl Popper', *Government and Opposition* 1976, vol. 11 no. 3, p. 337–355.

Greenberg, Udi, *The Weimar Century: German Émigrés and the Intellectual Foundations of the Cold War*, Princeton: Princeton University Press 2014.

Grift, Liesbeth van der, *Voorwaarts en vergeten. De overgang van fascisme naar communisme in Oost-Europa, 1944-1948* (Onwards and forgotten. The transition from fascism to communism in Eastern Europe, 1944-1948), Amsterdam: Ambo 2010.

Grimm, Dieter, 'Freedom of Speech in a Globalized World', p. 11–22, in Ivan Hare and James Weinstein (eds.), *Extreme Speech and Democracy*, Oxford: Oxford University Press 2010.

Guidelines on Prohibition of Political Parties and Analogous Measures, European Commission for Democracy through Law (Venice Commission), adopted 10-11 December 1999, Strasbourg 2000.

Guiora, Amos N., *Freedom from Religion: Rights and National Security*, Oxford: Oxford University Press 2009.

Haersolte, R.A.V. van, 'John Rawls', p. 209–228, in P.B. Cliteur and M.A. Loth (eds.), *Rechtsfilosofen van de twintigste eeuw* (Legal philosophers of the twentieth century), Arnhem: Gouda Quint 1992.

Halberstam, Daniel, and Christoph Möllers, 'The German Constitutional Court Says "Ja zu Deutschland"', *German Law Journal* 2009, vol. 10 no. 8, p. 1242–1258.

Hale, Piers J., 'Of Mice and Men: Evolution and the Socialist Utopia: William Morris, H.G. Wells, and George Bernard Shaw', *Journal of the History of Biology* 2010, vol. 43 no.1, p. 17–66.

Halmai, Gábor, 'Unconstitutional Constitutional Amendments: Constitutional Courts as Guardians of the Constitution?', *Constellations* 2012, vol. 19 no. 2, p. 182–203.

Harmsen, Ger, 'W.A. Bonger', in *Biografisch Woordenboek van het Socialisme en de Arbeidersbeweging in Nederland* 2001, available via http://hdl.handle.net/10622/14811943-2157-4C93-8548-004AA292ACC8.

Hartmans, Rob, *Vaarwel dan! Essays over intellectuelen en hun illusies* (Farewell then! Essays on intellectuals and their illusions), Soesterberg: Aspekt 2000.

Hartmans, Rob, *Vijandige broeders? De Nederlandse sociaal-democratie en het nationaal-socialisme, 1922-1940* (Enemy brothers? Dutch social democracy and National Socialism, 1922-1940), Amsterdam: Ambo 2012.

Harvey, Paul, 'Militant Democracy and the European Convention on Human Rights', *European Law Review* 2004, vol. 29 no. 3, p. 407–420.

Haupt, Claudia E., 'The Scope of Democratic Public Discourse: Defending Democracy, Tolerating Intolerance, and the Problem of Neo-Nazi Demonstrations in Germany', *Florida Journal of International Law* 2008, vol. 20 no. 2, p. 169–217.

Heerikhuizen, Bart van, *W.A. Bonger*, p. 114–146, in Jan Bank, Paul Talma, Martin Ros and Bart Tromp (eds.), *Het vierde jaarboek voor het democratisch-socialisme* (The fourth yearbook for democratic socialism), Amsterdam: De Arbeiderspers/Wiardi Beckmann Stichting 1983.

Hendriks, Frank, *Vitale democratie: theorie van democratie in actie* (Vital democracy: theory of democracy in action), Amsterdam: Amsterdam University Press 2006.

Herzog, Michael, 'Can Hamas Be Tamed?', *Foreign Affairs* 2006, vol. 85, p. 83–94.

Hirsch Ballin, Ernst, *De Grondwet in politiek en samenleving. Rechtsstaatlezing 2013* (The Constitution in politics and society. Constitutional lecture 2013), The Hague: Boom Lemma Uitgevers 2013, p. 36.

Hoelzl, Michael, and Graham Ward, 'Introduction', p. x–xxviii, in Carl Schmitt, *Dictatorship (Die Diktatur. Von den Anfängen des modernen Souveränitätsgedankens bis zum proletarischen Klassenkampf)*, Cambridge: Polity Press 2014.

Hoeven, Johannes van der, 'Het staatkundig staatsbestel' ('The political constitution'), *Socialisme and Democratie* 1959, vol. 16 no. 9, p. 497–505.

Holmes, Stephen, 'Andras Sajó (ed.), Militant Democracy.' (review), *International Journal of Constitutional Law* 2006, vol. 4 no. 3, p. 586–591.

Hong, Quoc Loc, 'Democracy, Freedom of Speech and the Twin Challenges of the Exception', p. 329–366, in Afshin Ellian and Gelijn Molier, *The State of Exception and Militant Democracy in a Time of Terror*, Dordrecht: Republic of Letters Publishing 2012.

Invernizzi Accetti, Carlo, and Ian Zuckerman, 'What's Wrong with Militant Democracy?', *Political Studies* 2017, vol. 65, p. 182–199.

Issacharoff, Samuel, 'Fragile Democracies', *Harvard Law Review* 2007, vol. 120, p. 1405–1467.

Jabloner, Clemens, 'Hans Kelsen', p. 67–76, in Arthur J. Jacobsen and Bernhard Schlink (eds.), *Weimar: A Jurisprudence of Crisis*, Berkeley: University of California Press 2002.

Jacobsen, Arthur J., and Bernhard Schlink, 'Constitutional Crisis: The German and the American Experience', p. 1–39, in Arthur J. Jacobsen and Bernhard Schlink (eds.), *Weimar: A Jurisprudence of Crisis*, Berkeley: University of California Press 2002.

Jansen, Annette, 'Zelfcensuur, wen er maar aan' ('Self-censorship, get used to it'), *Trouw*, 24 January 2015.

Jansen, Corjo, with collaboration from Derk Venema, *De Hoge Raad en de Tweede Wereldoorlog: Recht en rechtsbeoefening in de jaren 1930-1950* (The Supreme Court and World War II: Law and the practice of law in the years 1930-1950), Amsterdam: Boom 2011.

Janssens, David, 'Leo Strauss: filosofie, protectie, tirannie en de vraag naar het kwaad' ('Leo Strauss: philosophy, protection, tyranny and the demand for evil'), p. 93–107, in G.J. Buijs and H.E.S. Woldring (eds.), *Grote politieke denkers. Hun strijd tussen goed en kwaad: een rondblik* (Great political thinkers. Their battle between good and evil: an exploration), Zoetermeer: Uitgeverij Meinema 2001.

Jones, Sam, 'Basque Separatist Group ETA Announces Dissolution', *The Guardian* (online), 2 May 2018.

Jonge, A.A. de, *Crisis en critiek der democratie, anti-democratische stromingen en de daarin levende denkbeelden over de staat in Nederland tussen de wereldoorlogen* (Crisis and criticism of democracy, antidemocratic trends and their inherent concepts of the state in the Netherlands in the interbellum), Assen: Van Gorcum 1968.

Josephus Jitta, A.C., letter to George van den Bergh, 29 September 1936, in the personal archive of George van den Bergh, owned by Van den Bergh's heirs.

Josephus Jitta, A.C., 'Zelfverdediging der democratie' ('Self-defence of democracy'), *De Groene Amsterdammer*, 10 October 1936.

Jost, Sebastian, 'Europas Richter urteilen über Draghis Milliarden-Plan', *Die Welt* (online), 16 June 2015.

Jurgens, E.C.M., 'De "erkenning" van het COC' ('The "recognition" of the COC'), *Nederlands Juristenblad* 1969, vol. 44, p. 76–78.

Jurgens, E.C.M., 'Over de illusie dat rechterlijke toetsing van de wet aan onze huidige Grondwet zinvol is' ('On the illusion that judicial review of the law with respect to our current constitution is worthwhile'), p. 117–123, in Paul Cliteur, Hans Franken and Wim Voermans (eds.), *Naar een Europese Grondwet* (Towards a European Constitution), The Hague: Boom Juridische Uitgevers 2004.

Jurgens, Erik, 'Het verschil tussen *rechtsstaat* en *rule of law*: inzichtelijk rapport van de Venice Commission van de Raad van Europa' (The difference between *rechtsstaat* and the *rule of law*: insightful report by the Venice Commission of the Council of Europe), *NTM/NJCM-bulletin* 2011, p. 867–872.

Kas, Annemarie, 'Deal met drugscrimineel die na 15 jaar bewindslieden de kop kostte' ('Deal with drug criminal that cost the ministers their heads after 15 years'), *NRC Handelsblad*, 10 March 2015.

Kas, Annemarie, 'Senaat verwerpt enkelband van Teeven na "genadeloze" kritiek' ('Senate votes down Teeven's electronic tag after "merciless" criticism'), *NRC Handelsblad*, 24 September 2014.

Keane, John, *The Life and Death of Democracy*, London: Pocket Books 2010.

Kelsen, Hans, 'Foundations of Democracy', *Ethics* 1955, vol. 66 no. 1, p. 1–101.

Kelsen, Hans, 'On the Essence and Value of Democracy (*Vom Wesen und Wert der Demokratie*)', p. 84–109, in Arthur J. Jacobsen and Bernhard Schlink (eds.), *Weimar: A Jurisprudence of Crisis*, Berkeley: University of California Press 2002.

Kelsen, Hans, 'Verteidigung der Demokratie', p. 229–237, in *Verteidigung der Demokratie: Abhandlungen zur Demokratietheorie*, Tübingen: Mohr Siebeck 2006.

Kelsen, Hans, *Vom Wesen und Wert der Demokratie*, Tübingen: Mohr 1920.

Kennedy, Ellen, 'Introduction: Carl Schmitt's *Parlementarismus* in Its Historical Context', p. xiii–l, in Carl Schmitt, *The Crisis of Parliamentary Democracy* (*Die geistesgeschichtliche Lage des heutigen Parlamentarismus*), Cambridge (M.A.): MIT Press 1988.

Kimmage, Michael, 'Do the Roots of the Cold War Alliance Lie in Weimar Germany?' (review of Udi Greenberg, *The Weimar Century: German Émigrés and the Intellectual Foundations of the Cold War*, Princeton: Princeton University Press 2014), *The New Republic* (online), 8 December 2014.

Kinneging, Andreas, *Geografie van goed en kwaad* (Geography of good and evil), Houten/Antwerp: Spectrum 2005.

Kirchick, James, 'Wrong Way down the Danube: How Hungary's Democratic Backsliding Threatens Europe', *Foreign Affairs*, 10 July 2012.

Kirshner, Alexander, *A Theory of Militant Democracy: The Ethics of Combatting Political Extremism*, New Haven and London: Yale University Press 2014.

Klamt, Martin, *Die Europäische Union als Streitbare Demokratie: Rechtsvergleichende und europarechtliche Dimensionen einer Idee*, München: Herbert Utz Verlag 2012.

Klamt, Martin, 'Militant Democracy and the Democratic Dilemma: Different Ways of Protecting Democratic Constitutions', p. 133–158, in Fred Bruinsma and David Nelken (eds.), *Explorations in Legal Cultures*, Reed Business NV 2007.

Klei, Ewout, and Remco van Mulligen, *Van God Los: einde van de christelijke politiek?* (Rid of God: The end of Christian politics?), Amsterdam: Nieuw Amsterdam 2014.

Knegtmans, Peter-Jan, 'De jaren 1919-1946' ('The years 1919-1946'), p. 63–117, in Maarten Brinkman, Madelon de Keizer and Maarten van Rossem (eds.), *Honderd jaar sociaal-democratie in Nederland 1894-1994* (One hundred years of social democracy in the Netherlands 1894-1994), Amsterdam: Bert Bakker 1994.

Koçak, Mustafa, and Esin Örücü, 'Dissolution of Political Parties in the Name of Democracy: Cases from Turkey and the European Court of Human Rights', *European Public Law* 2003, vol. 9 no. 3, p. 399–424.

Kommers, Donald P., 'The Jurisprudence of Free Speech in the United States and the Federal Republic of Germany', *Southern California Law Review* 1980, p. 657–695.

Koole, Ruud, 'Hijgende vragen, vlotte babbels: de symbiose van politiek en media' ('Gasping questions, smooth chatter: the symbiosis of politics and media'), p. 101–114, in Jo Bardoel, Chris Vos, Frank van Vree and Huub Wijfjes, *Journalistieke cultuur in Nederland* (Journalistic culture in the Netherlands), Amsterdam: Amsterdam University Press 2009.

Koopmans, Tim, 'Some Comparative Comments on Judicial Review', p. 45–49, in E.J.H. Schrage (ed.), *Judicial Review*, Nijmegen: Paul Scholten Instituut/Ars Aequi Libri 2002.

Kornai, János, 'Hungary's U-turn: Retreating from Democracy', *Journal of Democracy* 2015, vol. 26 no. 3, p. 34–48.

Kortmann, C.A.J.M., *Constitutioneel Recht* (Constitutional Law, revised by P.P.T. Bovend'Eert, J.L.W. Broeksteeg, B.P. Vermeulen and C.N.J. Kortmann), Deventer: Kluwer 2012.

Kostal, R.W., 'The Alchemy of Occupation: Karl Loewenstein and the Legal Reconstruction of Nazi Germany, 1945-1946', *Law and History Review* 2011, vol. 29 no. 1, p. 1–52.

Krabbe, Hugo, *De Moderne Staatsidee* (The modern idea of the state), The Hague: Martinus Nijhoff 1915.

Krabbe, Hugo, *'Ongezonde Lectuur'* ('Unhealthy reading'), Groningen: J.M. Wolters 1913.

Kramer, H.L.M., 'De democratische staat en de niet-democratische partijen' ('The democratic state and the non-democratic parties'), *Nederlands Juristenblad* 1936, p. 820–824. (Kramer 1936a)

Kramer, H.L.M., 'Democratie en meerderheidsbeslissing' ('Democracy and majority decision'), *Nederlands Juristenblad* 1936, p. 991–995. (Kramer 1936b)

Krastev, Ivan, 'Democracy as Self-Correction', *Transatlantic Academy Paper Series 2012-2013*, 10 December 2012.

Krotoszynski, Jr., Ronald J., 'A Comparative Perspective on the First Amendment: Free Speech, Militant Democracy, and the Primacy of Dignity as a Preferred Constitutional Value in Germany', *Tulane Law Review* 2003-2004, vol. 87, p. 1549–1609.

Laborde, Cécile, 'Pluralism, Syndicalism and Corporatism: Leon Duguit and the Crisis of the State (1900-25)', *History of European Ideas* 1996, vol. 22 no. 3, p. 227–244.

Lachmayer, Konrad, and Gerhard Thallinger, 'Conference Report—Widening the Scope: Reflections on the Human Rights Law Session of the XVth Academy of European Law', *German Law Journal* 2004, vol. 5 no. 9, p. 1155–1169.

Langemeijer, G.E., 'De democratische staat en de niet-democratische partijen' ('The democratic state and the non-democratic parties'), *Nederlands Juristenblad* 1936, p. 881–886. (Langemeijer 1936a)

Langemeijer, G.E., 'Naschrift' ('Postscript'), *Nederlands Juristenblad* 1936, p. 995. (Langemeijer 1936b)

Lawson, Rick, 'Overvloed en onbehagen: de Universele Verklaring en de Europese bescherming van de mensenrechten' ('Abundance and unease: the Universal Declaration and European protection of human rights'), *Internationale Spectator* 2008, vol. 62 no. 12, p. 659–662.

Leenknegt, G., 'Commentaar op artikel 8 van de Grondwet' (Commentary on article 8 of the constitution), in E.M.H. Hirsch Ballin and G. Leenknegt (eds.), *Artikelsgewijs commentaar op de Grondwet* (Commentary on the constitution), online edition 2017, www.nederlandrechtsstaat.nl.

Legg, Andrew, *The Margin of Appreciation in Human Rights Law: Deference and Proportionality*, Oxford: Oxford University Press 2012.

Levy, Jacob T., 'Montesquieu's Constitutional Legacies', p. 115–138, in Rebecca Kingston (ed.), *Montesquieu and His Legacy*, State University of New York (SUNY) Press 2009.

Loewenberg, Gerhard, 'The Influence of European Émigré Scholars on Comparative Politics, 1925–1965', *American Political Science Review*, vol. 100 no. 4, p. 597–604.

Loewenstein, Karl, 'Autocracy versus Democracy in Contemporary Europe, I', *American Political Science Review* 1935, vol. 29 no. 4, p. 571–593. (Loewenstein 1935a)

Loewenstein, Karl, 'Autocracy versus Democracy in Contemporary Europe, II', *American Political Science Review* 1935, vol. 29 no. 5, p. 755–784. (Loewenstein 1935b)

Loewenstein, Karl, 'It Is Later Than You Think; The Need for a Militant Democracy by Max Lerner' (discussion), *American Political Science Review* 1939, vol. 33 no. 3, p. 519–521.

Loewenstein, Karl, 'Legislation for the Defense of the State in Chili', *Columbia Law Review* 1944, vol. 44 no. 3, p. 366–407.

Loewenstein, Karl, 'Legislative Control of Political Extremism in European Democracies I', *Columbia Law Review* 1938, vol. 38 no. 4, p. 591–622.

Loewenstein, Karl, 'Militant Democracy and Fundamental Rights, I', *American Political Science Review* 1937, vol. 31, no. 3, p. 417–432. (Loewenstein 1937a)

Loewenstein, Karl, 'Militant Democracy and Fundamental Rights, II', *American Political Science Review* 1937, vol. 31 no. 4, p. 638–658. (Loewenstein 1937b)

Loichemol, Hervé, 'Une fatwa contre Voltaire?', *Le Monde*, 14 February 2006.

Loof, Jan-Peter, 'Restricting Free Speech in Times of Terror: An ECHR Perspective', p. 185–216, in Afshin Ellian and Gelijn Molier (eds.), *Freedom of Speech under Attack*, The Hague: Eleven Publishing 2015.

Macklem, Peter, 'Militant Democracy, Legal Pluralism, and the Paradox of Self-determination', *International Journal of Constitutional Law* 2006, vol. 4 no. 3, p. 488–516.

Magee, Bryan, *Popper*, London: Woburn Press 1974.

Mair, Peter, *Ruling the Void: The Hollowing of Western Democracy*, London: Verso Books 2013.

Maldonado-Denis, Manuel, 'Ortega y Gasset and the Theory of the Masses', in *Western Political Quarterly* 1961, vol. 14 no. 3, p. 676–690.

Malik, Kenan, 'Met zelfcensuur help je minderheden juist niet' ('You won't help minorities by self-censorship'), *De Volkskrant*, 10 January 2015.

Malkopoulou, Anthoula, 'Ostracism and Democratic Self-defense in Athens', *Constellations* 2017, vol. 24, p. 623–636.

Malkopoulou, Anthoula, 'The Self-Limiting Theory of Militant Democracy' (review of Kirshner, *Militant Democracy*), *Rediscriptions* 2016, vol. 19 no. 1, p. 108–112.

Malkopoulou, Anthoula, and Ludvig Norman, 'Three Models of Democratic Self-Defence: Militant Democracy and Its Alternatives', *Political Studies* 2017, vol. 66 no. 2, p. 442–458.

Maloney, Andrew, 'Democracy, Political Parties and the Will of the People', p. 53–67, in Claudio Michelon, Gregor Clunie, Christopher McCorkindale and Harris Psarras, *The Public in Law: Representations of the Political in Legal Discourse*, Farnham: Ashgate 2012.

Mancini, Susanna, 'The Tempting of Europe, the Political Seduction of the Cross: A Schmittian Reading of Christianity and Islam in European Constitutionalism', p. 111–135, in Susanna Mancini and Michel Rosenfeld (eds.), *Constitutional Secularism in an Age of Religious Revival*, Oxford: Oxford University Press 2014.

Mandel, Daniel, 'Preemptive Appeasement', *The Weekly Standard*, 20 September 2007.

Mansfield, Harvey, *A Student's Guide to Political Philosophy*, Wilmington: ISI Books 2001.

Marcuse, Herbert, and Karl Popper, *Sociale hervorming of sociale revolutie? Een confrontatie* (*Revolution oder Reform? Herbert Marcuse und Karl Popper. Eine Konfrontation*), Baarn: Het Wereldvenster 1971.

Mareš, Miroslav, 'Czech Militant Democracy in Action. Dissolution of the Workers' Party and the Wider Context of This Act', *East European Politics and Societies* 2012, vol. 26 no. 1, p. 33–55. (Mareš 2012a)

Mareš, Miroslav, 'How Does Militant Democracy Function in Combating Right-Wing Extremism? A Case Study of Slovakian Militant Democracy and the Rise of *Kotleba—People's Party Our Slovakia*', in Afshin Ellian and Bastiaan Rijpkema (eds.), *Militant Democracy: Political Science, Law and Philosophy*, New York: Springer *forthcoming* 2018.

Mareš, Miroslav, 'Right-Wing Extremism in the Czech Republic', *Friedrich Ebert Stiftung*, September 2012, p. 3. (Mareš 2012b)

Margolis, Emanuel, 'Soviet Views on the Relationship between National and International Law', *International and Comparative Law Quarterly* 1955, vol. 4, no. 1, p. 117–118.

Markovitch, Milan P., *La doctrine sociale de Duguit: ses idées sur le syndicalisme et représentation professionnelle*, Paris: Éditions Pierre Bossuet 1933.

Mayer, Franz, 'Rebels without a Cause? A Critical Analysis of the German Constitutional Court's OMT Reference', *German Law Journal* 2014, vol. 15 no. 2, p. 112–146.

McAuley, James, 'Hungary Votes to Keep Prime Minister and Right Wing in Power', *The Washington Post* (online), 8 April 2018.

McCormick, John, *Carl Schmitt's Critique of Liberalism: Against Politics as Technology*, Cambridge: Cambridge University Press 1997.

McCormick, John, 'Identifying or Exploiting the Paradoxes of Constitutional Democracy? An Introduction to Carl Schmitt's Legality and Legitimacy', p. xiii–xlii, in Carl Schmitt, *Legality and Legitimacy* (*Legalität und Legitimität*), Durham and London: Duke University Press 2004.

McDonough, Frank, *Hitler and the Rise of the Nazi Party*, Abingdon/New York: Routledge 2014.

McElligott, Anthony, *Rethinking the Weimar Republic: Authority and Authoritarianism 1916-1936*, London: Bloomsbury 2014.

McGuinness, Damien, '"Russian Agent" Row Hits Latvia Election', *BBC* (online), 10 April 2014.

Meada, Ko, 'Two Modes of Democratic Breakdown: A Competing Risks Analysis of Democratic Durability', *Journal of Politics* 2010, vol. 72 no. 4, p. 1129–1143.

Meeus, Tom-Jan, 'De hang naar foutloosheid die zich tegen politici keert' ('The predilection for flawlessness which backfires on politicians'), *NRC Handelsblad*, 21 December 2013.

Meiklejohn, Alexander, *Free Speech and Its Relation to Self-Government*, New York: Harper Brothers 1948.

Melching, Willem, and Marcel Stuivenga, 'Revolutie en consolidatie 1933-1934' ('Revolution and consolidation 1933-1934'), p. 34–38, in Willem Melching and Marcel Stuivenga (eds.), *Joseph Goebbels: Hitlers spindoctor, een selectie uit de dagboeken 1933-1945* (Joseph Goebbels: Hitler's spin doctor, a selection from the diaries 1933-1945), Amsterdam: Bert Bakker 2011.

Mertens, Thomas, *Mens and Mensenrechten: basisboek rechtsfilosofie* (Humans and human rights: handbook on legal philosophy), Amsterdam: Boom 2012.

Mill, James, 'Government', p. 857–889, in Edwin A. Burtt, *The English Philosophers from Bacon to Mill*, New York: The Modern Library 1939.

Mill, J.S., 'On Liberty', p. 41–132, in Alan Ryan (ed.), *Mill: Norton Critical Edition*, New York/London: W.W. Norton 1997.

Minkenberg, Michael, 'From Pariah to Policy-Maker? The Radical Right in Europe, West and East: Between Margin and Mainstream', *Journal of Contemporary European Studies* 2013, vol. 21 no. 1, p. 5–24.

Minkenberg, Michael, 'Repression and Reaction: Militant Democracy and the Radical Right in Germany and France', *Patterns of Prejudice* 2006, vol. 40 no. 1, p. 25–44.

Moe, Christian, '*Refah* Revisited: Strasbourg's Construction of Islam', p. 235–271, in W. Cole Durham, Jr., Rik Torfs, David M. Kirkham and Christine Scott, *Islam, Europe and Emerging Legal Issues*, Farnham: Ashgate 2012.

Molier, Gelijn, 'De Vereniging Martijn mag toch bestaan: over de scheiding van recht en moraal' ('The Vereniging Martijn may exist after all: on the separation of law and morality'), *Nederlands Juristenblad* 2013, p. 1502–1509.

Molier, Gelijn, 'De vrijheid van meningsuiting: "it's politics all the way down"' ('Freedom of expression: "it's politics all the way down"'), p. 205–242, in Afshin Ellian, Gelijn Molier and Tom Zwart (eds.), *Mag ik dit zeggen? Beschouwingen over de vrijheid van meningsuiting* (May I say this? Views on freedom of expression), The Hague: Boom Juridische Uitgevers 2011.

Molier, Gelijn, 'Drie typen van weerbare democratie' ('Three types of militant democracy'), in Afshin Ellian, Gelijn Molier and Bastiaan Rijpkema (eds.), *De strijd om de democratie: essays over democratische zelfverdediging*, Amsterdam: Boom 2018.

Molier, Gelijn, 'Het verbod van een politieke partij: een anomalie in een democratie?' ('The ban of a political party: an anomaly in a democracy?'), *Nederlands Juristenblad* 2016, nr. 34, p. 2438–2446.

Molier, Gelijn, 'Syrië-gangers wacht "strijdbare democratie"' ('"Militant democracy" awaits Syria-goers'), *Civis Mundi* 2014, no. 22.

Molier, Gelijn, and Bastiaan Rijpkema, 'Germany's New Militant Democracy Regime: National Democratic Party II and the German Federal Constitutional Court's "Potentiality" Criterion for Party Bans', *European Constitutional Law Review* 2018, vol. 14 no. 2, p. 394–409.

Molier, Gelijn, and Bastiaan Rijpkema, 'Naar een afzonderlijke bepaling inzake het partijverbod' (Towards an independent legal provision regarding party bans), *Nederlands Juristenblad* 2017, vol. 92 no. 10, p. 662–664.

Montesquieu, *The Spirit of the Laws (De l'esprit des lois)*, Cambridge: Cambridge University Press 1989.

Moravcsik, Andrew, 'The Origins of Human Rights Regimes: Democratic Delegation in Postwar Europe', *International Organization* 2000, vol. 54 no. 2, p. 217–252.

Moroff, Anika, 'Party Bans in Africa—An Empirical Overview', *Democratization* 2010, vol. 17 no. 4, p. 618–641.

Mouffe, Chantal, 'Carl Schmitt and the Paradox of Liberal Democracy', *Canadian Journal of Law and Jurisprudence* 1997, vol. 10 no. 1, p. 21–33.

Mudde, Cas, 'No, We Are NOT All Charlie (and That's a Problem)', *Open Democracy* (online), 7 January 2015.

Müller, Jan-Werner, 'A "Practical Dilemma Which Philosophy Alone Cannot Resolve"? Rethinking Militant Democracy: An Introduction', *Constellations* 2012, vol. 19 no. 4, p. 536–539.

Müller, Jan-Werner, *Constitutional Patriotism*, Princeton/Oxford: Princeton University Press 2007.

Müller, Jan-Werner, 'Defending Democracy within the EU', *Journal of Democracy* 2013, vol. 24 no. 2, p. 138–149. (Müller 2013a)

Müller, Jan-Werner, 'Militant Democracy', p. 1253–1269, in Michel Rosenfeld and Andras Sajó (eds.), *The Oxford Handbook of Comparative Constitutional Law*, Oxford: Oxford University Press 2013. (Müller 2013b)

Müller, Jan-Werner, *Safeguarding Democracy inside the EU, Transatlantic Academy Paper Series 2012-2013*, no. 3, 20 February 2013. (Müller 2013c)

Müller, Jan-Werner, *Wat is populisme?* (translation of *What is populism?*, with a new preface), Amsterdam: Nieuw Amsterdam 2017.

Müller, Jan-Werner, 'Who Is the European Prince? A More or Less Machiavellian Meditation on the European Union', *Social Research: An International Quarterly* 2014, vol. 81 no. 1, p. 243–267.

Napel, Hans-Martien ten, 'Het EHRM en de "waarlijk democratische regeringsvorm"' ('The ECHR and the "true shape of democratic government"'), *NJCM-Bulletin* 2007, vol. 32 no. 8, p. 1090–1106.

Navot, Suzie, 'Fighting Terrorism in the Political Arena: The Banning of Political Parties', *Party Politics* 2008, vol. 14 no. 6, p. 745–762.

Neumann, Volker, 'Carl Schmitt', p. 280–289, in Arthur J. Jacobsen and Bernhard Schlink (eds.), *Weimar: A Jurisprudence of Crisis*, Berkeley: University of California Press 2002.

Niesen, Peter, 'Anti-Extremism, Negative Republicanism, Civic Society: Three Paradigms for Banning Political Parties—Part I', *German Law Journal* 2002, vol. 3.

Niesen, Peter, 'Banning the Former Ruling Party', *Constellations* 2012, vol. 19 no. 4, p. 540–561.

Nieuwenhuis, A.J., 'Partijverbod en supraconstitutionalisme in rechtsvergelijkend perspectief' ('Party bans and supraconstitutionalism from a comparative legal perspective'), p. 199–213, in J.L. de Reede and J.H. Reestman (eds.), *Op het snijvlak van recht en politiek: Opstellen aangeboden aan prof. mr. L. Prakke* (On the cutting edge of law and politics: Papers presented to Professor L. Prakke), Deventer: Kluwer 2003.

Nieuwenhuis, A.J., 'Tussen grondrechtelijke vrijheid en parlementaire onschendbaarheid: de vrijheid van meningsuiting van de parlementariër' ('Between constitutional freedom and parliamentary inviolability: the parliamentarian's freedom of expression'), *Tijdschrift voor Constitutioneel Recht* 2010, vol. 1 no. 1, p. 4–23.

Noorloos, Marloes van, 'Extreme Speech in a Religious Context: A Legal Theoretical Perspective on the Case Law of the European Court of Human Rights', p. 163–183, in Afshin Ellian and Gelijn Molier (eds.), *Freedom of Speech under Attack*, The Hague: Eleven Publishing 2015.

Notitie antidemocratische groeperingen (Memorandum on antidemocratic factions), *Kamerstukken II* (Dutch Parliamentary Papers II) 2014/2015, 29 279, 226, p. 1–20.

Oakes, Guy, 'Translator's Introduction', p. ix–xxxv, in Carl Schmitt, *Political Romanticism (Politische Romantik)*, Massachusetts/London: MIT Press 1986.

Opinion on the New Constitution of Hungary, Commission for Democracy through Law (Venice Commission), adopted in the 87e plenary session, 17-18 June 2011.

Oppenheimer, Martin, 'Social Control Mechanisms in a Modern Welfare State: The Case of the Federal Republic of Germany', *Critical Sociology* 1977, vol. 7 no. 1, p. 65–68.

Orenstein, Mitchell A., Péter Krekó and Attila Juhász, 'The Hungarian Putin?', *Foreign Affairs*, 8 February 2015.

Ortega y Gasset, José, *The Revolt of the Masses (La rebelión de las masas)*, New York/London: W.W. Norton 1993.

Ost, François, 'De sfinx aan de stadspoorten: enkele vragen om een debat te openen over anti-democratische partijen' ('The sphinx at the city gates: a few questions to open up the debate on antidemocratic parties'), p. 179–191, in Maurice Adams and Patricia Popelier (eds.), *Recht en democratie: de democratische verbeelding in het recht* (Law and democracy: the democratic illusion of law), Antwerp: Intersentia 2004.

Pans, Ralph, 'George van den Bergh, 1890-1966', p. 174–202, in Jan Bank, Paul Kalma, Martin Ros and Bart Tromp, *Het zesde jaarboek van het democratisch-socialisme* (The sixth yearbook of democratic socialism), Amsterdam: De Arbeiderspers/ Wiardi Beckmanstichting 1985.

Papier, Hans-Jürgen, and Wolfgang Durner, 'Streitbare Demokratie', *Archiv des öffentlichen Rechts* 2003, vol. 128, p. 340–371.

Parekh, Bhikhu, *Contemporary Political Thinkers*, Oxford: Martin Robertson 1982.

Parrington, John S., 'H.G. Wells and the World State: A Liberal Cosmopolitan in a Totalitarian Age', *International Relations* 2003, vol. 17 no. 2, p. 233–246.

Pech, Laurent, and Kim Lane Scheppele, 'Poland and the European Commission, Part III: Requiem for the Rule of Law', *Verfassungsblog*, 3 March 2017.

Pedahzur, Ami, *The Israeli Response to Jewish Extremism and Violence: Defending Democracy*, Manchester: Manchester University Press 2002.

Perry, Jos, 'De jaren 1849-1919' ('The years 1849-1919'), p. 10–61, in Maarten Brinkman, Madelon de Keizer and Maarten van Rossem (eds.), *Honderd jaar sociaal-democratie in Nederland 1894-1994* (One hundred years of social democracy in the Netherlands 1894-1994), Amsterdam: Bert Bakker 1994.

Pfersmann, Otto, 'Shaping Militant Democracy: Legal Limits to Democratic Stability', p. 47–68, in András Sajó (ed.), *Militant Democracy*, Utrecht: Eleven Publishing 2004.

Ploeg, Tymen van der, 'Hoe moeilijk is het om een vereniging te verbieden? Deel 2: de zaak Martijn' ('How difficult is it to ban an association? Part 2: the Martijn case'), *Nederlands Juristenblad* 2013, p. 2808–2810.

Poelje, G.A. van, 'Bewogen Staatsrecht' ('Turbulent Constitutional Law'), in G.A. van Poelje, *Opstellen aangeboden aan Prof. Mr. Van den Bergh ter gelegenheid van zijn aftreden als hoogleraar in het Nederlandse Staatsrecht aan de Universiteit van Amsterdam* (Essays presented to Professor Van den Bergh on the occasion of his retirement from the position of professor of Dutch constitutional law at the University of Amsterdam), Alphen aan den Rijn: N. Samson 1960.

Polak, Henri, 'Kroniek', *Het Volk*, 10 October 1936.

Popper, Karl, *Conjectures and Refutations*, New York: Routledge 2002. (Popper 2002a)

Popper, Karl, 'On Democracy', p. 360–369, in Jeremy Shearmur and Piers Norris Turner (eds.), *After the Open Society: Selected Social and Political Writings*, London/New York: Routledge 2008. (Popper 2008b)

Popper, Karl, 'On Toleration', p. 314–328, in Jeremy Shearmur and Piers Norris Turner (eds.), *After the Open Society: Selected Social and Political Writings*, London/New York: Routledge 2008. (Popper 2008a)

Popper, Karl, 'The Open Society and the Democratic State', p. 231–248, in Jeremy Shearmur and Piers Norris Turner (eds.), *After the Open Society: Selected Social and Political Writings*, London/New York: Routledge 2008. (Popper 2008c)

Popper, Karl, *The Open Society and Its Enemies*, Princeton/New York: Princeton University Press 2013.

Popper, Karl, *The Poverty of Historicism*, London: Routledge 2002. (Popper 2002b)

Preuss, Ulrich K., 'Political Order and Democracy: Carl Schmitt and His Influence', p. 155–179, in Chantal Mouffe (ed.), *The Challenge of Carl Schmitt*, London/ New York: Verso 1999.

Preuss, Ulrich, 'The Implications of "Eternity Clauses": The German Experience', *Israel Law Review* 2011, vol. 44, p. 429–448.

Quinault, Roland, 'Winston Churchill and Democracy', p. 27–46, in David Cannadine and Roland Quinault (eds.), *Winston Churchill in the Twenty First Century*, Cambridge: Cambridge University Press 2004.

Rawls, John, *A Theory of Justice* (Revised edition), Cambridge (M.A.): Harvard University Press 1999.

Remarks by the President in Year-End Press Conference, 19-12-2014, available via https://www.whitehouse.gov/the-press-office/2014/12/19/remarks-president-year-end-press-conference.

Rensmann, Thilo, 'Munich Alumni and the Evolution of International Human Rights Law', *European Journal of International Law* 2011, vol. 22 no. 4, p. 973–991.

Rensmann, Thilo, 'Procedural Fairness in a Militant Democracy: The "Uprising of the Decent" Fails before the Federal Constitutional Court', *German Law Journal* 2003, vol. 4 no. 11, p. 1117–1136.

Report by the Commissioner for Human Rights, Mr. Thomas Hammarberg, on his visit to the Netherlands, 21-25 September 2008, Strasbourg, 11 March 2009.

Report on the Rule of Law, European Commission for Democracy through Law (Venice Commission), 10-11 March 2011 (86th Plenary Session).

Rijpkema, Bastiaan, 'Democratie als zelfcorrectie *revisited*: nadere aantekeningen bij de weerbare democratie' (Democracy as self-correction revisited: further remarks on militant democracy), p. 31–59, in Afshin Ellian, Gelijn Molier and Bastiaan Rijpkema (eds.), *De strijd om de democratie: essays over democratische zelfverdediging* (The battle for democracy: essays on democratic self-defence), Amsterdam: Boom 2018.

Rijpkema, Bastiaan, 'Dierenrechten als politiek-filosofisch probleem' ('Animal rights as a problem of political philosophy'), p. 131–151, in Bastiaan Rijpkema and Machteld Zee (eds.), *Bij de beesten af! Over dierenrecht en onrecht* (Brutish! On animal rights and injustice), Bert Bakker 2013.

Rijpkema, Bastiaan, 'Popper's Paradox of Democracy', *Think* 2012, vol. 11, p. 93–96.

Roach, Kent, 'Anti-Terrorism and Militant Democracy', p. 171–207, in András Sajó (ed.), *Militant Democracy*, Utrecht: Eleven Publishing 2004.

Robinson, Richard, 'Dr. Popper's Defense of Democracy', *Philosophical Review* 1951, vol. 60 no. 4, p. 487–507.

Roessel, Aukje van, 'Zelfcorrectie' ('Self-correction'), *De Groene Amsterdammer*, 8 April 2015.

Rosenblum, Nancy, 'Banning Parties: Religious and Ethnic Partisanship in Multicultural Democracies', *Law and Ethics of Human Rights* 2007, vol. 1 no. 1, p. 17–57.

Rosnai, Yaniv, 'Unconstitutional Constitutional Amendments—The Migration and Success of a Constitutional Idea', *American Journal of Comparative Law* 2013, vol. 61, p. 657–719.

Rule of Law: European Commission Acts to Defend Judicial Independence in Poland, European Commission Press Release, 20 December 2017, available at http://europa.eu/rapid/press-release_IP-17-5367_en.htm.

Rummens, Stefan, 'Deliberation Can Be Rough', p. 269–289, in Afshin Ellian and Gelijn Molier (eds.), *Freedom of Speech under Attack*, The Hague: Eleven Publishing 2015.

Rummens, Stefan, and Koen Abts, 'Defending Democracy: The Concentric Containment of Political Extremism', *Political Studies* 2010, vol. 58, p. 649–665.

Rummens, Stefan, and Koen Abts, 'Politiek extremisme en de weerbaarheid van de democratie' ('Political extremism and the militancy of democracy'), *Ethische Perspectieven* 2008, vol. 18 no. 4, p. 512–536.

Ryan, Alan, 'Introduction', p. ix-xxii, in Karl Popper, *The Open Society and Its Enemies*, Princeton/New York: Princeton University Press 2013.

Ryan, Alan, *On Politics: A History of Political Thought from Herodotus to the Present*, London: Penguin 2012. (Ryan 2012a)

Ryan, Alan, *The Making of Modern Liberalism*, Princeton: Princeton University Press 2012. (Ryan 2012b)

Sadurski, Wojciech, *Constitutionalism and the Enlargement of Europe*, Oxford: Oxford University Press 2012.

Sadurski, Wojciech, *Freedom of Speech and Its Limits*, Dordrecht: Kluwer Academic 1999.

Sajó, András, 'From Militant Democracy to the Preventive State', *Cardozo Law Review* 2006, vol. 27 no. 5, p. 2255–2294.

Sajó, András, 'Militant Democracy and Emotional Politics', *Constellations* 2012, vol. 19 no. 4, p. 562–574.

Sajó, András, 'Militant Democracy and Transition towards Democracy', p. 209–230, in András Sajó (ed.), *Militant Democracy*, Utrecht: Eleven Publishing 2004.

Salafisme in Nederland: diversiteit en dynamiek (Salafism in the Netherlands: diversity and dynamic), AIVD/NCTV (Dutch General Intelligence and Security Service/Dutch National Coordinator for Security and Counterterrorism), The Hague 2015.

Sasse van IJsselt, Paul van, 'Sharia en de democratische paradox; terugkeer van de crisistoon' ('Sharia and the democratic paradox: return of the crisis tone'), *Nederlands Juristenblad* 2006, vol. 81 no. 34, p. 1952–1953.

Schaik, Mirjam van, and Jasper Doomen, 'De toekomst van godslastering' ('The future of blasphemy'), *Nederlands Juristenblad* 2014, no. 30, p. 2110–2116.

Schmitt, Carl, *Constitutional Theory (Verfassungslehre)*, Durham: Duke University Press 2008.

Schmitt, Carl, *Dictatorship (Die Diktatur. Von den Anfängen des modernen Souveränitätsgedankens bis zum proletarischen Klassenkampf)*, Cambridge: Polity Press 2014.

Schmitt, Carl, *Die geistesgeschichtliche Lage des heutigen Parlamentarismus*, München/Leipzig: Duncker and Humblot 1926.

Schmitt, Carl, *Legality and Legitimacy (Legalität und Legitimität)*, Durham and London: Duke University Press 2004.

Schmitt, Carl, *Political Romanticism (Politische Romantik)*, Massachusetts/London: MIT Press 1986.

Schmitt, Carl, *Political Theology: Four Chapters on the Concept of Sovereignty (Politische Theologie)*, Chicago/London: Chicago University Press 2005.

Schmitt, Carl, *The Crisis of Parliamentary Democracy (Die geistesgeschichtliche Lage des heutigen Parlamentarismus)*, Cambridge (M.A.): MIT Press 1988.

Schmitt, Carl, 'The Dictatorship of the Reich President According to Art 48 of the Reich Constitution' (translated by Ellen Kennedy), *Constellations* 2011, vol. 18 no. 3, p. 299–323.

Schreuerman, William E., *Carl Schmitt: The End of Law*, Oxford: Rowman and Littlefield 1999.

Schuijt, G.A.I., 'Ten geleide' ('Editorial'), p. 7–10, in G.A.I. Schuijt and D. Voorhoof (eds.), *Vrijheid van meningsuiting, racisme en revisionisme* (Freedom of expression, racism and revisionism), Ghent: Academia Press 1995.

Schumpeter, Joseph, *Capitalism, Socialism and Democracy*, London/New York: Routledge 2010.

Scruton, Roger, 'The Nation-State and Democracy', p. 75–87, in Mark Dooley (ed.), *The Roger Scruton Reader*, New York: Continuum 2011.

Sherborne, Michael, *H.G. Wells: Another Kind of Life*, London/Chester Springs: Peter Owen 2010.

Sottiaux, Stefan, '"Bad Tendencies" in the ECHR's "Hate Speech" Jurisprudence', *European Constitutional Law Review* 2011, vol. 7 no. 1, p. 40–63.

Sottiaux, Stefan, 'Democratie en grondrechten: de inhoudelijke en procedurele democratiemodellen van Dworkin en Habermas' ('Democracy and fundamental rights: the substantive and procedural models of Dworkin and Habermas'), p. 39–64, in Maurice Adams and Patricia Popelier (eds.), *Recht en democratie: de democratische verbeelding in het recht* (Law and democracy: the democratic illusion of law), Antwerp: Intersentia 2004.

Stam, Jip, 'Leve de onafhankelijke geesten. Waarom het individuele mandaat van parlementariërs de democratie weerbaarder maakt' ('Long live the independent minds. Why the free mandate of MPs makes democracy more militant'), *Liberale Reflecties* (Liberal Reflections) 2017, vol. 58 no. 1, p. 15–22.

Stark, Franz, 'Woord na' ('Afterword'), p. 43–47, in Herbert Marcuse and Karl Popper, *Sociale hervorming of sociale revolutie? Een confrontatie (Revolution oder Reform? Herbert Marcuse und Karl Popper. Eine Konfrontation)*, Baarn: Het Wereldvenster 1971.

Stegbauer, Andreas, 'The Ban of Right-Wing Extremist Symbols According to Section 86a of the German Criminal Code', *German Law Journal* 2007, vol. 8 no. 2, p. 173–184.

Steinvorth, Daniel, and Volkhard Windfuhr, 'Morsi's Grab for Power: Egyptian Revolutionaries Take on Radical Islam', *Der Spiegel* (online), 26 November 2012.

Stephen, Leslie, *The English Utilitarians*, in three volumes (volume II: *James Mill*), London/New York: Continuum 2006.

Tames, Ismee, *'Oorlog voor onze gedachten': oorlog, neutraliteit en identiteit in het Nederlandse publieke debat, 1914-1918* ('War for our ideas': war, neutrality and identity in the Dutch public debate, 1914-1918, diss. Amsterdam UvA), Hilversum: Verloren Uitgeverij 2006.

Tardi, Gregory, 'Political Parties' Right to Engage in Politics', p. 81–111, in András Sajó (ed.), *Militant Democracy*, Utrecht: Eleven Publishing 2004.

Tavris, Carol, and Elliot Aronson, *Mistakes Were Made (But Not by Me): Why We Justify Foolish Beliefs, Bad Decisions, and Hurtful Acts*, Orlando: Harcourt 2007.

Taylor, Martha, 'Implicating the Demos: A Reading of Thucydides on the Rise of the Four Hundred', *Journal of Hellenic Studies* 2002, vol. 122, p. 91–108.

Tempel, Bastiaan van den, *Democratische vrijheid en socialistisch recht* (Democratic freedom and socialist justice, diss. Amsterdam Uva), Haarlem: Tjeenk Willink 1933.

Terpstra, Doekle, '"Nee" tegen kwade boodschap Wilders' ('"No" to Wilders' malicious message'), *Trouw*, 30 November 2007.

Thange, Fernand, *Multiculturalisme kritisch bekeken* (A critical look at multiculturalism), Antwerp/Apeldoorn: Garant 2010.

Thiel, Markus, 'Comparative Aspects', p. 380–424, in Markus Thiel (ed.), *The 'Militant Democracy' Principle in Modern Democracies*, Farnham: Ashgate 2009. (Thiel 2009b)

Thiel, Markus, 'Introduction', p. 1–14, in Markus Thiel (ed.), *The 'Militant Democracy' Principle in Modern Democracies*, Farnham: Ashgate 2009. (Thiel 2009a)

Thiel, Markus, 'Militant Democracy and State of Emergency in Germany', p. 273–327, in Afshin Ellian and Gelijn Molier (eds.), *The State of Exception and Militant Democracy in a Time of Terror*, Dordrecht: Republic of Letters Publishing 2012.

Thiel, Markus (ed.), *The 'Militant Democracy' Principle in Modern Democracies*, Farnham: Ashgate 2009.

Thienel, Rudolf, 'Militant Democracy—Can Democracy Defend Itself?', p. 63–69, in Harald Eberhard, Konrad Lachmayer, Gerald Ribarov and Gerhard Thallinger (eds.), *Perspectives and Limits of Democracy: Proceedings of the 3rd Vienna Workshop on International Constitutional Law*, Nomos/facultas.vuw 2008.

Thomassen, J.J.A., 'Democratie, problemen en spanningsvelden' ('Democracy, problems and areas of tension'), p. 15–33, in J.J.A. Thomassen (ed.), *Hedendaagse democratie* (Contemporary democracy), Alphen aan den Rijn: Samsom/H.D. Tjeenk Willink 1991.

Thomassen, J.J.A., and R.B. Andeweg, 'Fractiediscipline. Vooroordelen en misverstanden.' ('Party discipline. Prejudices and misunderstandings'), p. 154–175, in G. Voerman (ed.), *Jaarboek Documentatiecentrum Nederlandse Politieke Partijen 2005* (Yearbook of the Documentation Centre for Dutch Political Parties 2005), Groningen: Documentatiecentrum Nederlandse Politieke Partijen 2007.

Thornton, Stephen, 'Karl Popper', *Stanford Encyclopedia of Philosophy* (online), edition: summer 2014, available at http://plato.stanford.edu/archives/sum2014/entries/popper/.

Tinnevelt, Ronald, 'Rawls over de rechtvaardigheid van samenleving en wereld' ('Rawls on the justice of society and the world'), p. 449–477, in Marin Terpstra (ed.), *Onenigheid en Gemeenschap: basisboek politieke filosofie* (Discord in society: a handbook of political philosophy), Amsterdam: Boom 2012.

Tracy, B. Strong, 'Foreword: The Sovereign and the Exception: Carl Schmitt, Politics, Theology, and Leadership', p. vii-xxxiii, in Carl Schmitt, *Political Theology: Four Chapters on the Concept of Sovereignty (Politische Theologie)*, Chicago/London: Chicago University Press 2005.

Tromp, Bart, 'Anti-democratische stromingen' ('Antidemocratic trends'), p. 84–104, in J.J.A. Thomassen (ed.), *Hedendaagse democratie* (Contemporary democracy), Alphen aan den Rijn: Samsom/H.D. Tjeenk Willink 1991.

Turkey: opinion on the amendments to the Constitution adopted by the Grand National Assembly on 21 January 2017 and to be submitted to a national referendum on 16 April 2017, European Commission for Democracy through Law (Venice Commission), 10-11 March 2017 (110th Plenary Session).

Tyulkina, Svetlana, *Militant Democracy: Undemocratic Political Parties and Beyond*, London/New York: Routledge 2015.

Urbinati, Nadia, and Carlo Ivernizzi Accetti, 'Editor's Introduction', p. 6–40, in Hans Kelsen, *Essence and Value of Democracy* (translated by Brian Graf), Lanham: Rowman and Littlefield 2013.

Uyl, Jeroen den, and Has Bakker, 'Geef ook politici de kans om van fouten te leren' ('Give politicians a chance to learn from mistakes too'), *Trouw*, 24 April 2015.

Uzman, Jerfi, *Constitutionele remedies bij schending van grondrechten: Over effectieve rechtsbescherming, rechterlijk abstineren en de dialoog tussen rechter en wetgever* (Constitutional remedies in the case of violation of fundamental rights: On effective protection of rights, judicial abstention and the dialogue between judge and legislator, diss. Leiden), Deventer: Kluwer 2013.

Vaicaitis, Vaidotas A., 'Role of (sic) Lithuanian Constitutional Court during (sic) Period of "Transitional Democracy"', p. 89–102, in Harald Eberhard, Konrad Lachmayer and Gerhard Thallinger, *Transitional Constitutionalism: Proceedings of the 2nd Vienna Workshop on International Constitutional Law*, Nomos/facultas. wuv 2007.

Vanden Heede, Pieter, 'Het Europees Hof voor de Rechten van de Mens en het Partijverbod: dansen op een slap koord' ('The European Court of Human Rights and the Party Ban: dancing on a slack rope'), p. 193–232, in Maurice Adams and Patricia Popelier (eds.), *Recht en democratie: de democratische verbeelding in het recht* (Law and democracy: the democratic illusion of law), Antwerp: Intersentia 2004.

Van den Bergh, George, 'De demokratische staat en de demokratische partijen (afscheidsrede uitgesproken op 2 juli 1960)' ('The democratic state and the democratic parties [valedictory lecture of 2 July 1960]'), p. 82–90, in George van den Bergh, *Verzamelde staatsrechtelijke opstellen (supplement bij de derde bundel)* (Collected constitutional law papers [supplement to the third collection]), Alphen aan den Rijn: Samsom N.V. 1961.

Van den Bergh, George, *De democratische Staat en de niet-democratische partijen* (The democratic state and the nondemocratic parties, inaugural lecture, Amsterdam UvA), Amsterdam: De Arbeiderspers 1936 (Van den Bergh 1936a).

Van den Bergh, George, *Democratie: beginsel en doel, rede uitgesproken op het congres 1936 van de SDAP* (Democracy: principle and goal, speech given at the 1936 SDAP conference), Amsterdam: De Arbeiderspers 1936 (Van den Bergh 1936b).

Van den Bergh, George, *Hoofdlijnen van het Nederlandse Staatsrecht, met nog een zestal staatsrechtelijke opstellen* (Outlines of Dutch constitutional law, with six extra papers on constitutional law), Haarlem: H.D. Tjeenk Willink and Zn 1958.

Van den Bergh, George, *Wat te doen met antidemocratische partijen? De oratie van George van den Bergh uit 1936* (What to do with antidemocratic parties? The inaugural lecture of George van den Bergh, 1936), with an introduction by Bastiaan Rijpkema, a foreword by René Cuperus and an afterword by Paul Cliteur, Amsterdam: Elsevier Boeken 2014.

Van der List, G.A. 'Karl Popper', p. 59–71, in P.B. Cliteur and G.A. van der List (eds.), *Filosofen van het hedendaags liberalisme* (Philosophers of contemporary liberalism), Kampen: Kok Agora 1990.

Velde, Henk te, *Van regentenmentaliteit tot populisme: politieke tradities in Nederland* (From authoritarianism to populism: political traditions in the Netherlands), Amsterdam: Bert Bakker 2010.

Verfassungsshutzbericht 2013, Berlin: Bundesministerium des Innern 2013.

Verhofstadt, Dirk, *De Liberale Canon: Grondslagen van het liberalisme* (The liberal canon: foundations of liberalism), Antwerp: Uitgeverij Houtekiet 2015.

Verseck, Keno, 'Hungary in the Crossfire: Orbán Lashes Out at Critics in European Parliament', *Der Spiegel* (online), 19 January 2012.

Verslag van de Staatscommissie, ingesteld bij Koninklijk Besluit van 24 januari 1936, No. 41, aan welke is opgedragen de voorbereiding van eene partieele herziening van de Grondwet (Report by the government commission set up by Royal Decree on 24 January 1936, No. 41, tasked with preparation of a partial revision of the Constitution), The Hague: Algemeene Landsdrukkerij 1936.

Vis, J.C.P.M., *Politiek en democratie: een inleiding* (Politics and democracy: an introduction), Groningen: Wolters-Noordhoff 1988.

Visser, Robert, *In dienst van het algemeen belang: Ministeriële verantwoordelijkheid en parlementair vertrouwen* (Serving the general interest: Ministerial accountability and parliamentary confidence, diss. Leiden), Amsterdam: Boom 2008.

Voermans, W.J.M., and J.H. Gerards, with collaboration from M.L. van Emmerik and H.-M.Th.D. ten Napel, *Juridische betekenis en reikwijdte van het begrip 'rechtsstaat' in de legisprudentie and jurisprudentie van de Raad van State* (Legal significance and scope of the concept of 'constitutional state' in the legisprudence and jurisprudence of the Council of State), The Hague: Raad van State 2011.

Waldron, Jeremy, *Law and Disagreement*, Oxford: Oxford University Press 1999.

Waling, Geerten, *Zetelroof: fractiediscipline en afsplitsingen in de Tweede Kamer 1917-2017* (Seat robbery: party discipline and party ruptures in the House of Representatives 1917-2017), Uitgeverij Vantilt 2017.

Walker, Clive, 'Militant Speech about Terrorism in a Smart Militant Democracy', *Mississippi Law Journal* 2011, vol. 80 no. 4, p. 1395–1453.

Weber, Eric Thomas, *Democracy and Leadership: On Pragmatism and Virtue*, Plymouth: Lexington Books 2013.

Weezel, Max van, and Kleijwegt, Margalith, 'Piet Hein Donner: "De meerderheid telt!"' ('Piet Hein Donner: "The majority counts!"'), *Vrij Nederland*, 16 September 2006.

Weitz, Eric D., *Weimar Germany: Promise and Tragedy*, Princeton: Princeton University Press 2013.

Wells, H.G., 'A Liberal World Organization', p. 29–39, in H.G. Wells, *After Democracy: Addresses and Papers on the Present World Situation*, London: Watts and Co 1932.

Wells, H.G., *Anticipations*, London: Chapman and Hall 1914.

Wells, H.G., 'Liberalism and the Revolutionary Spirit', p. 1–28, in H.G. Wells, *After Democracy: Addresses and Papers on the Present World Situation*, London: Watts and Co 1932.

Wenar, Leif, 'Rawls', p. 393–411, in David Estlund (ed.), *The Oxford Handbook of Political Philosophy*, Oxford: Oxford University Press 2012.

Wichers Hoeth, H.C., *De democratie en niet-democratische partijen* (Democracy and non-democratic parties, master's thesis), 1980.

Wilde, Marc de, 'Safeguarding the Constitution with and against Carl Schmitt' (discussion of Ellen Kennedy, *Constitutional Failure: Carl Schmitt in Weimar*, Durham: Duke University Press 2004, and Giorgio Agamben, *State of Exception*, Chicago: University of Chicago Press 2005), *Political Theory* 2006, vol. 34 no. 4, p. 510–515.

Wilde, Marc de, 'The State of Emergency in the Weimar Republic. Legal Disputes over Article 48 of the Weimar Constitution', *Legal History Review* 2010, vol. 78, p. 135–158.

Wilde, Marc de, *Verwantschap in Extremen: Politieke Theologie bij Walter Benjamin en Carl Schmitt* (Affinity in Extremes: Political theology of Walter Benjamin and Carl Schmitt, diss. Amsterdam UvA), Amsterdam: Vossiuspers/Amsterdam University Press 2008.

Wilkinson, Michael, 'Authoritarian Liberalism in the European Constitutional Imagination: Second Time as Farce?', *European Law Journal* 2015, vol. 21 no. 3, p. 313–339.

Wilkinson, Michael, 'From Karlsruhe, with Love? Questioning the Constitutionality of Unconventional Monetary Policy' (October 2014), *London School of Economics Law—Policy Briefing Paper*, no. 6.

Wise, Judith, 'Dissent and the Militant Democracy: The German Constitution and the Banning of the Free German Workers Party', *University of Chicago Law School Roundtable* 1998, vol. 5, p. 301–343.

Wit, Th. W.A. de, 'Carl Schmitt: het risico van het politieke kwaad' ('Carl Schmitt: the risk of political evil'), p. 59–76, in G.J. Buijs and H.E.S. Woldring, *Grote politieke denkers. Hun strijd tussen goed en kwaad: een rondblik* (Great political thinkers. Their battle between good and evil: an exploration), Zoetermeer: Uitgeverij Meinema 2001.

Woolls, Daniel, 'Basque Separatist, Arnaldo Otegi, Convicted of Terrorism in Spain', *The Huffington Post* (online), 16 September 2011.

Woude, W. van der, *Democratische waarborgen* (Democratic safeguards), Deventer: Kluwer 2009.

Young, Michael G., 'Kent Roach. The 9/11 Effect: Comparative Counter-Terrorism' (discussion), *Terrorism and Political Violence*, vol. 25 no. 5, p. 852–854.

Zoethout, Carla, 'Hugo Krabbe over recht, staat en staatsrecht' ('Hugo Krabbe on law, state and constitutional law'), *Recht en Kritiek* 1991, vol. 17 no. 4, p. 468–481.

Table of cases

European Court of Human Rights

ECHR 7 December 1976 (Handyside/United Kingdom).
ECHR 30 January 1998, 133/1996/752/951 (United Communist Party of Turkey/Turkey).
ECHR 13 February 2003, 41340/98, 41342/98 and 41344/98, NJ 2005, 73, incl. note E.A. Alkema (Refah Partisi/Turkey).
ECHR 16 March 2006, 58278/00, (Zdanoka/Latvia).
ECHR 20 June 2009, 25803/04 and 25817/04 (Batasuna: Herri Batasuna/Spain).
ECHR 12 June 2012, 31098/08 (Hizb ut-Tahrir/Germany).
ECHR 10 July 2012, 58369/10 (Staatkundige Gereformeerde Partij/Netherlands).
ECHR 14 March 2013, 26261/05 and 26377/06 (Kasymakhunov and Saybatalov/Russia).

Germany

Bundesverfassungsgericht 23 October 1952, *E* 2, 1 (SRP-Verbot).
Bundesverfassungsgericht 17 August 1956, *E* 5, 85 (KPD-Verbot).
BVerfG 18 March 2003, 2 BVB 1/01 (NPD I).
Bundesverfassungsgericht 26 February 2014, 2 BvE 2/13.
Bundesverfassungsgericht 17 January 2017, 2 BvB 1/13 (NPD II).

Netherlands

Royal decree 24 June 1970, AA 1971, 253, incl. note E.C.M. Jurgens.
District Court of Amsterdam 18 November 1998, *NJ* 1999, 377 (Nationale Volkspartij/CP'86).
Supreme Court 18 April 2014, AB 2014/38 (concl. A-G L. Timmermans) incl. note G. Molier and J.G. Brouwer (Vereniging Martijn).
Distict Court The Hague, 26 April 2016, ECLI:NL:RBDHA:2016:12789.

Index